DIRTY ASSETS

Adopting a multi-disciplinary and comparative approach, this book focuses on the emerging and innovative aspects of attempts to target the accumulated assets of those engaged in criminal and terrorist activity, organized crime and corruption. It examines the 'follow-the-money' approach and explores the nature of criminal, civil and regulatory responses used to attack the financial assets of those engaged in financial crime in order to deter and disrupt future criminal activity as well as terrorism networks. With contributions from leading international academics and practitioners in the fields of law, economics, financial management, criminology, sociology and political science, the book explores law and practice in countries with significant problems and experiences, revealing new insights into these dilemmas. It also discusses the impact of the 'follow-the-money' approach on human rights while also assessing effectiveness.

The book will appeal to academics and researchers of financial crime, organized crime and terrorism as well as practitioners in the police, prosecution, financial and taxation agencies, policy-makers and lawyers.

T0303989

Dirty Assets
Emerging Issues in the Regulation of Criminal and Terrorist Assets

Edited by

COLIN KING
University of Manchester, UK

CLIVE WALKER
University of Leeds, UK

Routledge
Taylor & Francis Group

LONDON AND NEW YORK

First published 2014 by Ashgate Publishing

Published 2016 by Routledge
2 Park Square, Milton Park, Abingdon, Oxfordshire OX14 4RN
711 Third Avenue, New York, NY 10017, USA

First issued in paperback 2016

Routledge is an imprint of the Taylor & Francis Group, an informa business

British Library Cataloguing in Publication Data
A catalogue record for this book is available from the British Library

The Library of Congress has cataloged the printed edition as follows:
King, Colin
  Dirty assets : emerging issues in the regulation of criminal and terrorist assets / by Colin
King and Clive Walker.
     pages cm. -- (Law, justice and power)
  Includes bibliographical references and index.
  ISBN 978-1-4094-6253-8 (hardback)
1. Terrorism--Finance--Law and legislation--Criminal provisions.
2. Organized crime--Finance--Law and legislation--Criminal provisions. 3. Terrorism-
-Finance--Law and legislation--European Union countries--Criminal provisions. 4.
Terrorism--Prevention--Law and legislation. I. Walker, Clive (Professor) II. Title.
  K5223.K57 2014
  345'.0773--dc23

                                                                            2013025919

ISBN 13: 978-1-138-24755-0 (pbk)
ISBN 13: 978-1-4094-6253-8 (hbk)

Contents

List of Figures

List of Tables

Notes on Contributors

Thomas Baumert is Professor of Economics at the Catholic University of Valencia and Head of the Research Institute 'Jovellanos'. His research areas include the economics of terrorism, especially on the impact of terrorist attacks on financial markets. Among others, he co-edited the much acclaimed book *La hora de los economistas* (Ecobook, 2010) and (with Mikel Buesa) *The Economic Repercussions of Terrorism* (Oxford University Press, 2010). He is also a member of the Cátedra de Economía del Terrorismo at the Complutense University of Madrid ('CET-UCM'). *Email*: tbaumert@ucm.es

Matthias J. Borgers is Professor of Criminal Law and Criminal Procedure at VU University Amsterdam. In 2001 his (cum laude) PhD thesis on the confiscation of criminal proceeds was published. It was awarded the SNS Bank Award and the Modderman Award. Borgers has written numerous publications on Dutch criminal law (especially criminal procedure and sentencing) and European criminal law. His current research interests lies in, *inter alia*, the (repressive and precautionary) role of criminal law in the fight against terrorism. In his inaugural lecture Professor Borgers elaborated the concept of the risk society in relation to the criminal law approach to combatting terrorism. Matthias Borgers is a substitute judge in the Amsterdam Court of Appeal. *Email*: m.j.borgers@vu.nl

Mikel Buesa is Professor of Applied Economics at the Complutense University of Madrid and Chair of the Economics of Terrorism (CET-UCM). He has published widely on the subject of terrorism and the economy, and is president of two Spanish civic organizations devoted to promotion of intellectual and political work on counter-terrorism. He has co-edited (with Thomas Baumert) *The Economic Repercussions of Terrorism* (Oxford University Press, 2010) and is the author of *ETA, S.A.* (Planeta, 2011). Professor Buesa has been honoured with the Spanish Order of Constitutional Merit. *Email*: mbuesa@ccee.ucm.es

Karen Bullock is Senior Lecturer in Criminology in the Department of Sociology at the University of Surrey. Her research interests include aspects of contemporary policing and crime prevention theory and practice, most recently contemporary forms of community policing, intelligence-led policing and on the impact of the 1998 Human Rights Act on the police service. She conducted a large-scale empirical study of the confiscation regime in England and Wales on behalf of the Home Office (see K. Bullock, D. Mann, R. Street and C. Coxon, *Examining Attrition in Confiscating the Proceeds of Crime* (Home Office Research Report 17,

2009) and, edited with Ronald V. Clarke and Nick Tilley, *Situational Prevention of Organised Crimes* (Willan Publishing, 2010). *Email*: k.bullock@surrey.ac.uk

Indira Carr is Professor of Law at the University of Surrey. She specializes in International Trade Law and for the past eight years has been researching the topic of corruption in international business generally and more specifically of corruption in developing countries. This has inevitably led her to examine legal and political issues surrounding money laundering and asset recovery. Professor Carr's corruption-related research has been funded by the Arts & Humanities Research Council and the British Academy. Along with a colleague from the Business School (Professor David Goss), she set up the Corruption Research Group in 2010. Interdisciplinary in nature, its membership is drawn from academia, international organizations, the professions and CSOs. This Group holds workshops at regular intervals. Further information is available at: http://www.surrey.ac.uk/corruption. *Email*: i.carr@surrey.ac.uk

Laura K. Donohue is Professor of Law at Georgetown Law and Director of Georgetown's Center on National Security and the Law. She writes on the history of national security and counter-terrorist law in the United States and United Kingdom. Her most recent book, *The Cost of Counterterrorism: Power, Politics, and Liberty* (Cambridge: Cambridge University Press, 2008) analyses the impact of American and British counter-terrorist law on life, liberty, property, privacy and free speech. She is currently writing a book on the history of national security law. Her articles focus on biometric identification; state secrets; surveillance, data collection and analysis; extended detention and interrogation; anti-terrorist finance and material support; biological weapons; scientific speech; and the history of quarantine law. Professor Donohue has held fellowships at Stanford Law School's Center for Constitutional Law, Stanford University's Center for International Security and Cooperation, and Harvard University's John F. Kennedy School of Government, where she was a Fellow in the International Security Program as well as the Executive Session for Domestic Preparedness. In 2001 the Carnegie Corporation included her in its Scholars Program, funding the project, Security and Freedom in the Face of Terrorism. She took up the award at Stanford, where she taught in the Departments of History and Political Science and directed a project for the United States Departments of Justice and State and, later, Homeland Security, on mass-casualty terrorist incidents. In 2008–2009 she clerked for Judge John T. Noonan, Ninth Circuit Court of Appeals. Professor Donohue is a Life Member of the Council on Foreign Relations, an Advisory Board Member of the ABA Standing Committee on Law and National Security, and an Advisory Board Member of the Electronic Privacy Information Center ('EPIC'). She obtained her BA in Philosophy (with Honours) from Dartmouth College, her MA in Peace Studies (with Distinction) from the University of Ulster, Northern Ireland, her JD (with Distinction) from Stanford Law School, and her PhD in History from the University of Cambridge. *Email*: lkdonohue@law.georgetown.edu

Rositsa Dzhekova is an analyst on criminological and policy research at the Center for the Study of Democracy ('CSD'), which is an interdisciplinary public policy institute dedicated to the values of democracy and market economy based in Sofia, Bulgaria. As the leading think tank in the region, CSD has been a pioneer in several areas traditionally perceived as inviolable parts of the public arena, such as anti-corruption institutional reform, organized crime and national security. Rositsa's current work is related to conventional and organized crime, corruption, border security and home affairs policy issues. She has contributed to a number of EU-commissioned studies and research projects, including the first Bulgarian Organised Crime Threat Assessment, a study on the practices of EU member states in management and disposal of confiscated criminal assets, a study on the anti-corruption measures in EU border control, as well as on assessing corruption in law enforcement. Previously she worked as a researcher and consultant at the business risk consultancy, Control Risks, in Berlin and London. As part of the Corporate Investigations team there, she worked on several projects related to corruption and compliance audits, fraud investigations, integrity due diligence, asset-tracing and litigation support for clients operating in South-Eastern Europe and the German-speaking countries. In 2010 she also worked in the political risk analysis team of Control Risks, where she provided daily forecasts and in-depth risk assessments on political stability, corruption, state capture, organized crime, security and terrorism risks in the Balkan region. Rositsa studied Political Science at the Freie Universität, Berlin, specializing in European integration and development cooperation. *Email*: rositsa.dzhekova@csd.bg

Christina Eckes is Associate Professor in EU Law at the University of Amsterdam and senior researcher at the Amsterdam Centre for European Law and Governance ('ACELG'). In 2012/2013, she was Emile Noël Fellow-in-Residence at New York University. Her current research project *Outside-In: Tracing the Imprint of the European Union's External Actions on Its Constitutional Landscape* is funded by the Netherlands Organisation for Scientific Research ('NWO'). She has widely published on EU external relations and EU counter-terrorist sanctions, including a monograph entitled *EU Counter-Terrorist Policies and Fundamental Rights – The Case of Individual Sanctions* (Oxford University Press, 2009). *Email*: C.Eckes@ uva.nl

Michelle Gallant is Associate Professor and former Associate Dean (Research and Graduate Studies) at the Faculty of Law, University of Manitoba. She teaches in the areas of taxation law, international law, conflict resolution, money laundering, terrorist finance and tax havens. Her research interests and publications cover a range of fields including taxation law and policy, global governance and money laundering, and international law and conflict resolution. She is the author of the book *Money Laundering and the Proceeds of Crime: Economic Crime and Civil Remedies* (Edward Elgar Publishing, 2005). Dr Gallant serves on the Peace and Conflict Studies ('PACS') Committee, which governs the PhD Program in Peace and Conflict Studies. She is also a Commissioner on the Manitoba Law Reform Commission. *Email*: Michelle.Gallant@ad.umanitoba.ca

Andrew Goldsmith is Strategic Professor in Criminology and Criminal Justice at the Flinders Law School, Adelaide. He was previously Executive Director of the Centre for Transnational Crime Prevention, University of Wollongong. He is the founder of the Illicit Networks Workshop. He has degrees in law, criminology and sociology, including an SJD from the University of Toronto and an LLD from the London School of Economics. His research interests include criminal and corrupt organizations, police governance, transnational policing and new social media. *Email*: andrew.goldsmith@flinders.edu.au

David Gray is Manager, Proceeds of Crime Litigation with the Australian Federal Police, Canberra. He was admitted to practice in 1982 and practised as a commercial litigator before joining the Office of Public Prosecutions (Victoria) as a senior lawyer preparing criminal cases for trial and appearing as in-house prosecutor. In 2002 he was appointed manager of the Proceeds of Crime Directorate OPP until his retirement in December 2011. In January 2012 he was appointed to his current position. *Email*: David.Gray@afp.gov.au

Jackie Harvey is Professor of Financial Management and Director of Business Research at Newcastle Business School, Northumbria University. Her research is focused in the area of criminal financial management, in particular money laundering. Her early work considered costs and benefits of regulatory compliance whilst recently she has focused on the effectiveness of the Anti-Money Laundering Framework. She is on the Editorial Board for the European Cross-Border Crime Colloquium. Before becoming an academic, Professor Harvey spent 10 years working for a major merchant bank, followed by a three-year posting as fiscal policy adviser (under the auspices of the British Government) to the Ministry of Finance in Belize. *Email*: jackie.harvey@northumbria.ac.uk

Robert Jago is Senior Lecturer in Law at the University of Surrey. His teaching and research interests lie in the fields of criminal law and criminal justice. He has extensive experience in the field having worked on research projects evaluating young offender regimes (University of Cambridge), the management, monitoring and assessment of dangerous and sexual offenders (Cardiff University) and parenting support (University of Kent). His research interests are broad and include the psychological impact of the ASBO on young people and the extension of the vote to prisoners. He is currently exploring the sentencing of those sentenced for corruption offences. He is a co-author of *Politics of the Common Law* (Routledge, 2008). *Email*: r.jago@surrey.ac.uk

Colin King is Lecturer in Law at the University of Manchester. He completed his PhD – 'The Confiscation of Criminal Assets: Tackling Organised Crime Through a "Middleground" System of Justice' – at the University of Limerick, where he also taught constitutional law. In 2006, he worked as a research intern at the Office of the Director of Public Prosecutions in Dublin. He has made submissions to the Irish Law Reform Commission (Consultation Paper on Search Warrants) and the Department of Justice and Law Reform (White Paper Discussion Document on Organised and White Collar Crime). Colin has received funding awards from the Irish Research Council for the Humanities and Social Sciences, the University of Limerick Research Board, the JP McManus Scholarship Foundation, the Modern Law Review and the Worldwide Universities Network. *Email*: colin.king@manchester.ac.uk

Stuart Lister is Senior Lecturer in Criminal Justice at the Centre for Criminal Justice Studies in the School of Law, University of Leeds. His research interests come together around exploring the changes and continuities in the provision, role, function and effectiveness of contemporary policing and security endeavours. He is author of the report *Street Policing of Problem Drug Users* (with T. Seddon, E. Wincup, S. Barrett and P. Traynor for the Joseph Rowntree Foundation, 2008), *Plural Policing: The Mixed Economy of Visible Security Patrols* (with A. Crawford, S. Blackburn and J. Burnett; Policy Press, 2005), *The Extended Policing Family: Visible Patrols in Residential Areas* (with A. Crawford; York Publishing, 2004), and *Bouncers: Violence and Governance in the Night-time Economy* (with D. Hobbs, P. Hadfield and S. Winlow; Oxford University Press, 2003). *Email*: S.C.Lister@leeds.ac.uk

Daniele Piva graduated in 2002 in Law (summa cum laude) from the University of Roma Tre. After his degree he was involved in teaching and research on criminal law at the universities of Roma Tre, Sapienza, and L.U.M.S.A. He completed his PhD ('Tecniche di individuazione del soggetto attivo del reato. Contributo all'analisi della responsabilità penale nelle organizzazioni complesse con particolare riferimento all'impresa giornalistica') at the University of Rome 'Tor Vergata'. From 2006 he worked as a professor in criminal law at the Scuola di Specializzazione per le Professioni Legali in the University of Roma Tre. In 2008 and 2009 he obtained a research post as a criminal law specialist at the University of Roma Tre. In 2007, 2008 and 2009 he visited the Max Planck-Institut für ausländisches und Internationales Strafrecht at Freiburg (Germany) and in 2008 was awarded a fellowship by the Deutscher Akademischer Austauschdienst. Daniele Piva is author of many publications (papers, articles, etc.), he has also given papers at many academic congresses. In 2011 he published a monograph on corporate criminal liability with the title *La Responsabilità del 'Vertice' per Organizzazione Difettosa nel Diritto Penale del Lavoro* (Jovene). In 2012 he obtained a research post as a criminal law specialist at the University Sapienza. *Email*: daniele.piva@tiscali.it

Russell G. Smith has qualifications in law, psychology and criminology from the University of Melbourne and a PhD from King's College London. He was a solicitor in Melbourne, and then a lecturer at the University of Melbourne before taking up a position at the Australian Institute of Criminology where he is now Principal Criminologist and Head of the Transnational and Organised Crime Program. He has published extensively on aspects of financial crime, money laundering, computer crime and professional regulation. *Email*: Russell.Smith@aic. gov.au

Clive Walker is Professor of Criminal Justice Studies at the School of Law, University of Leeds, where he has served as the Director of the Centre for Criminal Justice Studies (1987–2000) and as Head of School (2000–2005, 2010). He has written extensively on terrorism issues, with a PhD (University of Manchester, 1982), and numerous published books and papers not only in the UK but also several other jurisdictions. He has been a visiting professor at many universities, including George Washington and Stanford Universities in the USA, and Melbourne and New South Wales in Australia. His latest book on terrorism is a comprehensive study of *Terrorism and the Law* (Oxford University Press, 2011), work for which was funded by an AHRC fellowship. He is currently the special adviser to the Home Office's Independent Reviewer of Terrorism Legislation and has served as a special adviser to the UK Parliamentary select committee which scrutinized what became the Civil Contingencies Act 2004. A book commentating upon this act, *The Civil Contingencies Act 2004: Risk, Resilience and the Law in the United Kingdom*, was published by Oxford University Press in 2006. *Email*: law6cw@leeds.ac.uk

PART I:
Introductory Matters

Chapter 1

Emerging Issues in the Regulation of Criminal and Terrorist Assets

Colin King and Clive Walker

Background

Increasing apprehensions surrounding organized crime, terrorism and corruption have given rise to a realization that conventional policing methods are insufficient on their own to deter, or at least disrupt, those engaged in criminal activities. It is thought that a more proactive approach is needed, since a 'criminal law' approach will not, alone, suffice.[1] One consequence has been a focus on the financial assets of those engaged in criminal activities. In the United Kingdom, the Proceeds of Crime Act 2002 ('POCA') enacted a sweeping array of powers that allow the authorities to target such illicit assets. This legislation provides a number of avenues through which criminals can be targeted by a focus on the money trail, namely: anti-money laundering provisions,[2] post-conviction confiscation,[3] civil recovery in the absence of a criminal conviction,[4] and taxation of assets.[5] The 2002 Act also established the short-lived Assets Recovery Agency, though most of its functions have since been transferred to the Serious Organised Crime Agency ('SOCA').[6] SOCA has since been supplanted by the National Crime Agency.[7]

---

1   Cabinet Office and Home Office, *Extending Our Reach: A Comprehensive Approach to Tackling Serious Organised Crime* (London: Stationery Office, 2009); M. Kilchling, 'Tracing, Seizing and Confiscating Proceeds from Corruption (and other Illegal Conduct) Within or Outside the Criminal Justice System' (2001) 9(4) *European Journal of Crime, Criminal Law and Criminal Justice* 264; F.E. Jansen and G.J.N. Bruinsma, 'Policing organized crime: A new direction' (1997) 5(4) *European Journal on Criminal Policy and Research* 85.

2   Proceeds of Crime Act 2002, Pt 7.

3   Proceeds of Crime Act 2002, Pt 2.

4   Proceeds of Crime Act 2002, Pt 5.

5   Proceeds of Crime Act 2002, Pt 6.

6   Serious Organised Crime and Police Act 2005.

7   Crime and Courts Act 2013.

The ever-evolving framework to deal with organized crime, corruption and other threats reflects the difficulties faced by conventional policing stratagems.[8] The focus on financial assets now forms a central aspect of policing strategies, supplementing perceived inadequacies of traditional criminal procedure and punishment. The same line of thinking has been applied to the financial assets of terrorist organizations, with greater emphasis and attention since 9/11. There are significant differences between the phenomena of crime and terrorism, but this distinction has not prevented cross-fertilization between the codes.[9]

'Follow the money' strategies also reflect a move away from the 'national' to the 'transnational' – as befits a late modern society in which transnational crime is perceived as a growing threat.[10] At the international level, key instruments include, *inter alia*, the Warsaw Convention from the Council of Europe,[11] the revised Financial Action Task Force Recommendations,[12] the EU's Third Money Laundering Directive,[13] and UN interest especially in the field of terrorism,[14] but

---

8   Home Office, *New Powers Against Organised and Financial Crime* (London: Stationery Office, 2006); Home Office, *One Step Ahead: A 21st Century Strategy to Defeat Organised Crime* (London: Stationery Office, 2004).

9   Terrorists and organized criminals are mentioned together in the HM Government, *A Strong Britain in an Age of Uncertainty: The National Security Strategy* (London: Cm 7953, Stationery Office, 2010) e.g. para. 3.2. A major influence behind the design of early anti-terrorism financial legislation was the US RICO legislation (18 USC s 1963; 21 USC s 853): see M. Zander, *Confiscation and Forfeiture Law* (London: Police Foundation, 1989); C.P. Walker, *The Prevention of Terrorism in British Law* (2nd ed., Manchester: Manchester University Press, 1992) ch. 7.

10   HM Government, *Local to Global: Reducing the Risk from Organised Crime* (London: Stationery Office, 2011); A. Edwards and P. Gill, *Transnational Organised Crime: Perspective on Global Security* (London: Routledge, 2003); P. Andreas and A.E. Nadelmann, *Policing the Globe: Criminalization and Crime Control in International Relations* (Oxford: Oxford University Press, 2006); G.F. Madsen, *Transnational Organized Crime* (London: Routledge 2009); UNODC, *The Globalization of Crime: A Transnational Organized Crime Threat Assessment* (Vienna, 2010); B. Bowling and J. Sheptycki, *Global Policing* (London: Sage, 2012).

11   Council of Europe Convention on Laundering, Search, Seizure and Confiscation of the Proceeds from Crime and on the Financing of Terrorism 2005.

12   International Standards on Combating Money Laundering and the Financing of Terrorism and Proliferation, issued in February 2012.

13   Directive 2005/60/EC of the European Parliament and of the Council of 26 October 2005 on the prevention of the use of the financial system for the purpose of money laundering and terrorist financing. In February 2013, the European Commission issued a further Proposal for a Directive of the European Parliament and of the Council on the prevention of the use of the financial system for the purpose of money laundering and terrorist financing. Strasbourg, 5.2.2013 COM(2013) 45 final. SWD(2013) 21 final.

14   See United Nations International Convention for the Suppression of the Financing of Terrorism (A/RES/54/109 of 9 December 1999) and UN Security Council Resolution 1373 of 28 September 2001.

also in relation to transnational crime[15] and corruption.[16] International actors, such as the Financial Action Task Force ('FATF'),[17] the Committee of Experts on the Evaluation of Anti-Money Laundering Measures and the Financing of Terrorism ('MONEYVAL'),[18] the Group of States Against Corruption ('GRECO'),[19] the European Criminal Assets Bureau and the Camden Asset Recovery Inter-Agency Network ('CARIN'),[20] also play an important role here. Movement in the international arena reflects the need for a transnational response cutting across not only the boundaries of states and institutions within them but also conventional legal boundaries (such as civil, criminal and regulatory). As criminal gangs become increasingly flexible and international, so too have State and international responses adapted likewise.

A number of these new and sophisticated state dispositions around 'follow the money' approaches have given cause for concern. Points of doubt and contention include: effectiveness and measurement of impact; impact on the rule of law and due process rights; the imposition of costs on the legitimate economy; and the limited accountability of specialist teams and bodies. Therefore, this book examines the nature of criminal, civil and regulatory responses to illicit assets, with hybridity and innovative approaches and institutions as key recurrent themes, as are questions as to the legitimacy, purposes and impacts of key mechanisms.

Over the course of the past two decades, much has been written about 'follow the money' approaches, especially anti-money laundering legislation, principally measures enacted to tackle the process by which the origins of ill-gotten gains are disguised and cleansed so as to appear legitimate.[21] As other elements in the

---

15   United Nations Convention Against Transnational Organized Crime (General Assembly resolution 55/25 of 15 November 2000).

16   See United Nations Convention Against Corruption (General Assembly resolution 58/4 of 31 October 2003).

17   http://www.fatf-gafi.org/ (accessed 1 August 2013).

18   http://www.coe.int/t/dghl/monitoring/moneyval/default_en.asp (accessed 1 August 2013).

19   http://www.coe.int/t/dghl/monitoring/greco/default_en.asp (accessed 1 August 2013).

20   Camden Asset Recovery Inter-Agency Network (CARIN), *The History, Statement of Intent, Membership and Functioning of CARIN. Manual* (Hague: Europol, 2012).

21   See, for example, W.C. Gilmore, *Dirty Money. The Evolution of International Measures to Counter Money Laundering and the Financing of Terrorism* (4th ed., Strasbourg: Council of Europe Publishing, 2011); N. Ryder, 'The Financial Services Authority and Money Laundering: A Game of Cat and Mouse' (2008) 67(3) *Cambridge Law Journal* 635; P.C. van Duyne, M.S. Groenhuijsen and A.A.P. Schudelaro, 'Balancing financial threats and legal interests in money-laundering policy' (2005) 43 *Crime, Law and Social Change* 117; M. Levi, 'Money Laundering and its Regulation' (2002) *Annals of the American Academy of Political and Social Science* 181; J.A. Blum et al., *Financial Havens, Banking Secrecy and Money Laundering* (United Nations Office for Drug Control and Crime Prevention, 1998); P. Williams, 'Money Laundering' (1997) 5(1) *South African Journal of International Affairs* 71.

'follow the money' strategy are afforded increased prominence, there is a need to focus on emerging and innovative aspects of attempts to target the accumulated assets of those engaged in criminal and terrorist activity. This book, then, focuses on some of these emerging issues. The book adopts a multi-disciplinary and comparative approach, with contributions from law, economics, financial management, criminology, sociology and political science. The authors and issues were deliberately selected to focus on emerging and cutting-edge issues. The comparative nature of the book is enhanced by the exploration of law and practice in countries with deep problems and experiences, about which little has yet been revealed to English-speaking audiences.

Some of the issues covered in this book were explored at a symposium, 'The Confiscation of Assets: Policy, Practice and Research', hosted by the School of Law, University of Leeds in April 2011 and funded by the *Modern Law Review*. This funding allowed the editors to explore an original agenda, and so some of the more familiar names in this field were not asked to submit a contribution to this book. The symposium attracted an audience from a mixture of academic and practitioner backgrounds and ensuing discussion has also fed into the chapters in this book. The book, then, will be of interest to a wide audience, not only academics and researchers who specialize in areas such as financial crimes, organized crime and terrorism, but also practitioners in the police, prosecution and specialized financial and taxation agencies, policymakers and lawyers. The book also brings a fresh approach to human rights issues (including powers and constraints affecting the State in its responses to crime and terrorism) and political science (including the working and worth of new forms of hybrid institutional formations and governance within criminal justice).

Rationale

In 2000, the then Prime Minister Tony Blair stated 'For too long, we paid insufficient attention to the financial aspects of crime. We must remember that many criminals are motivated by money and profit.'[22] This reflects the greater emphasis that would subsequently be placed on targeting illicit assets as a central tenet of modern crime control strategies.

'Follow the money' techniques have developed significantly in recent decades. Money laundering offences remain a key aspect of this approach, though there is now a greater realization that other innovative techniques offer their own benefits. For example, while post-conviction confiscation and civil forfeiture techniques both have long histories these have now been adapted in the fight against organized crime, in particular. There is often a degree of confusion regarding such

---

22   Performance and Innovation Unit, *Recovering the Proceeds of Crime* (London: Cabinet Office, 2000), Foreword by the Prime Minister Tony Blair.

terminology though, not helped by the diverse approaches in different jurisdictions and at the international level. According to Golobinek:[23]

> There are differences in the fundamental nature of legislation on confiscation with regard to criminal law, civil or administrative law. Confiscation regimes can be part of the sentencing procedure of the defendant. In that case, conviction is usually required. In some States, proceeds can be confiscated in civil forfeiture proceedings (mostly in common law based countries) independently or in parallel to related criminal proceedings.

For example, in some jurisdictions (e.g. Bulgaria – see Chapter 5) the term 'civil forfeiture' refers to the use of civil processes to confiscate assets subsequent to a criminal conviction, whereas in other jurisdictions (e.g. Ireland – see Chapter 7) the term is used to describe forfeiture of assets in the absence of criminal conviction (a non-conviction based approach). Not only are there differences in terminology, so too are there differences in, for example, evidential rules (such as the burden and standard of proof), the requirement of a direct link between 'crime' and seizure of assets, the calculation of profits (gross or net) and the function of confiscation (preventive or punitive).[24] This book, then, is enriched by a comparative approach to methods adopted and experiences learned in other jurisdictions in their applications both to criminals and terrorists.

Targeting illicit assets is often claimed to have multiple benefits: demonstrating that crime does not pay; underpinning confidence in the criminal justice system; removing negative role models from society; disrupting criminal networks and markets; acting as a deterrent through reduced returns; improving crime detection rates; and assisting in the fight against money laundering and its associated harms.[25] It has been said that: 'Asset recovery is not an end in itself but a mechanism for achieving headline objectives such as crime reduction and, potentially, lowering the fear of crime.'[26] In addition, it is often thought that asset recovery[27] is cost-

---

23   R. Golobinek, *Financial Investigations and Confiscation of Proceeds of Crime: Training Manual for Law Enforcement and Judiciary* (Strasbourg: Council of Europe, 2006) 13.

24   R. Golobinek, fn 23 above, 13.

25   Performance and Innovation Unit, *Recovering the Proceeds of Crime* (London: Cabinet Office, 2000) 16. See also HM Inspectorate of Constabulary, HM Crown Prosecution Service Inspectorate and HM Inspection of Court Services, *Payback Time: Joint Review of Asset Recovery since the Proceeds of Crime Act 2002*, report available at: http://www.hmcpsi.gov.uk/documents/reports/CJJI_THM/BOTJ/PaybackTIme_Rep_Nov 04.pdf, paras 1.1–1.4.

26   HM Inspectorate of Constabulary, HM Crown Prosecution Service Inspectorate, and HM Inspection of Court Services, *Payback Time*, fn 25 above, 7.

27   'Asset recovery' is wider than 'confiscation'. The 'asset recovery' process includes the asset tracing phase (e.g. national financial investigations, the work of Asset Recovery Offices) and the disposal phase (e.g. sale of an asset in a public auction or re-use of the

effective in that the costs associated with operating such a regime or running a dedicated asset-recovery organization would be covered by the monetary sums recovered.[28] In 2000, the use of asset-recovery techniques in the UK was described as:

> an underused avenue of attack on crime, with an accompanying early and significant impact. In failing to take full account of the profit motive, the UK criminal justice system is at present overlooking a powerful lever in the fight against crime.[29]

That situation, though, is now changing with the money trail a key element in contemporary policing. A decade on from the enactment of the UK's Proceeds of Crime Act 2002 (and a decade or more on from 9/11) provides an ideal point at which to engage with emerging issues in the regulation of criminal and terrorist assets, from a multi-disciplinary and comparative perspective.

An early review of the Proceeds of Crime Act identified several shortcomings: poor awareness on the part of police forces about the new asset recovery powers and relevance to reducing volume crime; inconsistent take-up of those powers; inconsistent monitoring of performance; no consolidated collection of appropriate statistics; and significant attrition rates.[30] A decade on, while there have been some improvements (such as increased awareness and uptake of confiscation powers – though, arguably, still relatively low), many of these concerns remain valid. Contributions to this book demonstrate, for example, that statistical inconsistencies remain, thereby hampering detailed scrutiny of the asset recovery regime. This point is confirmed by a recent *Impact Assessment* carried out for the European Commission, which states:

---

asset for public purposes). European Commission, *Commission Staff Working Paper. Accompanying Document to the Proposal for a Directive of the European Parliament and the Council on the Freezing and Confiscation of Proceeds of Crime in the European Union. Impact Assessment* (Brussels, 12.3.2012. SWD(2012) final) para. 2.1.1.

28   See, for example, Performance and Innovation Unit, *Recovering the Proceeds of Crime* 23; HM Crown Prosecution Service Inspectorate, HM Inspectorate of Court Administration and HM Inspectorate of Constabulary, *Joint Thematic Review of Asset Recovery: Restraint and Confiscation Casework* (2010) Criminal Justice Joint Inspection, report available at: http://library.npia.police.uk/docs/hmcpsi/AssetRecovery.pdf, para. 6.12. There are two trains of thought in relation to cost-effectiveness: first, that there is benefit in sending out a message that 'crime does not pay', and second, that the cost of recovery should be weighed against the likely value of recovery. HM Inspectorate of Constabulary, HM Crown Prosecution Service Inspectorate and HM Inspection of Court Services, *Payback Time*, fn 25 above, para. 3.47.

29   Performance and Innovation Unit, *Recovering the Proceeds of Crime* (London: Cabinet Office, 2000) 16.

30   HM Inspectorate of Constabulary, HM Crown Prosecution Service Inspectorate and HM Inspection of Court Services, *Payback Time*, fn 25 above.

Statistics on confiscation and asset recovery activities are scarce. ... Reliable data sources on the number of ongoing freezing and confiscation procedures (especially those to be executed in other Member States), the turnover of criminal organisations, the costs of judicial procedures or the administrative costs related to asset management or data collection activities are even scarcer. Therefore, the economic impacts of the foreseen actions are often difficult to quantify.[31]

In addition, the assumptions underpinning the increased focus on the money trail are open to criticism.[32] Further, while the policy discourse suggests that 'the confiscation system is at least partially effective, insofar as it delivers large sums of cash from the hands of convicted defendants into the public purse, in a manner which is just to defendants, according to the POCA regime',[33] there equally persists an ongoing debate both as to whether current approaches and operations are in fact effective and whether they are fair. While official discourse tends to emphasize the potential for expanding and improving the system,[34] a recurrent theme throughout this book is the need for restraint, that there is a need for considered reflection upon current techniques and how they are implemented in practice.

In summary, the contributions in this book challenge the asset recovery policy discourse. Equally, measures of 'success' and 'impact' are questioned. Practical implementation is also considered. This book thus offers a critique of emerging and contentious issues that permeate debate: within different fields, primarily the civil, criminal and regulatory realms; across different boundaries, namely 'criminal' and 'terrorism'; at the national and transnational level; in both civil and common law jurisdictions; and between policy, practice and research.

Core Themes and Contents

This book consists of three parts – Part I introduces the edited collection, Part II examines criminal and civil responses to illicit assets, while Part III examines responses to the financing of terrorist activity.

---

31   European Commission, *Commission Staff Working Paper*, fn 27 above, para. 2.1.2.

32   R.T. Naylor, 'Wash-out: A critique of follow-the-money methods in crime control policy' (1999) 32 *Crime, Law and Social Change* 1; H. Nelen, 'Hit them where it hurts most? The proceeds-of-crime approach in the Netherlands' (2004) 41 *Crime, Law and Social Change* 517.

33   HM Crown Prosecution Service Inspectorate, HM Inspectorate of Court Administration and HM Inspectorate of Constabulary, *Joint Thematic Review of Asset Recovery: Restraint and Confiscation Casework* (2010) Criminal Justice Joint Inspection, report available at: http://library.npia.police.uk/docs/hmcpsi/AssetRecovery.pdf, para. 2.1.

34   See, for example, HM Government, *Local to Global: Reducing the Risk from Organised Crime* (London: Stationery Office, 2011) para. 77 et seq.

Within the context of criminal and civil responses, Matthias Borgers examines in Chapter 2, 'Confiscation of the proceeds of crime: the European Union framework', how the confiscation of proceeds of crime has increasingly drawn the attention of the European Union. Borgers sets out the European framework, examining measures providing for confiscation of assets and for international cooperation. The European Union has recognized that mutually compatible practices enhance cooperation, thereby facilitating steps to confiscate dirty assets. The spur behind this was its concern to combat organized crime.[35] Throughout, Borgers considers how relevant measures have been implemented in practice drawing upon empirical studies conducted by both the European Union[36] and by researchers. The EU itself has recognized some of the difficulties in this regard. Not all member states have implemented, or adequately implemented, their obligations in relation to harmonizing powers of confiscation.[37] Significantly, present laws are only concerned with post-conviction confiscation. As will be seen in later chapters, a non-conviction based approach is becoming increasingly prominent in many jurisdictions, but the EU does not currently impose any obligations to implement such an approach.

One way of enhancing cooperation between Member States at a practical level is the obligation to establish central contact points – Asset Recovery Offices – to facilitate tracing and identification of proceeds of crime. While the EU, presently, only concerns itself with post-conviction confiscation Matthias Borgers makes the important point that cooperation might be possible where one Member State, but not another, is relying upon non-conviction based measures. While this is potentially of huge significance, Borgers argues that the mandates of national Asset Recovery Offices are actually quite limited. While the Council Decision concerning cooperation between Asset Recovery Offices[38] does seem to be effecting change in this regard, there are other measures that allow for exchange of information and intelligence between law-enforcement authorities which are not specifically tied to asset recovery cases.[39] Other measures such as the European evidence warrant offer further potential in confiscation cases, leading to the potential for confiscation processes to be integrated into the 'normal' set of EU criminal justice cooperation instruments.

Overall, Borgers is of the view that EU legislation on the confiscation of the proceeds of crime amounts to a reasonably coherent structure of regulations,

---

35   See, for example, 'Action Plan for combating organised crime' (OJEC 1997, C 251/1); 'Joint Action on money laundering' (OJEC 1998, L 333/1).

36   'Final Report on the first evaluation exercise – mutual legal assistance in criminal matters', published in OJEC 2001, C 216/14.

37   OJEU 2005, L 68/49.

38   OJEU 2007, L 332/103.

39   For example, Council Framework Decision 2006/960/JHA of 18 December 2006 on simplifying the exchange of information and intelligence between law enforcement authorities of the Member States of the European Union.

subject to two important limitations, namely that those regulations concerning organizational aspects are relatively modest in scope and pay little attention to legal safeguards for affected parties. Borgers also expresses some misgivings pertaining to the absence of specific obligations relating to cooperation in asset recovery cases, especially non-conviction based measures of asset forfeiture.

While Borgers views the EU post-conviction regime as a reasonably coherent structure, Karen Bullock and Stuart Lister in Chapter 3, 'Post-conviction Confiscation of Assets in England and Wales: Rhetoric and Reality' are more critical of the regime of confiscation law in England and Wales over the last 30 years. This regime represents a telling development within criminal justice policy in England and Wales, culminating in the Proceeds of Crime Act 2002, and its underpinning rationale is intuitively appealing – to deprive perpetrators of criminal acts of the benefit of their wrongdoing. But Bullock and Lister, quite rightly, call for rigorous scrutiny of both the legislative regime and its operation.

Despite the expansive approach adopted in England and Wales towards post-conviction confiscation provisions, in practice there have remained practical difficulties, including a reluctance to pursue confiscation before the courts, inexperience amongst police and lawyers, alongside judicial reticence. Even where confiscation has been ordered, the value realized tends to be of low value, all difficulties which were recognized a decade or so ago.[40] Furthermore, Bullock and Lister take issue with the very assumptions on which the post-conviction confiscation regime in England and Wales has been built and doubt whether they stand up to critical examination. Such assumptions include that: offenders retain part of their criminal income; confiscation will have a positive impact in reducing crime levels; and confiscation will prevent criminals from infiltrating the legitimate economy. They draw attention to the risks of overstating the supposed benefits of the confiscation regime as well as the absence of any meaningful data relating to this regime. The confiscation regime is exposed to further criticism when the authors examine the creeping and punitive effect of post-conviction confiscation under the Proceeds of Crime Act 2002. While preceding policy discourse drew attention to the organizers of crime, Bullock and Lister demonstrate how both law and policy is now expanding its net to ensnare both the 'big fish' as well as the 'small fry'. This gives rise to a number of concerns, such as: the punitive nature of confiscation; proportionality; the absence of due process safeguards given the hybrid civil/criminal nature of the proceedings; evidential implications relating to the presumption of innocence and the right to silence; the undermining of judicial independence; and difficulties in contesting a confiscation order whilst serving a prison sentence. They conclude by suggesting that the appeal of confiscation to the State lies in its expressive and moral qualities – the assertion that crime should not pay – as much as its instrumentality for controlling crime.

---

40 Performance and Innovation Unit (PIU), *Recovering the Proceeds of Crime* (London: Cabinet Office, 2000).

The focus on criminal assets has a long history in Italy. A recent *Impact Assessment* prepared for the European Commission reports findings that organized crime revenues in Italy are estimated at €150 billion per year and the costs of corruption at €50–60 billion per year.[41] In Chapter 4, 'Anti-Mafia Forfeiture in the Italian System', Daniele Piva examines how forfeiture is used in the fight against organized crime in the Italian context. He outlines a very complex super-structure of legislation which includes not just one type of 'forfeiture' but three principal forms of forfeiture: as a security measure, as a preventive measure and as a sanction. After outlining relevant procedural issues, Piva considers some assumptions underpinning forfeiture, including the 'social dangerousness of the individual', deriving from association with Mafia-type organizations and possession of assets disproportionate to lawful income/economic activities. Even where 'social dangerousness' is no longer at issue, for example where a person is dead, abroad, or incarcerated, forfeiture can still be sought, which Piva argues accords with the reasonableness principle.

A pressing issue for many jurisdictions is the 'end product' of asset recovery. In Italy, the administration of seized/ forfeited goods is handled by the National Agency for the administration and destination of seized and forfeited goods ('ANBSC'), which has experienced a number of difficulties in relation to: staff and money shortages; increasing number of seizures; statutory obligations to pursue preventive measures; lack of coordination across different bodies. Further problems exist in relation to the rights of third parties. Agencies in other jurisdictions have faced many similar problems, for example the Bulgarian Commission for Establishing Property Acquired from Criminal Activity (discussed in Chapter 5). Piva also examines the impact of European developments on the Italian forfeiture regime, contending that the recent proposal for a Framework Decision would, in the main, have little impact on the Italian regime as Italy already has in place a far-reaching model. Piva thus suggests that the Italian approach could be taken as a role model for future European developments in this field.

In contrast to the far-reaching model in Italy, perceived deficiencies in national criminal process are reflected, and perhaps amplified, in Chapter 5, 'Civil forfeiture of criminal assets in Bulgaria', where Rositsa Dzhekova outlines attempts to target proceeds of crime in the Bulgarian context. Two significant factors influenced recent developments in Bulgaria, namely: pressure for reform from the European Union prior to Bulgaria's accession in 2007, and the election of a new government on an anti-corruption agenda. In 2005, Bulgaria enacted the Law on Forfeiture of Proceeds of Criminal Activity ('LFPCA'). A new Commission for Establishing Property Acquired from Criminal Activity ('CEPACA') was also established.

Dzhekova argues that there has been a lack of political will to implement an effective system to target criminal assets, stemming from not only a lack of strategic vision and thinking but also from the significant influence of corruption and organized crime groups in preserving their vested interests. These shortcomings

---

41   European Commission, *Commission Staff Working Paper*, fn 27 above, para. 4.1.

are reflected in the watering-down of the LFPCA, the early drafts of which allowed for assets to be forfeited even where a criminal conviction had not been secured. This model was based on the Irish approach (see Chapter 7), and similar models also operate in a number of other jurisdictions such as Australia (see Chapter 6) and Canada (see Chapter 8). However, at the drafting stage, this provision was dropped, so that a criminal conviction was still a prerequisite under the LFPCA as enacted. The approach adopted under the LFPCA was that assets could be forfeited in civil proceedings but only subsequent to a criminal conviction. As mentioned earlier, the term 'civil forfeiture' here must be distinguished from the use of the term in other jurisdictions, where the term often refers to a non-conviction based approach to forfeiture of assets.[42] Dzhekova examines this process of civil forfeiture and associated institutional features. The agency tasked with implementing LFPCA is the Commission for Establishing Property Acquired from Criminal Activity ('CEPACA'). This agency is predominantly staffed by accountants and lawyers, in contrast to specialist agencies like the Serious Organised Crime Agency in the UK, the Criminal Assets Bureau in Ireland and the Criminal Assets Confiscation Taskforce in Australia where a multi-agency approach, including police officials, is favoured. The CEPACA then is hampered by not having investigatory powers that are associated with law-enforcement agencies, but is instead reliant on police and/ or prosecution agencies to supply evidence concerning criminal assets. In practice, such cooperation is rarely forthcoming, which adds to the problems of tight financial constraints and results in a 'reverse prioritizing' of small-scale cases. This point echoes the argument advanced by Bullock and Lister, in Chapter 3, in relation to 'small fry' criminals. A special issue discussed by Dzhekova is the management and disposal of seized assets, which offers a valuable lesson to other jurisdictions about the dangers of dissipation and corruption.

The regime under the LFPCA was generally seen to be in need of significant change. In November 2012, a new Law on the Forfeiture of Illegally Acquired Assets ('LFIAA') was enacted, which did adopt a non-conviction based asset forfeiture approach. There remains a notable difference between the Bulgarian non-conviction based approach and the non-conviction based approach in other jurisdictions discussed in this collection. In Bulgaria, there is still a requirement that a person be indicted for criminal wrongdoing. It remains to be seen how the LFIAA will work in practice.

The Bulgarian experience is especially useful in that a tool favoured in certain common law jurisdictions – a non-conviction based approach – is now being transplanted into a civil law jurisdiction. Developments in Bulgaria reflect a recent global trend towards a non-conviction based approach to asset forfeiture.[43] The next three chapters examine jurisdictions where a non-conviction

---

42   In the UK the term 'civil recovery' is used. See Part 5 of the Proceeds of Crime Act 2002.

43   See S. Young (ed.), *Civil Forfeiture of Criminal Property: Legal Measures for Targeting the Proceeds of Crime* (Cheltenham: Edward Elgar, 2009).

based approach has been effectively implemented, though not without their own share of criticisms. The chosen jurisdictions – Australia, Ireland and Canada – offer significant and original insights into the non-conviction based approach in common law jurisdictions. In a number of respects, these jurisdictions provide valuable lessons to other jurisdictions which may be contemplating adopting a non-conviction based approach or considering reform of existing laws. Two, Australia and Ireland, were identified as models of international best practice in a recent report commissioned by the US National Institute of Justice.[44] Australia and Canada are of further interest as federal jurisdictions, which is significant given suggestions that the European Union is considering a non-conviction based approach to targeting criminal assets.

In Chapter 6, 'Criminal Asset Recovery in Australia', Andrew Goldsmith, David Gray and Russell Smith examine recent developments in the Australian context. They demonstrate how concerns surrounding the growth of organized crime resulted in alternative law-enforcement approaches, a shift away from conviction-based schemes to non-conviction based schemes. The Australian experience is especially interesting due to the range of models existing there. Goldsmith et al. outline the approaches across the different jurisdictions, that is, the six states, two territories and the Commonwealth. The latest weapon adopted is the use of unexplained wealth orders at the federal level.[45] There have been a number of other significant changes in the Australian approach to proceeds of crime. The establishment of the multi-agency Criminal Assets Confiscation Taskforce in 2011 allows for a coordinated and integrated approach to targeting illicit assets, reducing duplication across different agencies.

Australia provides further insight into the effectiveness of the non-conviction based approach to asset forfeiture. The authors suggest that the supposed effectiveness of this approach against organized crime is unrealistic and that its implementation is far more difficult than might be expected. Drawing upon experiences at the state level, the authors claim that the application of unexplained wealth order legislation has been narrower than originally envisaged, but also that the new approach has allowed authorities to successfully target assets that would previously have been out of reach. Measuring the success of proceeds of crime approaches has proved difficult in many jurisdictions, and Australia is no different. The authors note how success in Australia is not measured simply on the basis of monetary amounts realized, but also encompasses disruptive effects on crime groups, referrals to revenue agencies, and, further, the capacity to handle more complex cases will also be taken into consideration. They do acknowledge, however, that evidence-based policy in this area remains weak. They also recognize how some scholars view the non-conviction based approach to asset recovery as

---

44   Booz Allen Hamilton, *Comparative Evaluation of Unexplained Wealth Orders: Prepared for the US Department of Justice, National Institute of Justice* (Washington, DC, 2011).

45   Crimes Legislation Amendment (Serious and Organised Crime) Act 2010.

unpalatable due to the circumvention of the establishment of criminal liability as the hitherto proper threshold for State forfeiture of assets, although many others adopt a contrary view. The next two chapters are firmly located in the former perspective.

In Chapter 7, '"Hitting Back" at Organized Crime: The Adoption of Civil Forfeiture in Ireland', Colin King examines how the Irish asset forfeiture regime has also been moulded against a backdrop of political and popular concerns surrounding organized criminal activity. His chapter focuses on the use of non-conviction based asset forfeiture to 'hit back' at the upper echelons of organized crime groups in Ireland. This Irish model, including the Irish legislation, the innovative multi-agency Criminal Assets Bureau, as well as judicial dicta, has played a central role in the expansion of the non-conviction based approach across the common law world.

The enactment of the Irish proceeds of crime model formed part of a raft of measures to tackle organized crime in the 1990s. King examines the demonstrative shift towards repressive policymaking in Ireland, with politicians notably vociferous in playing up the organized crime threat, demanding changes to the criminal justice system, calling for a recalibration of the scales of justice and criticizing the judiciary for being out of touch with reality. Ultimately, a non-conviction based approach was enacted to overcome such deficiencies. King, though, questions whether the threat of organized crime was as serious as it was portrayed in the political arena and then examines the principal arguments relied upon to justify the non-conviction based approach, as well as the criticisms that have been levied against this approach, before considering judicial reaction in Ireland. King then considers the effectiveness of civil forfeiture against organized criminal activities, though is obstructed by the limited data available upon which to ground a proper assessment, a concern echoed in Chapter 6.

Measuring the success of initiatives such as civil forfeiture is, of course, difficult. The next chapter on civil forfeiture in Canada, by Michelle Gallant, explores and reinforces this difficulty. Simply focusing on monetary returns tells little in and of itself. In Chapter 8, 'Civil Processes and Tainted Assets: Exploring Canadian Models of Forfeiture', Gallant maps the development of civil forfeiture in the Canadian provinces. Similar to Australia and Ireland, concern surrounding organized criminal activities heralded in the non-conviction based approach in Canada. Interestingly, alongside this, a second rationale for the Canadian adoption of civil forfeiture is based on the interests of victims of crime. Gallant considers the constitutional restraints under which civil forfeiture must operate in Canada, namely the federal/state division of powers and constitutionally protected rights under the Canadian Charter of Rights and Freedoms. This framework came before the Canadian Supreme Court in *Chatterjee v Attorney General of Ontario*,[46] where the court upheld the constitutionality of the Ontario civil forfeiture law. Gallant also identifies a number of prospects and problems for civil forfeiture in Canada.

---

46   [2009] 1 SCR 624.

She suggests that civil forfeiture now parallels, and has the potential to supplant, criminal law. Yet, despite its far-reaching potential, civil forfeiture has received little attention in Canada. While there are merits, Gallant argues that there are many reasons to approach this measure with caution. While civil forfeiture has been used against those suspected of involvement in drug trafficking, Gallant also outlines unexpected applications, such as seizure of vehicles linked to racing activities on public roads and property of individuals alleged to be culpable of assault – activities unconnected to organized crime groups. Gallant suggests that civil forfeiture is therefore being expanded and is critical of this tendency to cast a broad net over the assets of offenders rather than just illicit assets.

In Chapter 9, 'Asset Recovery: Substantive or Symbolic?', Jackie Harvey returns to asset recovery in the UK. She notes how the enactment of the Proceeds of Crime Act 2002 introduced wide-ranging powers, far beyond anti-money laundering provisions. That Act also provides a comprehensive regime of both criminal and civil recovery. Similar to Bullock and Lister (Chapter 3), Harvey argues that the policy discourse rested on unsound presumptions. Harvey takes this further, arguing that the existence of enforcement agencies, and indeed the creation of new agencies, results in a self-reinforcing, self-perpetuating rationale and legitimacy. Harvey then examines the 'scattered evidence' of the success of asset recovery. Despite unrealistic expectations, monetary recoveries have been modest. Not only does the asset-recovery regime cost more than it recovers, the persons targeted by the Proceeds of Crime Act tend to be low-level operators (as argued by Bullock and Lister in Chapter 3). Harvey then interrogates data obtained from the Serious Organised Crime Agency ('SOCA') and the Home Office. Detailing difficulties in obtaining such data, Harvey further notes that data supplied by SOCA does not reconcile with data in published SOCA sources. Nor is there consistency with data obtained from the Home Office, published on the Joint Asset Recovery Database ('JARD'). Putting aside difficulties in reconciling different sets of data, Harvey points to significant increases in both the volume of cash seizures and the volume of confiscation orders in recent years. Despite these increases, the average size of seizures has tended to decrease, which leads Harvey to conclude that those being subjected to the legislation are the less sophisticated operators. This reinforces suspicions that while asset-recovery laws might be intuitively appealing, they do not necessarily work well in practice.

There is a tendency when discussing criminal assets to think of assets held by drug dealers as the paradigm example. Reference to 'organized crime' usually conjures images of a 'Godfather' type figure directing others to commit the illegal activity in question and amassing huge fortunes from these crimes. As a result, crimes of the powerful and corrupt may fade into the shadows, despite their prevalence and even larger scale. In Chapter 10, 'Corruption, the United Nations Convention Against Corruption ('UNCAC') and Asset Recovery', Indira Carr and Robert Jago examine how asset recovery can be used to target illicit assets obtained through corrupt actions, especially topical now given recent revolutions in Arab countries such as Egypt, which resulted in the summary overthrow of several kleptocratic dictators. The problem then arises that these political elites have siphoned off assets for their personal use, often diverting the proceeds to foreign, more stable jurisdictions for safekeeping. Their home countries later seek the return of those assets, but the recovery of assets can be challenging, even when sympathetic and well-governed Western countries are involved, as Carr and Jago illustrate. In light of these complexities, the United Nations Convention against Corruption 2003[47] devotes great attention to asset recovery, as does a number of other international instruments. Carr and Jago examine the international anti-corruption framework, before outlining specific measures, such as the use of shell companies, used to hide ownership of assets.

In making their assessment of the regime, Carr and Jago explore theoretical justifications for asset recovery, namely: retribution, deterrence, reparation and rehabilitation, drawing upon examples such as Siemens' use of bribery to secure lucrative contracts and the siphoning of assets from Nigeria by Sani Abacha. They contend that it is not possible to declare any primary justification in cases of corruption and that each case must be taken on its own merits. The UN Convention against Corruption is considered by drawing upon the case of Ferdinand Marcos to illustrate difficulties in asset recovery. While, Carr and Jago suggest, the UNCAC puts in place stringent measures to prevent laundering of assets and to facilitate recovery, the Convention's effectiveness ultimately still rests on the political will to properly implement and enforce these provisions.

In Part III of the book, measures designed to tackle the financing of terrorism are considered. This group of chapters advances our objectives by providing selective surveys of a problem which has become highly prominent since 11 September 2001, and which remains a prime preoccupation of the financial and political worlds. There was some interest in terrorism finance before 2001. For example, the Chief Constable of the Royal Ulster Constabulary claimed in 1988 that 'Money is a crucial factor in the continuance of terrorism'.[48] However, beyond the United Kingdom few paid much heed, and by the time of the attacks on 11 September only four States (including the United Kingdom) had ratified the UN's International Convention for the Suppression of the Financing of Terrorism 1999.[49] However, the attacks in 2001 energized international and domestic agendas, though the data which shows that terrorism is a highly geared enterprise or that the subsequent measures have much impacted on the flow of finance is often lacking. Nevertheless, terrorism has become a major focus of the United Nations ever since that time, with the subject of the threat of terrorism finances becoming prominent in its pronouncements. Thus, the seminal UN Security Resolution 1373 of 28 September 2001 presents as its first demand in paragraph 1 that 'all States

---

47   UNGA resolution 58/4 of 31 October 2003.

48   Chief Constable for the R.U.C., *Annual Report for 1987* (Belfast, 1988) p. xiii. For the UK's response, see C.P. Walker, *The Prevention of Terrorism in British Law* (2nd ed., Manchester: Manchester University Press, 1992) ch. 7.

49   A/RES/54/109 of 9 December 1999.

shall: (a) Prevent and suppress the financing of terrorist acts; (b) Criminalize the wilful provision or collection, by any means, directly or indirectly, of funds ...; (c) Freeze without delay funds and other financial assets or economic resources ...; (d) Prohibit their nationals or any persons and entities within their territories from making any funds, financial assets or economic resources or financial or other related services available ...' These demands added to the sanctions regimes already put in place against the Taliban and al-Qa'ida,[50] and have been treated as peremptory international norms enforced through the Security Council's Counter-Terrorism Committee.[51] This strong lead has been taken up by other international bodies. The European Union has been conspicuously enthusiastic, inventing in 2002 its own version of sanctions regimes (described in Chapter 14), as well as cooperating in mass financial surveillance through 'SWIFT' – the Society for Worldwide Interbank Financial Telecommunication, an organization, based in Brussels, that holds information for nearly 9,000 financial institutions about the millions of electronic financial transactions that take place daily.[52] Another major global player in the terrorism financing specialism has been the Financial Action Task Force ('FATF'), which in October 2001 quickly issued eight Special Recommendations on Terrorist Financing, revised to nine in 2004 and revised again in 2012.[53] They demand State action on: implementation of UN instruments; national criminal law; civil law freezing and confiscation of assets; reporting suspicious transactions; international cooperation; monitoring alternative remittance systems, wire transfers and cash couriers; and tighter regulation of non-profit organizations such as charities.

In keeping with the objectives of this book, bringing fresh perspectives and especially comparative perspectives, Part III does not attempt to describe the whole field[54] but seeks to provide original insights into some of the most acute

50   UNSCR 1267 of 15 October 1999 and 1333 of 19 December 2000. Currently in force are UN Security Council Resolutions 1989 of 17 June 2011 and Resolution 2083 of 17 December 2012. For enforcement, see Security Council Committee pursuant to resolutions 1267 (1999) and 1989 (2011) concerning Al-Qaida and associated individuals and entities (http://www.un.org/sc/committees/1267/, accessed 1 August 2013).

51   http://www.un.org/en/sc/ctc/ (accessed 1 August 2013).

52   See Agreement between the European Union and the United States of America on the processing and transfer of Financial Messaging Data from the EU to the US for the purposes of the Terrorist Finance Tracking Program (Brussels, 2010); European Commission, *Proposal for a Council Decision* (COM(2010) 316 final).

53   http://www.fatf-gafi.org/topics/fatfrecommendations/documents/international standardsoncombatingmoneylaunderingandthefinancingofterrorismproliferation-the fatfrecommendations.html (accessed 10 April 2013).

54   See instead C. Eckes, *EU Counter-Terrorist Policies and Fundamental Rights: The Case of Individual Sanctions* (Oxford: Oxford University Press, 2009); M. Levi, 'Combating the financing of terrorism' (2010) 50 *British Journal of Criminology* 650; M. Pieth (ed.), *Financing Terrorism* (Heidelberg: Springer, 2010); C. Walker, *Terrorism and the Law* (Oxford: Oxford University Press, 2011); C.C. Murphy, *EU Counter-*

controversies in order to determine whether the law-making and enforcement which has profusely flowed since 2001 is effective or fair. In that spirit, the collection begins with an inquiry by Clive Walker in Chapter 11 into 'Terrorism financing and the policing of charities: who pays the price?' As mentioned, the FATF has taken a special interest in the relationship between charitable funding and terrorism. However, it is the approach of the UK's Charity Commission which is used as the case study for this chapter, aided by original research into its partially unpublished enquiries and documentation. The mechanisms for the policing of charities in regard to terrorism financing, including by the Charity Commission, are evident and extensive, but, as well as providing an exposition of these instruments, the key question tackled in this chapter is 'who pays the price' for that policing? It is found that the impact of policing is very uneven, an outcome which raises doubts about the strategies being deployed and whether different tactics might be more suitable. In pursuance of this theme, there is an analysis of where the policing burden falls in terms of internal and external policing as well as an analysis of modes of policing in terms of 'green-light' and 'red-light' approaches.[55] In view of the notoriety of terrorism, it is surprising to learn that the approach of the Charity Commission is decidedly 'green-light'. As a result of this serial indulgence, various persistent abuses have been discovered and often publicized by the mass media in lurid terms. The effect is that individual trustees may be sanctioned but the charities themselves often are allowed to continue, and service organizations which assist them, such as banks, also seem to escape official attention. Because of widespread criticism of the effectiveness of the Charity Commission, some of which arises internationally from US diplomatic sources and has been disclosed through the agency of Julian Assange's Wikileaks, there are belated signs of greater efforts by the Charity Commission to issue clearer and stronger guidance and also special funding to assist Muslim charities to improve their regulatory standards.

Taking the problem forwards, Walker suggests that two obvious reactions should be avoided: either to swing entirely towards criminal prosecution and asset forfeiture and thereby downplay competing public goods arising from voluntarism; or to expect the Charity Commission to act in a more punitive fashion contrary to its statutory remit and entrenched 'partnership' culture. Therefore, a suggested third way is to further the value of financial investigation to facilitate intelligence-gathering. Prosecution and confiscation remain ultimate possible outcomes but

---

Terrorism Law: Pre-Emption and the Rule of Law (Oxford: Hart Publishing, 2012); I. Cameron (ed.), *EU Sanctions: Law and Policy Issues Concerning Restrictive Measures* (Cambridge: Intersentia, 2013); Independent Reviewer of the Terrorism Legislation (D. Anderson), *First and Second Reports on the Operation of the Terrorist Asset Freezing etc Act 2010* (London: 2011 and 2012) and HM Treasury, *Responses* (London: Cm 8287 and 8553, 2012 and 2013).

55   See especially C. Harlow and R. Rawlings, *Law and Administration* (3rd ed., Cambridge: Cambridge University Press, 2009) ch. 1.

should be less pressing than objectives such as disruption and the gathering of leads about terrorism activities rather than just financing. In this way, it is hoped to deliver information about terrorism networks and to close off the facilitation of violence but without hurting worthy causes being pursued by humanitarian activists.

Given that it was the prime target for the September 11 attacks, one might expect the US Government to have taken decisive action against terrorism. Leaving aside the military aspects of the 'Global War on Terror', some of which are still keenly experienced in the form of Guantánamo Bay detentions and drone strikes, there have also been extensive and drastic legal responses to terrorism finances,[56] especially those contained in Title III of the USA PATRIOT Act, ss 803 to 815, also known as the International Money Laundering Abatement and Anti-Terrorist Financing Act 2001,[57] which added to the offences of material support in 18 USC s 2339A, enacted in 1994,[58] and in 18 USC s 2339B, enacted in 1996.[59] These criminal law sanctions are but the tip of a bulky enforcement iceberg, which includes export controls under the Arms Export Control Act 1976,[60] the US Terrorist Finance Tracking Program[61] (already mentioned in relation to 'SWIFT'), the Financial Crimes Enforcement Network ('FinCEN') of the US Treasury Department's Office of Terrorism and Financial Intelligence which processes the Currency Transaction Reports and Suspicious Transaction Reports,[62] and the Office of Foreign Assets Control ('OFAC') of the US Department of the Treasury which administers and enforces sanctions against listed persons and organizations suspected of terrorism.[63]

Laura Donohue in Chapter 13, 'US Efforts to Stem the Flow of Funds to Terrorist Organizations: Export Controls, Financial Sanctions and Material Support', seeks to provide analysis and critique of these key operations in this vast array of financial governance, as well as plotting the different emphases between them in different periods. She uncovers that following the attacks of 9/11, the US shifted its emphasis from export controls to financial sanctions and material support prosecutions. But these favoured mechanisms have resulted in many distasteful features and effects. As for financial sanctions, after 9/11 there was an unseemly rush to list individuals and entities based on undisclosed evidence

---

56   The financing of the attacks is considered by the National Commission on Terrorist Attacks upon the United States, *Report* (Washington, DC: GPO, 2004).

57   PL 107-56. See also Suppression of the Financing of Terrorism Convention Implementation Act 2002 (PL 107-197 s 301).

58   Violent Crime Control and Law Enforcement Act 1994, PL 103-322, s 120005.

59   Antiterrorism and Effective Death Penalty Act 1996, PL 104-132, s 303.

60   PL 94-329.

61   See Executive Order 13224 and the United Nations Participation Act of 1945 s 5 (22 USC 287c).

62   http://www.fincen.gov/ (accessed 1 August 2013).

63   http://www.treasury.gov/resource-center/sanctions/Pages/default.aspx (accessed 1 August 2013).

of involvement, while the designated people and organizations were given no notice and had no opportunity to contest their listings. Due process has been almost entirely absent (a complaint later sustained by the courts in the UK and the EU regarding their equivalent sanctions systems). Material support has grown even more prominent, but the various offences are found to be equally beset with constitutional and legal problems, including over-reach (almost amounting to a crime of terrorism and with an increasingly attenuated connection between being a terrorist and engagement in violence), a lack of due process and incursions into free speech and free association.[64]

Another instance of national reactions to the financing of terrorism, though with a much longer history than the American experience, is drawn from Spain. The Basque terrorist group ETA (*Euskadi Ta Askatasuna*) also provides a fascinating case study. Another reason for attention is that, perhaps like the Irish Republican Army in Northern Ireland, ETA is embedded within some domestic communities rather than representing an international or transnational threat as was the early conception of the threat from al-Qa'ida.[65] The result is to open up to ETA an enticing variety of funding opportunities, which have been seized upon with notable ingenuity and adaptability by ETA over 50 years. In response, Thomas Baumert and Mikel Buesa discuss Spanish counter-measures in Chapter 13, 'Dismantling terrorist economics: the Spanish experience'. The chapter plots the many facets of ETA financing and how they have affected wide sections of Basque society, including public institutions as well as individual victims (and the businesses from which is extorted a 'revolutionary tax' or 'compulsory contribution'). Other funds are raised through kidnapping, robberies (including from banks) and a wide variety of other illicit operations, such as drug trafficking and other forms of illegal trading. Some of the most inventive and insidious tactics have involved the use of political parties and other municipal and social organizations to act as fronts for the receipt of public funding, amounting to over half of ETA's income between 1993 and 2002. Newspapers have also been sources of both political and financial funding. Estimates are made by the authors of the overall intake, and it is claimed that the banning of *Batasuna* and the judicial investigation of many of the organizations operating in ETA's orbit, throttled significantly the terrorist's economic inflow after 2002. However, the public authorities, especially the Basque government, are accused of complacency in allowing 'economic oxygen' to flow to ETA, which was able to convert its sources of income to a

---

64   But see *Holder v. Humanitarian Law Project*, 561 U.S. ____ (2010).

65   There is now greater appreciation of the phenomenon of 'insider' lone wolves or 'neighbour' terrorists. See C. Walker, '"Know Thine Enemy as Thyself": Discerning friend from foe under anti-terrorism laws' (2008) 32 *Melbourne Law Review* 275; M. Crone and M. Harrow, 'Homegrown terrorism in the west' (2011) 23 *Terrorism & Political Violence* 521; EU Counter-Terrorism Coordinator, *Preventing Lone Wolf Terrorism* (Brussels, 2012); B. Barnes, 'Confronting the one-man wolf pack' (2012) 42 *Boston University Law Review* 1613.

semi-legal status. Despite the evident enforcement problems of dealing with such embedded terrorism, the authors contend that a continuous economic throttling of the terrorist network, by tying down the different sources of income one by one, no matter how insignificant they may seem from the overall perspective, and by all legal means available, remains a vital task for government. It is indeed a vital point in relation to hierarchical, ethnically-based terrorist groups like ETA, and the counter-terrorism lessons learnt through responding to it should not be entirely forgotten because they do not fit the heterarchical and disestablished profile of most emanations of *jihadi* terrorism that precisely.

Finally, though the United Nations has been the prime international agenda setter, one might argue that, within its jurisdiction, the European Union has been more active and has secured more direct achievements. Therefore Chapter 14, 'EU Counter-Terrorist Sanctions: The Questionable Success Story of Criminal Law in Disguise', by Christina Eckes, examines European counter-terrorist sanctions. She immediately encounters many of the same criticisms put forward by Donohue in Chapter 12, above all breaches of the fundamental rights to due process. These shortcomings are built into the fabric of the system and cannot easily be overcome by subsequent reformulations, which have included: the introduction of a delisting procedure;[66] the focal point;[67] the regular review of the listings;[68] the ombudsperson;[69] and expanded humanitarian exemptions.[70] This condemnation is made on the basis that sanctions substantially amount to a criminal charge within the meaning of Article 6 of the European Convention on Human Rights ('ECHR') rather than temporary emergency measures. The careful analysis undertaken by Eckes suggests that autonomous EU counter-terrorist sanctions do constitute criminal law in substance and that they are in many ways built on, and interlinked with, *national* criminal law. The result is that these sanctions measures are vulnerable to legal challenge, and the courts are becoming increasingly bold in their willingness to traduce the handiwork of international bodies such as the European Union or even the United Nations.[71] In addition, the chapter considers the efficiency of sanctions. But it is found that there is limited data and no proper efficiency evaluations and that even the limited effectiveness assessments that have

---

66   First introduced by: Guidelines of the Al Qaida Sanctions Committee for the conduct of its work, adopted on 7 November 2002, as amended on 10 April 2003, 21 December 2005, 29 November 2006, 12 February 2007, 9 December 2008, 22 July 2010, 26 January 2011 and 30 November 2011 ('Guidelines'), para. 7; available at: http://www. un.org/sc/committees/1267/pdf/1267_guidelines.pdf (accessed 21 March 2013).

67   UN SC Res 1730 (2006), para. 1.

68   UN SC Res 1822 (2008), paras 25–26.

69   UN SC Res 1904 (2009).

70   UN SC Res 1452 (2001).

71   See Kadi I [2008] ECR I-06351; Cases C584/10 P, C593/10 P and C595/10 P *Kadi II* 18 July 2013; *Her Majesty's Treasury v Mohammed Jabar Ahmed and others (FC); Her Majesty's Treasury v Mohammed al-Ghabra (FC); R (on the application of Hani El Sayed Sabaei Youssef) v Her Majesty's Treasury* [2010] UKSC 2.

been conducted are flawed and in any event do not also consider the efficiency of these long-term policies which, rather like the bleak 'Global War on Terror' have no end in sight.

PART II:
Criminal and Civil Responses to Illicit Assets

Chapter 2

Confiscation of the Proceeds of Crime: The European Union Framework

Matthias J. Borgers

Introduction

Opportunities for confiscating the proceeds of crime have been attracting increasing attention in the European Union. This attention manifests itself in three different ways. First, confiscation was mentioned as one of the methods for combating certain types of crime, such as money laundering, drug trafficking, defrauding community funds and organized crime. This is reflected in various legislative instruments which recommend provisions for confiscation.[1] Second, the recovery of criminal money is increasingly seen as an independent issue not linked to a specific type of crime. This is evidenced, *inter alia*, by the Framework Decision on confiscation, which requires member states to put in place effective legislation for confiscation with respect to a variety of criminal acts.[2] Similarly, attention is also being paid to international cooperation in confiscation cases, as evidenced by the Framework Decision on the execution in the European Union of orders freezing property or evidence[3] and the Framework Decision on the execution in the European Union of confiscation orders.[4] Finally, confiscation and confiscation legislation are also seen as part of the efforts to combat terrorist financing.[5]

This chapter provides an overview of the European Union's various legal instruments and initiatives that are of importance to international cooperation in confiscation cases. Legal instruments specifically aimed at confiscation cases, as well as other regulations relevant to cooperation, will be discussed. Where

---

1 For a detailed overview see Gilmore, W.C., *Dirty Money. The Evolution of International Measures to Counter Money Laundering and the Financing of Terrorism* (4th ed., Strasbourg: Council of Europe, 2011).

2 Council Framework Decision 2006/783/JHA of 6 October 2006 on the application of the principle of mutual recognition to confiscation orders.

3 Council Framework Decision 2003/577/JHA of 22 July 2003 on the execution in the European Union of orders freezing property or evidence.

4 Council Framework Decision 2006/783/JHA of 6 October 2006 on the application of the principle of mutual recognition to confiscation orders.

5 See the European Council 'Declaration on combating terrorism' of 25 March 2004, Council document 7906/04, especially part 5(a), and 'The fight against terrorist financing' of 9 December 2004, Council document 14180/4/04, parts 14, 15 and 27.

possible, based on EU evaluations, the chapter will indicate the working of these legal instruments to date. Using this overview, the chapter will identify a system of standards and benchmarks that are, or should be, applied within the European Union as standards, or minimum standards, for proper international cooperation in confiscation cases. Finally, the chapter will briefly discuss developments that can be expected in the near future.

Initiatives and Instruments Specifically Aimed at Confiscation Cases

Joint Action on Money Laundering

The first instrument specifically aimed at confiscation cases is the Council of the European Union's Joint Action regarding money laundering, the identification, tracing, freezing, seizing and confiscation of instrumentalities and the proceeds of crime ('Joint Action').[6] The Joint Action was a result of the Action Plan for combating organized crime.[7] One of the recommendations of this Action Plan concerns efforts to strengthen the tracing and seizure of illegal assets and the enforcement of court decisions on asset confiscations.

The preamble of the Joint Action on money laundering states, *inter alia*, that mutually compatible practices make cooperation at a European level more efficient as regards the confiscation of proceeds of crime. Reference is made to the need to speed up procedures for judicial cooperation in combating organized crime and considerably shortening the time limits for submitting and responding to requests for action, thereby reinforcing the reference in the Action Plan for combating organized crime. It is worth detailing the actual obligations laid down in the Joint Action as these obligations are still of great importance in structuring the practice of international cooperation today.[8]

Table 2.1   Joint action on money laundering obligations

Article 1	(1): Member States must ensure – within certain limitations – that no reservations are made in respect of Articles 2 and 6 of the Council of Europe Convention on Laundering, Search, Seizure and Confiscation of the Proceeds from Crime. As a result (among other things) confiscation of proceeds from criminal acts must be made possible on a large scale.

6   OJEC 1998, L 333/1.
7   OJEC 1997, C 251/1.
8   The provisions of the Joint Action still apply, although some were revoked by the Framework Decision on money laundering. Most of the revoked provisions, however, have been replaced by comparable, but somewhat more explicitly formulated provisions. See second sub-heading of the section of this chapter.

Article 1	(2): Member States must make provision for the possibility of substitute value confiscation (in addition to or instead of confiscation of objects), both in national proceedings and in international cooperation. This includes requests for the enforcement of foreign confiscation orders.
Article 1	(3): Member States must make provision to allow suspected proceeds from crime to be identified and traced at the request of another Member State, if a criminal act is suspected of having been committed. Such assistance should be given at the earliest possible stage in an investigation.
Article 2	Each Member State must make provision for a user-friendly guide, including information about which authority can provide advice on legal assistance, and specifying what assistance a Member State is able to provide in confiscation cases. The guide must also include details on any significant restrictions on providing legal assistance and the information that requesting States must supply. Each Member State's guide will – with the intervention of the Council – be translated into all the official languages and distributed to the Member States, the European Justice Network (EJN) and Europol. Member States must keep the guide up-to-date.*
Article 3	Member States must give the same priority to all requests for legal assistance relating to asset identification, tracing, freezing, seizing and confiscation as is given to similar measures in national proceedings.
Article 4	Member States shall encourage direct contacts between the parties involved in the legal assistance. The cooperation must adhere to the following rules: • if a formal request for legal assistance is necessary, the requesting State must ensure that it is correctly prepared and observes the applicable requirements of the requested State; • Member States must not submit requests for legal assistance unless the precise nature of the assistance is known; • a request for legal assistance marked 'urgent' or indicating a deadline must explain the reason for the urgency or deadline; • if it is not possible to comply in full with a request for legal assistance, the requested Member State will make every effort to comply with the request in another way.
Article 5	(1): Member States will, insofar as this is not contrary to national law, take all necessary steps to minimise the risk of assets being dissipated. This includes measures that serve to freeze or seize assets expeditiously so that a subsequent request for confiscation is not frustrated.
Article 5	(2): If completion of a request for legal assistance requires an investigation to be conducted in a region other than the region dealing with the request, the Member State will ensure, insofar as this is not contrary to national law, that the necessary assistance can be provided without any need for a further written request.
Article 5	(3): If completion of a request for legal assistance requires further investigation on a related issue and the requesting State submits a supplementary written request, the requested State will, insofar as this is not contrary to national law, expedite execution of such supplementary request.

Article 6	This Article sums up a number of measures that serve to guarantee international cooperation in general. Under these measures:

- Member States will acquaint their judiciary with 'best practices' in international cooperation in asset recovery cases;
- Member States will ensure that the parties involved in international cooperation receive appropriate training;
- The Presidency and interested Member States will organise seminars to promote and develop 'best practices' and to encourage compatibility between the various procedures.

Note: * This user-friendly guide resembles the 'Statements of good practice' that member states have made, or have to make, based on the Joint Action on good practice in mutual legal assistance in criminal matters, OJEC 1998, L 191/1. For these statements, see Council document SN 1371/00.

This summary shows that the Joint Action on money laundering contains a constellation of legal and practical standards and principles designed to guarantee effective and efficient international cooperation in confiscation cases. The next issue is how it has been implemented in practice.

Empirical material on the practical operation of these legal and practical standards and principles is available in the form of the evaluation study conducted on the basis of the Joint Action establishing a mechanism for evaluating the application and implementation at national level of international undertakings in the fight against organized crime.[9] The first evaluation exercise that took place based on the Joint Action addressed 'mutual legal assistance and urgent requests for the tracing and seizure of assets'.[10] Given the importance of seizure for international cooperation in asset recovery cases, the results of this evaluation exercise are relevant to the present study.

The evaluation study was conducted by studying the situation in all the then member states, *inter alia*, by means of a questionnaire and working visits. Based on the results, reports on all member states were issued.[11] After these reports were completed, the Council of the European Union adopted a final report on 28 May 2001.[12] This report provides a reasonably positive overview of legal assistance in the European Union but makes several recommendations for improving existing practices. Specifically as regards international cooperation in confiscation cases, these recommendations have a clear overlap with the principles and standards included in the Joint Action on money laundering. More specifically, the Council insists upon: early and unconditional ratification of the conventions relevant to legal

---

9   OJEC 1997, L 344/7.

10   'Final Report on the first evaluation exercise – mutual legal assistance in criminal matters', published in OJEC 2001, C 216/14.

11   These reports can be found on the Council's website: http://consilium.europa.eu.

12   'Final Report on the first evaluation exercise – mutual legal assistance in criminal matters', published in OJEC 2001, C 216/14.

assistance;[13] the need for an accelerated procedure for tracing bank accounts;[14] fast, efficient and, where possible, informal legal assistance procedures, and provisions to ensure that a specific measure applied at the request of another member state is not executed less efficiently than the same measure in a domestic procedure;[15] the exchange of 'best practices' with the aim, among other things, of improving cooperation between member states;[16] and the desirability of developing and making available a standard form for outgoing requests for legal assistance.[17]

Framework Decision on Money Laundering

The Framework Decision on money laundering, the identification, tracing, freezing, seizing, and confiscation of instrumentalities and the proceeds of crime[18] ('Framework Decision on money laundering'), adopted by the Council on 26 June 2001, directly builds on the Joint Action on money laundering. Under Article 5 of the Framework Decision on money laundering, a number of the provisions – Articles 1, 3, 5 (1) and Article 8(1) – of the Joint Action on money laundering are revoked, while the Framework Decision prescribes largely similar, but somewhat more tightly formulated, obligations or obligations expressed in more mandatory terms.[19] A different approach is taken for the obligations of Article 1(3) and Article 5(1) of the Joint Action, which have not been included (even in an adapted form) in the Framework Decision on money laundering. Essentially these concern the obligations for member states, at the request of another member state, to identify and trace suspected proceeds of crime and to take all measures to minimize the risk of assets being dissipated. These obligations were explicitly included in the initial proposal for the Framework Decision.[20] However, it was later decided to include these obligations in the Framework Decisions on mutual recognition such

---

13   Compare Recommendation 1 and Article 1(1), Joint Action on money laundering.

14   Compare Recommendation 3 and Article 1(3), Joint Action on money laundering.

15   Compare Recommendations 5, 8 and 15, and Articles 3, 4 and 5(2) and (3), Joint Action on money laundering.

16   Compare Recommendation 7 and Article 6, Joint Action on money laundering.

17   Compare Recommendation 9 and Article 4, Joint Action on money laundering.

18   OJEC 2001, L 182/1.

19   An example of such a tightening of the rules is the replacement of the words 'in minor cases' in Article 1(2) of the Joint Action on money laundering by 'that value would be less than EUR 4000' in Article 3 of the Framework Decision on money laundering. The time limit for transposing the Framework Decision used in Article 6(1) of the Framework Decision on money laundering is an example of more mandatory terms in comparison to the limited open-end arrangement used in Article 8(2) of the Joint Action on money laundering.

20   Council document 10232/00. See also Council documents 9903/00 and 9903/00 ADD 1.

as the Framework Decision on freezing property or evidence[21] and the Framework Decision on mutual recognition of confiscation orders.[22] These legal instruments, however, do not include an obligation with respect to the tracing and identification of suspected proceeds of crime. It is unclear why the Framework Decision does not provide for an equivalent of this obligation. The provisions in the Joint Action on money laundering that have not been revoked are, for that matter, still in force.[23]

Framework Decision on Freezing Property or Evidence

The Framework Decision on the execution in the European Union of orders freezing property or evidence (also referred to as the Framework Decision on freezing property or evidence, or the Framework Decision on freezing) was adopted on 22 July 2003.[24] This Framework Decision reflects the view commonly held within the European Union that mutual recognition is the 'cornerstone' of judicial cooperation in Europe.[25] The Framework Decision on freezing lays down rules whereby a member state must recognize and execute on its territory a freezing order issued in criminal proceedings by a judicial authority of another member state (under Article 1).

The Framework Decision aims to establish a simplified procedure for executing orders to freeze property or evidence in member states other than the member state in which the relevant decision was taken. With respect to the confiscation of the proceeds of crime, this means that it should be relatively easy to seize property deriving from a criminal act or, as the case may be, property that has a value corresponding, either wholly or partially, to such proceeds. The most important features of this simplified procedure are outlined below.

An important principle of the simplified procedure (according to Article 3(2)) is that the dual criminality requirement is not imposed with respect to quite a number of criminal acts, insofar as they are covered by the freezing order. If an act is not included in the relevant list, a member state can nevertheless apply the dual criminality requirement as a condition (under Article 3(4)). In outline, the simplified procedure is as follows. The judicial authority issuing the freezing order sends the freezing order, together with a standardized certificate, directly

---

21   Council Framework Decision 2003/577/JHA of 22 July 2003 on the execution in the European Union of orders freezing property or evidence.

22   Council Framework Decision 2006/783/JHA of 6 October 2006 on the application of the principle of mutual recognition to confiscation orders.

23   The European Parliament insisted that these provisions would also be included in the Framework Decision on money laundering. See the report of 25 October 2000, PE 294.241. It cannot be inferred from public Council documents why the Council of the European Union did not adopt the European Parliament's suggestion. Compare Council document 14897/00.

24   OJEU 2003, L 196/45.

25   See V. Mitsilegas, 'The constitutional implications of mutual recognition in criminal matters in the EU' (2006) 43 *Common Market Law Review* 1277.

to the judicial authority in the other member state authorized to execute the order (under Article 4). The order will subsequently be executed immediately, unless one of the exhaustive grounds for refusal listed in Article 7 is present, or one of the exhaustive grounds for suspension listed in Article 8, applies. Under Article 3(3), the decision whether to proceed with the execution must be taken 'as soon as possible and, whenever practicable, within 24 hours of receipt of the freezing order'. If additional coercive measures, such as a search, must be taken for execution of the freezing order, the measures will be applied with due observance of the executing member state's relevant rules (under Article 5(3)). This usually means that a request for legal assistance, or a supplementary request, will be necessary if such coercive measures are to be applied.

In principle, the property will remain frozen until a request for execution of a confiscation order is received (according to Article 6(1) in conjunction with Article 10(1)), although restricting conditions may be imposed under certain circumstances. The Framework Decision on mutual recognition of confiscation orders, which is discussed below, also embeds the principle of mutual recognition with respect to execution, and so such execution can also be via a simplified procedure.

Framework Decision on Confiscation

The Framework Decision on the confiscation of crime-related proceeds, instrumentalities and property ('Framework Decision on confiscation') was adopted by the Council on 24 February 2005.[26] The most important objective of this Framework Decision is the harmonization of the powers of confiscation in the different member states of the European Union. The preamble of the Framework Decision on confiscation shows this harmonization to be important for two reasons. First and foremost, it is stated that, notwithstanding the obligations flowing from the Convention on laundering, search, seizure and confiscation of the proceeds from crime and the Framework Decision on money laundering, not all member states have provided (or adequately provided) for the opportunity to confiscate proceeds from criminal acts carrying a prison sentence of more than one year. Furthermore, the Framework Decision aims at ensuring that member states have effective rules governing the confiscation of proceeds from crime, *inter alia*, in relation to the onus of proof regarding the source of assets held by a person convicted of an offence related to organized crime. The obligations included in this Framework Decision further elaborate on the minimum conditions that member states must incorporate in their legislation.

At present, harmonization of the laws of the member states as regards confiscation only entails the imposition of confiscation sanctions by a court following proceedings relating to one or more criminal acts.[27] The Framework

---

26 OJEU 2005, L 68/49.
27 Compare Article 1 of the Framework Decision on confiscation.

Decision does not pertain to forms of confiscation outside the framework of criminal proceedings, such as civil forfeiture or civil recovery in British and Irish law.[28]

Framework Decision on Mutual Recognition of Confiscation Orders

A Framework Decision that pertains to confiscation and international cooperation in confiscation cases is the Framework Decision on the application of the principle of mutual recognition to confiscation orders ('Framework Decision on mutual recognition of confiscation orders'), which was adopted on 6 October 2006.[29] The objective of this Framework Decision is clear from the preamble (paragraph 8):

> The purpose of this Framework Decision is to facilitate cooperation between Member States as regards the mutual recognition and execution of orders to confiscate property so as to oblige a Member State to recognise and execute in its territory confiscation orders issued by a court competent in criminal matters of another Member State.

This Framework Decision builds on the Framework Decision on freezing property or evidence by developing a procedure whereby confiscation orders in many cases can and must be executed in another member state in a straightforward manner, in other words, without requiring complicated legal assistance requests. Implementing such a procedure obviously requires that the procedure be incorporated into domestic legislation in all the member states. However, it is also pointed out in paragraph 10 of the preamble that the proper practical operation of this procedure requires close liaison between the competent national authorities. Furthermore, member states are required to use all available means in order to identify the correct location of property, including the use of all available information systems.[30]

The procedure as embodied in the Framework Decision on mutual recognition of confiscation orders is largely similar to the procedure of the Framework Decision on freezing property or evidence. Here, too, it is an important principle, set out in Article 6, that there is no requirement for dual criminality with respect to several criminal acts, insofar as they underlie the confiscation order. For other offences, the executing state may make the recognition and execution of a confiscation order subject to the condition (under Article 6(3)) that the acts giving rise to the confiscation order constitute an offence which permits confiscation under the law of the executing state. The procedure to be followed in such circumstances is for the confiscation order, together with the relevant certificate, to be sent, in accordance with the provisions of Articles 4 and 5, to the authority in the member

---

28   Although the Framework Decision on confiscation, as evidenced by Article 3(4), does not preclude this either.

29   OJEU 2006, L 328/59.

30   Preamble para. 12.

state(s) authorized to execute the order. The order will subsequently be executed immediately, unless one of the grounds for refusal exhaustively listed in Article 8 is present, or one of the grounds for suspension exhaustively listed in Article 10 applies.

Although the Framework Decision on mutual recognition of confiscation orders is not discussed in detail here, it is still useful to touch upon a few particulars. First and foremost, it follows from the system of grounds for refusal that not every confiscation order should be eligible for the simplified form of execution, as referred to above, in another member state. Article 8(2)(g) includes as a valid ground for refusal the situation in which, in the opinion of the executing state, the confiscation order issued applies the extended powers of confiscation referred to in Article 2(d)(iv), in other words, powers going beyond those referred to in Article 2(d)(i–iii). This means refusal is possible, providing it does not concern confiscation of the proceeds of a criminal act (or a wholly or partly corresponding value), confiscation of instrumentalities with respect to that criminal act, or another form of confiscation as referred to in Article 3(1) and (2) of the Framework Decision on confiscation.[31] Mutual recognition, therefore, is not mandatory for every possible confiscation order.[32]

A much debated topic when the Framework Decision on mutual recognition of confiscation orders was being established was 'asset sharing'. The final version of the relevant regulation was laid down in Article 16.[33] Insofar as the execution pertains to an amount of money the proceeds will, in principle, be shared on a 50–50 basis between the issuing state and the executing state. If the amount obtained is below €10,000 the entire amount will accrue to the executing state. There are two options if the executing state obtains property from the execution: either the property will be sold, after which the sale proceeds will be divided in accordance with the above allocation formula; or the property will be transferred to the issuing state. In principle, it is the executing state's decision as to which option to pursue.[34] The issuing and executing states may alternatively jointly agree to another division or allocation.[35] It should be noted with respect to asset sharing that the costs of the execution will not be refunded. Other than in special cases, these costs will be borne by the executing state under Article 20.

---

31   The first two forms of confiscation have also been included in Article 2 of the Framework Decision on confiscation, but only as far as it concerns acts carrying a prison sentence of more than one year. As regards confiscation as meant in Article 3(2) of the Framework Decision on confiscation, it must be pointed out that, according to the fourth paragraph of that Article, such confiscation can also take place in a non-criminal procedure.

32   Compare also COM(2008) 766 final, p. 5.

33   The explanation given in the main text of this provision is merely an outline of the possibilities. Compare Article 16(2)(c) and (3) for special cases.

34   Unless the confiscation pertains to an amount of money and the execution results in property being obtained. In that case, transfer of the property is only possible with the issuing state's consent.

35   Article 16(4).

A noteworthy aspect lacking in the normal legal assistance treaties is a specific regulation for execution in more than one member state. Following an extensive debate, a detailed regulation to that effect was included in Article 5 of the Framework Decision on mutual recognition of confiscation orders. Briefly put, this enables execution in more than one member state on a relatively broad scale.

Council Decision Concerning Cooperation between Asset Recovery Offices

The Council Decision on cooperation between Asset Recovery Offices of the member states ('Decision on cooperation between Asset Recovery Offices') was adopted on 6 December 2007.[36] It concerns a decision as referred to in Article 34(2)(c) of the EU Treaty of 1992, which is not aimed at harmonizing the laws of the member states but essentially pertains to the structuring of day-to-day practice. The Decision on cooperation between Asset Recovery Offices follows the establishment of the Camden Assets Recovery Inter-Agency Network ('CARIN'), whose objectives include the task of establishing a network of central contact points for the purpose of recovering criminal money.[37] CARIN is an informal network and has no authority to take binding decisions. The Decision supports CARIN's initiative by placing EU member states under an obligation to establish central contact points. Based on Article 1(1) of the Decision, each member state is required to set up or designate a 'national Asset Recovery Office' ('ARO'). The task of each national ARO is essentially to facilitate the tracing and identification of proceeds of crime that may be seized or confiscated during criminal or civil proceedings. Although the intention of the initial draft decision was for each member state to have only one national ARO, Article 1(2) now allows for two AROs to be set up or designated. Even if other authorities in a member state are also charged with tracing and identifying proceeds of crime, the member state can only appoint a maximum of two AROs as contact points.

The purpose of the national ARO is to exchange information or 'best practices', either on request or otherwise (under Article 2(1)).[38] As regards the exchange of information, Article 3 of the Decision refers to the rules to be adopted pursuant to the Framework Decision on simplifying the exchange of information and intelligence between law-enforcement authorities of EU member states.[39] This Framework Decision pertains to police cooperation in the European Union, more specifically the exchange of information between police authorities. The exchange of information is restricted to information that can be obtained without the use

---

36 Council Decision 2007/845/JHA (OJEU 2007, L 332/103).

37 See https://www.europol.europa.eu/content/publication/camden-asset-recovery-in ter-agency-network-carin-manual-1665 (accessed 10 February 2013).

38 Council Decision, Article 2(1).

39 Council Framework Decision 2006/960/JHA of 18 December 2006 on simplifying the exchange of information and intelligence between law enforcement authorities of the member states of the European Union.

of coercive powers, and information exchanged cannot automatically be used as evidence in criminal proceedings. The reference to this Framework Decision indicates that the Decision on cooperation between Asset Recovery Offices is restricted to the exchange of information at a police level.[40] This information has to be useful in tracing and identifying proceeds of crime. Under Article 4 of the Decision, information may be spontaneously exchanged within the limits of the applicable national law of the member state supplying the information. Article 6 obliges the national AROs to exchange 'best practices' with respect to the tracing and identification of proceeds of crime.

As stated above, national AROs primarily have the task of facilitating cooperation in the exchange of information.[41] This exchange may involve their relaying an incoming request to another authority within the same member state. Council documents pertaining to the Decision show, however, that the aim is for national AROs to be more than a post box and, therefore, to have the expertise needed to assist in the execution of requests.[42] The structures and procedures of the national AROs, however, are not regulated. The status of the national AROs – administrative, law enforcement, judicial authority – is not of any relevance, providing it does not hamper cooperation.[43]

The Decision on cooperation between Asset Recovery Offices obviously aims to promote international cooperation in asset recovery cases in a practical manner. Noteworthy, too, is that the reference to a 'civil procedure' in Article 1(1) makes it clear that cooperation should also be possible with member states using forms of non-conviction based confiscation such as civil forfeiture or civil recovery.[44] At the same time, however, the restrictions in this respect should not be overlooked. In contradistinction to the initial draft decision,[45] the responsibilities of the national AROs in the Decision are explicitly restricted to exchanging information at a police level.[46] In this way, the Decision ignores the fact that a

---

40 This restriction brings along that there is no obligation to provide information and intelligence to be used as evidence before a judicial authority. There is also no right to use such information or intelligence for that purpose. Where a member state has obtained information or intelligence, and wishes to use it as evidence before a judicial authority, it has to obtain consent of the member state that provided the information or intelligence. Council Framework Decision 2006/960/JHA of 18 December 2006 on simplifying the exchange of information and intelligence between law enforcement authorities of the Member States of the European Union, Article 1(4).

41 Council documents 7259/06 ADD 1, p. 5 and 6589/2/06 REV 2, p. 2.

42 Council document 5644/06, p. 2.

43 Council Decision, Article 2(2).

44 Compare Council document 15628/05 ADD 1, p. 5.

45 Compare Article 2 under 1 of the initial draft decision, Council document 15628/05, which refers to the 'widest possible cooperation' between the national AROs.

46 Because of this restriction it is not problematic for a member state that does not have a system of non-conviction based confiscation to cooperate with a member state that does have such a system.

significant part of international cooperation in confiscation cases takes place at a judicial level, for instance where such cooperation concerns the seizure of assets (by means of a European freezing order) or investigative measures. Viewed in that light, national AROs can play only a restricted role in cooperation, or in any case a more restricted role than CARIN envisages. Member states can, of course, decide at their discretion to expand the responsibilities of their national AROs. The possibility of having two national AROs in a member state also raises questions since this arrangement could easily result in a division of competences, which in turn could be a complicating factor in cooperation.[47] Given the limited mandate of the national AROs, it is also somewhat surprising that no provision has been made for the designation of only one national ARO. Council documents do not reveal why the possibility of designating two national AROs in one member state was created, other than to reflect pre-existing arrangements.

In a report in 2011, the Commission expresses general satisfaction regarding the manner in which member states have executed the Decision on cooperation between Asset Recovery Offices.[48] The report states that most national AROs employ relatively few staff, and that in practice their opportunities to gather financial data in particular are limited. It also points out that the infrastructure for a fast and, importantly, entirely secure exchange of information is lacking, although bodies such as Europol are working on this problem.

Other Initiatives and Instruments

No Specific Legal Instrument for the Exchange of Information

The initiatives and instruments described above are specifically aimed at confiscation cases and international cooperation in confiscation cases. It is remarkable that the emphasis is on the possibilities of (prejudgment) seizure, including tracing and identifying assets, and on executing confiscation orders. Exchanging information relevant to the imposing of confiscation orders is not an area of special attention in that respect, as explained below. The Decision on cooperation between Asset Recovery Offices seems to be breaking this tradition because it pays explicit attention to the exchange of information, both on request and spontaneously. It should, however, be pointed out that, with regard to the exchange of information on request, this Decision seeks to tie in with the Framework Decision on simplifying the exchange of information and intelligence

---

47 In that respect, see also Council document 5644/06, p. 2.

48 Report from the Commission to the European Parliament and to the Council based on Article 8 of the Council Decision 2007/845/JHA of 6 December 2007 concerning cooperation between Asset Recovery Offices of the Member States in the field of tracing and identification of proceeds from, or other property related to, crime (COM(2011) 176 final).

between law-enforcement authorities in EU member states,[49] even though this Framework Decision is not specifically tailored to asset recovery cases.

An explanation for the low profile assigned to the exchange of information could be that the gathering of information mainly occurs during the criminal investigation underlying the criminal proceedings and this is also when the confiscation order is made.[50] This suggests that at the EU level there is no strict distinction between 'traditional' legal process and financial information gathering. The gathering of information for the purposes of deciding whether to issue a confiscation order must be done on the basis of 'normal' instruments for legal assistance and international cooperation.

A case in point is the Framework Decision on the European evidence warrant for obtaining objects, documents and data for use in proceedings in criminal matters.[51] This Framework Decision introduces the principle of mutual recognition with respect to member states' obtaining evidence. Neither the provisions relating to the evidence warrant, nor the Explanatory Memorandum to the Framework Decision or the draft Framework Decision indicate the extent to which the evidence warrant is meant to gather information for the purpose of making confiscation decisions. The same applies in the case of the Framework Decision on simplifying the exchange of information and intelligence between law-enforcement authorities in EU member states.

The lack of a Framework Decision for gathering information for the purpose of making confiscation decisions raises the question as to whether gathering that information can be seamlessly integrated into the 'normal' set of instruments. Or, to phrase it differently, can the desired gathering of information specifically for the purpose of confiscation decisions be interpreted as information gathering for the purpose of a criminal case? There are potentially two key obstacles. First, information that is useful for confiscation decisions is not necessarily relevant to the criminal case itself, in other words for the decision about the suspect's criminal responsibility. This may include information needed, for example, to calculate the total amount of criminal money obtained, including calculations not based on the proceeds of each criminal act but instead on calculations of the results of activity (or even presumed activity) over a period of time.[52] Secondly, it is

---

49   Council Framework Decision 2006/960/JHA of 18 December 2006 on simplifying the exchange of information and intelligence between law enforcement authorities of the Member States of the European Union.

50   Compare Council recommendation of 25 April 2002 on improving investigation methods in combating organized crime: simultaneous investigations into drug trafficking by criminal organizations and their finances/assets, OJEC 2002, C 114/01. This document also recommends seeking to determine the proceeds of drug trafficking organizations from the start of the criminal investigation.

51   OJEU 2008, L 350/72.

52   Calculations covering a period of time are often used for forms of confiscation allowing a shift of the burden of proof. Compare in this respect Article 3(2) of the Framework Decision on confiscation.

important to note that in some legal systems the confiscation order is imposed in a procedure that is more or less separate from the 'main' criminal procedure. Such a procedure could take place, or still be ongoing, after final judgment on the indictment has been issued. These two peculiarities should not be taken to mean that international cooperation on the exchange of information for the purpose of confiscation decisions is problematic in each and every case. Empirical research has not found international cooperation to be hampered in this respect.[53] It should also be pointed out that the question of whether cooperation takes place in a particular case depends in part on the legal instrument invoked, the wording used in that legal instrument and the requested state's interpretation of the wording. One factor in that interpretation may be that the Decision on cooperation between Asset Recovery Offices takes it as self-evident that the exchange of information in asset recovery cases can take place on the basis of normal legal instruments (regarding police cooperation).

Legal Assistance in the European Union

Although mutual recognition is viewed as the cornerstone of international cooperation in criminal cases within the European Union, much of this cooperation currently still takes place by way of traditional legal assistance. This legal assistance is based first and foremost on the various international treaties, while there is also the Convention on Mutual Assistance in Criminal Matters between the member states of the European Union of 29 May 2000.[54] This Convention was supplemented by a Protocol on 16 October 2001,[55] and both have now entered into force (on 23 August 2005). Although these documents do not contain specific provisions with respect to international cooperation in asset recovery cases, that does not alter the fact that the Protocol in particular can be of special importance in such cooperation. Indeed the Protocol contains a specific procedure for legal assistance relating to the gathering of information on bank accounts for the purposes of combating economic crime, money laundering and organized crime. In general terms, this procedure allows information on bank accounts and transactions on specific bank accounts during specific periods of time to be obtained. The legal assistance can also involve monitoring possible future transactions on a bank account.

There are several bodies in the European Union that, each in their own way, seek to promote efficient processes for legal assistance, regardless of whether the legal assistance is based on the Convention or the Protocol. These are Europol, the European Judicial Network ('EJN') and Eurojust.

---

53 M.J. Borgers and J.A Moors, 'Targeting the proceeds of crime: Bottlenecks in international cooperation' (2007) 15 *European Journal of Crime, Criminal Law and Criminology* 1.

54 OJEC 2000, C 197/1.

55 OJEC 2001, C 326/1.

One of Europol's tasks is to promote effective cooperation between member states in preventing and combating various serious offences.[56] The exchange of information via liaison officers is one of the available means. The task of Europol's Criminal Assets Bureau is to assist member states in locating assets outside national borders, with an aim of freezing these assets. In addition, the Bureau supports the investigations undertaken by member states and can assist joint investigation teams. The focus in performing this task seems to be on coordinating contacts between the responsible police and judicial authorities in the member states and on the exchange of information. This entails facilitating cooperation between the member states rather than seeking to replace the existing legal assistance procedures.

The EJN[57] and Eurojust[58] are both responsible for promoting international judicial cooperation within the European Union. One of the important tasks in this respect involves ensuring that the appropriate people in the various member states are brought into contact with each other. EJN uses a network of contact points in the member states to fulfil this task, while Eurojust is a centralized organization with seconded magistrates. International cooperation in confiscation cases is not an area of special attention for either EJN or Eurojust.

Synthesis

The standards and minimum standards applying within the European Union with respect to proper international cooperation in confiscation cases can be represented functionally, based on the various European instruments and initiatives discussed in this contribution. The foundations for this cooperation are contained in the Joint Action on money laundering and its successor, the Framework Decision on money laundering. These two foundations (stripped of all details and further conditions),

---

56   Council Decision of 6 April 2009 establishing the European Police Office (Europol) (2009/371/JHA) Article 3: 'The objective of Europol shall be to support and strengthen action by the competent authorities of the Member States and their mutual cooperation in preventing and combating organised crime, terrorism and other forms of serious crime affecting two or more Member States.'

57   See Council Decision 2008/976/JHA of 16 December 2008 on the European Judicial Network.

58   Under the Treaty on European Union, Article 85 requires Eurojust 'to support and strengthen coordination and cooperation between national investigating and prosecuting authorities in relation to serious crime affecting two or more Member States' while Article 86 states that 'in order to combat crimes affecting the financial interests of the Union, the Council, by means of regulations adopted in accordance with a special legislative procedure, may establish a European Public Prosecutor's Office from Eurojust'. See also Council Decision 2009/426/JHA of 16 December 2008 on the strengthening of Eurojust and amending Decision 2002/187/JHA setting up Eurojust with a view to reinforcing the fight against serious crime.

taken alongside the recommendations in the final report of the evaluation exercise regarding combating organized crime, require member states to comply with the following obligations:

Table 2.2   European obligations to cooperate in confiscation cases

A	Member States must provide for ample confiscation possibilities by law, including the possibility of value confiscation.
B	Member States must make provisions for the possibility of tracing suspected proceeds from crime at the request of another Member State* – *inter alia* by means of investigating bank accounts and bank transactions – and for freezing the assets concerned pending the outcome of confiscation proceedings.
C	Member States must, in a number of ways, proceed expeditiously as regards legal assistance with respect to the identification, tracing, freezing, seizing and confiscation of assets. Among other things, it is important that:

- the same priority is given to legal assistance requests as is given to similar measures in national proceedings;
- formalities and any necessary supplementary requests for legal assistance are dealt with as soon as possible;
- the requesting State is adequately informed about the processing of the legal assistance request and possible obstacles;
- Member States requesting legal assistance from another Member State ensure that the request is specific and substantiated, in accordance with applicable regulations;
- Member States take steps to guarantee efficient responses to legal assistance requests, *inter alia*, by providing a user-friendly guide, promoting direct contacts between the parties involved and providing appropriate training.

Note: * As noted under the second sub-heading of the second section of this chapter, the provision to that effect was removed from the Joint Action by the Framework Decision on money laundering, without being replaced by a similar obligation. It may be, however, that the removal of this obligation was unintentional.

Aspects of the other Framework Decisions discussed in this chapter build on this group of obligations. The Framework Decision on confiscation further substantiates what is set out above under A in Table 2.2. The Framework Decision on freezing property or evidence aims – by replacing legal assistance by mutual recognition – to guarantee the possibility of prompt seizing and, in doing so, ties in with what is set out under B and C. The standardization of the manner in which a freezing order is given also promotes what is set out under Civ. Along the same lines, the Framework Decision on mutual recognition of confiscation orders ties in with what is set out under B and C. In addition to these Framework Decisions, the Protocol to the Convention on mutual assistance in criminal matters between the member states of the European Union is important for identifying assets and so can be linked to what is set out under B. At the European level, the facilitating role of Europol, EJN and Eurojust is also important with regard to the execution of, and response to, requests for legal assistance. The national AROs referred to in the Decision on cooperation between Asset Recovery Offices have an important facilitating role to play, specifically as regards the exchange of information at a police level. The setting-up or designation of AROs, therefore, is linked to what is set out under C, albeit that it pertains only to police cooperation and not judicial legal assistance. The exchange of 'best practices' by AROs ties in with what is set out under Cv.

If the various obligations discussed above are compared to the possibilities laid down in various 'classical' international treaties on cooperation in criminal cases (for instance: the (Council of Europe's) European Convention on Mutual Assistance in Criminal Matters[59] and the Convention on Mutual Assistance in Criminal Matters between the Member States of the European Union[60]), European legislation can be seen to a greater or lesser extent to be consistent with existing treaty obligations. This does not mean, however, that the added value of the European regulations vis-à-vis the treaty obligations is modest. The European regulatory framework has a clear added value in two respects. First, the European regulations are related in part to how international cooperation is structured (as set out under C above). Secondly, the European regulations are constructed in part around the principle of mutual recognition, which aims to simplify and accelerate international cooperation.

To a certain extent, therefore, the legal instruments referred to in this chapter provide assurance that member states will ultimately comply with the obligations as laid down in the Joint Action on money laundering and the Framework Decision on money laundering. Of course, this requires the Framework Decisions discussed here to be implemented correctly – and the implementation legislation to be correctly executed – as well as requiring the Protocol and the Decision to be applied through national legislation. This also means that sufficient tools and resources must be available to enable compliance with the various obligations. The requirements for an expeditious and efficient response to legal assistance requests have been tightened further by the requirement that mutually recognized decisions be promptly executed. In that sense, the obligations flowing from the Joint Action on money laundering and the Framework Decision on money laundering have been intensified.

Overall, European legislation can be seen as comprising a reasonably coherent structure of regulations with respect to legal instruments for and organizational aspects of international cooperation. These regulations obviously also have their limitations. With a view to the practice of international cooperation in confiscation cases, it is useful to discuss two of these limitations separately.

---

59   European Convention on Mutual Assistance in Criminal Matters, Strasbourg, 20 April 1959 (CETS 30).

60   Council Act of 29 May 2000 establishing in accordance with Article 34 of the Treaty on European Union the Convention on Mutual Assistance in Criminal Matters between the Member States of the European Union, OJEC 2000, C 197/1.

First, the regulations as regards the organizational aspects are relatively modest in scope. At present, they are limited to a few provisions with respect to, *inter alia,* the prioritization of legal assistance requests and the provision of information and advice. Detailed regulations on various components of day-to-day practice – the available capacity, the manner in which contacts are established and so on – are lacking. The Decision on cooperation between Asset Recovery Offices, however, marks an important step towards a system of national AROs and contact points to facilitate international cooperation in asset recovery cases. Yet, at the same time, the AROs' mandate is fairly limited.

Secondly, European regulations pay little attention to legal safeguards for interested parties. Although several Framework Decisions stipulate that member states must put the necessary legal remedies in place,[61] judging by the documents pertaining to the various European legal instruments, the issue of the general system of legal protection is barely addressed. It is, for instance, debatable whether it is reasonable that a Dutch party wishing to oppose, say, the execution of a Spanish freezing order in the Netherlands can only complain about the substantial reasons of that freezing order in Spain. From a practical viewpoint, it will not be easy for the Dutch individual – not least because of the language barrier – to obtain proper assistance or legal representation in Spain.

It should also be pointed out that, on a number of issues, no specific obligations as regards international cooperation in asset recovery cases have yet been set. This applies first and foremost in the case of the exchange of information relating to the making of confiscation decisions. This exchange needs to take place on the basis of the 'regular' legal instruments, including conventions on mutual assistance. The bottlenecks that can result from this have been outlined under the third heading in this chapter. However, the Protocol to the Convention on mutual assistance in criminal matters between the Member States of the European Union introduced a regulation, partly to combat laundering, that allows information to be obtained on bank accounts and bank transactions.[62] The Decision on cooperation between Asset Recovery Offices, too, provides some practical rules for exchanging information at a police level in asset recovery cases. Secondly, there is no regulation in European legislation for forms of extrajudicial confiscation, such as settlement pursuant to Article 511c of the Dutch Code of Criminal Procedure.[63] Thirdly, the

---

61 See, for example, Article 11 of the Framework Decision on freezing property or evidence.

62 Protocol to the Convention on Mutual Assistance in Criminal Matters between the Member States of the European Union established by the Council in accordance with Article 34 of the Treaty on European Union (Official Journal C 326 of 21.11.2001) Articles 1 and 2.

63 The Prosecutor may, as long as the investigation in the case is not closed, enter into a written settlement with the accused or convicted person for them to pay a sum of money to the state or to transfer of property in partial or total fulfilment of Article 36e of the Criminal Code for the confiscation of an illegally obtained asset.

European legal instruments are barely tailored for cooperation with respect to forms of confiscation other than post-criminal conviction confiscation. Powers of civil forfeiture or civil recovery for example are, therefore, not taken into account. This is somewhat surprising because although the various Framework Decisions consider confiscation a sanction imposed for one or more criminal acts, Article 3(4) of the Framework Decision on confiscation allows scope for confiscation in a non-criminal context. It is also remarkable in this respect that the Decision on cooperation between AROs regards cooperation in the area of non-conviction based forfeiture as fairly self-evident.

Conclusion: Looking to the Future

How will the collection of European rules on cooperation in asset recovery cases discussed above develop in the future? Several comments may be offered, based on the Commission's communication entitled *Proceeds of organized crime: Ensuring that 'crime does not pay'* and the recent proposal for a Directive on the freezing and confiscation of proceeds of crime in the European Union.[64] These documents set out several ambitions for furthering European policy on recovering the proceeds of crime. The draft Directive aims to make it easier for member states to confiscate and recover the profits from cross-border serious and organized crime, by setting minimum rules for member states with respect to freezing and confiscation of criminal assets through direct confiscation, value confiscation, extended confiscation, non-conviction based confiscation (in limited circumstances) and third-party confiscation. It is true that this harmonization of the member states' freezing and confiscation regimes facilitates mutual trust and effective cross-border cooperation.[65] Nevertheless, it is striking that hardly any new legislation is being proposed as regards the cooperation between member states. Instead, in the Commission's communication the focus seems to be on improving the practical execution of cooperation, while also promoting closer contacts between AROs and improving the opportunities to exchange information. This ambition ties in thoroughly with what has emerged in this chapter: current European legislation forms a reasonably coherent structure of regulations with respect to legal instruments for and organizational aspects of international cooperation. What really matters, therefore, is for good use to be made of this structure.

---

64 COM(2011) 766 final; COM(2012) 85 final.
65 COM(2012) 85 final, p. 4.

Chapter 3

Post-Conviction Confiscation of Assets in England and Wales: Rhetoric and Reality

Karen Bullock and Stuart Lister

Introduction

This chapter critically analyses the development and operation of the regime of post-conviction confiscation of assets in England and Wales. As this area of law is triggered on conviction of a predicate offence in a higher criminal court, this chapter contrasts with those contributions to this book which focus on civil forfeiture of assets (in which a conviction is unnecessary). That said, post-conviction confiscation should be viewed alongside (pre-conviction) asset forfeiture and anti-money laundering legislation as a key component of so-called 'follow the money' approaches to crime control, the rationale for which is to reduce crime by attacking the financial infrastructure of criminal enterprise.[1]

Whilst few would disagree with the explicit intention of 'confiscation', to deprive offenders of the financial benefit of their criminal activity, this chapter posits that the assumptions which underpin the strategy, and how it has been enacted in legislation as well as operationalized in practice, ought to be subject to more rigorous conceptual, normative and empirical scrutiny. The purpose of this chapter therefore is to offer caution about how 'asset confiscation' (or 'asset recovery', as it is frequently and euphemistically referred to in the UK) functions as a key crime control strategy of the late modern era. This chapter is constructed in two parts. The first examines the policy rhetoric of post-conviction confiscation of assets, identifying its role in the rationalization of the confiscation regime in England and Wales, before outlining the evolution of the legal mechanisms by which the state seizes the proceeds of crime. The second part examines the 'reality' of the contemporary regime of confiscation, critiquing the assumptions underpinning its capacity to reduce serious, acquisitive crime, as well as the legal rules governing confiscation hearings. We conclude by suggesting the value of the 'confiscation' strategy lies more in its communicative properties, by enabling the State to reassert its moral certitude within criminal justice policy, than its instrumental properties as an effective technology of crime control.

---

1   M. Gallant, *Money Laundering and the Proceeds of Crime: Economic Crime and Civil Remedies* (Cheltenham: Edward Elgar, 2005).

The Rhetoric of Post-Conviction Confiscation

Rationalizing the Confiscation of Criminal Assets

Governments justify confiscating the 'proceeds of crime' by linking that sanction to a set of postulated desirable outcomes which are sustained and reinforced by various assumptions about individual motivations for committing crime and how crime might be controlled. These aims and assumptions are identified in this opening section in order to contextualize our later and more critical discussion of the law and practice of confiscation in England and Wales.

The first aim of post-conviction confiscation is simply to ensure that offenders do not profit from crime. An influential report published in 2000 by the Cabinet Office's Performance and Innovation Unit ('PIU') within the UK government, to which we refer to throughout this chapter, observed 'the removal of assets from those living off crime is a valuable end in itself in a just society'.[2] This moral argument, encapsulated in the normative assertion that 'crime should not pay', conceptualizes confiscation as a means of restoring the *status quo* of legitimate economic relations prior to the commission of the original offence. Confiscation is therefore held to have a reparative function, righting a moral wrong, by remedying an injustice.[3]

As confiscation is widely assumed to have an instrumental, regulatory effect on behaviour, a second aim is to reduce or control crime. The most common argument here is that the prospect of losing their 'ill-gotten gains' dissuades offenders from committing crimes.[4] This control effect is also presumed to operate through various other mechanisms, including reducing the capital available to criminals to invest in illicit enterprise, removing criminal role models from communities and promulgating the message that 'crime does not pay'.[5] Indeed, the intended audiences of the criminal confiscation strategy feature heavily in its rationalization within government policy:

> Perhaps as importantly for the future well-being of society, preventing overt criminals from living off the proceeds of crime can deter impressionable young people from entering or expanding their involvement in criminality. At all levels

---

2   Performance and Innovation Unit (PIU), *Recovering the Proceeds of Crime* (London: Cabinet Office, 2000) para. 1.2.

3   For discussion of this point in the context of the use of civil procedures to seize assets see Gallant (fn 1) 30–31.

4   Home Office, *Rebalancing the Criminal Justice System in Favour of the Law-abiding Majority: Cutting Crime, Reducing Re-offending and Protecting the Public* (London: Home Office, 2008).

5   PIU (fn 2) para. 1.2.

successful criminals who are seen to be living lives of relative luxury, act as dysfunctional role models for their peers and juniors.[6]

A final oft-stated aim of confiscation is to inhibit the corrosive effects of 'organized crime' on financial systems, for instance, through the infiltration and corruption of legitimate business and markets. By attacking the capacity of criminal wealth to penetrate the legitimate economic sphere, so the argument runs, markets will become more stable, more reliable and less prone to 'the detrimental effects of counterfeiting and other illegitimate acts'.[7]

Whilst these three aims represent the central tenets of the policy discourse surrounding the 'proceeds of crime approach', they are built on at least three assumptions about the nature of crime and mechanisms through which it can be controlled. Let us briefly describe each in turn.

The first assumption is that criminal acts are motivated by profit and, as a consequence, they can be prevented if their financial incentive is eliminated. This assertion has been informed by contemporary modes of governance. As western Governments have become increasingly actuarial in how they seek to govern political or social problems, so they have tended to view criminality and its precursor motivations less as the consequence of social, cultural and economic conditions embedded in the structure of societies and more as the outcome of a rational choice in which the decision to offend can be distilled to a cost-benefit calculation, irrespective of the biography of individual actors.[8] The criminal act, according to this logic, is freely determined by an internal assessment of the risks and rewards associated with it. The PIU report of 2000 drew heavily on this economic model of offending to explain how confiscation could be a powerful tool of crime control policy:

> ... many financially-motivated crimes result from a relatively rational risk/ reward analysis. In these circumstances, crimes are committed when there is a combination of opportunity and the motivation that results from concluding that the expected overall benefit from the crime is higher than the perceived total risks and costs. The costs of securing the desired benefit from crime must also appear lower than those involved in acquiring the benefit through legitimate means.[9]

---

6   Her Majesties Inspectorate of Constabulary (HMIC), *Payback Time: Joint Review of Asset Recovery since the Proceeds of Crime Act 2002* (London: Home Office, 2004) para. 1.4.

7   Ibid., at fn 5.

8   P. O'Malley, 'Risk, Power and Crime Prevention' (1992) 21 *Economy and Society* 252.

9   PIU (fn 2) para. 3.16.

The second assumption is that 'traditional' law-enforcement methods of detection and prosecution, specifically the deterrent and preventative value of incarceration, do not effectively tackle the activities of elite professional criminals. According to this logic, so vast are the profits available from the organization and commission of serious, acquisitive crime, such as drug trafficking, that those receiving custodial sentences may find it difficult not to re-offend on their release; alternatively, they may seek to continue their criminal enterprise whilst in prison, either personally or via co-conspirators who have avoided police attention.[10] Nor does a prison sentence stop criminals from enjoying their unlawfully-earned wealth once they are released. Confiscation, by contrast, is said 'to hit the criminal where it hurts', denying them access to the fruits of their criminal labour whilst reducing their access to capital to (re)invest in further illicit ventures. Unsurprisingly, law-enforcement agencies have come to view confiscation as a pragmatic and effective alternative to traditional techniques that stress deterrence through incarceration.[11]

The third assumption pervading the policy rhetoric of criminal confiscation, presupposes that significant profits are derived from criminal activity and thus available for confiscation. This belief is closely linked to the escalation of the global trade in illegal drugs over the last 30 years.[12] In England and Wales, though, the recent policy discourse has taken a wider focus. An inspection of 'asset recovery' practices within the criminal justice system, led by Her Majesties' Inspectorate of Constabulary, for instance, stated: 'Over 70% of all crime is acquisitive in nature and estimates of the total value of the proceeds of such crime vary widely. The most-often quoted figure is the equivalent of 2% of the national gross domestic product – around £18 billion.'[13] These kinds of 'official' estimates, which Naylor sceptically describes as being 'mainly based on hype and hysteria',[14] have been widely cited to support the international development of confiscation regimes. One outcome is that governments have predicted that confiscation regimes will – at the very least – recoup their running costs. The PIU report, for example, optimistically stated that its proposals had 'the potential to be relatively cost-effective … asset confiscation policies can generate significant revenue flows that reduce the net costs to the criminal justice system'.[15]

---

10   Ibid., para. 2.4.

11   M. Levi and L. Osofsky, *Investigating, Seizing and Confiscating the Proceeds of Crime*, Police Research Group Crime, Detection and Prevention Series Paper 61 (London: Home Office, 1995); J.W.E. Sheptycki, 'Global law enforcement as a protection racket: Some sceptical notes on transnational organized crime as an object of global governance', in A. Edward and P. Gill (eds), *Transnational Organised Crime: Perspectives on Global Security* (London: Routledge, 2003).

12   Gallant (fn 1) 7.

13   HMIC (fn 6) para. 1.1.

14   T. Naylor, 'Criminal Profits, Terror Dollars, and Nonsense' (2007) 23 *Crime & Justice International* 27 at 28; see also J. Harvey, 'Just how effective is money laundering legislation?' (2008) 21 *Security Journal* 189.

15   PIU (fn 2) 16.

The Development of Confiscation Law

The historical development of contemporary confiscation law in England and Wales can be traced back to 'Operation Julie', a large scale police investigation into drug trafficking in the mid-1970s, which highlighted weaknesses in the ability of the state to confiscate the proceeds of crime. In *Cuthbertson* (the criminal trial arising from 'Operation Julie'), the House of Lords ruled 'with considerable regret' that the proceeds of the defendants' unlawful drug trading could not be forfeited under the Misuse of Drugs Act 1971.[16] It was held that existing forfeiture law, such as under this legislation, did not allow for the profits of the conspiracy to be confiscated but only for the forfeiture of effects directly connected to the original criminal act.[17] Subsequently the 'Hodgson Committee', which was formed to consider the inadequacies of confiscation law as highlighted in *Cuthbertson*, recommended the introduction of a statutory power to enable the courts to confiscate the proceeds of an offence or offences for which a defendant had been convicted (or had taken into consideration), as well as several ancillary powers including pre-trial restraint to enable the courts to prevent defendants moving and concealing their assets.[18] The Hodgson Committee's report led to the Drug Trafficking Offences Act 1986 which established a regime of confiscation law broadly similar to that which currently operates in England and Wales. As Table 3.1 (overleaf) shows subsequent pieces of primary legislation have enabled the state, *inter alia*, to apply the 'proceeds of crime' label ever more widely and also to confiscate them more efficiently.

Despite the enactment of a variety of confiscation provisions, research conducted in the mid-1990s identified several concerns about confiscation law and practice.[19] Confiscation cases were not routinely put before the courts, which the researchers attributed, *inter alia*, to a lack of expertise on confiscation law among police and lawyers combined with a perception among the judiciary that the matter was marginal to the primary proceedings of the Court. When they were sanctioned, confiscation orders tended to be of low value, as upper level offenders were seldom prosecuted and most convicted defendants in confiscation hearings had few 'recoverable' assets of value.[20]

---

16   *R v Cutherbertson* [1981] AC 470 at p. 479 *per* Lord Diplock.

17   For a detailed discussion of the legal arguments see P. Alldridge, *Money Laundering Law: Forfeiture, Confiscation, Civil Recovery, Criminal Laundering and Taxation of the Proceeds of Crime* (Oxford: Hart Publishing, 2003) 74–75.

18   D. Hodgson, *Profits of Crime and their Recovery* (London: Heinemann, 1984) 4.

19   See M. Levi and L. Osofsky, *Investigating, Seizing and Confiscating the Proceeds of Crime*, Police Research Group Crime, Detection and Prevention Series Paper 61 (London: Home Office, 1995) vi.

20   Ibid.

Table 3.1   The development of UK confiscation legislation*

Year	Statute	Provisions
1986	Drug Trafficking Ac	Confiscation provisions for drug trafficking offences and first drug money laundering offence
1988	Criminal Justice Act	Confiscation provisions for all non-drug indictable and specified summary offences
1990	Criminal Justice (International Co-operation Act)	Mutual legal assistance, further drug money laundering offences and drug cash seizure on import or export
1993	Criminal Justice Act	(Other forms of) money laundering offences and enhancements to all crime confiscation provisions
1994	Drug Trafficking Act	Consolidating the drug provisions and removing mandatory confiscation
1994	Criminal Justice and Public Order Act	Bringing forward the date from which the Criminal Justice Act (1993) confiscation provisions apply
1995 1995 1996	Proceeds of Crime Act Proceeds of Crime (Scotland) Act Proceeds of Crime (Northern Ireland) Order**	Further alignment of all crime confiscation provisions with Drug Trafficking Act 1994; notably use of assumptions in crime lifestyle cases
1998	Crime and Disorder Act	Amendment to Criminal Justice Act for confiscation orders on committal for sentence

Note: * PIU (fn 2) 27. There is separate legislation on terrorism financing. See Part III of this book; ** SI 1996/1299.

A significant milestone in the evolution of the contemporary confiscation regime was the aforementioned PIU report of 2000. Embodying many of the assumptions identified in the earlier sections of this chapter the then Prime Minister, Tony Blair, stated in the foreword to the report that:

> Through implementing the recommendations in this report, we shall help turn the tide against criminals. We will deter people from crime by ensuring that criminals do not hang on to their unlawful gains. We will enhance confidence in the law by demonstrating that nobody is beyond its reach. We will make it easier for courts to recover the proceeds of crime from convicted criminals. And we will return to society the assets that have been unlawfully taken. All this will need to be achieved in a way that respects civil liberties; we will ensure that is the case.[21]

---

21   PIU (fn 2) 3.

The report argued that seizing assets from those convicted or suspected of criminal activity was an important but under-exploited tool of law enforcement. Crucially, it criticized inconsistencies and shortcomings in the then contemporary legislative provisions, which it attributed to the piecemeal development of confiscation law. Accordingly, by advocating a simpler and more consistent legal approach, the report recommended that the confiscation rules previously established for drug trafficking cases should be applicable to those convicted of non-drug offences.[22] Its recommendations, which formed the basis of the Proceeds of Crime Act 2002, included the introduction of new structures to promote a more joined-up strategic approach and a greater focus on financial investigation designed to institutionalize the confiscation approach throughout law-enforcement agencies, to be supported by new powers to enable the courts more easily to confiscate the proceeds of crime.

The Proceeds of Crime Act 2002 came into force on the 24 March 2003. It is a consolidating Act designed to provide 'an all-encompassing web to catch anyone who moves, hides, converts or otherwise has possession of cash or property that represent the proceeds of crime'.[23] As such, it intended to bring confiscation law in from the margins, placing it centrally within criminal justice policy responses to crime and insecurity.[24] The next section of this chapter sets out the key legal and policy mechanisms within the current confiscation regime.

Contemporary Criminal Confiscation Law

In England and Wales, the principal mechanism by which the state seizes the proceeds of crime is the confiscation order. Under section 4 of the Proceeds of Crime Act 2002, a confiscation order is obtained (exclusively) in the Crown Court within two years of a conviction and is additional to any sentence. The order is the outcome of a financial investigation, usually conducted by specialist police officers, which determines the extent to which a defendant has 'benefited' from crime and the value of the assets they have available for confiscation. Whilst the court determines the value of a confiscation order it must be equal to the value of a defendant's 'criminal benefit', which we define shortly, unless the defendant can demonstrate that the value of assets they have available for confiscation is less than this. In this event, the value of the confiscation order becomes equivalent to the latter not the former (i.e. the 'realizable value'). The original benefit figure, however, remains important since the prosecution can, at a later date, apply to the court to recalculate the available amount if the defendant is later shown to have

---

22   Ibid., 63; for a discussion of the generic process by which legislation specifically introduced to tackle serious offences is over time generalized to cover a wider range of offences see Alldridge (fn 17) 10.

23   HMIC (fn 6) para. 2.

24   Alldridge (fn 17) v.

acquired further assets. Importantly, therefore, the value of the confiscation order does not necessarily represent the actual benefit derived from crime but is, in effect, a debt to the Court which the defendant must settle with assets however derived. Failure to do so within a specified timescale can result in a prison sentence, to run concurrently or consecutively to any sentence imposed on conviction for the original offence.

'Criminal benefit' under section 76 of the Proceeds of Crime Act 2002 is the monetary value attached to a defendant's 'particular criminal conduct' or, alternatively, their 'general criminal conduct' which results from a criminal lifestyle. This important legal distinction determines how the benefit figure is determined. The value of criminal benefit in 'particular criminal conduct' cases may only include an estimate of the benefit from the offence(s) being prosecuted and any others taken into consideration. For example, if a defendant has been convicted of the theft of a car worth £25,000, the prosecutor may request a confiscation order for such an amount. The calculation of a 'criminal lifestyle' confiscation order is markedly different and may rely on assumptions under section 10 and Schedule 2.

Under Schedule 2 of the Proceeds of Crime Act, a defendant is defined as having a criminal lifestyle if the offence (or any of the offences) (a) concerns drug trafficking, money laundering, directing terrorism, people trafficking, arms trafficking, counterfeiting, intellectual property crimes, pimping or operating brothels, blackmail or inchoate offences, or (b) constitutes conduct forming part of a 'course of criminal activity' (adjudged to be where a defendant is convicted in the same proceedings of at least three offences, or has been convicted on two occasions in the previous six years from which he or she has benefitted by at least £5000) or (c) was committed over a period of at least six months and from which the defendant has benefited by at least £5000.

Once a 'criminal lifestyle' is established, the benefit arising from it is considered widely, over the six-year period previous to the start of proceedings, on the basis of the following set of (mandatory) assumptions: that any property transferred to the defendant at any time after the relevant day (the first day of the period of six years before proceedings were started) was obtained by criminal conduct; that any property held by the defendant at any time after the date of conviction was obtained was a result of his general criminal conduct; that any expenditure incurred by the defendant at any time after the relevant day was met from property obtained by him as a result of his general criminal conduct; and that, for the purpose of valuing any property obtained (or assumed to have been obtained) by the defendant, he obtained it free of any other interests in it.

Crucially, the normal burden of proof is overturned, so that it is for the defence to prove, to the civil standard of balance of probabilities, that these assumptions do not apply and/or that the defendant does not have the assets to meet the value of benefit figure alleged by the prosecution. If the defendant cannot (or does not) so prove, the court must make the confiscation order equal to the value of the benefit figure. Indeed, the court should only fail to apply the benefit figure where the assumption is shown to be incorrect, or there would be a serious risk of injustice if the assumption were made. The latter does not apply to hardship that might arise from the imposition of the order (such as the sale of the family home) but any injustice that might arise from the way that the assumptions are applied by the court (such as double-counting of assets).

The Reality of Post-Conviction Confiscation

Under this heading, we critically consider the postulations on which the confiscation regime rests, along with aspects of its operation. We first explore the posited outcomes and assumptions. Secondly, we identify some implications for defendants caught up within confiscation proceedings, focusing on its 'creeping' and 'punitive' nature. Finally, we examine what outputs the regime has achieved in practice, drawing on data showing the number and value of confiscation orders sanctioned. In doing so, we draw attention to impacts on those offenders who are the focus of confiscation hearings, as well as to the difficulties of enforcing confiscation orders.

The Assumptions of Criminal Confiscation

In our view, the assumptions of confiscation are, at best, unprovable and, at worst, fundamentally flawed. We concur with Nelen that 'the solution to tackle the alleged dangers of organised crime was formulated before the problem had been properly analysed and taken seriously into account'.[25] In short, the confiscation regime in England and Wales, as in other jurisdictions, has been built on assumptions which do not necessarily stand up to critical examination. Let us revisit the aims and assumptions identified above but view them through a more critical lens.

First, as confiscation aims to seize the proceeds of crime, its functionality relies on offenders retaining part of their crime-derived income and making it available for the courts to confiscate. Unfortunately for the success of the policy, many offenders do not appear to save or invest in ways that facilitate confiscation. The inherent hedonism and status trappings of the 'criminal lifestyle', coupled with concerns about detection by law enforcement, mean that 'most professional criminals seem to be profligate spenders'.[26] Consequently, at the point of arrest they often possess little of value for the state to restrain and, in turn, confiscate, a point we return to throughout the closing sections of this chapter.

---

25   H. Nelen, 'Hit them where it hurts most? The proceeds-of-crime approach in the Netherlands' (2004) 41 *Crime, Law and Social Change* 517 at 522.

26   R. Naylor, 'Wash-out: A critique of follow-the-money methods in crime control policy' (1999) 32 *Crime, Law, and Social Change* 1 at 11; see also P. Adler, *Wheeling and Dealing: An Ethnography of an Upper-level Drug Dealing and Smuggling Community* (2nd ed., New York: Columbia University Press, 1993).

Secondly, although confiscation aims to reduce crime overall, there is little evaluation evidence of its impact on crime levels, both at the local and national level. Indeed, several commentators have cast doubt on its crime-control value. Lea suggests many offenders are 'driven to criminal enterprise by a culture of drugs and short-term hedonism as a way of adapting to poverty and lack of worthwhile legitimate career opportunities' and that 'it will take more than a few asset seizures to achieve anything beyond a short term reduction in crime'.[27] In contrast to the rhetoric of criminal confiscation, with limited access to alternative and legitimate career paths, professional criminals may seek to recoup what has been confiscated from them by returning to the types of (unlawful) labour they know best. More troublingly, confiscation may stimulate further, potentially more harmful, criminal activity, particularly if criminal debts have been left unpaid.[28] As markets in (unlawful) commodities function largely on credit and trust, law-enforcement interventions such as asset confiscation might upset their stability and thus risk inciting violence between participants in the market.[29]

A final aim of confiscation is to prevent any corrosive, or indeed catastrophic, effects of criminal wealth on legitimate business, financial markets and the wider economic system. This threat is no doubt over-stated for well-developed and largely settled market economies, but it may be more acute in developing and weaker economies where the state and market are more fragile and less resilient[30] or in communities where deep-rooted conflict is a recurring feature.[31] Critics of the confiscation approach have argued that in western liberal democracies the methods and consequences of criminal entrepreneurs investing illicit assets in the legitimate economy are unlikely to have any significant malign or corrupting influence, as this outcome would risk attracting law-enforcement attention and therefore jeopardize the safe dispersal of those assets.[32] Moreover, serious and professional criminals do not routinely wish to gain any broader foothold in the urban domains of economic or political power; instead, as Nelen describes it, 'they fancy a certain life style and are somewhat "addicted" to the luxury that comes with it'.[33] Doubtless, however, the apocalyptic depictions of 'organized crime'

---

27 J. Lea, 'Hitting criminals where it hurts: Organised crime and the erosion of due process' (2004) 30 *Cambrian Law Review* 81 at 88.

28 J.W.E. Sheptycki, *Review of the Influence of Strategic Intelligence on Organized Crime Policy and Practice* (London: Home Office, 2004).

29 D. Hobbs and G. Pearson, *Middle Market Drug Distribution* (London: Home Office, 2001).

30 See further Chapter 5.

31 See the reports of the Organised Crime Task Force: http://www.octf.gov.uk/ (accessed 10 February 2013).

32 R. Naylor, 'Wash-out: A critique of follow-the-money methods in crime control policy' (1999) 32 *Crime, Law, and Social Change* 1 at 12.

33 H. Nelen, 'Hit them where it hurts most? The proceeds-of-crime approach in the Netherlands' (2004) 41 *Crime, Law and Social Change* 517 at 523; see also D. Hobbs, *Bad Business* (Oxford: Oxford University Press, 1995).

routinely promulgated by government officials, law-enforcement agencies and media outlets serve a 'bureaucratic function' enabling the state to rationalize the escalation of its crime control apparatus.[34] As well as aiming to secure certain outcomes, as described above, the theory of 'criminal confiscation' rests on a series of linked assumptions, which we now turn to consider.

The first assumption is that crime is committed because offenders expect to profit from it. Whilst this is likely to be true for acquisitive and market-based forms of crime, arguably it only tells part of the story. It does not necessarily follow that the threat of asset confiscation will persuade offenders to end their criminal behaviour. Criminality is not always rational. Weighing up the risks and rewards associated with a specific course of illicit action does not fit neatly with the often reckless, sometimes compulsive and routinely opportunistic outlook of much criminality.[35] Moreover, the construction of deviant identities by professional criminals and the material and cultural trappings associated with the often hedonistic lifestyle, offer sensual attractions that extend beyond the accumulation of sustained wealth.[36] For many, the distal threat of confiscation is unlikely to hang heavy over their deliberations as they contemplate their next foray into the criminal marketplace.

The second, and related, assumption underpinning asset confiscation concerns the utility of 'traditional' law-enforcement methods in tackling serious, acquisitive crime. Again, however, there is a lack of evidence that confiscation is a greater deterrent than a long term custodial sentence. Nelen links the uncritical acceptance of this assumption by legislators and law-enforcement officials to 'romantic myths about organized crime', specifically that serious criminals perceive a period of imprisonment to be merely a 'cost of doing business'.[37] It is however difficult to unpick the relative effects of the threats of prison and asset confiscation on offenders. As Levi notes: 'Because of the length of their sentences, the more serious offenders would not have had much opportunity to display or to discount the effects of confiscation, which anyway would be hard to separate from the possible deterrent effects of lengthy imprisonment.'[38]

There may also be 'counterproductive' side-effects of legal innovations such as confiscation provisions. The previous comments regarding the extent to which offending is profitable notwithstanding, as offenders become accustomed to the threat of financial investigation and confiscation, the more resourceful and

---

34   M. Levi, 'Perspectives on "Organised Crime": An Overview' (1998) 37 *Howard Journal* 335 at 337.

35   K.J. Hayward, 'Situational Crime Prevention and its Discontents: Rational choice theory versus the "culture of now"' (2007) 41 *Social Policy and Administration* 232.

36   J. Katz, *Seductions of Crime: The Moral and Sensual Attractions of Doing Evil* (New York: HarperCollins, 1988).

37   H. Nelen, 'Hit them where it hurts most? The proceeds-of-crime approach in the Netherlands' (2004) 41 *Crime, Law and Social Change* 517 at 525.

38   M. Levi, 'Taking the Profit Out of Crime' (1997) 5 *European Journal of Crime, Criminal Law and Criminal Justice* 228 at 235.

'professional' among them are motivated to conceal any assets they hold, by moving them abroad or legally placing them in the name of another.[39] Such actions are reminiscent of what commentators have referred to as an 'arms race' in which offenders perpetually adapt their practices to circumvent new legal provisions and law-enforcement techniques.[40] Alternatively, the risk of confiscation itself may, perversely, spur offenders to adopt a profligate approach to 'earning and burning' their illegal income.[41] The faster such income is spent, the less is available for the purpose of confiscation.

Proponents of confiscation also make assumptions about the likelihood that it can disrupt the capacity of the serious crime community to invest in illicit enterprise. Yet this idea largely rests on a false construction of 'organized crime'. Elite professional criminals tend not to conspire to commit crime under the auspices of stable organizations, but they conjoin in flexible and temporal trading networks which lack the rigidity, formality and structure presumed in much of the policy discourse.[42] It is plainly spurious, therefore, to suggest that asset confiscation will disrupt the economic power of phantom-like 'criminal organizations' whose presence is felt most keenly on the pages of government dictat. Although at times confiscation may significantly hit the finances of some criminal entrepreneurs, it is highly unlikely to disrupt the functionality or the longevity of the criminal marketplace as a whole.[43]

Lastly, implicit within policy discourses is the assumption that the 'criminal economy' is awash with the proceeds of crime, which itself emphasizes the potential of confiscation to disrupt criminal activity. Yet accurately assessing the amount of unlawful money in circulation and, in turn, the potential or actual 'disruptive' impact confiscation might have is a wholly speculative exercise. Hence Naylor argues:

> [N]o-one really knows how much criminal income and wealth actually exists,
> how illegal gains are distributed or how (if at all) deleterious their impact on

---

39   J. Lea, 'Hitting criminals where it hurts: Organised crime and the erosion of due process' (2004) 35 *Cambrian Law Review* 81 at 89.

40   P. Ekblom, 'Gearing up against Crime: A Dynamic Framework to Help Designers Keep up with the Adaptive Criminal in a Changing World' (1997) 2 *International Journal of Risk, Security and Crime Prevention* 249.

41   R. Naylor, 'Wash-out: A critique of follow-the-money methods in crime control policy' (1999) 32 *Crime, Law, and Social Change* 1 at 11.

42   D. Hobbs, 'Going Down the Glocal: The Local Context of Organised Crime' (1998) 37 *Howard Journal of Criminal Justice* 407; G.W. Potter, *Criminal Organisation* (Long Grove, IL: Waveland Press, 1994); M. Woodiwiss and D. Hobbs, 'Organised Evil and the Atlantic Alliance: Moral Panics and the Rhetoric of Organized Crime Policing in America and Britain' (2009) 49 *The British Journal of Criminology* 106.

43   J.E.W. Sheptycki, 'Police Ethnography in the House of Serious and Organized Crime' in A. Henry and D.J. Smith (eds), *Transformations of Policing* (Aldershot: Ashgate, 2007).

legitimate society really is. As a result, no one can say with any degree of confidence what the actual impact of a follow-the-money strategy has or could have on its intended target.[44]

However large the criminal economy may actually be, confiscation is rationalized on an expectation that a proportion of its turnover is 'recoverable'. Yet official estimations, as we have seen, disregard the fact that much criminal income is spent long before the bureaucratic reach of the state can make any claim to it.[45] Unsurprisingly, a recent criminal justice inspectorate report found 'a number of defendants do not invest their gains in readily identifiable assets; they use them to support drug or gambling habits, fritter them away in other ways, or are smart in concealing them from view'.[46] This finding undermines not only the deterrence rationale of the confiscation strategy, but also governmental ambitions to ensure its cost-effectiveness.

We have seen that in England and Wales, as in other countries, public investment in the institutional apparatus of confiscation was partly justified by the assumption that it would become cost neutral. Estimates, however, suggests the wider 'asset recovery' regime costs about four times more to run than the revenue that it generates.[47] Significantly, owing to sizeable and un-recouped running costs, the Government chose in 2007 to merge the Assets Recovery Agency, which was established by the Proceeds of Crime Act 2002, Part I, with the Serious and Organised Crime Agency. This represented something of an embarrassing U-turn for the UK government, which had made much of the Assets Recovery Agency's potential to disrupt offending as well as to become self-financing. A report examining the reasons why the Assets Recovery Agency failed to meet this latter aim drew attention to, amongst other things, failure to generate referrals from the police, poor quality representation in court, obstacles in the Human Rights Act 1998 and weaknesses in the Agency's internal processes. Tellingly, despite the claims made for its impact on the 'champagne lifestyle' of criminals, at the point the agency had been established, no 'feasibility study was carried out to assess its likely performance'.[48] The fate of the much heralded but short-lived Assets Recovery Agency reminds us not only of the risks of overstating what

---

44   R. Naylor, 'Wash-out: A critique of follow-the-money methods in crime control policy' (1999) 32 *Crime, Law, and Social Change* 1 at 3.

45   K. Bullock, D. Mann, R. Street and C. Coxon, *Examining Attrition in Confiscating the Proceeds of Crime* (London: Home Office, 2009).

46   HMCPSI, HMICA and HMIC, *Joint Thematic Review of Asset Recovery: Restraint and Confiscation Casework* (2010) Criminal Justice Joint Inspection 53.

47   P. Sproat, 'The new policing of assets and the new assets of policing: A tentative financial cost-benefit analysis of the UK's anti-money laundering and asset recovery regime' (2007) 10 *Journal of Money Laundering Control* 277.

48   National Audit Office, *The Asset Recovery Agency* (2006-07 HC 253). See also House of Commons Committee of Public Accounts, *Assets Recovery Agency* (2006-07 HC 391) 5; and Chapter 9 of this book.

confiscation of those assets deemed to be the proceeds of crime can realistically hope to achieve, but also of the absence of any meaningful data on the costs and benefits of operating such a regime.

Implications for Defendants

In the context of concerns that much serious and acquisitive criminality is immune from traditional law-enforcement methods, a regime of confiscation law has been established that critics view as 'creeping' in scope, unduly punitive and incorporating insufficient legal protections for defendants.[49] This section considers the widening of confiscation powers, the civil–criminal hybrid nature of confiscation hearings and the procedural implications for defendants caught up in this regime.

The Proceeds of Crime Act 2002 continued the process by which the legal powers and rules of confiscation have become increasingly widely empowered by successive pieces of legislation. Despite the policy rhetoric invoking images of 'crime barons' being permanently separated from their 'large house, yacht and Ferrari', the regime now impacts on the 'small fry' as well as the 'big fish' within the spectrum of offenders.[50] Indeed, at the consultation stage of legislative proceedings, civil rights organizations called for the proposals to be regarded as exceptional, to be used only for serious offences and subject to stringent procedural safeguards to avoid their indiscriminate or excessive use.[51] We consider shortly whom the regime ensnares but should stress here that not only does the legislation enable the capture of low-level offenders, policy documentation and guidance has advocated the importance of doing so. As the post-Proceeds of Crime Act regime has been rolled out, the authorities have emphasized that the legislation can be used against any defendant who may have profited from crime. Guidance, for example, suggested that 'the main principle is that confiscation opportunities can arise in any crime where an offender has benefited, directly or indirectly, or gained a pecuniary advantage'.[52] As such, both confiscation law and policy have embraced a process akin to net-widening, wherein a sanction initially introduced to respond to 'upper level' offenders has been extended to incorporate lower level offenders.[53] That said, confiscation orders are not routinely obtained, a point that we shall return to shortly.

---

49 N. Nicol, 'Confiscation and the Profits of Crime' (1988) 52 *Journal of Criminal Law* 75; I., Lawrence, 'Draconian and Manifestly Unjust: how the confiscation regime has developed' (2008) 76 *Amicus Curiae* 22.

50 HMIC (fn 6) para. 1.

51 JUSTICE, *Briefing on the Proceeds of Crime Bill*, House of Commons Second Reading; Liberty, *Proceeds of Crime: Consultation on Draft Legislation* (London: 2001).

52 Association of Chief Police Officers and Centrex, *Practice Advice on Financial Investigation* (Wyboston: Centrex, 2006) 53.

53 S. Cohen, *Visions of Social Control* (Cambridge: Polity, 1985).

The broadening reach of confiscation law ought to be seen in the context of the punitive nature of the sanction. Gallant has observed the 'proceeds of crime' is an ill-defined concept which, as we have seen, is quantified by estimating the 'benefit' derived from criminal conduct, tempered by the value of assets a defendant has available for confiscation.[54] The nebulosity of the definition enables the boundaries of confiscation law to extend beyond the net 'profit' of crime, for instance, incorporating any expenses a defendant incurs in the execution of their crime (such as the costs of purchasing or distributing drugs). Consequently, the confiscation claims of the state – as enshrined in legislation and affirmed in a body of case-law – go beyond the reparative rationale embodied within its normative calling, asserting a punitive function and raising the prospect of double punishment.[55] Furthermore, the criminal lifestyle assumptions raise further acute concerns about proportionality. As these assumptions can draw in a defendant's income and expenditure stretching back six years, the seriousness of the offence(s) for which he or she has been convicted is decoupled from the value of assets to be confiscated.

Concerns over the punitive nature of the Proceeds of Crime Act 2002 are accentuated by a lack of due process safeguards for defendants (and their families), who, as an outcome of confiscation proceedings, can face severe hardship. The legislation places a considerable burden on defendants who, albeit that in criminal confiscation proceedings some crime has been established beyond reasonable doubt, 'are penalized for criminal conduct which is unproven; civil standards and methods of proof apply to most issues; assumptions of fact and reverse burdens of proof punctuate the various stages; hardship is never a consideration'.[56] As confiscation hearings represent a hybrid civil–criminal process, the applicable standard of proof overall for the prosecution is specified by section 3(7) to be the balance of probabilities. This represents a deliberate departure from the formula in the Drug Trafficking Act 1994 and Criminal Justice Act 1988 which both used the expression of requiring a level of proof the same as 'that applicable to civil proceedings'. Rees et al. argue that this shift was 'without doubt' intended to evade the flexibility of the civil standard and the principle that civil proceedings involving criminal allegations require a higher degree of proof.[57]

Once the prosecution has established proof on the balance of probabilities, the evidential burden is then on the defendant to demonstrate that the 'criminal lifestyle' assumptions, noted above, have been applied incorrectly or unjustly. As the independent civil rights organization, Liberty, has argued, it may be easier for a defendant to account for his or her finances than for the prosecution but it may

---

54   Gallant (fn 1).

55   Alldridge (fn 17).

56   E. Rees, R. Fisher and P. Bogan, *Blackstone's Guide to the Proceeds of Crime Act* (Oxford: Oxford University Press, 2008) 18.

57   Ibid., 28. An example of the higher standard is *R (McCann) v Manchester Crown Court* [2002] UKHL 39.

not be fair to oblige them to do so.[58] The implications bear upon the erosion of the presumption of innocence, which has given rise to successive legal challenges to confiscation cases under Article 6 of the European Convention of Human Rights.[59] Whilst these challenges have repeatedly failed on the basis that the confiscation order is part of the sentence (for an already-established conviction) rather than a new criminal charge, Ashworth offers the caveat that the criminal lifestyle assumptions cast unproven aspersions on a defendant's past behaviour stretching back six years.[60] Furthermore, the fact that defendants in confiscation hearings have already been convicted of a predicate offence may implicitly undermine the account they provide as to the origins of their assets. Furthermore, there is no absolute right of silence. Under section 17 of the 2002 Act, a defendant who does not reply to the prosecutor's statement, or indicate the extent to which he or she accepts the prosecutions allegations, should be treated as accepting all allegations as accurate. In criminal lifestyle cases then the onus is on the defendant to account for his or her expenditure over the six-year period: 'a daunting task for even the most scrupulous record-keeper and honest citizen'.[61]

Several commentators have also drawn attention to how the act undermines judicial independence. Like others, JUSTICE (a UK based human-rights campaign organization) expressed concern about the draconian nature of the powers set out in the (then) Bill as well as the broad range of offences to which they could apply, and argued that the potential impact should be mitigated by judicial discretion. Justice noted that under the provisions of the Bill, a court may be *required* to make a finding that a defendant has a criminal lifestyle, once he or she satisfies the criteria, even though those criteria may constitute relatively minor offending. It proceeded to argue that a court should instead be *empowered* to identify an individual as having a criminal lifestyle in order that the courts have the discretion to apply a just solution based on the particular circumstances of each case.[62] However, as we have seen, the act requires these assumptions to be applied. As Lawrence put it, 'judicial discretion has been stripped away so that, apart from where abuse of process can be found, it is practically non-existent'.[63]

Whilst there is a significant burden on the defendant and the potential to create hardship, defendants may find it difficult to contest confiscation orders,

---

58   Liberty, *Proceeds of Crime: Consultation on Draft Legislation* (London: 2001) para. 5.2.2.

59   Alldridge (fn 17) 149–150.

60   A.J. Ashworth and C. Ovey, 'Human rights: Whether imposition of confiscation order amounts to "criminal charge"' [2001] *Criminal Law Review* 817. See further S. Trechsel, *Human Rights in Criminal Proceedings* (Oxford: Oxford University Press, 2005) 34–35.

61   N. Nicol, 'Confiscation and the Profits of Crime' at 77.

62   JUSTICE, *Proceeds of Crime Bill, Part 2 – Committee Stage House of Lords: Proposed Amendments* (London: 2002) 2.

63   I. Lawrence, 'Draconian and Manifestly Unjust: How the confiscation regime has developed' at 23.

particularly as they tend to be preparing their defence from the confines of a prison cell. Lawrence is particularly scathing of the current procedural arrangements, noting how defendants frequently lack access both to their own records, business files and, moreover, defence practitioners. He asks, 'What chance in such circumstances has a defendant of concentrating on documentary detail and explanations, still less of proving anything against the odds to the satisfaction of a court?'[64] Lawrence goes on to suggest that defence practitioners are likely to be reluctant to take on confiscation cases as they are paid 'half the already grossly inadequate fees paid for the rest of the criminal work'.[65] In these circumstances, defendants may struggle to get representation at all.

Number and Value of Confiscation Orders

Despite the wide-ranging governmental attempt to promote the use of confiscation orders over the last decade, there is a deficit of reliable and robust data about their application. Data collected by different agencies do not always correspond, and there are analytical difficulties in reconciling the use of powers before and after the operation of the Proceeds of Crime Act 2002.[66] Nor are detailed analyses about confiscation orders, or how much money these sanctions raise for HM Treasury, routinely published. The Government's approach to informing the public about the perceived benefits of the approach has focused on publicizing examples of high-value confiscation orders rather than conducting systematic overviews of the operation of the regime. To help to remedy the deficiency of data on the number and value of confiscation orders, we were able to access some recent data under Freedom of Information requests to Her Majesty's Courts and Tribunals Service ('HMCTS').[67]

Table 3.2   Number and value of confiscation orders (2008–2011)*

Year	Number of orders	Overall value of orders	Average order value
2007/08	4,475	£134,592,086	£30,076
2008/09	5,392	£131,820,426	£24,447
2009/10	5,345	£126,493,429	£23,666
2010/11	6,242	£188,797,998	£30,246

Note: * Data received under Freedom of Information Act release by HMCTS.

---

64   Ibid., 24.

65   Ibid., 24.

66   See for example J. Harvey, 'Just how effective is money laundering legislation?' (2008) 21 *Security Journal* 189.

67   It is notable that data in Chapter 9 from SOCA does not entirely correspond.

Table 3.3 Sentenced defendants ordered to pay confiscation orders for drug trafficking offences by amount (1995–2009)

	1995	1996	1997	1998	1999	2000	2001	2002	2003	2004	2005	2006	2007	2008	2009
Total sentenced for trafficking offences	6,199	7,373	8,370	6,998	6,577	6,458	6,653	6,404	6,797	6,906	6,911	6,676	7,767	9,191	9,775
Total with confiscation order made (% of orders made of eligible offences)	1562 (25%)	1557 (21%)	1466 (18%)	1243 (18%)	1009 (15%)	836 (13%)	777 (12%)	694 (11%)	784 (12%)	709 (10%)	982 (14%)	961 (14%)	1,128 (15%)	1,486 (16%)	1,195 (12%)
Total value of confiscation order (£) (in 100,000s)*	18,337	10,471	5,620	6,970	16,107	5,002	7,980	14,048	6,992	16,170	7,896	11,412	8,859	20,530	5,429
Under £1,000 (number and % of total)**	1,117 (72%)	1,117 (72%)	1032 (70%)	855 (69%)	682 (68%)	525 (63%)	454 (58%)	428 (62%)	471 (60%)	378 (53%)	604 (62%)	590 (61%)	728 (64%)	1,043 (70%)	863 (72%)
£1,000–£3,000	224 (14%)	217 (14%)	224 (15%)	185 (15%)	147 (15%)	159 (19%)	155 (20%)	114 (16%)	130 (17%)	124 (17%)	196 (20%)	203 (21%)	213 (19%)	219 (15%)	178 (15%)
£3,000–£10,000	120 (8%)	118 (8%)	127 (9%)	111 (9%)	99 (10%)	69 (8%)	77 (10%)	70 (10%)	78 (10%)	102 (14%)	93 (9%)	84 (9%)	92 (8%)	104 (7%)	79 (7%)
£10,000–£30,000	56 (4%)	64 (4%)	56 (4%)	56 (5%)	45 (4%)	51 (6%)	47 (6%)	37 (5%)	57 (7%)	38 (5%)	49 (5%)	39 (4%)	46 (4%)	61 (7%)	39 (3%)
£30,000–£100,000	20 (1%)	32 (2%)	19 (1%)	26 (2%)	23 (2%)	20 (2%)	30 (4%)	25 (4%)	32 (4%)	44 (6%)	24 (2%)	30 (3%)	30 (3%)	34 (3%)	25 (2%)
£100,000–£300,000	12	6	6	7	9	11 (1%)	10 (1%)	13 (2%)	14 (2%)	15 (2%)	11 (1%)	7	13 (1%)	16 (1%)	8
£300,000–£1million	9	1	1	1	2	1	3	3	2	6	4	6	5	6	3
£1 million +	4	2	1	2	2	–	1	4	–	2	1	2	1	3	–
Average amount of a confiscation order (£)	11,740	6,725	3,834	5,608	15,964	5,984	10,270	20,242	8,918	22,807	8,041	11,875	7,853	13,815	4,543

Note: Adapted from Home Office, *Criminal Statistics England and Wales* (London: Home Office, 2000); Home Office, *Criminal Statistics England and Wales* (London: Home Office, 2003); Ministry of Justice, *Sentencing Statistics 2007 England and Wales* (London, 2008); Ministry of Justice, *Sentencing Statistics: England and Wales 2009* (London, 2010); * Rounded up to the nearest thousand; ** Percentages less than 1 per cent are not shown.

Table 3.2 shows the volume of confiscation orders sanctioned between 2008 and 2011 and their annual aggregated value. Over the whole period, the data show in both aspects an upward trajectory, suggesting the drive to mainstream the use of the sanction met with some success (though much more so in numbers than average amount). Table 3.2 also shows that across the four years of data the average value of a confiscation order was just over £27,000. More detailed and longer term data, stretching back to 1995, on confiscation orders obtained in drug trafficking cases have been published by the Government, and are illustrated in Table 3.3.

Table 3.3 shows the use of confiscation orders in drug trafficking cases between 1995 and 2009. The average size of orders in such cases is approximately £12,000, although significant variation from the mean is shown throughout the period. About two-thirds of the orders are for less than £1,000, and only a very few are for more than £1,000,000 (25 orders over the 14 year period). A similar picture was revealed by an analysis of 3,604 confiscation orders issued during the financial year 2006/2007, following an integration of the Joint Asset Recovery Database ('JARD'), which holds information on all cases where an order was granted (not merely in drug trafficking cases).[68] The analysis (see Figure 3.1) found wide variation in the value of confiscation orders, which ranged from £1 to well over £1 million. Importantly, however, it found that 45 per cent of orders were for less than £1,000 and less than 1 per cent of them were for more than £1 million. Furthermore, less than 1 per cent of all confiscation orders accounted for over 50 per cent of their aggregated value. By contrast, 50 per cent of confiscation orders accounted for less than 1 per cent of the aggregated value.[69] Consequently, although the average value of an order was just over £40,000, a few very large value orders masked the fairly low value of most. This analysis suggests that whereas a minority of defendants do have considerable sums of money to be confiscated, most do not. As we have stressed above, many offenders either fail to profit substantively from their criminal activity, or alternatively any monies that they do make are spent or successfully concealed from the authorities prior to their arrest.

These sets of data show that the courts do not sanction confiscation orders routinely, but when they do so the orders tend to be of low value. Despite a wide-ranging governmental project over the last decade to promote the use of confiscation orders,[70] it seems little has changed. Entrenched difficulties remain within the process of securing confiscation orders despite, *inter alia*, the introduction of new consolidating legislation, new institutional structures, additional resources to train, accredit and deploy specialist teams of financial investigators, and an incentive scheme by which HM Treasury 'returns' 50 per cent of confiscated funds to those prosecuting agencies involved in specific cases.[71]

---

68   Ibid.; K. Bullock, D. Mann, R. Street and C. Coxon, *Examining Attrition* (fn 45).

69   Ibid., 8.

70   See Home Office, *National Best Practice Guide to Confiscation Order Enforcement* (London: Home Office, 2010).

71   HMIC (fn 6).

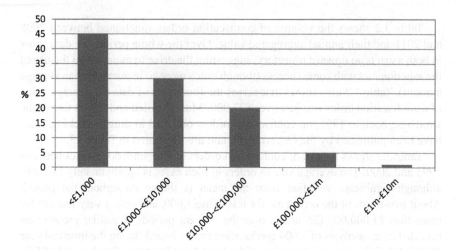

Figure 3.1   Value of confiscation orders sanctioned by percentage (2006/2007)

Note: From K. Bullock, D. Mann, R. Street and C. Coxon, *Examining Attrition* (fn 45).

The Focus of Confiscation Orders

Although there is little data on the types of offences for which defendants issued with confiscation orders are convicted, we do know that 'drug trafficking' cases account for just under two-thirds of the volume of all confiscation orders and about one-third of their aggregate value, with fraud accounting for another 10 per cent of all orders.[72] Importantly, however, 'drug trafficking' in this context refers to any drug offence (though not in the data shown in Table 3.3). We suggest the use of 'trafficking' in this context, which conjures up images of cross-border drug smugglers possessing sizeable resources to enable such activity, serves to mystify the main focus of the sanction. Our argument is that, despite political rhetoric depicting images of 'crime barons', the paradigm situation involves individuals possessing relatively few assets of value who mostly find themselves in confiscation hearings. This outcome is unsurprising as, over the last decade, central policy directives from government and law-enforcement agencies has repeatedly called for confiscation orders to be used against defendants from across the offending spectrum. Indeed, as we have suggested, the legislation is enabling in this regard. In so doing, official reports emphasize how the Proceeds of Crime Act 2002, being regarded as complex and specialist activity, is poorly understood and only partially exploited by criminal justice practitioners.[73] As a recent cross-inspectorate review

---

72   HMCPSI et al. (fn 46) fn 18; see also K. Bullock, D. Mann, R. Street and C. Coxon, *Examining Attrition* 6.

73   HMIC (fn 6); HMCPSI et al. (fn 46).

stated: 'The infrequency of referral of acquisitive crime, particularly at the lower end of the range of offending, suggests a lack of appreciation of how the proceeds of crime legislation could potentially assist across the crime spectrum, and may represent a significant gap in the use of the legislation.'[74] By advocating greater use of the sanction per se, rather than a narrower focus on those who profit most from crime, however, the strategy risks mostly drawing in to financial investigations and confiscations hearings those 'usual suspects' of police work, who tend to be easier to identify, investigate and prosecute than offenders from less socially and economically marginalized groups. Indeed, research has found that 'highly visible but relatively low-level drug dealers and/or users are routinely swept into the net of confiscation proceedings'.[75] This finding accentuates concerns over the proportionality of the response. An exceptional set of legal tools, introduced specifically to tackle the perceived perils of powerful 'organized' criminals, is being used against offenders who are likely to possess little of value to be confiscated.

The Enforcement of Confiscation Orders

It has been evident for some time that enforcing confiscation orders can be difficult. There is a high level of monetary attrition in which only a proportion of the aggregate value of all confiscation orders is realized by the courts. For example, between 1995 and 1999 only 40 per cent of all orders were fully enforced.[76] Examining the enforcement status of 1,390 orders imposed between April and August 2006 after one year, Bullock et al. found 88 per cent of them had been paid in part or in full, though the amount paid equated only to 38 per cent of the aggregate value of the orders.[77] Repayment levels varied significantly in respect of the value of the order, though they steadily declined as the value of orders increased. Whereas 98 per cent of confiscation orders valued at between £10 and £100 were paid in full, this figure fell to 35 per cent for those valued between £100,000 and £1 million.

The researchers identified several reasons for this attrition, including a shortfall between the expected value of assets when orders are made and the actual value they return when sold; the difficulties faced by imprisoned offenders when trying to sell their (often meagre) assets to pay an order; complications regarding the position of third parties in asset ownership; actions taken by some offenders to conceal their assets; and offenders absconding, dying, or being deported. Whilst such problems can routinely afflict the enforcement of all confiscation orders, as shown, there is a particular problem with those of high value. The difficulty of enforcing these orders is partly a function of the technical and financial complexity

---

74   Ibid.; HMCPSI et al. (fn 46) 22.

75   K. Bullock, 'The Confiscation Investigation' (2010) 4 *Policing: An International Journal of Policy and Practice* 7 at 12.

76   HMCPSI et al. (fn 46) para. 1.11.

77   K. Bullock, D. Mann, R. Street and C. Coxon, *Examining Attrition.*

of the arrangements behind the order and partly a function of the legal and administrative efforts to which defendants go to delay or avoid the paying of these orders.[78] Enforcement options, in practice, may be limited after an offender has served a default prison sentence. Further, some offenders are skilful at dispersing and concealing their assets, for example, by ensuring they are held in someone else's name or holding them abroad.

The difficulties of enforcing confiscation orders represent a persistent challenge for the courts with the implications of non-payment felt across the prosecuting agencies of the criminal justice process, as well as for the overall financial viability of the confiscation regime itself. The broader concern, however, is the emergence of a vicious cycle in which offenders perceive partial or non-payment to be a realistic option, thereby negating any deterrence value they associate with the sanction, which in turn may discourage law-enforcement and prosecuting agencies from pursuing confiscation, therein further reducing the likelihood that those convicted at court will be stripped of their assets. The assumptions underpinning the rationalization of confiscation presume a theory of implementation which is not always (or indeed often) realized.

Conclusion

This chapter has sought not only to contextualize but also to critique the emergence and practice of post-conviction confiscation of assets in England and Wales. It is no coincidence that the legal and institutional apparatus developed to enable this state activity has expanded (both in the UK and elsewhere) over the last two decades in tandem with the increasing level and range of harms associated with serious and professional criminals and, more recently, local and global terrorist networks. Regardless of whether these harms are real or perceived, they have helped to justify the development of a confiscation regime in England and Wales that is widely considered to be 'severe and unforgiving' in its intent and application.[79] The regime enables the state to seize assets from its citizens on the basis of far-reaching assumptions about the origins of those assets, presuming them to be the proceeds of crime without needing to link them to any (proven or unproven) criminal act. Moreover, the legal contest is governed by civil evidential standards and rules, despite the penal nature of the sanction, whilst loading the defendant with the burden of disproving the state's allegations. The structure of confiscation law is heavily tilted towards efficiency not rights, towards retribution not restoration. It is deeply ironic that a regime of law, which places moral certitude at its core, so flagrantly circumvents the normative conventions of criminal law

---

78   K. Bullock, 'Enforcing financial penalties: The case of confiscation orders' (2010) 49 *Howard Journal of Criminal Justice* 328.

79   E. Rees, R. Fisher and P. Bogan, *Blackstone's Guide to the Proceeds of Crime Act* (Oxford: Oxford University Press, 2008) 18.

and procedure. The draconian nature of the current regime of confiscation law in England and Wales is all the more problematic because of the type of offenders it routinely draws in. The analysis presented here suggests the drive to broaden the focus of the regime is, in contradiction to the original policy rhetoric, leading to confiscation hearings being mostly concerned with offenders from the lower, rather than the upper, echelons of criminal enterprise.

Whilst the purpose of this chapter has been to reflect critically on the law, policy and practice of confiscation, our analysis implicitly raises questions of its functional role within the politics of law and order. We suggest that the prominence given to confiscation by the state, despite the entrenched problems of implementation and enforcement, despite the financial cost of institutionalizing the approach, despite the myriad of legal challenges it has brought forth and despite the uncertainties over its effectiveness to deliver its crime-reduction goals, owes much to the symbolic and communicative properties the strategy expresses.[80] Confiscation, as a governmental strategy, speaks to its audiences of a powerful rhetoric of control over acquisitive criminality, but perhaps equally importantly reasserts a moral authoritarianism within the state's response to crime and insecurity. Its forthright normative stance presents to citizens a symbolic commitment that 'crime should not pay', a moral offering that is difficult to oppose but also which, in an era of penal populism and knee-jerk political posturing to be 'tough on crime', justifies the oppressive potential of the sanction.[81] Although the instrumentality of the confiscation agenda for controlling crime is uncertain, its moral symbolism is not.

---

80   E.V. Ericson and K.D. Haggerty, *Policing the Risk Society* (Oxford: Clarendon, 1997); see also A. Crawford, 'Dispersal Powers and the Symbolic Role of Anti-Social Behaviour Legislation' (2008) 71 *Modern Law Review* 753.

81   See also Alldridge (fn 17) 18–19.

Chapter 4

Anti-Mafia Forfeiture in the Italian System

Daniele Piva

Introduction

In recent years, anti-Mafia legislation has relied upon an increased use of forfeiture alongside a wide array of criminal law initiatives. Examples of such criminal law measures include white collar crimes, usury (lending money at extraordinary interest rates), money laundering, public officers' crimes against the public administration, tax fraud, customs crimes, international drug trafficking, transnational crimes and corporate liability. Yet, it is forfeiture which might be regarded as the most efficient tool in fighting organized crime. Forfeiture has now acquired a 'poly-functional' character, varying according not only to the context it is based on, but also on different assumptions and recipients. Nowadays in Italy, we should refer not just to a single concept of 'forfeiture', but discuss plural anti-Mafia 'forfeitures'. This is because we cannot unify in a single notion what, in effect, only shares the outcome of depriving somebody of an asset which is seized and subsequently acquired by the government. We must also consider increased international influences on the development of forfeiture, for example, the Resolution on organized crime in the European Union adopted by the EU Parliament on 25 October 2011[1] and the subsequent proposal for a Directive on the freezing and confiscation of proceeds of crime, set forth by the European Commission on 12 March 2012.[2]

---

1   European Parliament resolution of 25 October 2011 on organised crime in the European Union (2010/2309(INI)). See A. Balsamo and C. Lucchini, 'La risoluzione del 25 ottobre 2011 del Parlamento europeo: un nuovo approccio al fenomeno della criminalità organizzata. A proposito della Risoluzione del 25 ottobre 2011 sulla criminalità organizzata nell'Unione europea (2010/2309(INI)' (2011) *Diritto Penale Contemporaneo*: http://www. penalecontemporaneo.it/upload/Risoluzione%20Parlamento%20UE%20su%20c%20o% 20.pdf (accessed 11 April 2013).

2   COM(2012) 85 final.

**Forfeiture as the Main Tool to Tackle Organized Crime: From the
'Bond of Dependent Nexus' to the 'Assumption of Unlawful Sources'**

Within the Italian legal system, forfeiture measures can be clustered into three
main fields: forfeiture as a 'security measure', forfeiture as a 'preventive measure'
and forfeiture as a 'sanction'. In each category, the object of the seizure can range
from the money taken out of, the price, or the means of, a crime or goods of
alleged illicit provenance. Forfeiture as a security measure, as in article 240 of the
Italian Penal Code, notoriously centred on the need to prove a specific 'bond of
dependent nexus' ('*pertinenzialità*') between the goods and a crime.

This category has now been joined by so called 'widened forfeitures' that can
have as their object the entire assets of a person on the assumption of 'qualified
social dangerousness' arising from participation in the Mafia or Mafia-like
organizations. The best-known examples involve forfeiture as a 'preventive
measure', now entirely provided for in the Code of anti-Mafia and preventive
measures laws (*Codice delle leggi antimafia e delle misure di prevenzione*)[3] or
as an accessory sanction to other criminal procedures.[4] Both are equally founded
on the presumption that goods appearing to be the direct or indirect possession of
an individual are to be regarded as the 'offshoot' or 'reuse' of illicit endeavours,
where these goods are disproportionate to the person's legitimate profit-making,
economic activity or lifestyle, unless he can prove that they originate from lawful
sources. These ablative measures, chipping away assets from criminals, are
independent from any solid 'link' between alleged criminal deeds and ownership
of the goods. Forfeiture is based solely on the assumption that the source of the
goods is unlawful, in the framework of a 'trial against assets', rather than on
bringing criminal proceedings against the person. Forfeiture, then, can occur in
the absence of criminal conviction.

Under article 12-*sexies* of *Decreto-legge* (D.L.) 306/1992, all goods for which
no justification is provided can be seized as a sanction, irrespective of the when
they were acquired. When forfeiture as a preventive measure is at stake, case-law
is split into two categories. The first category requires a link between acquisition
of the goods and time considered necessary to establish whether or not assets
were acquired by the individual at the time the suspect allegedly joined a criminal

---

3   d.lgs.159/2011. See previously L. 646/1982 within L. 575/1965. See F. Menditto,
*Lo schema di decreto legislativo del codice delle leggi antimafia e delle misure di
prevenzione (Livri I, II, IV e V): esame, osservazioni e proposte* (2011) 3 ff., *Diritto Penale
Contemporaneo*: http://www.penalecontemporaneo.it/materia/-/-/-/742-lo_schema_di_decr
eto_legislativo_del_codice_delle_leggi_antimafia_e_delle_misure_di_prevenzione__libri
_i__ii__iv_e_v___esame__osservazioni_e_proposte/ (accessed 11 April 2013).
4   D.L. 306/1992, art. 12-*sexies* (converted into L. 356/1992).

organization or at a subsequent date.[5] The other, more recent, category is concerned with the 'dependent nexus link' between goods whose lawful source is unproven and persons who represent a social danger. Here, all assets of the said individuals are subject to preventive confiscation, even those acquired prior to the judicial ascertainment of social dangerousness, as long as legal proceedings leading to the imposition of a personal preventive measure are introduced.[6]

Setting a time-frame which is related to when a person joined a criminal organization comes from the fact that while article 12-*sexies*, D.L. 306/1992 requires conviction (or even plea bargaining under article 444 of the Code of Penal Procedure) for crimes set forth in article 416-*bis* of the Penal Code, in order to apply a preventive measure, a merely circumstantial ascertainment is sufficient under article 29 of the *Decreto legislativo* (d.lgs.) 159/2011. Moreover, as a preventive measure is unrelated to the commencement of a criminal trial, the criminal standard of proof 'beyond any reasonable doubt' (as specified in article 533 of the Code of Penal Procedure) is not required. What is required are mere circumstances, objectively assessable, driving towards a judgment of reasonable probability that the individual is part of a criminal organization.

In this way, a time-link embodies the bond between social dangerousness and the unlawful source of assets. Without that, forfeiture as a preventive measure would turn into an even harsher sanction which, despite the widespread support

---

5   See Cass., Sez. I, 4 July 2007, n. 33479, in *dejure.giuffre.it*; Sez. I, 16 April 2007, n. 21048, in *Guida al dir.*, 27/2007, 82; Sez. V, 23 March 2007, n. 18822, in dejure. giuffre.*it*; Sez. I, 5 October 2006, n. 35481, in *Cass. pen.*, 10/2007, 3870; Sez. V, 13 June 2006, n. 24778, in *dejure.giuffre.it*; Sez. VI, 29 September 2005, n. 41195, in *Arch. nuov. proc. pen.*, 2/2006, 182. For case-law, see A. Maugeri, *Profili di legittimità costituzionale delle sanzioni patrimoniali (prima e dopo la riforma introdotta dal decr. N. 92/2008): la giurisprudenza della Corte Costituzionale e della Suprema Corte* in F. Cassano (ed.), *Le misure di prevenzione patrimoniali dopo il 'pacchetto sicurezza* (Bari: Neldiritto, 1999) 39 ff., and *Dalla riforma delle misure di prevenzione alla confisca generale dei beni contro il terrorismo* in O. Mazza and F. Viganò (eds), *Il 'pacchetto sicurezza' 2009 (commento al d.l. 23 febbraio 2009, n. 11 conv. in legge 23 aprile 2009 n. 38 e alla legge 15 luglio 2009, n. 94)* (Turin: Giappichelli, 2009) 425.

6   See Cass., Sez. I, 29 May 2009, n. 34456, in *dejure.giuffre.it*; Sez. II, 22 April 2009, n. 20906, in *Cass. pen.*, 7-8/2010, 2830; Sez. II, 16 April 2009, n. 25558, ibid., 4/2010, 1647; Sez. II, 8 April 2008, n. 21717, ibid., 5/2009, 2158; Sez. Un., 19 January 2004, ibid., 2004, 1188.

in case-law,[7] would inevitably put it in conflict with constitutional principles of 'legality' and 'fair trial',[8] as well as the presumption of innocence.[9]

Moreover, the subjective scope of application and the net of possible subjects are wider in three respects in preventive measure than in 'sanction' forfeiture on the basis of article 12-*sexies* of D.L. 306/1992. First, although forfeiture as an accessory sanction typically requires a person to be convicted of crimes related to Mafia activities or crimes committed that benefit from conditions set forth in article 416-*bis* or in order to help Mafia organizations, the array of behaviour provided for in article 16, d.lgs. 159/2011 is much larger. The list includes all legal forms of 'generic' social dangerousness related to ongoing economic criminal deeds or to derivation of economic means of sustenance from illicit deeds. The effect is that, other than its traditional preventive effect, anti-Mafia forfeiture constitutes, in accordance with modern tendencies in criminal policy, a key factor for the repression of both social deviance and crime committed by the most powerful people.[10] Secondly, with preventive forfeiture, it is possible to go after assets owned by a person who has deceased during the proceedings, within five years after their death.[11] By contrast, if a person dies during the course of a criminal trial then the law precludes conviction.[12] Where this happens the crime becomes extinct. Further, it also results in the subsequent restitution of seized goods. Finally, it is noticeable that preventive measures are not subject to the principle of non-retroactivity in criminal law.[13] Rather, according to article 200 of

---

7   See for all Cass., Sez. I, 15 June 2005, in *Cass. pen.*, 2006, 3326; Sez. II, 31 January 2005, ibid.; Sez. II, 4 April 1999, ibid., 2000, 1411 (with criticisms by P.V. Molinari, *Confisca antimafia: si estende il dialogo con il morto*); Sez. I, 24 November 1998, ibid., 1999, 558 (with notes by P.V. Molinari, *Confisca antimafia e dialogo con il morto*), Sez. Un., 3 July 1996, ibid., 1996, 1963 (with notes by P.V. Molinari, *Ancora sulla confisca antimafia: un caso di pretesa giustizia sostanziale* contra legem).

8   As per the Trib. Napoli, Sez. Mis. Prev., 6 July 2011: http://www.penalecontemporan eo.it/area/3-/-/-/862-ancora_in_tema_di_confisca_di_prevenzione__sull__onere_proba torio_in_materia_di_illecita_provenienza_dei_beni__sulla_connessione_temporale_tra_ epoca_di_acquisto_dei_beni_e_manifestazione_della_pericolosit____sulla_confisca_di_ ramo_d__azienda_di_societ_/ (accessed 11 April 2013).

9   As per A. Maugeri, *Le moderne sanzioni patrimoniali tra funzionalità e garantismo* (Milan: Giuffré, 2001) 838 and 'Proposta di direttiva in materia di congelamento e confisca dei proventi del reato: prime riflessioni': http://www.penalecontemporaneo.it/materia/-/-/- /1400-proposta_di_direttiva_in_materia_di_congelamento_e_confisca_dei_proventi_del_ reato__prime_riflessioni/ (accessed 11 April 2013, p. 16).

10   With regard to the preventive measures addressed also to those individuals who systematically evade taxes, even if based on lawful business incomes, see Trib. Chieti, 12 July 2012: http://www.penalecontemporaneo.it/upload/1346509978Provvedimento%20 Chieti.pdf (accessed 17 April 2013).

11   article 18 par. 1 e 2, d.lgs. 159/2011.

12   article 12-*sexies*.

13   article 25 of the Italian Constitution (Cost.).

the Penal Code, they are governed by the law in force at the time of application, as they, and security measures alike, are not imposed as a consequence of a well-determined deed but because of the developed lifestyle of an individual which raises the suspicion of him being socially dangerous.[14]

Despite their complicated variations, these legal provisions of forfeiture are basically alike, as shown by the use of identical words to describe forfeitable assets,[15] and the same legal provisions apply, as on how to carry out seizure and take care of the goods. Where both measures might arise, the choice about which to apply would be with the authority holding the power to request the seizure.[16]

Assumptions behind Forfeiture as a Preventive Measure

The main assumption behind the application of seizure and forfeiture as preventive measures lies in the social dangerousness of the individual. This assumption derives from association with Mafia-driven organizations and the possession, directly or otherwise, of assets disproportionate with lawfully acquired incomes and legal economic activity, to the extent that is probable that these goods derive from unlawful endeavours or constitute the re-use thereof.[17] In particular, what is needed is an established fact giving rise to a probability that a person has partaken in a Mafia-driven organization[18] and a presumption of 'on-going dangerousness' according to which participation is adequately demonstrated; there is no further need for a judge to give reasons on the point unless evidence of exit from the organization has emerged. It is not enough to show that time has passed since joining the criminal enterprise or active participation in criminal deeds.

Direct or indirect ownership of goods means that, even without their formal registration to a party or even without any physical contact with the asset, the goods appear to be possessed by the individual, when he has the capacity to determine their use and destination at his own will.[19] For example, it is possible to forfeit the

---

14 See Cass., Sez. II, 14 May 2009, n. 33597, in *dejure.giuffre.it*; Sez. I, 8 November 2007, n. 7116, in *dejure.giuffre.it*.

15 Respectively at comma 1, article 12-*sexies* and comma 3 article 2-*ter* L. 575/1965 and now placed at comma 1 of article 24 d.lgs. 159/2011.

16 For provisions dealing with overlap, see art. 30 of d.lgs. 159/2011, subject to art. 104-*bis* disp att. Code of Penal Procedure.

17 article (s.) 20 comma 1 and 24 comma 1, d.lgs. 159/2011.

18 See Corte Cost., sentences n. 2 – 23 June 1956, n. 23 – 23 March 1964 and n. 113 – 21 May 1975, all part of *dejure.giuffre.it*; as well as Cass., Sez. I, 20 March 1995, n. 1675, in *Riv. polizia*, 1996, 591; Sez. I, 8 March 1994, in *Cass. pen.*, 1995,1358; Sez. I, 28 April 1995, n. 2583, in *Giust. pen.*, 1996, III, 114.

19 Cass., Sez. V, 17 March 2000, n. 1520, in *Cass. pen.*, 2001, 1327; Sez. VI, 23 January 1996, n. 398, in *Giust. pen.*, 1997, III, 380. See A. Aiello, *La tutela civilistica dei terzi nel sistema della prevenzione patrimoniale antimafia* (Milan: Giuffré, 2005) 102 ff.; F. Cassano, 'La tutela dei diritti nel sistema della prevenzione' in G. Fiandaca and

branch of a corporation formally owned by a legal person, where it is made clear that it is the 'dangerous individual' who actually runs it and that asset derives from unlawful activities. This is so even where the 'dangerous individual' is not the registered owner of the business.[20] Given this approach, investigations prior to preventive measures nowadays comprehensively consider the spouse, siblings, people who lived with the subject in the previous five years, corporations, and partnerships the assets of which dangerous individuals appear to be able to handle, fully or in part, directly or indirectly.[21] These people may not be named owners of the goods;[22] unless otherwise proven, every transaction or handover – even for payment – towards children, spouse or persons living together, relatives, and contacts in the two years preceding a judicial petition for a preventive measure are considered as non-genuine.[23]

Despite these rules, there is no inversion of the burden of proof as assumptions behind the preventive measure are based upon factual elements characterized by gravity, precision and concurrence that the prosecution must establish[24] to the satisfaction of the court. If necessary, this may happen by ordering further investigations. Third parties are free to raise any issue, even bald allegations. Regardless of representations coming from parties, it is for the judge to pick out and highlight facts showing that some assets are disproportionate in respect of the subject's income or economic activity, and to gather enough clues to establish that the assets concerned derive from illicit activities or constitute re-use thereof. This point about the burden of proof applies also in respect of the decision on forfeiture, where the possibility to 'justify' goods as derived from lawful activities[25] does not constitute a real 'burden' or, even less, an 'obligation' that courts may impose on the third-party owner.[26]

Another assumption, on which may be founded a preventive measure, is 'disproportion' between lifestyle, working placement and officially declared or

---

C. Visconti (eds), *Scenari attuali di mafia. Analisi e strategie di intervento* (Turin: Giappichelli, 2010) 418; A. Mangione, *La misura di prevenzione patrimoniale fra dogmatica e politica criminale* (Padua: Giuffré, 2001) 268.

20   Trib. Napoli, Sez. Mis. Prev., 6 July 2011, cit.

21   article 19 comma 3, d.lgs. 159/2011.

22   article 35 comma 3.

23   article 26 comma 2, lett. a. Fraudulent or sham transfers of assets will be applied as per art. 12-*quinquies* D.L. 306/1992. See F. Giunta and E. Marzaduri, *La nuova normativa sulla sicurezza pubblica – aggiornata alla legge 15 July 2009, n. 94* (Milan: Giuffré, 2010) 261.

24   In this sense, making reference to the previous legislation, Cass. 28 March 2002, in *Cass. pen.*, 2003, 612; 4 June 2003, ibid., 2005, 2066; 18 September 2002, in *Dir. pen. proc.*, 2003, 1108; 10 November 1997, in *Giust. pen.*, 1998, II, 512; 16 April 1996, in *Cass. pen.*, 1997, 849; 18 May 1992, ibid., 1993, 2377.

25   article 24 comma 1, d.lgs. 159/2011.

26   See article 34 comma 1 d.lgs. 159/2011 on judicial administration of assets.

apparent income. Contrary to some case-law,[27] these differences all have to occur when imposing forfeiture as a preventive measure each time the sources of assets are lawful and traceable, but unrelated to income statements. Otherwise, there would be a danger, in some degree, of punishing people, for example, for tax evasion alone.[28]

If disproportion is a key element on its own, to be evaluated when the assessment of social dangerousness is at stake,[29] it can become conclusive when seizure is involved. Indeed, disproportion can operate as a stand-alone assumption for the application of freezing,[30] to the point that 'sufficient clues' are needed only to demonstrate the unlawful source or re-use of goods. Bearing in mind that this element can be considered as stand-alone (and sufficient) evidence,[31] we should also recognize that the disproportion has to relate to each and every one of the assets and/or the funds used in their purchase. Otherwise, it could be possible, through an aggregation of goods, to elude the necessary detection of what in fact constitutes proceedings or re-use of proceeds of illicit deeds.[32] On the other hand,

---

27   *Among others*, regarding forfeiture *ex* art. 12-*sexies* D.L. 206/1992, Cass., Sez. I, 14 October 1996, n. 5202, in *Cass. pen.* 1997, 3495.

28   See Cass., Sez. VI, 31 May 2011, n. 29926: http://www.penalecontemporaneo. it/materia/1-/16-/-/1086-sulla_rilevanza_dei_redditi_non_dichiarati_al_fisco_ai_fini_del_ sequestro_e_della_confisca_di_cui_all___art__12_sexies_del_d_l__n__306_92__conv__ dalla_l__n__356_92/ (accessed 11 April 2013), with notes by F. Menditto, *Sulla rilevanza dei redditi non dichiarati al fisco ai fini del sequestro e della confisca di cui all'art. 12-*sexies *del d.l. n. 306 del 1992.* See further G. Locatelli, *La confisca del patrimonio di valore sproporzionato. Note all'art. 12-*sexies *della l. 7.8.1992, nr. 356*, in *Il Fisco*, 1996, 8304.

29   Trib. Napoli, Sez. Mis. Prev., 6 July 2011, cit.

30   article 2-*ter* comma 2 L. 575/1965 (as amended by article 3 L. 24 July 1993 n. 256) – article 20 comma 1 d.lgs. 159/2011.

31   Opposite to the previous regulation, see Cass., Sez. II, 23 June 2004, n. 35628, in *Cass. pen.*, 9/2005, 2704. For more details: A. Cairo, *Le misure di prevenzione patrimoniali* in R. Tartaglia (ed.), *Codice delle confische e dei sequestri* (Rome: Neldiritto, 2012) 1044 ff.; A. Balsamo, V. Contraffatto and G. Nicastro, *Le misure patrimoniali contro la criminalità organizzata* (Milan: Giuffré, 2010).

32   Among others, compare to Cass., 21 March 1999, in *Cass. pen.*, 2000, 1048; 1 March 1991, in *Giur. it.*, 1992, Penal Code 299. A cause-effect link is required between the typical behaviour of the 'Mafia' and an unlawful gain or a co-existence of social dangerousness and the purchasing of the assets; see Cass. 24 February 2011, n. 10219: http://www.penalecontemporaneo.it/materia/-/-/-/718-sulla_confisca_di_prevenzione_ex_ art__2_ter_l__575____65__nozione_di___reimpiego___e_necessario_rispetto_dell__ art__42_cost_/ (accessed 11 April 2013), with notes by A. Maugeri, *Sulla confisca di prevenzione ex art. 2 ter l. 575/'65 (nozione di reimpiego e necessario rispetto dell'art. 42 Cost.)*; 3 February 1998, in *Arch. n. proc. pen.*, 1998, 424 (with notes by P. Grillo, *Fra misure di prevenzione personale e misura di prevenzione patrimoniale nella legislazione antimafia*). The following support the 'garantismo' (legal rights-based) case-law approach: A. Aiello, *La tutela civilistica dei terzi nel sistema della prevenzione patrimoniale antimafia* (Milan: Giuffré, 2005) 204; A. Gialanella, *La confisca di prevenzione antimafia, lo sforzo*

when forfeiture is concerned, article 24 never demands the criterion of sufficient clues, seeking instead assets that derive from unlawful endeavours or constitute the re-use thereof. This approach surely seems to call for a proof tighter than 'sufficient clues',[33] possibly coinciding with that of article 192 Code of Penal Procedure.[34] Further, when the legislature really wanted to advance the potential idea behind the two measures, it did so by using the same formula as in article 20, as happens in judicial administration regulations where Courts pronounce forfeiture of goods which 'there is reason to believe are the outcome of illicit deeds or constitutes the reuse thereof'.[35]

The Separated Application of Forfeiture with Regard to Personal Preventive Measures

The effectiveness of seizure and forfeiture as preventive measures is noticeably improved by the provision[36] of a possible disjointed application of personal and patrimonial preventive measures, regardless of the social dangerousness of the

---

sistematico della giurisprudenza di legittimità e la retroguardia del legislatore in F. Cassano (ed.), *Le misure di prevenzione patrimoniali* 202 and *I patrimoni di mafia – La prova, il sequestro, la confisca, le garanzie* (Naples: Edizioni Scientifiche Italiane, 1998) 124; P.V. Molinari and U. Papadia, *Le misure di prevenzione nella legge fondamentale, nelle leggi antimafia e nella legge antiviolenza nelle manifestazioni sportive* (Milan: Giuffré, 2002) 519; L. Pascali and D. Cherubini, *La misura di prevenzione patrimoniale nella normativa antimafia. Il problema della tutela civile dei creditori* (Bari: Cacucci, 1999) 71; F. Cassano, *Misure di prevenzione patrimoniali* 54.

33   With regard to the need of a proof of the goods' illicit provenance see, for example, Cass., Sez. II, 22 April 2009, n. 20906, cit.; Sez. II, 23 June 2004, cit., according to which 'the ... judge proceeding with the forfeiture cannot rely upon simple clues only ... but ... must demonstrate the goods' illicit provenance through very sound statements'. Compare F. Menditto, *Lo schema di decreto legislativo del codice delle leggi antimafia e delle misure di prevenzione (Libri I, II, IV e V): esame, osservazioni e proposte* (fn 3) 55.

34   See A. Maugeri (ed.), *La riforma delle misure* 156; Gialanella, *La confisca di prevenzione antimafia, lo sforzo sistematico della giurisprudenza di legittimità e la retroguardia del legislatore* in F. Cassano (ed.), *Le misure di prevenzione patrimoniali* 202 and *I patrimoni di mafia – La prova, il sequestro, la confisca, le garanzie* (Naples: Edizioni Scientifiche Italiane, 1998) 133; as well as in case-law, see *Cass.*, 16 January 2007, n. 5234, in *Guida al dir.*, 2007, 1067, according to which 'with regard to both the ownership of the goods and their illicit provenance, a different level of demonstration is required as far as a seizure or a forfeiture is concerned. In case of seizure, an evaluation of "reasonable probability" is necessary and sufficient, while in case of forfeiture, the relevant demonstration (even if made through a presumptive proof) has to meet the following requirements: gravity, precision and concurrence'.

35   article 34 comma 7.

36   This provision was already set forth in L. 125/2008 at article 2-*bis* comma 6-*bis* L. 575/1965 and today in article 18 comma 1 d.lgs. 159/2011.

individual at the time of request for application.[37] These may arise where the subject is dead,[38] living abroad,[39] already enduring custodial security measures or supervised release,[40] where personal preventive measures have ceased or been revoked and, more generally, where social dangerousness is no longer at issue at the time of forfeiture.

Erasing a link between personal and patrimonial preventive measures does not mean that forfeiture can be imposed without judicial ascertainment that social dangerousness was present when goods were acquired and that the possible ending of such status cannot stand in the way of depriving of goods any persons who illicitly acquired them.[41] Accordingly all pronouncements from the Constitutional Court that have affirmed links between personal and patrimonial preventive measures are fully compliant with the reasonableness principle,[42] even though some waivers thereof have been tolerated, ultimately calling on the legislator to reconsider its criminal policy choices.[43]

The Administration and Destination of Seized and Forfeited Goods

Another issue that merits discussion is the destination of the goods forfeited from organized crime,[44] with 'social use' being the first goal, aimed at returning assets to the community from which they had been unlawfully derived and thus creating

---

37 For a wider overview about the amendments with the D.L. 92/2008, see L. Filippi and M.F. Cortesi, *Novità sulle misure di prevenzione* in A. Scalfati (ed.), *Il Decreto sicurezza – d.l. n. 92/2008 convertito con modifiche in legge n. 125/2008* (Turin: Giappichelli, 2008) 254; P. Giordano, 'Senza controllo sull'effettiva applicazione la filosofia dell'inasprimento non basta' in *Guida al dir.*, 32/2008, 81.

38 See Trib. Napoli, 15 July 2011, entirely issued in http://www.penalecontemporaneo. it/tipologia/8-/-/-/860-in_tema_di_confisca_di_prevenzione_nei_confronti_degli_eredi_ del_proposto/ (accessed 11 April 2013).

39 See article 18 comma 4, d.lgs. 159/2011.

40 Again, article 18 comma 5, d.lgs. 159/2011.

41 See F. Menditto, *Lo schema di decreto legislativo del codice delle leggi antimafia e delle misure di prevenzione (Libri I, II, IV e V): esame, osservazioni e proposte* (fn 3) 48.

42 See Corte Cost., ord. 23 June 1988, n. 721, in *Foro it.*, 1989, I, c. 2035; sent. 28 December 1993, n. 465, in *Cass. pen.*, 1994, 884; sent. 8 October 1996, n. 335, ibid., 1997, 334 (with notes by P.V. Molinari, *Una parola forse definitiva su confisca antimafia e morte della persona pericolosa*); as well as, more recently, ord. 29 November 2004, n. 368, ibid., 2005, 800 (with notes by P.V. Molinari, *Ancora una volta bocciata la giurisprudenza creativa in tema di confisca antimafia*).

43 See F. Menditto, *Lo schema di decreto legislativo del codice delle leggi antimafia e delle misure di prevenzione (Libri I, II, IV e V): esame, osservazioni e proposte* (fn 3) 52.

44 L. 7 March 1996, n. 109.

opportunities for growth and development. Of most interest is the institution,[45] the Agenzia Nazionale per l'amministrazione e la destinazione dei beni sequestrati e confiscati ('ANBSC') ('National Agency for the administration and destination of seized and forfeited goods'). In advance of the final judicial decision ordering forfeiture, the final destination of goods will already be known.[46] This agency centralizes the different tasks of administration, custody and planning, which had previously been handled by different institutions both from the judicial (by a delegate judge) and administrative authorities (the 'Agenzia del Demanio' and the 'Prefettura' in the relevant locality). The aim is to save time between the initial seizure and final distribution of the assets, to cut handling costs, as well as to alleviate the burden of work on judicial authorities.

The main problem with ANBSC arises from ongoing organizational staff and money shortages, exacerbated by ever bigger number of seizures and, even more, the automatic application of preventive measures provided for in article 23-*bis* L. 646/1982. This provides that 'a Public Prosecutor initiates a criminal proceeding against somebody for crimes provided for in article 416-bis Penal Code or in article 75 Law 22 December 1975, n. 685, and immediately gives notice to the Prosecutor-in-Chief of the place where the person lives, he must initiate – if he has not already done so – a proceeding for the imposition of preventive measures'.[47]

Another problem is a lack of coordination and control mechanisms between the ANBSC and the proceeding judge, especially with regard to the progress of proceedings, possible discovery of new assets to seize and payments to third parties.

Furthermore, the ANBSC is still not competent to deal with the seizure and confiscation of goods pursuant to article 321 comma 2 of the Code of Penal Procedure and article 240 of the Penal Code or article 12-*sexies* D.L. 306/1992, as these are dealt with by the judge who has to name an administrator.[48]

---

45   See D.L. 4 February 2010, n. 4; http://www.benisequestraticonfiscati.it/Joomla/ (accessed 17 April 2013).

46   About the Agency's duties, see A. Roberto, A. Cisterna, M.V. De Simone, et al., *L'Agenzia Nazionale per i patrimoni di mafia. Amministrazione e destinazione dei beni confiscati dopo l'entrata in vigore dei regolamenti* (Sant'Arcangelo di Romagna: Maggioli, 2012).

47   Illustrative of the operating difficulties that the ANBSC faced straight after its constitution, as provided for under art. 4 of the above mentioned D.L., 15 February 2011, the Agency signed an agreement to let the Agenzia Demanio (State Property Agency: http://www.agenziademanio.it, accessed 17 April 2013) deal with the preliminary investigation activities aimed at managing the goods seized from organized crime, together with all the activities linked to and necessary for administrative and transactional proceedings, as well as legal arguments at any trial stage and level or extrajudicial proceedings, while remaining the single body entitled to define any overt act.

48   article 12-*sexies* comma 4-*bis*. See further article 116 comma 2 del d.lgs. 159/2011.

The Safeguarding of Third Parties and the Relationship with Bankruptcy Proceedings within the Anti-Mafia Code

The safeguarding of third parties' property rights has always given rise to a dilemma, since opposing third-party interests – often both public and private – clash.[49] Yet, there is a need to avoid the possible constitution of 'fake' credits in favour of third parties, designed to elude preventive measures, and it is important to ensure that third parties' rights do not frustrate the legitimate public destination (devolution to state ownership) that is the main effect of a final forfeiture order. Therefore, the law has always imposed a burden on claimants to show that their property rights come not only from acts with an ascertained date before seizure, but also from 'good faith' or 'non-guilty reliance', as proof of having absolutely nothing to do with the criminal organization or, alternatively, with the illicit deeds from which the asset derives.[50] The law further holds that preventive measure prevail over any other enforceable proceedings and thus the other pending procedures are deemed non-actionable, though the claimant of property and/or guarantee rights affecting seized or forfeited goods is awarded the option of resort to the ordinary remedies provided for in civil law.[51]

In this light, the Supreme Court case-law has often held that seizure and other preventive measures do not impinge upon other people's property and guarantee rights.[52] Third parties are allowed to intervene in the relevant procedures to set

49 Within its 2011 Report, the ANBSC pointed to its biggest technical problem regarding the seized goods' destination as being about the existence of mortgages (1457 of the 2944 properties to be allocated).

50 See Cass., Sez. Un., 28 April 1999, in *Foro it.*, 1999, II, c. 580 regarding the forfeiture *ex* art. 644 Penal Code; Cass., 11 February 2005, in *Cass. pen.*, 2006, 638; Cass. 9 March 2005, ibid., 634; as well as Cass. civ., 29 October 2003, in *Dir. fall. soc. comm.*, 2004, p 16. See further F. Cassano, '*Azioni esecutive su beni oggetto di sequestro antimafia e buona fede dei creditori*' in *Il Fallimento*, 2002, 661 ff. For the difficulty for third parties in disproving bad faith, see L. Petrillo, *La tutela del terzo creditore ipotecario su beni confiscati: prime aperture* in *Merito*, 2006, 48; G. Izzo, '*Criticità nella confisca di prevenzione*' in *Impresa*, 2005, 1309.

51 See recently, Trib. Palermo, Sez. Mis. Prev., 11 April 2011: http://www.penal econtemporaneo.it/materia/-/-/-/717-a_proposito_di_ipoteche_giudiziali_iscritte_da_ societ___creditrici_su_beni_immobili_oggetto_di_confische_definitive_di_prevenzione/, with notes by A. Maugeri, *A proposito di ipoteche giudiziali iscritte da società creditrici su beni immobili oggetto di confische definitive di prevenzione*. For the action of 'unjustified enrichment', as a remedy at the mortgage-holder's disposal, see the positions taken by the Milan Court, Circular of 22 May 2008; F. Cassano, *Confisca antimafia e tutela dei diritti dei terzi* in *Cass. pen.*, 2005, 2161 ff.

52 Compare Corte Cost., 19 May 1994, n. 190, in *Il Fallimento*, 1994, p 804; as well as re preventive seizure, Cass., Sez. II, 4 June 2003, n. 24265, in *Cass. pen.*, 2004, 4161 (s.m.). A similar approach is taken in Cass. civ., Sez. I, 12 November 1999, n. 12535, in *Giust. civ. Mass.*, 1999, 2231; Sez. I, 3 July 1997, n. 5988, ibid., 1997, I, 2733.

forth their representation.[53] Furthermore they are allowed to request the repeal of a final forfeiture judgment when it is affected with 'genetic invalidity', as forfeiture does not rule out assets being returned to legitimate owners or, at least, the grant of compensation for a loss.[54] Third parties can also file an 'execution incident' procedure before competent judicial authorities to obtain an ascertainment of whether the third party's rights are still valid on the basis that they derive from good faith, with burden of proof lying on the third parties.[55]

Moreover, rectifying a discrepancy that had long been highlighted in case-law, the legislator intervened, even before article 25 d.lgs. 159/2011 came into force, with article 10 d.l. 92/2008,[56] according to which 'per equivalent' forfeiture could be applied to preventive measures where goods had been lawfully transferred to good faith third parties, immediately before seizure.

There is also the possibility of a judicial tribunal determining – with the consent of affected public administrations – the amount of money good-faith third parties should be awarded, where the asset is forfeited, in order to free landed properties from bonds or guarantees affecting the property in accordance with legislation on 'public interest expropriation'.[57]

The same principles were put into section IV d.lgs. 159/2011 in which the law maintains that forfeiture does not impair third parties' rights deriving from acts beyond a certain date ahead of seizure, as well as guaranteeing rights originated ahead thereof if certain elements are met. The first element is if the remaining assets of the individual are not enough to fulfil obligations; secondly, if the credit is not linked to illicit deeds or constitutes the product or the reuse thereof, unless the third party is proven to have ignored such link; finally, if the background obligation is adequately proved, where credit derives from 'payment promises', 'debt recognition' or cheques.[58]

---

53   See Cass., Sez. I, 11 February 2005, n. 12317, in *Guida al dir.*, 32/2008, 111. Sez. II, 4 March 2000, n. 998, in *Cass. pen.*, 2000, 2770 ff. (with notes by P.V. Molinari, '*Tutela del terzo creditore di un diritto reale di garanzia nel procedimento di prevenzione con riferimento al sequestro e alla confisca antimafia*').

54   Cass., Sez. Un., 19 December 2006, n. 57, in *Cass. pen.*, 4/2007, 1429 ff. (with notes by P.V. Molinari, '*La riparazione dell'errore giudiziario in tema di confisca antimafia: un annoso contrasto giurisprudenziale finalmente risolto*').

55   Cass., Sez. I, 21.11.2007, n. 45572, where this principle has been extended to forfeiture as per the art. 12-*sexies*, D.L. 306/1992. For more detail, see Cass., 29 April 2011, n. 30326, in *dejure.giuffre.it*; as well as Trib. Palermo, Sez. Mis. Prev., 18 January 2011, in http://www.penalecontemporaneo.it/area/3-/17-/-/846-misure_di_prevenzione_pat rimoniale__tutela_dei_terzi_e_nozione_di_buona_fede/ (accessed 11 April 2013) with notes by A. Maugeri, *Misure di prevenzione patrimoniale: tutela dei terzi e nozione di buona fede*.

56   Now in Law 24 July 2008, n. 125.

57   See article 5 comma 1, lett. *a)*, D.L. 4/2010 as it introduced, at article 2-*ter* comma 5 L. 575/1965.

58   See article 52.

In relation to personal or *in rem* rights of enjoyment, forfeiture eliminates them, but legitimate creditors are given adequate compensation.[59] Good-faith owners of common goods can avail themselves of pre-emption rights on shares leftover (unless the there is a possibility that, because of the degree of criminal infiltration, the asset may wind up back in the possession of the organized crime groups, even through intermediaries) or, as an alternative, can be given the equivalent of the market value of their share, as long as public finances allow.[60]

As for relations existing at the time of seizure, the execution of contracts is suspended until a judicial administrator, properly authorized by the judge delegate, declares either to take over the contract or to void the contract, unless, in those with immediate *in rem* effects, ownership of rights has already passed over.

A third party, in order to obtain a remedy, possibly through the restitution of assets can rely upon article 630 of the Code of Penal Procedure for the repeal of a conclusive forfeiture judgment, whenever it appears, on the basis of new evidence and not merely on a fresh assessment of existing evidence, that the assumptions for it were effectively never there.[61] More remarkably, there may be an ascertainment of third parties' rights within a preventive proceeding at which they are summoned to appear.[62] The aim is to confer protection even through the goods' disposal when the sums otherwise obtained, gathered or received, are insufficient[63] but subject to the State's need to acquire goods which are free from burdens of any kind.[64] Nevertheless, the legislation still lacks enough safeguards for *in rem* guarantees held by third parties, so that case-law has always been forced to deal with it them by a compromise-driven style, trying to reconcile the good faith of third parties with the urge not to stop or impede the final remission of forfeited goods to the State.

Still the main issue remains that forfeiture determines that guaranteed property rights of third parties must regress into a credit and that such credit is legally constrained at 70 per cent of the value of the seized/forfeited goods as appears in the judicial administrator's evaluation or, if less, the proceedings from sale.[65] In this way, a forfeiture order does affect good-faith parties' rights, by placing on the individual the burden to legally intervene in order to protect his own right in a much less satisfactory fashion as compared to the one obtaining before. On this point, the legislator was determined to protect the State's interest in acquiring goods without any burdens, also avoiding any risk (for example, through straw

---

59   article 52 commi 4 e 5.
60   article 52 commi 7 e 8.
61   See article 28 and 46 d.lgs. 159/2011.
62   article 23, 55 comma 3, article 57 d.lgs. 159/2011.
63   article 60 comma 1, d.lgs. 159/2011.
64   article 46 comma 1, d.lgs. 159/2011.
65   See article 53.

men or obliging new owners), that the asset could return into the hands of the 'dangerous individual'.[66]

D.lgs. 159/2011 finally provides for the relationships between preventive measures and bankruptcy proceedings, distinguishing cases where default was declared after seizure[67] or prior to seizure,[68] always affording the public interest in the fight against organized crime priority over other civil claims. In the first case, seized goods are separate from bankruptcy assets and are handled according to anti-Mafia provisions. In the latter case, relevant assets are put aside, but creditors are allowed to take shares, after the judicial administrator has determined, within a 90 day period from seizure, a specific payment schedule which takes into account the sums possibly already earned during bankruptcy procedures.

The Residual Limits to the Effectiveness of the Anti-Mafia Forfeiture within the Italian Legislation

Apart from its undue reliance on mere 'suspicion', the Italian anti-Mafia forfeiture legislation has also been challenged on a range of other grounds. The first of these is the unreasonable length of preventive measure proceedings. The time limit for final conversion of seizure into forfeiture is one year and six months, and the length of time is longer where an appeal is brought.[69] Importantly then, the Italian system has not provided for specialized judges or court or, at least, a fast-track system.[70] In addition, there is the possibility of objecting to the territorial competency of the preventive judge[71] at any given moment, as determined by the criterion of the individual's place of residence, as it is believed to be the place from where his social dangerousness emanates. Furthermore, preventive proceedings are characterized by slowness in processes, since the courts have to seek to ascertain third parties' rights and deal with possible linked criminal trials or bankruptcy procedures.

From a procedural standpoint, the process of the empowerment of bailiffs to enact seizures requires even more time and also opens up the risk of leaks to the

---

66   But see the transitional measures in article 117 comma 1, d.lgs. 159/2011.

67   article 63.

68   article 64.

69   See articles 24 comma 2 and 26, comma 6, d.lgs. 159/2011. See further P. Grillo, *Durata massima del sequestro di prevenzione e provvedimento di confisca dopo il d.lgs. n. 159 del 2011. Note sui termini per la definizione del procedimento finalizzato alla confisca di prevenzione*: http://www.penalecontemporaneo.it/tipologia/0-/-/-/1388-/ (accessed 11 April 2013).

70   Compare article 132-*bis* disp. att. c.p.p. See F. Menditto, *Lo schema di decreto legislativo del codice delle leggi antimafia e delle misure di prevenzione (Libri I, II, IV e V): esame, osservazioni e proposte* (fn 3) 112 s.

71   In this sense compare, for example, Cass., Sez. V, 31 March 2010, n. 19067, in *C.E.D. Cass.*, n. 247504.

media, which is potentially disruptive of the beneficial effects of the measure, especially when assets are located in different places.[72] Alongside these problems, proper coordination is still lacking, due to a possible overlap in initiatives from different competent authorities (the Public Prosecutor, the head of the local police and the Director of the Anti-Mafia task force).

Next, despite some isolated and extraordinary decisions concerning rogatory letters,[73] the forfeiture of goods located abroad is adversely affected by the lack of a mutual acknowledgment principle in international law, corresponding to that contained in Framework decision 2006/783/JHA, European Union Council, 6 October 2006 on forfeitures following criminal proceedings. The cooperation tools provided for in the Council of Europe's Convention of 8 November 1990 on Laundering, Search, Seizure and Confiscation of the Proceeds from Crime[74] cannot help either, as they are limited to seizure and forfeiture decrees that, although deriving from preventive measures, are adopted by judicial authorities and may be deemed 'criminal' as they are designed to pursue goods representing the crime proceeds or criminal tools.[75] However, even though comparable to common law civil forfeiture (as in England, Scotland, Ireland, USA and Australia), forfeiture as a preventive measure in the Italian legal system still involves investigation and standard of proof typical of criminal proceedings. There is thus a need for the shared legislation on 'forfeiture without conviction' pursuing the path already taken with Framework Decision 2005/212/JHA, which deals with 'Confiscation of Crime-Related Proceeds, Instrumentalities and Property'.

Another problem is represented by the enduring lack of a crime of 'self-generated-money laundering' making it impossible, at present, to go after investments made by organized crime with capital raised by the commission of typical crimes. While various parliamentary initiatives have been instigated, this desire to tackle criminality often clashes with constitutionally protected rights.

---

72 A. Balsamo, A., *Il 'Codice antimafia' e la proposta di direttiva europea sulla confisca: quali prospettive per la misure patrimoniali nel contesto europeo?*: http://www.penalecontemporaneo.it/area/3-societa/-/-/1641-il___codice_antimafia___e_la_propos ta_di_direttiva_europea_sulla_confisca__quali_prospettive_per_le_misure_patrimoniali_ nel_contesto_europeo/ (accessed 11 April 2013).

73 See the statement of the French *Cour.de Cassation, Chambre Criminelle*, 13 November 2003) about the case *Crisafulli-Friolo*; and also Swiss Tribunal penal federal, II, 21 January 2011: http://www.penalecontemporaneo.it/materia/3-/38-/-/757-il_tribunale_ penale_federale_svizzero_accoglie_una_rogatoria_della_procura_di_milano_finalizzata_ alla_confisca___di_prevenzione___di_conti_bancari/ (accessed 11 April 2013), with notes by E. Nicosia, E., 'Il Tribunale penale federale svizzero accoglie una rogatoria della Procura di Milano finalizzata alla confisca "di prevenzione" di conti bancari'.

74 Ratified by Italy with Law 9 August 1993, n. 328.

75 See A. Maugeri, *Proposta di direttiva in materia di congelamento e confisca dei proventi del reato: prime riflessioni* (fn 9) 3.

Lastly, the most pervasive limits of anti-Mafia forfeiture concern the handling, administration and destination of seized goods. The ANBSC has an excessive workload and lacks means.

The EU Commission Proposal 'On the Freezing and Confiscation of Proceeds of Crime'

The slowness with which EU Members have implemented Framework Decisions 2005/212/JHA, 2003/577/JHA and 2006/783/JHA,[76] together with the need to keep the level of the fight against organized crime as high on the agenda as possible, has pushed the EU Commission to put forward the proposal of a Framework Decision, under article 83.1, TFEU, on different forms of forfeiture.[77]

The first issue considered is forfeiture following criminal conviction of instrumentalities and proceeds of the crime (article 3). This measure would not have any relevant impact on the Italian legislation which already provides for such forfeiture both for the crime of Mafia-style organization and for those typically in the range of a said conspiracy (money lending at exceptionally high interest rates, money laundering, bribery, drug trafficking and so on). If anything, the effect would be to make such measures more widespread since, at present, article 240 of the Penal Code only deems it an option[78] and article 735-*bis* Penal Code provides for it only when the decision of a foreign authority has to be implemented in Italy.

Of much more relevance to the Italian legal system is article 4 of the proposal, which provides for the adoption of 'measures to enable it to confiscate, either wholly or in part, property belonging to a person convicted of a criminal offence where, based on specific facts, a court finds it substantially more probable that

---

76   See D. Fondaroli, *Le ipotesi speciali di confisca nel sistema penale – Ablazione patrimoniale, criminalità economica, responsabilità delle persone giuridiche* (Bologna: Bononia University Press, 2007) 79 ff.

77   European Commission, Proposal for a Directive of the European Parliament and of the Council on the freezing and confiscation of proceeds of crime in the European Union, COM(2012) 85 final, Brussels, 12 March 2012. F. Mazzacuva, *Sulla posizione della Commissione LIBE del Parlamento europeo alla proposta di direttiva relativa al congelamento e alla confisca dei proventi di reato*: http://www.penalecontemporaneo.it/materia/-/-/-/2424-la_posizione_della_commissione_libe_del_parlamento_europeo_alla_proposta_di_direttiva_relativa_al_congelamento_e_alla_confisca_dei_proventi_di_reato/.

78   See G. Grasso, 'Art. 240 Penal Code' in M. Romano, G. Grasso and T. Padovani (eds), *Commentario sistematico del Codice penale*, vol. III (Milan: Giuffré, 2011), 604 ff.; F. Vergine, *Confisca e sequestro per equivalente* (Milan: Ipsoa, 2009) 14 ff.; A. Gaito, *Nuovi modelli di intervento penale: sequestro e confisca per equivalente* in *Giur. it.*, 2009, 2066 ff.; V. Manes, *Nessuna interpretazione conforme al diritto comunitario con effetti in malam partem* in *Cass. pen.*, 2010, 101; V. Maiello, *La confisca per equivalente non si applica al profitto del peculato* in *Dir. pen. proc.*, 2010, 433; A. Maugeri, *Le moderne sanzioni patrimoniali tra funzionalità e garantismo* (fn 9) 144 ff.

the property in question has been derived by the convicted person from similar criminal activities than from other activities'. This represents a standard different from that designated for forfeiture as a preventive measure. Mere clues (including disproportion between economic activity and lifestyle) are not enough, as the law calls for 'specific facts'. This sort of forfeiture only concerns goods deriving from 'similar criminal activities' and not crimes 'of another nature'. Further, there is no reference to any time limit; with respect to Mafia-like organizations the said link is reduced to the simple fact that the organization continues to commit crimes.[79]

Inspired by article 54.1, of the UN Convention on Bribery,[80] article 5 of the proposed Framework Decision introduces 'forfeiture without conviction' in relation to a situation in which no criminal trial is possible because the defendant is a fugitive or deceased. Article 5 consists of an autonomous *in rem* proceeding where criminal trials *in personam* are useless. This tool has a general preventive function as it could strike the Mafia even when crimes are committed abroad or by fugitives,[81] even without individual liability being established in a criminal trial. As already pointed out, however, Italian legislation already grants broader possibilities through preventive measures. In fact, Italian legislation can be used not only against individuals suspected of participating in criminal organizations (so called 'qualified dangerous persons') but also against those believed to be usually engaged in criminal deeds (so called 'generically dangerous persons').[82] Thus, the possibility of forfeiture of the product, price and/or proceeds of a crime should be widened so as to include cases when restitution is needed of that which the suspect has no right to hold.

No particular comment need be made about article 6 of the proposal, concerning measures necessary to proceed with forfeiture (with or without conviction) toward third parties to whom assets deriving from crimes – or even from lawful deeds when forfeiture is at risk of being eluded – have been transferred. The safeguarding of third parties seems to be the same as has already provided for in the Italian legislation for a long time.

The Commission's proposal next provides for asset-freezing with the aim of ensuring execution of forfeiture despite any intended dispersion, cover up

---

79   See further A. Maugeri, *Proposta di direttiva in materia di congelamento e confisca dei proventi del reato: prime riflessioni* (fn 9) 14 ff.

80   See Chapter 10.

81   A. Maugeri, *Le moderne sanzioni patrimoniali tra funzionalità e garantismo*, cit., 871 s.

82   On this approach A. Maugeri, *Proposta di direttiva in materia di congelamento e confisca dei proventi del reato: prime riflessioni* (fn 9) 29; A. Maugeri, *La riforma delle sanzioni patrimoniali: verso un actio in rem?* in O. Mazza and F. Viganò (eds), *Il 'Pacchetto sicurezza' 2009 (Comments to d.l. 23 February 2009, converted in law 23 April 2009, n. 38 and law 15 July 2009, n. 94)*, (fn 5) 131 ff. A. Maugeri, *L'actio in rem assurge a modello di 'confisca europea' nel rispetto delle garanzie CEDU*: http://www.penalecontemporaneo. it/materia/-/-/-/2422-l___actio_in_rem_assurge_a_modello_di____confisca_europea____ nel_rispetto_delle_garanzie_cedu/.

or transfer outside of, the local jurisdiction.[83] In cases of urgency, the judicial authority can issue a decree (subject to validation) as provided for in article 22 d.lgs. 159/2011. In connection with this decree there may be a need to guarantee defense rights and to limit the proceeding's publicity, especially when orders are adopted without hearing the affected parties.[84]

As a whole, the Framework Decision proposal seems to contain limited innovations compared to the anti-Mafia forfeiture law which is already provided for in Italy. Indeed, the Italian approach could be taken as a role model for forth-coming European initiatives since it sets forth the essential elements of a patrimonial procedure truly autonomous from any criminal basis with greater boldness.[85] With such an approach, there would be no need at all to ascertain crimes which form the basis of asset acquisition; instead, the process would be founded on evidentiary standards of criminal derivation, albeit minimized.[86]

If anything, the new EU legislation could offer an opportunity to amend the anti-Mafia Code by filling in the gaps and easing out loopholes but possibly 'step backwards' where preventive measures and the preventive requirements behind them assumed too much over individual safeguards. Above all, just think about the temporary suspension from administration of assets against persons suspected simply of continuing in economic endeavours that 'could make easier' activities exclusively for those subject to the request for application of preventive measures, or currently facing trial for crimes related to organized crime:[87] a measure that, despite being almost ignored when article 3-*quater* L. 575/1975 used to be in force, has already displayed the ability to strike at, on the basis of mere indications of 'partnership' with Mafia interests, for instance not just single assets, but an

---

83   article (s.) 7 ss.

84   See Filippi, L., *Il diritto di difesa nel procedimento di prevenzione patrimoniale* in F. Cassano (ed.), *Misure di prevenzione patrimoniale* 487; F. Palumbo, *Le misure di prevenzione viste dall'avvocato*, ibid., 555 ff.; A. Mangione, *Le misure di prevenzione anti-mafia al vaglio dei principi del giusto processo*, ibid., 21.

85   See further Maugeri, A., *Le moderne sanzioni patrimoniali* (fn 9) 883 ff.

86   See further L. Fornari, *Criminalità del profitto e tecniche sanzionatorie. Confisca e sanzioni pecuniarie nel diritto penale moderno* (Padua: Cedam, 1997) 222; A. Maugeri, *Proposta di direttiva in materia di congelamento e confisca dei proventi del reato: prime riflessioni* (fn 9) 13, nn 38 and 39; A. Maugeri, *La lotta contro l'accumulazione di profitti illeciti: recenti orientamenti* in *Riv. trim. dir. pen. econ.*, 2007, 541 ff.; A. Maugeri, *La conformità dell'actio in rem con il principio del mutuo riconoscimento* in *La gestione dei beni confiscati alla criminalità organizzata (le questioni di diritto civile, penale e amministrativo)* in S. Mazzarese and A. Aiello, *Le misure patrimoniali antimafia* (Milan: Giuffré, 2010), 187 ff.; G. Abbadessa and F. Mazzacuva, *La giurisprudenza di Strasburgo 2008–2010: il diritto di proprietà (art. 1 Prot. 1 CEDU)*: http://www.penalecontemporaneo.it/foto/1959RIVISTA.pdf#page=329&view=Fit; A. Balsamo, *Il rapporto tra forme 'moderne' di confisca e presunzione di innocenza: le nuove indicazioni della Corte europea dei diritti dell'uomo* in *Cass. pen.*, 2007, 3936.

87   article 34 comma 2.

entrepreneur's patrimony as whole, irrespective of its whether its source is lawful or unlawful.[88]

---

88   Compare to C. App Catania, 21 November 1997, in *Cass. pen.*, 1998, 2726; C. App Palermo, 1 October 1996, ibid., 1997, 2257. See further A. Maugeri, *Proposta di direttiva in materia di congelamento e confisca dei proventi del reato: prime riflessioni* (fn 9) 45 ff.; A. Maugeri, *Profili di legittimità costituzionale delle sanzioni patrimoniali (prima e dopo la riforma introdotta dal decr. N. 92/2008): la giurisprudenza della Corte Costituzionale e della Suprema Corte* (fn 5) 97 ff.; R. Scarpinato, *Le indagini patrimoniali*, ibid., 245; C. Visconti, *Contro le mafie non solo confisca ma anche 'bonifiche' giudiziarie per imprese infiltrate: l'esempio milanese (working paper). Un nuovo modello di contrasto alle infiltrazioni mafiose nelle attività economiche 'sane'? In margine a un recente provvedimento della Sezione Misure di prevenzione del Tribunale di Milano*: http://www.penalecontemporaneo. it/materia/-/-/-/1174-contro_le_mafie_non_solo_confisca_ma_anche___bonifiche____ giudiziarie_per_imprese_infiltrate__1___esempio_milanese__working_paper/ (accessed 11 April 2013).

Chapter 5

Civil Forfeiture of
Criminal Assets in Bulgaria

Rositsa Dzhekova

Introduction

Over the past two decades a number of Western European countries (such as Ireland, Italy and the UK) have introduced civil procedures for the forfeiture of proceeds of crime in order to overcome the limitations and the slow pace of the criminal justice process when dealing with criminal assets. In a similar vein, Bulgaria has put a criminal assets forfeiture system in place, institutionally backed up with a specialized agency that brings forfeiture proceedings in the civil courts. At the same time, the country's efforts to tackle rampant corruption and organized crime by strengthening law-enforcement agencies and the judiciary were subjected to intensive external scrutiny before and after its accession to the European Union in 2007. Along with criminal justice and penal policies, forfeiture of criminal assets has become one of the key areas where the European Commission has strongly pressed for reform.[1] Public and European Union expectations were fuelled even more when the centre-right party GERB (*Grazhdani za Evropeysko Razvitie na Balgariya* – Citizens for the European Development of Bulgaria) entered government in 2009 and subsequently put the adoption of a more effective forfeiture regime high on its (populist) agenda. This led to legislative changes, especially the introduction of a non-conviction based ('NCB') procedure (previously, confiscation was not possible without a conviction in related criminal proceedings). Although the current legislation on asset forfeiture provides enough tools for the forces of the law to 'go after the money' of criminals, its practical implementation has faced several challenges and has not satisfied public expectations.

Political and public demands for harsher measures against organized crime and the illicit enrichment of high-level political officials highlighted several deficiencies in the practical implementation of the forfeiture legislation. Some of these deficiencies were of a technical or legislative nature, such as the limited investigative powers of the specialized agency in charge of asset forfeiture, the contradictory judicial practice of the courts, the general weaknesses of the

---

1 See for instance Report from the Commission to the European Parliament and the Council, *On Progress in Bulgaria under the Cooperation and Verification Mechanism* COM(2012) 411 final.

judiciary and the difficulty in obtaining criminal convictions. Other obstacles, however, are symptoms of the reluctance of the political and administrative elites to counter organized criminal networks. As law-enforcement and asset forfeiture priorities are not properly aligned, the lack of capacity and of willingness on the part of the law-enforcement bodies, which are politically influenced, to prioritize investigations into organized crime threatens to cripple the forfeiture process in the long term.

The Law on Forfeiture of Illegally Acquired Assets has become one of the most debated and challenged pieces of legislation in the country's recent history, reflecting the political resistance towards measures attempting to effectively target organized crime and illegal enrichment of high-level officials. The asset forfeiture process is burdened with disproportionally high expectations to compensate for the ineffectiveness of the forces of the law to tackle serious organized crime and high-level corruption. As a result, although the legal system has provided the Commission for Establishing of Property Acquired from Criminal Activity ('CEPACA')[2] with sufficient tools, it quickly reached its practical limits. The recent introduction of a revised non-conviction based regime is unlikely to overcome these problems.

This chapter examines the practical obstacles to the implementation of civil forfeiture in Bulgaria, taking into consideration key institutional, legislative and policy factors that shape the application of the Law on Forfeiture of Proceeds of Criminal Activity.[3] It argues that the socio-cultural specifics of organized crime in Bulgaria, as well as the broader context of the existing policies for countering organized crime, have a strong determinant effect on the resistance to an effective and efficient forfeiture regime.

This chapter draws on several EU-funded research and policy implementation projects carried out by the Center for the Study of Democracy ('CSD') over the past decade, in which the author participated as a member of the research team. The first project took place between 2010 and 2012 and aimed at developing the first *Bulgarian Serious and Organised Crime Threat Assessment*.[4] The other two projects, carried out between 2010 and 2013, examined existing practices in Bulgaria for the disposal of confiscated criminal assets, identifying weaknesses and deficiencies in the asset forfeiture procedure from the investigatory to the final disposal phase, as well as exploring the potential for the social reuse of such

---

2   Комисията за установяване на имущество, придобито от престъпна дейност *(КУИППД)*, after November 2012 renamed in Комисия за отнемане на незаконно придобито имущество (КОНПИ): http://www.cepaca.bg/ (accessed 2 April 2013). The EU interim report translates this as the 'Commission for the Identification and Forfeiture of Criminal Assets'.

3   State Gazette, No. 19 of 1 March 2005.

4   Center for the Study of Democracy, *Serious and Organised Crime Threat Assessment (2010–2011)* (Sofia: CSD, 2012).

assets.[5] Additional analysis was derived from the 2010 study, *Examining the Links between Organised Crime and Corruption.*[6]

Key Parameters of the Asset Recovery Regime

Criminal Confiscation

Bulgarian law provides for both criminal confiscation and civil forfeiture of criminal assets. These regimes are not interchangeable but can be applied cumulatively. Under Article 37(1)3 of the Penal Code,[7] criminal confiscation is a punishment. It is not dependent on a person's ability to provide evidence about the origin of their assets, which is required for civil forfeiture. Criminal confiscation is applied to exhaustively enumerated crimes under the Penal Code.[8] Under the criminal confiscation regime, property is appropriated by the criminal court upon request from the Prosecution Service as part of the punishment. Criminal confiscation is an auxiliary punishment – it is never the only one that a court can impose. In the majority of cases, criminal confiscation is not mandatory. Mandatory confiscation is provided for only in Article 253 of the Penal Code in the case of laundered profits:[9]

> (6) The object of crime or the property into which it has been transformed shall be forfeited to the benefit of the state, or where absent or alienated, its equivalent shall be awarded.

However, there are no statistics publically available on how often confiscation of assets under this provision has been imposed. Given the small number of money laundering cases brought to court (19 in 2009, 22 in 2010 and 31 in 2011),[10] it is unlikely that this instrument has achieved its intended result. According to the Committee of Experts on the Evaluation of Anti-Money Laundering Measures and the Financing of Terrorism ('MONEYVAL') evaluation of Bulgaria for 2011, the total amount of the proceeds from money laundering confiscated was

---

5   See Center for the Study of Democracy, *Money Laundering and Criminal Asset Confiscation*: http://www.csd.bg/index.php?id=1426 (accessed 20 December 2012).

6   Center for the Study of Democracy, *Examining the Links between Organised Crime and Corruption* (Sofia: CSD, 2010).

7   Subject to amendments promulgated in State Gazette No. 20 on 9 March 2012.

8   See articles 114(2), 159(5), 159G, 195(2), 196(2), 196A, 199(1), 199(2)3, 201, 202(3), 203(2), 205(2), 206(4)(7), 210(2), 211, 212(7), 212B(2), 213A(3)(4), 214(1-3), 227G, 242(5), 252(1)(2), 255(3), 256(2), article 277A(8), 278(6), 279(3), 302A, 307D(2), 346(5), 414(2) of the Penal Code.

9   MONEYVAL, *Third Round Detailed Assessment Report on Bulgaria* (MONEYVAL (2008) 02, Council of Europe, Strasbourg, 2008) 56.

10   Statistics provided by the Supreme Prosecution Service.

€5.7 million in 2009 and €7.6 million in 2010, with significantly lower amounts in the preceding years.[11] However, these amounts do not account for property other than financial funds. This indicates that confiscation in relation to money laundering cases is imposed only where the proceeds of the crime are easy to trace and recover.

In all other cases, it is at the criminal court's discretion whether to impose it at all.[12] The value of the 184 confiscation claims filed in court by the office of prosecution in 2011 was €1.9 million, but there are no statistics on the actual value confiscated under the Criminal Procedure Code (Article 72) publicly available.

The prosecution rarely seeks criminal confiscation as a penalty. Prosecutors, for career reasons, are focused mainly on securing a conviction in relation to the predicate crime. The professional assessments that prosecutors receive are completely unaffected by the presence or absence of a criminal asset recovery. Such financial investigations are seen as an additional burden. There are also institutional culture obstacles within the prosecution (and the police). The state prosecution generally thinks of itself as a traditional 'power structure', whose primary purpose is the prosecution of the (predicate) crime. Another reason for the limited application of criminal confiscation is that the police rarely investigate the assets of the crime suspect or the finances of organized or white-collar criminals. The preventive effect of imposing confiscation sanctions is not perceived as part of the prosecution's key responsibilities. As a result, the police have not developed the practice of investigating criminal assets per se,[13] and more often than not they only seize the physical instrumentalities of crime which they come across during investigations.

Therefore, the dissuasive potential of confiscation has not been effectively implemented in Bulgaria, which means that, after serving their prison sentence criminals can continue their criminal activity, because their financial clout remains largely untouched. This result again means that the civil forfeiture process[14] has failed to meet the expectation that it would become the primary mechanism for removing the financial incentives of organized crime.

---

11   MONEYVAL, *Bulgaria. Progress Report and Written Analysis by the Secretariat of Core Recommendations* (MONEYVAL (2011) 5, Council of Europe, Strasbourg, 2011).

12   For example, article 114(2) of the Penal Code states that the 'court *may* impose confiscation' (emphasis added). Similarly, see Penal Code articles 159(5), 159G, 195(2).

13   P. Gounev, 'Bulgaria – case study report' in Matrix Insight, *Assessing the Effectiveness of EU Member States' Practices in the Identification, Tracing, Freezing and Confiscation of Criminal Assets* (London: Matrix Insight, 2009) 127 et seq.

14   The term 'civil forfeiture' is used in Bulgaria to denote post-conviction forfeiture within the civil process (discussed below). This must be distinguished from the non-conviction based (NCB) approach, which does not require criminal conviction before forfeiture can occur.

Background to the Civil Forfeiture Process

Targeting criminal assets has become a politically important topic in Bulgaria over the past decade. In 2002 the first draft law on forfeiture of assets derived from criminal activity was put forward by the Ministry of Interior. The draft bill prompted negative reactions from all sides of the political spectrum, but the fiercest criticism came from lawyers and judges on the grounds of possible use of the forfeiture regime for political and economic retribution.[15]

It was not until 2005, and after several revisions, that the Law on Forfeiture of Proceeds of Criminal Activity ('LFPCA') was adopted.[16] Given that Bulgaria had been facing a high volume of organized crime during the period of the transition to democracy, the adoption of the LFPCA in 2005 came at a late stage. By that point, large parts of the ill-gotten gains generated during the 1990s had already been transferred to the legal economy, and the statute of limitations had expired for much of the wrongdoing. A commonly cited argument against the creation of a special law on asset forfeiture during public debates prior to 2005 was that the Law on Civil Property of 1990[17] already provided a solid base for civil confiscation. Minor adjustments in this law would have been sufficient for building a robust instrument for forfeiture, as it also allowed the reversal of the burden of proof.[18] Although this piece of legislation provided for a civil deprivation mechanism for assets whose value exceeded the legal income of the person concerned,[19] this instrument was rarely applied in practice. Between 1997 and 2005 there were only 32 claims filed in court on the basis of this provision.[20] However, pressure exerted on Bulgaria on the part of the EU to undertake more effective action to curb organized crime and corruption prior to the country's EU accession eventually led to the adoption of the asset forfeiture legislation.

---

15   In 2002 and 2004, CSD organized a series of round tables and discussions on the draft LFPCA with experts and relevant stakeholders from the public and non-government sector. Criticisms were levied by, *inter alia*, Svetla Tsacheva (judge at the Supreme Judicial Council), Borislav Belazelkov (judge at the Supreme Court of Cassation), Neli Kutskova (chairperson, Sofia District Court) and Georgi Atanasov (lawyer). See http://www.csd.bg/ artShowbg.php?id=1393 and http://www.csd.bg/artShow.php?id=12718) (accessed 2 April 2013).

16   State Gazette, No. 19 of 1 March 2005.

17   State Gazette, No. 26 of 30 March 1976, repealed by State Gazette No. 19 of 1 March 2005.

18   S. Stoychev, G. Petrunov, A. Velev and M. Veselinova, *Civil Confiscation in Bulgaria (2005–2010)* (Sofia: RiskMonitor Foundation, 2011) 10; Group of States against Corruption (GRECO), *Second Evaluation Report on Bulgaria* (Strasbourg: GrecoEval II Rep (2004)13 E, Council of Europe, 2005) 4.

19   Law on Civil Property, chapter 3, Articles 34, 36.

20   S. Stoychev, G. Petrunov, A. Velev and M. Veselinova, *Civil Confiscation in Bulgaria* 10.

The LFPCA established the Commission for Establishing of Property Acquired from Criminal Activity ('CEPACA').[21] It repealed the Law on Citizens' Property, but left as an alternative the criminal confiscation measures existing under the Criminal Code.[22] The LFCPA provided for post-conviction forfeiture within a civil process under the Civil Procedure Code. Therefore it is commonly referred to in Bulgaria as 'civil forfeiture'. This regime remained in place until November 2012, when the Law on Forfeiture of Illegally Acquired Assets[23] introduced a procedure for non-conviction based (NCB) forfeiture. This represents a novel approach because the requirement of prior conviction was removed: forfeiture claims can be brought before civil courts following charges brought by the Prosecution Service under the provisions of the Penal Code that fall within the scope of the law, independently of the final outcome of the criminal process. This new regime is referred to as NCB forfeiture. Given that the NCB forfeiture regime under the Law on Forfeiture of Illegally Acquired Assets was only enacted in November 2012, there are understandably little results to date. As such, the analysis in this chapter is based on the procedural and judicial practice accumulated between 2005 and 2012.

When in draft, the 2005 legislation on civil forfeiture initially took the Irish Proceeds of Crime Act 1996 as a model which envisioned forfeiture of criminal assets within a civil procedure that is not bound to prior criminal conviction.[24] The main rationale behind the Irish approach, much like non-conviction based forfeiture regimes in other countries, was to deploy forfeiture as a proactive 'crime control strategy', departing from intervention only as a consequence of convictions.[25] As such, the idea of the initial Bulgarian draft was to transplant a NCB regime typical of common-law countries into a civil-law context.[26] However the initial proposal did not retain the NCB provision during the parliamentary debates, and the requirement for a criminal conviction was re-introduced in the bill that was adopted in 2005. Nevertheless, the forfeiture regime introduced through the LFPCA was considered by legal practitioners to be a more 'severe' piece of legislation than the existing moderate forfeiture regimes in many civil

---

21   Chapter 3. See http://www.cepaca.bg/?act=content&id=80 (accessed 2 April 2013).

22   See http://www.cepaca.bg/?act=content&id=242 (accessed 2 April 2013).

23   Закон за отнемане в полза на държавата на незаконно придобито имущество (ЗОПДНПИ), promulgated in State Gazette No. 38 of 18 May 2012, amended No. 82 of 26 October 2012, amended No. 102 of 21 December 2012, amended No. 103 of 28 December 2012, amended by No. 15 of 15 February 2013.

24   See Chapter 7 of this book.

25   F. McKenna and K. Egan, 'Ireland: A multi-disciplinary approach to proceeds of crime' in S.N.M. Young (ed.), *Civil Forfeiture of Criminal Property. Legal Measures for Targeting the Proceeds of Crime* (Cheltenham: Edward Elgar Publishing, 2009) 55 et seq.

26   Venice Commission, *Interim Opinion on the Draft Act on Forfeiture in Favour of the State of Illegally Acquired Assets of Bulgaria* (Strasbourg: CDL-AD(2010)010 of 16 March 2010, Council of Europe, 2010) para. 21.

law countries, as it provides the authorities with extended powers to go after criminals' assets.

The Bulgarian model has several distinctive features not only in relation to the legal framework, but also in terms of powers and resources at the disposal of the specialized agency, the Commission on Establishing Property Acquired through Criminal Activity ('CEPACA'), which is tasked with investigating criminal assets and bringing civil court claims for forfeiture. Although the LFPCA envisions forfeiture of assets in a civil procedure, the initiation of these proceedings is bound to the criminal justice process. The investigation procedures run by the CEPACA have to be carried out in parallel with, or following, criminal proceedings. The CEPACA brings requests to the civil courts to apply freezing orders on the property in question, under the condition that a penal prosecution procedure against the suspect has started (under article 21). However, the CEPACA can request deprivation of criminal assets only after the criminal proceedings are concluded and the suspect convicted (under article 27).

There are three key prerequisites for starting a forfeiture procedure (Article 3): (1) a criminal procedure has been started in relation to the 33 crime categories as defined in the Criminal Code (or in some specific cases: the prosecution has been terminated, suspended or cannot be started); (2) the criminal assets need to valued at more than €30,000 which (3) can be reasonably assumed to have been acquired from criminal activity (similar to the 'balance of probabilities' principle in the UK).

Institutional Features of Civil Forfeiture

The CEPACA is comprised of five members, who are supported by 255 administrative staff. The Commission members are appointed on a 3:1:1 quota principle under Article 12: respectively from the National Assembly, the Prime Minister and the President. The nominee of the Prime Minister is also appointed chair of the CEPACA. From the outset this structure was heavily criticized, as it embodies a disproportionate dependence on the Prime Minister. Furthermore, its credibility has been severely weakened throughout its existence due to inadequate control and oversight mechanisms.

As the CEPACA is not part of the prosecution authority, nor subordinate to the police or the judiciary, it has the potential to become a highly specialized and autonomous body. When drafting the LFPCA, the lawmakers realized that embedding the function of asset forfeiture institutionally into other ministries or the judiciary was not a desirable option. The state prosecution system, for instance, was seen as corrupt, unruly and largely out of control. The 1991 Constitution placed the state prosecution within the judiciary, but prosecutors enjoyed immunity from criminal pursuit, with limited exceptions. Prosecutors were appointed and promoted via a powerful independent body, the Supreme Judicial Council, which means that the prosecution is almost 'untouchable' on the part of the executive and parliament. At the same time, the then General Prosecutor enjoyed an almost unprecedented level of decision-making power, which enabled him to exercise an effective influence over the bringing forward or dropping of investigations and indictments, as well as over the nature and content of charges brought to court. The prosecution system was largely perceived as 'rogue' – difficult to predict and control, due to its tendency to selectively pursue certain economic crimes but conceal others. It had been identified as the weak point in the judicial system. In order to institutionally circumvent the prosecution service, the political establishment looked for an alternative, a more reliable body specializing in the tracing and forfeiture of criminal assets.

However, the initial idea of a strong, independent and highly specialized forfeiture agency was modified and softened before the adoption of the LFPCA. The initial draft of the bill prompted fears within the political and economic elites that the pending law would create a 'monster', an instrument for political repression and economic retribution which was powerful yet difficult to control. The LFPCA was therefore opposed from the outset since the economic elites who accumulated wealth via rigged privatization deals, tax evasion and contraband in the 1990s feared they may be threatened by their political opponents. These fronts of resistance to the development of the proposed legislation in 2003–2004 were not only spontaneous and chaotic, but were fed by paid media campaigns and targeted 'lobbying' through public relations agencies. The numerous amendments of the draft LFPCA between 2003 and its final adoption in 2005 put in place weaker provisions that significantly disempowered the CEPACA and the forfeiture procedure.

The CEPACA is currently the only substantive body tasked with inspections and civil forfeiture of criminal assets. It has three main responsibilities under Article 13: (1) conducting preliminary inspections in order to identify illegally acquired assets; (2) requesting injunctions against assets in court; and (3) requesting asset forfeiture. The police, prosecution and the courts are supposed to notify the Commission of newly-opened investigations or issued sentences in relation to the crimes listed in the LFPCA. All new and ongoing cases are presented on a weekly basis to the five-member body, which decides whether to open an investigation, request a freezing order or file a forfeiture claim in court. The CEPACA currently has 255 employees, 160 of whom are accountants and lawyers tasked with investigations, based in 11 territorial offices across the country.[27] There are no police officers or prosecutors, and the CEPACA has no police powers. The main rationale is that the CEPACA's functions are mainly document-based, so no police powers are needed (though in more complex cases, this absence might prove problematic). Additionally, on a purely cultural level the CEPACA inspectors do

---

27 Commission for Establishing of Property Acquired from Criminal Activity (CEPACA), *Report on the Activity of the Commission for Establishing of Property Acquired from Criminal Activity for the Period January 2011 – December 2011* [in Bulgarian] (CEPACA, Sofia, 2011).

not enjoy the same status as the police, and are not recognized as 'equals' by law-enforcement bodies.

Several problems related to the investigation, freezing and forfeiture phases can be flagged up as impeding the CEPACA's work. Many of these are of a technical and organizational nature, such as the investigative powers and tools at the disposal of the CEPACA, but others relate to the cooperation of the CEPACA with the pre-trial authorities, as well as to the interpretation of the law by the courts. These will be discussed in the next section.

Practical Obstacles to Asset Recovery

Deficiencies in the Investigation Phase

Article 3 of the LFPCA lists 33 crime categories (as defined in the Criminal Code) concerning which the CEPACA is able to carry out inspections. According to Article 21 of the LFPCA, the courts, the prosecution or the police, are supposed to hand over information on newly-opened investigations or on cases where the courts have issued a sentence. In practice, however, the CEPACA is notified in most cases after a criminal conviction has been issued, which means that it starts its inquiries at a very late stage, long after the criminal has become aware that his criminal activities, and eventually his assets, will be (and are) targeted by the authorities. The problem is that law-enforcement and judicial bodies simply do not observe this requirement of the LFPCA.[28] This failure is to some extent confirmed through interviews with inspectors from the CEPACA, as well as through the comparison of statistical data (see Table 5.1 below). As a result, the number of individuals inspected by the CEPACA is much lower than the sum total of defendants in criminal cases in the same category of crime. In most criminal cases related to human trafficking, dangerous drug use and trafficking and organized crime, the prosecution does not seek to trace and identify the property of the defendant but simply forwards the case to the CEPACA. This is done mainly in investigations of money laundering as the predicate crime, where the priority is to recover the most obvious assets. It is much less likely that cases are not forwarded because the prosecution has established that some of the conditions of the LFPCA have not been met (such as the €30,000 threshold of unexplained wealth).

---

28 P. Gounev, 'Bulgaria – case study report' in Matrix Insight, *Assessing the Effectiveness of EU Member States' Practices*, 129.

Table 5.1   Comparing suspect and defendants in criminal trials and asset forfeiture investigations 2006–2011

Crime category (Penal Code)		2006	2007	2008	2009	2010	2011
Organized crime group (Art. 321, 321a)	Investigated by CEPACA	4	19	20	27	32	23
	Defendants in criminal court cases (broader definition)	n/a	n/a	n/a	355	547	598
Trafficking in human beings (Art. 159 a–d)	Investigated by CEPACA	9	3	2	11	7	7
	Defendants in criminal court cases	6	7	7	12	22	23
Fraud (Art. 209–213)	Investigated by CEPACA	10	13	22	22	36	38
	Defendants in criminal court cases (broader definition)	1002	904	790	825	924	795
Bribery (Art. 301–307a)	Investigated by CEPACA	2	2	7	8	5	5
	Defendants in criminal court cases	95	107	100	142	140	119
Extortion (Art. 213a–214a)	Investigated by CEPACA	8	6	11	2	5	4
	Defendants in criminal court cases	105	98	62	97	89	86
Production, possession, dealing in drugs (Art. 354a–c)	Investigated by CEPACA	8	7	5	5	11	12
	Defendants in criminal court cases	1942	1291	1080	1340	1537	1465
Money laundering (Art. 253–253b)	Investigated by CEPACA	3	5	6	7	5	5
	Defendants in criminal court cases	0	9	36	33	42	45
Contraband (Art. 242–242a)	Investigated by CEPACA	3	1	9	2	4	9
	Defendants in criminal court cases	155	140	106	150	154	179

Note: Supreme Prosecutor's Office, CEPACA, National Statistical Institute.

Another explanation could be the huge backlog of notifications at some of the territorial units of the CEPACA, which are only reviewed after a delay, but even then the discrepancy remains disproportionally high. The swift processing of the notifications from the pre-trial authorities is to some extent also hampered by the fact that there is no standard format for the reporting of the necessary information by the police, prosecution and courts. Often the only details sent to the CEPACA are the name and personal ID of the defendant, as well as the nature of and the number of the court case/investigation. All documentary evidence has to be collated and, if necessary, completed by the CEPACA.

A related problem is the lack of resources and powers within the CEPACA to investigate all incoming cases, and the need for proper prioritization of inspections. In this way, decision-making is rarely aligned with law-enforcement priorities. There are no criteria or strategic guidelines as to the priorities for incoming cases which are to be investigated.[29] Instead, cases are reviewed according to their incoming order. In fact, there is a 'reverse prioritizing' of cases: the simpler, small-scale inspections go to the top of the list, because they promise quick resolutions and inflate the statistics on completed cases.[30]

Overall, the forfeiture procedure has been described by interviewees from the CEPACA and some legal practitioners as a highly bureaucratically-driven process. This applies not only to the practical implementation of procedures, but also in the way cases are approached. If the CEPACA were to look into all the cases that fall under its mandate it would be so overloaded with work that it would be forced to prioritize and develop some sort of strategic approach, a policy direction addressing the question as to what this law should achieve. However, the existing practice indicates that cases are being handled as they come in – there is no sense of setting priorities and judging cases on their overall merits. It is much like a box-ticking exercise: as one interviewee put it, 'The whole mentality of autonomous bureaucracies is that in theory they pretend to apply the law blindly, as their role is not to judge, but to treat all cases equally. This wrongly understood strict compliance with the law in reality works the other way around – easier cases go on top of the list.' Later it will be shown that the rationale of 'reversed prioritizing' is to a great extent reflected in the general approach of the policy on targeting organized and white-collar crime, which is grounded in socio-historical roots.

Reach and Scope of Investigations into Criminal Assets

The scope and reach of inquiries into criminal assets carried out by the CEPACA is largely limited by the fact that the inspectors have almost none of the investigatory powers that law-enforcement officers enjoy. They may not search premises, collect evidence, use wiretaps and so on. They rely entirely on the police to collect any non-public evidence, to establish the non-family third parties to whom assets may

---

29   Interview with a former inspector from CEPACA, 2012.
30   Similar points are made elsewhere in chapters 3 and 9.

have been transferred, or determine whether assets have been transferred outside Bulgaria. The CEPACA is not one of the 'investigatory authorities' listed in the Criminal Procedure Code.[31]

Yet, the police, though they do have legal powers, hardly ever make any effort to collect evidence or trace criminal assets. The limited capacity of the forces of the law to effectively target organized and economic crime is clearly evident in money-laundering investigations. A few dozen specialists at the State Agency for National Security ('SANS' – Държавната агенция Национална сигурност)[32] and the Chief Directorate "Combating Organized Crime" (CDCOC)[33] can hardly take charge of the thousands of cases of money laundering which should be investigated. This shortage of resources directly results from the fact that money laundering is insufficiently prioritized by law-enforcement bodies and is not prosecuted systematically. Instead, it arises almost always only as an accessory crime to a main offence, often being dropped if the main offence is dropped.[34] For example, less than 1 per cent of all drug-trafficking offences are accompanied by an investigation into the financial aspects of the crime.[35] The lack of capacity and expertise within the law-enforcement system contributes to the low number of cases. A slight increase in the cases prosecuted and convicted in the past few years does not reflect on their quality – high-profile cases remain an exception.[36]

As a result, investigations into criminal assets are not the joint effort of prosecution/police and the CEPACA. Prosecutors see forfeiture as an additional burden that has been placed upon them, and which they continue to resist. Also, there is the perception that prosecutor's role is reduced in favour of the CEPACA, which results in burdensome cooperation and mistrust. Access to classified information is another source of disquiet which became particularly controversial during the drafting of the new forfeiture law in 2011. Since the investigators of the CEPACA deal with confidential information during the investigation phase, the question was raised as to whether they should receive access to classified information. This is important for improving their cooperation with law-enforcement bodies as it would allow them to be seen as equals by police and prosecution and would eliminate mistrust stemming from the potential risk of trading in information on the part of the CEPACA staff. However, granting security clearance (whether automatically

---

31   P. Gounev, 'Bulgaria – case study report' in Matrix Insight, *Assessing the Effectiveness of EU Member States' Practices* 127.

32   See http://www.dans.bg/en (accessed 2 April 2013).

33   See http://www.mvr.bg/en/AboutUs/StructuralUnits/National+MoI+Services/GD BOP/default.htm (accessed 2 April 2013).

34   Commission Staff Working Document SWD(2012) 232 final, 18 July 2012.

35   Interview with senior financial investigations officer.

36   Interviews with a prosecutor focused on money laundering and a senior intelligence officer from the State Agency National Security. See also G. Petrunov, *Money Laundering in Bulgaria: The Policy Response* (Sofia: RiskMonitor Foundation, 2010); Center for the Study of Democracy, *CSD Brief No 21: Investigation of Money Laundering: An Institutional Approach* (Sofia, 2010).

after joining the CEPACA, or upon application and a full security check) has not been included as a standard requirement in the framework regulating the CEPACA's responsibilities, powers and obligations, even after some key members of the Commission were denied access after a standard security check.

A final problem is that the inspectors working at the CEPACA are mostly lawyers and economists who have received only limited training in relation to performing more complex financial investigations and forensic analysis. In 2010 and 2011 some minor improvements were made, such as a joint manual issued by SANS, the CEPACA, the Chief Directorate "Combating Organized Crime", the prosecution and the Financial Investigation Unit, for investigating money laundering,[37] as well as the formation of joint working groups in relation to key investigations, including officers from different law-enforcement agencies focused on financial investigations, as well as prosecutors.

Procedural Obstacles

The CEPACA faces difficulties even in relation to the documentary checks it undertakes. The most pressing issue is the lack of a centralized electronic property register. Only a very small number of all 110 Asset Registration Agencies ('ARA') have electronic registers.[38] In all other jurisdictions, the CEPACA has to send written letters (per case) to each agency office. Poorly maintained property records and a lack of data additionally slows down the process. In addition, the ARA keep records only for deals carried out during the past 10 years, so any attempt to trace assets acquired earlier is difficult. The lack of a centralized bank register further complicates the asset-tracing exercise. Again, the CEPACA needs to send letters to over 30 banks and other financial institutions to acquire information. However, it is often the case that banks go on to inform their clients (especially major account holders) regarding such requests for the sharing of information regarding their accounts, as there is no specific legislation prohibiting them from doing so.[39] After it identifies the bank account, the CEPACA then has to request a court order to lift the bank secrecy rules so it can obtain access to account information. Frequent delays have been reported within the different steps of this procedure, while banks do not always fully cooperate in the process.

---

37   Center for the Study of Democracy, Разследване на изпиране на пари. Наръчник [*Investigation of money laundering. Manual*], designated for internal use by the employees of the Bulgarian Ministry of Interior, SANS and CEPACA (CSD, Sofia, 2010). See also CSD Policy Brief No. 21, Investigation of Money Laundering: an Institutional Approach (Sofia, 2010): http://www.csd.bg/artShow.php?id=15028 (accessed 2 April 2013)

38   See Law amending the Law on Cadastre and Property Register Act (prom. State Gazette No. 34 of 25 April 2000, amended No. 39 of 20 May 2011): http://www.cadastre.bg/node/5378.

39   An example of such a prohibition can be found in s.333A of the (UK) Proceeds of Crime Act 2002.

Furthermore, the commission lacks a standardized methodology for the evaluation of property value and instead resorts to external evaluation experts. As a result, the properties are often overvalued, which is evident from the discrepancy in the values of the injunction requests and those actually ordered for forfeiture by the courts.[40]

Judicial Practice

The interpretation of the law by the courts has proved controversial in many cases. Some courts have sought evidence on the causal link between the asset and the crime committed, while others did not adhere to the lower burden of proof. It is often the case that courts do not adhere to the reversed burden of proof and still require the CEPACA to provide evidence to prove the connection between the predicate crime and the criminal assets. In that sense, the LFPCA has not been as robustly enforced in the courts as it was envisioned it would be.

Furthermore, as civil proceedings are heard before the local courts, undue influence and corruption pose a risk. As such, the unsatisfactory results achieved through the implementation of the LFPCA are to a great extent related to the slow and highly inefficient judicial process at a local level. Criminal trials can last for several years and rarely end in a conviction, while the CEPACA cannot forfeit the property until the final conviction is issued. From the outset the CEPACA targeted smaller criminals in the main, ones who do not use complex financial schemes and do not have the resources to influence the judicial process in their favour. In practice, the major criminals who have access to good criminal defence attorneys are not affected by the regime, as they are in the position to prolong criminal trials for years. Some tactics commonly used to manipulate the criminal justice process include delays due to a change of lawyers, the unavailability of selected defence lawyers, the changing of judges, the lack of key witnesses (often due to threats from defendants), and the corruption of medical personnel to secure the release of defendants on remand.

The difficulties described above are reflected in the slow progress achieved by the CEPACA in its initial years. Between 2006 and 2008, the CEPACA successfully obtained a number of injunction orders, but did not manage to win any civil forfeiture claim in the courts. The first court orders for forfeiture of assets following claims from the CEPACA in accordance with the LFPCA took place in 2009, with proceeds amounting to €346,000. The following year 11 court decisions were issued (for a total value of €3,464,740), and 27 more followed in 2011 for €4.8 million (see Table 5.2 below).

---

40   S. Stoychev, G. Petrunov, A. Velev and M. Veselinova, *Civil Confiscation in Bulgaria (2005–2010)* (Sofia: RiskMonitor Foundation, 2011) 27 et seq.

Table 5.2   Investigations, forfeiture claims and value of confiscated property

Year	Investigations started	Forfeiture claims filed in court	Forfeiture claims won	Value of property under injunction (million EUR)	Value of confiscated property (million EUR)
2007	109	33	–	34	–
2008	126	57	–	33.9	–
2009	155	79	4	130	0.35
2010	177	82	11	137	3.5
2011	173	72	27	42.5	4.8
2012 (Jan–Oct)	n/a	n/a	25	n/a	5.7

Note: CEPACA, Annual reports 2006–2011.

Management and Disposal of Forfeited Assets

The issue of management and sale of confiscated and forfeited assets only came into the consideration of policymakers in 2010–2011. During that period, several public scandals broke out, involving well-known criminals who stripped and vandalized their property after it was seized by the CEPACA. It was clear that there was a legal void as the LFPCA arranged neither for the management nor the sale of confiscated assets. No resources were budgeted for the management or sale of confiscated assets.

Until the end of 2012, when the new Law on Forfeiture of Illegally Acquired Assets (LFIAA) was introduced, the Prosecution Service and the CEPACA sent court confiscation and forfeiture orders to the National Revenue Agency ('NRA'). The NRA sold the forfeited property, along with property seized within the criminal confiscation procedure, via public auctions executed under the Tax and Social Insurance Procedure Code ('TSIPC').[41] The proceeds from the sales were meant to go into the State Treasury. However, in a limited number of cases, the NRA was allowed to grant forfeited property, primarily motor vehicles, to other state agencies or ministries. For over a decade, the Ministers of Finance actively used these NRA powers and donated forfeited luxury vehicles in order to gain influence or trade favours with other ministers, with the offices of the Prime Minister or the President, and with police chiefs, mayors, or regional governors.

Under the new LFIAA regime the CEPACA is supposed to send information about forfeited property to an Inter-Institutional Council, composed of Deputy Ministers of Justice; Finance; Economy, Energy and Tourism; Labour and Social

---

41   SG No. 105/29.12.2005: http://www.customs.bg/document/3246 (accessed 2 April 2013).

Policy and Regional Development and Public Works.[42] According to Article 89 of the LFIAA, this Council will make proposals to the Council of Ministers as to how the property seized should be disposed of. A limited form of social re-use is still allowed, as state-funded institutions and local government bodies may also be beneficiaries and be granted confiscated assets.[43]

Recent studies have identified a number of further problems that the NRA has encountered in trying to dispose of confiscated or forfeited assets.[44] These obstacles are likely to remain in the foreseeable future, as the new LFIAA law and regulations do little to address them. For example, the existing law leaves a 'grey period' after the seizure of the property, during which no institution is in charge of safeguarding and managing the forfeited property. In the majority of cases, the seized proceeds are left for safeguarding with the investigated persons, who in some instances vandalize them. Next, two obstacles to ownership have been identified. When the state acquires mortgaged property, it also assumes the burden of debt. With the steep fall in the property values between 2009 and 2012, in some instances the state ended up being unable to cover the debt. The NRA has also found it close to impossible to sell partially forfeited property (such as a 50 per cent share in a house), where the other half is owned by a relation of the convicted criminal. Next, in cases of notorious criminals, buyers are often not interested in acquiring forfeited property out of fear of reprisals. Finally, there are technical restraints. The property registers in Bulgaria are often quite messy, as legal conflicts following the process of the return of previously nationalized property after 1990 and the lack of cadastral plans exacerbate more technical obstacles that slow down the disposal process (e.g. missing or inadequate data about the property in the court orders and/or in the ownership documents of the previous owner).

These impediments have resulted in very low proceeds from the sale of forfeited or confiscated property. The NRA may not provide specific values about the proceeds from the sale of forfeited or confiscated proceeds of crime. The bottom line is that out of 175 landed properties handed by the prosecution and the CEPACA to the NRA, at the end of 2011 only one had been disposed of – not by sale but by donation to a local authority. The NRA also donated 81 motor vehicles to other government agencies and 5467 cultural assets (whose value has not been estimated) to museums. In total, the 2011 NRA proceeds from the sale of all 'confiscated, forfeited, or abandoned' assets transferred to it by all government agencies (including the CEPACA) were only €4.2 million. This was slightly higher than the 2010 sales which were €3.8 million, but lower than the 2009 high of €6.4 million.[45] Even if we put these figures against estimated annual proceeds

---

42 Article 88 of the LFIAA.

43 Article 90 of the LFIAA.

44 CSD, *Management and Disposal of Confiscated Criminal Assets, Policy Brief No.33* (Sofia, 2012).

45 NRA data provided to the Center for the Study of Democracy in letter dated 24 January 2012.

of crime of at least €1.8 billion,[46] the impact of the confiscated proceeds of crime on criminal entrepreneurs still seems to be minimal.

Socio-Historical Factors with an Impact on Anti-Organized Crime Policies

The legal, technical and institutional impediments to the confiscation and forfeiture of criminal assets are indicative of the lack of a political will to implement an effective system. This lack of a political will is not merely an expression of a lack of vision and strategic thinking about countering organized crime in Bulgaria. It is the end result of a two-decade long situation of 'state capture', a period that started with the fall of communism in 1989. During this period, an oligarchy of former communist apparatchiks, criminal and 'grey' entrepreneurs seized economic power which they then used to maintain a political class that preserves their interests. Part of this 'trading in favours' involved the maintenance of a mutually beneficial status quo, where corrupt politicians and businessmen with unexplained wealth strived to preserve their illicit assets by constantly emasculating the criminal justice process. The ability of criminals to exercise such disproportionate influence over politics and the development of the criminal justice process is due to two major historical factors: the fusion of the former communist-era security apparatus into criminal networks and the merging of organized and white-collar criminals.

The involvement of former security officers in organized crime networks is one of the main factors that facilitates the continuance of corruption today. Bulgaria's 1989 political reforms were followed by the transformation of the communist-era Committee for State Security or CSS (the Bulgarian equivalent of the Soviet KGB). Apart from the structural reforms, substantial personnel cutbacks were made at all levels of the CSS. Between 1989 and 1991, over half its officers were dismissed, the majority of them from the political police and the Technological and Scientific Intelligence ('TSI') unit. An additional restructuring push in the period between 1991 and 1992 was carried out by the first non-Communist government. In the two waves of dismissals, a total of between 12,000 and 14,000 officers were laid off. In the following years, successive governments pushed through additional rounds of police staff layoffs totalling a further 10,000. Along with these changes, between 1989 and 2006, the Bulgarian army reduced its size, from around 250,000 to 38,000.[47]

A number of these redundant officers either directly switched sides and became involved in criminal activities[48] or set up private security firms which

---

46 Center for the Study of Democracy, *Serious and Organised Crime Threat Assessment* (Sofia, 2012).

47 Center for the Study of Democracy, *Partners in Crime: The Risk of Symbiosis between the Security Sector and Organized Crime in Southeast Europe* (Sofia, 2004) 7–8.

48 See M. Tzvetkova, *Wrestling for Supremacy. The Evolution of Extra-legal Protection in Bulgaria 1989–1999* (Oxford: DPhil Dissertation, 2008).

became involved in extortion racketeering or illicit market activities. Another group of these unemployed officers simply used their connections (especially TSI unit members) to start their own businesses. The majority of laid-off personnel maintained their personal connections with individuals within the police, the Ministry of Interior, or the prosecution service. This provided the conditions needed to maintain corrupt relations and to influence the construction of the criminal justice process. The involvement of former police officers in politics (as MPs, mayors, or government officials) became increasingly prevalent, and further strengthened the undue political influence of criminals or businessmen with a law-enforcement background.

The merging of white-collar and traditional organized criminals is the second key factor. The economic elite in Bulgaria has, for over two decades, maintained a large part of the economy in a grey zone, closely linked with the markets for illicit goods and services.[49] The history of the criminalized economic elite has been discussed at length elsewhere.[50] In the 1990s the main sources of such illicit enrichment were rigged privatization deals, the breaking of sanctions against Yugoslavia and involvement in grey/black economy enterprises such as protection rackets and the smuggling of excisable commodities, Chinese/Turkish and other consumer goods. In the past decade these criminal elites have abandoned much of these traditional criminal sources of income, and have become involved in various VAT fraud, tax avoidance schemes, EU funding and public procurement frauds.

The specifics of their criminal enterprises allowed this (criminal) economic elite to command a significant share of the economy. In the field of organized tax and excise fraud, for instance, the use of the legitimate business structure is a necessary part of the criminal activity. But even in other forms of organized crime (narcotics, prostitution, racketeering) the majority of the criminal groups control some legal business structure – not for the purpose of facilitating crimes, but simply as an investment and a way of laundering their criminal proceeds. Bulgarian criminal groups participate in the legal economy to a greater extent than their counterparts in Western Europe.[51] The strong foothold that these criminal elites have in the legal economy has allowed them to firmly establish their economic clout over the political class and the judiciary.

---

49   Center for the Study of Democracy, *The Hidden Economy in Bulgaria and the Global Economic Crisis* (Sofia, 2011).

50   Center for the Study of Democracy, *Organized Crime in Bulgaria: Markets and Trends* (Sofia, 2007); M. Tzvetkova, *Wrestling for supremacy. The evolution of extra-legal protection in Bulgaria 1989–1999* (Oxford: DPhil Dissertation, 2008); P. Gounev, *Backdoor traders: illicit entrepreneurs and legitimate markets* (London: PhD thesis, London School of Economics and Political Science, 2011); P. Gounev and T. Bezlov, 'Corruption and Criminal Markets' in P. Gounev and V. Ruggiero (eds), *Corruption and Organized Crime in Europe* (London: Routledge, 2012).

51   Center for the Study of Democracy, *Serious and Organised Crime Threat Assessment 2010–2011* (Sofia, 2012).

The mechanisms used by the criminal elites to undermine the development of a strong and effective criminal justice process have varied over time. One approach has been to suborn high-level government, police and judicial officials who then protect their interests. The other has been by suborning or lobbying members of parliament into (not) passing or amending hostile legislation or introducing provisions that deliberately weaken its enforcement.

New Forfeiture Legislation and the Way Forward

A significant increase in successful forfeiture claims and value of the property confiscated under the LFPCA occurred in 2011.[52] Under new management, the CEPACA started to seek closer cooperation with prosecution and law-enforcement bodies, in the form of joint working groups on key investigations. Although mainly occurring on an ad-hoc basis, these efforts were a step towards increasing inter-institutional trust and better recognition of the CEPACA.[53] Plans were made to establish a common electronic register of all properties under injunction. However, this momentum has been short-lived. The resignation of the Commission's director in early 2012, on the grounds of a lack of political support and resistance towards modernization and internal reform, marked a significant setback.[54] Until the entry into force of the new Law on Forfeiture of Illegally Acquired Assets in November 2012 (described below), which envisions dissolving the CEPACA and establishing a new Commission for Establishing Property Acquired through Illegal Activity ('CEPAIA') with new members, the body remained without a director, which significantly undermined its credibility and its ability to start new proceedings, as these actions require the signatures of all five members of the CEPACA. Furthermore, in 2010 and 2011 there were allegations related to the integrity of some of the CEPACA's members which have not been completely dispelled.

By 2008 it was generally accepted that the legislative framework required important changes in order to render the forfeiture process more effective. The CEPACA faced increasing public pressure to justify its existence. While the Commission did freeze assets valued at nearly €400 million, it actually forfeited a very small portion of these amounts (under €9 million). There has been a broad consensus that the main shortcoming of the system in place was that the forfeiture process started too late in the pre-trial phase, thus enabling defendants to transfer their assets before these could be seized. Furthermore, final seizure

---

52   Report from the Commission to the European Parliament and the Council, *On Progress in Bulgaria under the Cooperation and Verification Mechanism* (COM(2012) 411 final) 5.

53   Commission Staff Working Document SWD(2012) 232 final, 18 July 2012.

54   See Report from the Commission to the European Parliament and the Council, *On Progress in Bulgaria under the Co-operation and Verification Mechanism* (COM(2012) 411 final); *Commission Staff Working Document* (SWD(2012) 232 final) 34.

was completely dependent on a criminal conviction, which is hard to obtain given the ineffective and extremely slow judicial process. These features have negated the idea of putting the forfeiture process within the civil proceedings in order to reverse the burden of proof and lower the level of evidence required.

In July 2009, the centre-right Citizens for the European Development of Bulgaria ('GERB') won the national elections on a strong anti-corruption agenda. In December 2009, GERB proposed a new Law on the Forfeiture of Illegally Acquired Assets ('LFIAA'). The draft bill envisioned the introduction of non-conviction based seizure and forfeiture of assets derived from illegal activities, based on a combined system of criminal and civil law. Until its final adoption in 2012, this initially bold proposal underwent a process of amendment and numerous challenges from all sides of the political spectrum.

An initial attempt to adopt a stronger forfeiture bill failed in the Parliament in July 2011 and the draft was returned for adjustments. The strong polarization of the opinions of different interest groups indicated that the implementation of the law might face significant hurdles. The vast majority of NGOs opposed the changes based on human-rights concerns. There has also been an internal political battle as to who will be the leading power in determining the aspects of the new law. A day before the draft law had to be voted on in a second reading in Parliament, there were over 40 objections and proposals for changes. Most of these changes came from members within the ruling GERB, apart from those of the opposition forces. With intense political and public debate prior to the entry into force of the new LFIAA on 19 November 2012, the new NCB forfeiture regime has become one of the most debated and controversial pieces of legislation in Bulgaria's recent history.

Thus, there were attempts on several fronts to influence the decision-making process and reach a balance between a compliance with the increasingly vocal requests from the European Union to reform the regime, and removing or moderating the most controversial and bold provisions through an aggressive public campaign, or through back-door lobbying efforts. The method of using human-rights NGOs to campaign in favour of defence lawyers and contest key provisions of the draft on constitutional grounds resurfaced. The 'human rights cult'[55] has proved an effective commonly-used method for neutralizing proposals for harsher penal policies. As a result, several key provisions of the law, as well as the law in its entirety, have been challenged as unconstitutional (it is possible to bring challenges against laws that have been adopted before they enter into force).

In October 2012 the Constitutional Court issued a decision upon the request of a group of opposition MPs that it rule that the whole law, or several of its particular provisions, was unconstitutional on the basis of, *inter alia*, non-compliance with the provisions of the right to property and the right to respect for private and family life under the Constitution and the European Convention on Human Rights.

---

55 G. Petrunov, *Money Laundering in Bulgaria: The Policy Response* (Sofia: RiskMonitor Foundation, 2010) 28.

The Constitutional Court found the law, and the definition of unlawfully acquired property, to be generally compliant with the right to property since it concerns only property obtained through unlawful means. The checks preceding asset forfeiture are considered to contain sufficient guarantees not to cause violations of the right to private and family life.[56] However, unconstitutionality was sustained, *inter alia*, as regards Articles 24(3) and (4), which obliged all officials, and gave the right to all citizens, to report to the Asset Forfeiture Commission on administrative violations that resulted through the obtaining of a benefit in excess of BGN 150,000 (approximately €75,000).[57] Following the decision of the Constitutional Court, this provision was changed and currently envisions that only the authority that imposed an administrative penalty for such violations can notify the Commission, provided that the penalty has entered into force and that the benefit of € 75,000 cannot be forfeited otherwise. The extension of the Law to potential forfeitures for transactions that occurred during a period of up to 15 years before its start date was also pronounced unconstitutional as being excessive. The 15-year-period has been reduced to 10 years.[58] No decision has been issued as yet in relation to challenges to Articles 11(5), 75(1), and 76(2), pertaining to the appeal procedure, the right of relatives to participate in proceedings, among others.

The most significant change to the existing regime is that the CEPAIA will be able to initiate a civil procedure for seizure of such assets immediately after an indictment for a number of serious crimes, as well as administrative violations. The CEPAIA is not required to wait until the end of the criminal trial in order to file a forfeiture claim in court. The basis for the invocation of the LFIAA involves: a lack of financial balance between legitimate income and property in excess of €125,000 (instead of €30,000 under the old regime); and charges pending for crimes exhaustively enumerated in Article 22(1) of the LFIAA. Pursuant to Article 24(1), the new law also applies to any administrative violation that led to direct benefit in excess of €75,000 that cannot be forfeited under other laws.

Some further key changes introduced under the new Act raise concern. First, the catalogue of crimes that can trigger an asset forfeiture procedure was changed to include some additional offences, while others were removed. The law still does not cover all corruption offences, which has been seen as one of its weaknesses. One example is particularly telling – the law does not cover those provisions in the Criminal Code that target the trafficking in cultural and archaeological goods, but only the persons responsible for physical discovery ('digging out') of such goods, the low-level criminals. Consequently, the revenues acquired through the trade in such goods remain outside the scope of the NCB forfeiture procedure.[59] Second, questions remain as to whether the €125,000 threshold required to trigger

---

56   CC Decision No. 13 of 13 October 2012, SG No. 82 of 26 October 2012.
57   CC Decision No. 13 of 2012, SG No. 82 of 2012.
58   CC Decision No. 13 of 2012, SG No. 83 of 2012, amended SG No. 103 of 2012.
59   T. Kolarov, 'New Principles in the Criminal Assets Forfeiture Act' (2012) 2 *Judicial World* 100.

action is too high to be proven by the CEPAIA. Furthermore, the reduction of the review period to 10 years greatly limits the scope of the investigations. This also means that the proceeds generated during the large-scale privatization wave in the late 1990s and early 2000s cannot be targeted by the law. Third, while under the old regime the Prosecution Service and the police were the bodies that informed the CEPACA of any criminal charges that would trigger proceedings under the LFPCA, under the new law it is only the prosecution that notifies the CEPAIA of such charges. In practice this means that one of the sources of information on pre-trial actions has been removed. Furthermore, some practitioners from the CEPACA were concerned that the law did not explicitly oblige the prosecution to notify the CEPAIA of all relevant cases. This would mean that unless the CEPAIA improves its image dramatically and builds up a relationship of trust with the pre-trial authorities, they will retain their negative attitude towards the NCB forfeiture regime and will remain uncooperative or obstructive.

Overall, the success of the law will depend on its implementation by the institutions involved, in particular the formation of a strong and independent CEPAIA and the appointment of credible and professional staff, as well as inter-institutional cooperation with the administrative control bodies and prosecution agencies. Uncertainties remain regarding the ambiguous provision within the LFIAA related to the burden of proof (in theory the burden of proof should lie with the suspect, but the formulation is more vague than initially anticipated). On the one hand, Article 57(1) of the LFIAA requires, after a seizure order for the assets under investigation has been issued, that the investigated person be invited to present within 14 days a declaration on the type and value of the assets he/she or his/her family owns, as well as evidence on the source of the funds through which the assets were acquired and the circumstances of their acquisition. On the other hand, the LFIAA requires the state to present before the court all relevant facts and evidence to prove the existence of the preconditions that are required for a forfeiture decision to be issued by the court, placing the burden of proof on the Commission.[60] Thus, according to Article 77(4) of LFIAA, 'In the court proceedings the Commission shall present evidence on: [...] 5. other circumstances relevant to clarification of the origin of the assets and the manner in which the assets were acquired'. The old LFPCA did not explicitly contain such a requirement. Instead, Article 4(1) of the LFPCA envisioned the reversal of the burden of proof (according to which the suspect has to prove that the assets were not derived from criminal activity):[61] 'By order of this law property acquired during the checked period by persons about whom it has been established that the grounds of article 3 exist shall be divested and in the concrete case a grounded assumption can be made that the acquired property is connected with the criminal activity of persons

---

60   See N. Nikolov, *Civil Forfeiture According to the Law on Forfeiture of Illegally Acquired Assets. Thematic Comments on the New Aspects* (Sofia: Fenea, 2012) 169.

61   Ibid.

so far as a lawful source has not been established.'[62] Consequently, it remains in the hands of the courts to establish a consistent approach in the interpretation of the law and to allow for the reversed burden of proof.

Conclusion: Impact of the Bulgarian Asset Forfeiture Approach

Non-conviction based forfeiture and other features of extended confiscation face many legal and technical challenges in the countries where they are applied, and Bulgaria is no exception.[63] Cultural differences within the European Union may affect the general approach to confiscation.[64] Judges in some countries may consider confiscation to be the additional punishment of an already-convicted person and would be reluctant to apply it systematically, while some prosecutors rarely request confiscation in court.[65] Institutional culture also plays a role. Law-enforcement and prosecution agencies are often reluctant to take on new functions, and prefer to limit themselves to investigating and prosecuting the predicate crimes. As there is no clear distinction between the different goals of the two regimes (criminal confiscation and civil forfeiture), authorities attempting to forfeit criminal assets, such as the CEPACA (and since November 2012 – the CEPAIA) experience a number of practical difficulties, especially if they are not equipped with the necessary powers and independence of action.

Civil forfeiture is a relatively new concept in Bulgaria and is perceived by law-enforcement bodies, the prosecution and judges as a highly repressive measure. It is interpreted as a tool to persecute individuals by depriving them of their property, and not as a preventive tool that deprives the criminal of the capacity to engage in future criminal activities. Furthermore, with respect to the introduction of NCB forfeiture, Bulgaria has had difficulties similar to those in other European countries where, international and internal public pressure notwithstanding, some key characteristics of extended confiscation did not survive constitutional challenges, while in others alternatives were substituted.[66] Nonetheless, some studies point out that the specifics of the legal and socio-economic environments in different member states might require different legal tools.[67] For instance, the NCB can be

---

62   Promulgated SG No. 19 of 1 May 2005, amended SG No. 42 of 5 June 2009.

63   S.N.M. Young (ed.), *Civil Forfeiture of Criminal Property. Legal Measures for Targeting the Proceeds of Crime* (Cheltenham: Edward Elgar Publishing, 2009).

64   Matrix Insight, *Assessing the Effectiveness of EU Member States' Practices in the Identification, Tracing, Freezing and Confiscation of Criminal Assets* (London, 2009).

65   J. Forsaith, B. Irving, E. Nanopoulos and M. Fazekas, *Study for an Impact Assessment on a Proposal for a New Legal Framework on the Confiscation and Recovery of Criminal Assets. Final Report* (Brussels, RAND Corporation, European Union, 2012): http://ec.europa.eu/home-affairs/doc_centre/crime/docs/RAND%20EUROPE%20 Study%20Final%20Report.pdf (accessed 10 April 2013).

66   Ibid., 64 et seq.

67   Ibid.

the preferred model where criminal convictions are more difficult to obtain, or where the influence of corrupt officials may interfere with criminal investigations.[68] Other factors include variations in the nature of the threat of organized crime, the scope of police powers and their ability to generate more evidence, rules of evidence and standards of proof. Furthermore, extended confiscation might be unnecessary in countries with extended criminalization, for instance where money laundering is legally defined without reference to specific predicate offences.

In Bulgaria, the difficulty of obtaining criminal convictions in relation to serious organized and financial crimes (money laundering in particular) made the move, in 2012, towards non-conviction based forfeiture a logical step, after the previous conviction-based procedure had failed to produce the expected results. On the other hand, the new legislation is shaped and subsequently interpreted in such a way that most distinctive features and strengths of the civil, NCB forfeiture process, are effectively disempowered or deformed under the pretence of safeguarding human rights and preventing political repression. When looking behind the general human-rights rhetoric in Bulgaria, besides the traditional concerns, one can find a deeper rooted resistance towards more serious attempts to strengthen the penal process. The lack of political will produced an uncoordinated and underfinanced system, which at the same time was designed to target ambitious goals. As a result, the civil forfeiture regime in place has had no real dissuasive impact on organized crime. This lack of vision and proper prioritizing of policies to counter organized crime is a product of both the long period of state capture and undue political influence over the structures of law enforcement and the judiciary, as well as the merging of white-collar and traditional agents of organized crime. This second factor led to the formation of a strong economic elite actively participating in the legal economy and proactively using corruption in all aspects of political power to maintain their position. They gained access to the tools necessary for impeding and sabotaging harsher penal policies, as well as stricter regulations that could be used effectively against their financial strength.

The civil forfeiture regime has remained a hostage to this broader, unfavourable policy context for enacting measures to counter organized crime. The new regime, born of an urgent need to comply with international requirements and public scrutiny, is yet to produce any concrete results. However, as has been shown, the political debate has not changed significantly over the past decade, while the 'moderation' of several key provisions of the new non-conviction based approach clearly indicate that a strong functioning instrument for depriving criminals and administrative offenders of their assets is not welcomed and may face significant difficulties during implementation.

---

68   Ibid.; T.S. Greenberg, L.M. Samuel, W. Grant and L. Gray, *Stolen Asset Recovery. A Good Practices Guide for Non-conviction Based Asset Forfeiture* (Washington, DC: World Bank, 2009) 15.

Chapter 6

Criminal Asset Recovery in Australia

Andrew Goldsmith, David Gray and Russell G. Smith[1]

Introduction

In this chapter, we examine the approaches taken within Australian jurisdictions towards the proceeds of crime in the past 25 years, but with a particular focus on changes during the past decade. Features of the laws governing proceeds of crime and asset recovery will be examined to the extent that they set out key measures being adopted and implemented by law-enforcement and prosecution authorities in Australia. In addition, we shall consider some of the organizational and practical changes these agencies have undergone with the goal of taking away the illicit profits from organized crime.

What makes Australia potentially interesting in the context of this book is the range of models and diversity of experiences arising from the number of different jurisdictions involved (nine in total, comprising six states, two territories and the federal/Commonwealth). In turn, this presents a challenge to anyone attempting to provide an overview of developments in Australia in the space of a single chapter. Inevitably some selectivity of coverage is required. For this reason, we focus upon developments at the federal level but will draw comparisons with state and territory models in order to illustrate points of divergence as well as the emergence of shared approaches on some issues. In this regard, there are some relatively significant (if not unique) features of recent developments in Australia in the past few years (especially, the growth of unexplained wealth laws and the formation of multi-disciplinary and multi-agency task forces) that warrant some consideration in terms of their potential interest to non-Australian audiences.

The chapter is organized as follows. The next section puts criminal asset recovery and forfeiture in Australia into the context of policy concerns and public debates about the nature of organized crime and the threat that it poses to mainstream society and government. Then, we briefly examine the experience with conviction-based forfeiture schemes and the emerging widespread perception that the problems associated with accessing the profits required a broader response

---

1   The views expressed are those of the authors alone and do not necessarily represent the policies of the Australian Government or its agencies. This chapter is based in part upon papers presented by the second and third-named authors at the 30th Cambridge International Symposium on Economic Crime: Economic Crime – Surviving the Fall – Myths and Realities, Jesus College Cambridge, 3 September 2012.

than that offered by schemes of forfeiture premised upon securing a criminal conviction. In the following section, we chart the non-conviction based forfeiture schemes across Australian jurisdictions and outline the key features of some of the principal models implemented. Next, we turn to two recent phenomena of particular significance – the accelerating adoption of unexplained wealth provisions in addition to conviction-based and other non-conviction based measures, and the trend towards multi-agency task forces and the recruitment of teams with diverse skillsets. In the penultimate section, we reflect upon what these changes signify, and particularly the limited knowledge currently held about the effectiveness of these measures in meeting their goals. We shall suggest that what is occurring in the recent changes in criminal asset recovery in Australia is part of a broader visible shift in the philosophy and culture in law enforcement, from one that is punishment-oriented and criminal offence-focused to one that is developing new capabilities for crime prevention including disruption and the removal of incentives.

Organized Crime in Australia

Organized crime is now an officially designated national security concern in Australia.[2] In the past three decades, there has been a tremendous growth in government concern about the prevalence of organized crime and the actual and potential harms associated with its various forms. Much of this heightened awareness can be traced historically to official investigations into the incidence of drug trafficking and its effects.

Prior to the late 1970s, public awareness of organized crime was largely informed by occasional instances of violence, intimidation and/or scandal associated with gambling, prostitution and competition between business groups involved in the fruit and vegetable markets. While links to corruption of public officials and politicians emerged periodically, organized crime was seen largely as the activity of certain relatively long-standing ethnic enclaves operating on the margins rather than something deeply pervasive and affecting mainstream Australian society. However the huge profits derived from drug crimes saw a variety of new participants enter the field. While the 'foot soldiers' in the drug trade remained fairly visible to law enforcement and were easily targeted, a number of official inquiries between 1979 and the late 1980s came to share the view that the key players deriving the greatest profits were well-insulated from law enforcement attention and were therefore difficult to convict. Justice Woodward in his 1979 inquiry into drug trafficking in New South Wales (NSW) noted that 'while the high-level trafficker may avoid handling the drugs, he cannot avoid contact with

---

2   See Department of the Prime Minister and the Cabinet, *Strong and Secure: A Strategy for Australia's National Security* (Canberra, 2013) 9, 17.

the flow of money'.[3] Just a few years later, Frank Costigan QC, in his report into the infiltration of organized crime on the waterfront in Victoria, noted that 'the most successful method of identifying and ultimately convicting major organized criminals is to follow the money trail'.[4]

Since then, different approaches to following the money have been pursued in Australian jurisdictions. As we shall see, while differences in detail distinguish the approaches taken in different jurisdictions, there has been a shared philosophical and practical shift since the 1980s from reliance upon conviction-based schemes alone to the implementation of other measures in particular non-conviction based (i.e. civil) schemes.

The focus upon 'Mr Bigs', mainly in the area of drug trafficking, continues to shape organized-crime policy in Australia. This can be seen most recently in relation to the introduction in 2010 of unexplained wealth provisions at the Federal level that followed experimentation with this approach by some of the states and territories. These provisions are dealt with below. The elusive bosses of organized crime, because they remain relatively immune to regular law enforcement processes (charging and prosecution in the criminal courts), are now routinely invoked in policy circles to justify placing a host of new measures in the hands of law enforcement officials and agencies. While taking away illicit profits has remained central to policy in this area, two changes can be identified in the past decade that explains the growing urgency given to it in recent times.

The first is that organized crime, especially in its transnational forms, has been elevated to become a matter of national security significance since a statement by then Prime Minister Rudd in December 2008.[5] This has resulted in stepped up 'action plans' and 'strategic positions' at the national level, highlighting the need and support for new and renewed approaches to this problem. One example is the *Commonwealth Organised Crime Strategic Framework* that was launched on 25 November 2009 by the then attorney general and the minister for justice.[6] This policy focuses on identifying the threats to the nation from organized crime and on developing a whole-of-government approach to tackling this crime.

The second, related development is the shift in thinking in law enforcement circles towards a more proactive, preventive approach to handling organized crime. Law enforcement authorities have come to realize that securing convictions against organized-crime figures is of marginal deterrent value if the substantial ill-gotten gains, the product of the criminal activity, are not confiscated. This realization, together with mixed results in securing convictions of the Mr Bigs, has

---

3   Quoted in D. Lusty, 'Taxing the untouchables who profit from organised crime' (2003) 10 *Journal of Financial Crime* 209 at 215.

4   Royal Commission on the Activities of the Federated Ship Painters and Dockers Union, *Report* (Canberra: Australian Government Publishing Service, 1984) at 345.

5   Prime Minister, *National Security Statement* (Canberra, 2008).

6   See http://www.ag.gov.au/CrimeAndCorruption/OrganisedCrime/Documents/Orga nisedCrimeStrategicFrameworkOverview.pdf (accessed 18 April 2013).

resulted in a lesser emphasis upon criminal conviction as the means of securing confiscation.

Instead, a greater focus has been given to methods of prevention, including disruption and removing the profit from these activities. The Australian Federal Police Commissioner, Tony Negus, told a parliamentary inquiry in March 2012 that there 'have to be different ways of attacking the roots of serious and organized crime'.[7] In the search for new lines of attack, unexplained wealth has become the latest weapon favoured in Australia for attacking these roots.[8] Other key approaches include declarations that organizations are criminal organizations; orders controlling the activities of members of declared organizations and people involved in serious criminal activity; and the sharing of and protection from disclosure of criminal intelligence.[9]

Illicit Earnings and the Limits of Criminal Law

One key point to note is just how quickly and comprehensively the different jurisdictions in Australia have moved away from singular reliance upon conviction-based forfeiture schemes to endorse a range of non-conviction measures. The reasons for doing so are now briefly examined. What makes this shift particularly remarkable is the break with the criminal law principle that many believe has occurred in Australia. In essence, forfeiture no longer required the proof of a relevant criminal offence against a particular individual beyond reasonable doubt. While some scholars view changes in this area as unwarranted or unjustified moves away from the establishment of criminal liability as the threshold for forfeiture of assets, risking the confiscation of the assets of innocent persons,[10] many others disagree.[11] A large number of senior police officers and some prominent lawyers and judges, including those heading major inquiries into the challenges of confronting organized crime, have tended to take a pragmatic view, noting that criminal measures have not proved effective and that prevention requires a broader approach that is not limited to criminal-type proceedings

---

7   Parliamentary Joint Committee on Law Enforcement. *Inquiry into Commonwealth Unexplained Wealth Legislation and Arrangements* (Commonwealth of Australia, Canberra, 2012) at 9.

8   Ibid.

9   Australia, *Standing Committee on Law and Justice. Communique*, 12–13 April 2012. These measures have especially been used against outlaw motorcycle gangs; see G. Martin, 'Jurisprudence of secrecy' (2012) 14 *Flinders Law Journal* 189; T. Gavin, 'Extending the reach of Kable' (2012) 34 *Sydney Law Review* 395.

10   A. Gray, 'The Compatibility of Unexplained Wealth Provisions and "Civil" Forfeiture Regimes with Kable' (2012) 12 *QUT Law & Justice Journal* 18 and 'Forfeiture Provisions and the Criminal/Civil Divide' (2012) 15 *New Criminal Law Review* 32.

11   For the mixed view of the High Court of Australia, see *South Australia v Totani* [2010] HCA 39; *Wainohu v New South Wales* [2011] HCA 24.

with their associated higher evidentiary standards. In this regard, nothing much has changed it seems since Justice Moffitt stated in the 1980s that 'the path to conviction is slow, tortuous and expensive ... The criminal justice system is not adequate to secure the conviction of many organized crime figures'.[12] The scale of the problem has also been turned into a telling argument against the more traditional approaches. Given global and national assessments of the major risks associated with organized crime,[13] there is a strong sense that much more could, and needs, to be done. For example, scholars have estimated that conviction-based confiscation laws in Australia and the United Kingdom have barely impacted upon the wealth from organized crime. According to Lusty's estimate, it is 'less than 1 per cent of the billions derived or laundered by criminals within their borders each year'.[14]

Conviction-based forfeiture has been most successful in relation to the instruments of crime. Where the prosecution can show that property (even lawfully acquired property) has been used to facilitate the offences for which the person has been convicted, most Australian jurisdictions provide for forfeiture of that 'tainted' property upon conviction. If the property to be forfeited has been lawfully acquired (i.e. is not the proceeds of crime), the convicted person can get a 'discount' on their sentence on the basis that the forfeiture constitutes an additional 'punishment'. In this respect at least, Australia's proceeds of crime laws are much less 'draconian' than, for example, those applicable in the United Kingdom. In most cases, relatively little additional work by either the investigator or the prosecutor is required to obtain a forfeiture order in such circumstances. On the other hand, attempts to confiscate the *profits* of crime have been far less successful. There are a number of reasons for this, the most important being that in the traditional criminal prosecution model the primary role of police investigators is to investigate *the crimes* and the primary role of the prosecutors is to *prove the elements of the offences*. Because the core business of investigators and prosecutors is focused on the crimes (and not the profits derived from them), the investigation, analysis and argument needed to prove the profits derive from the relevant offences is usually well beyond the scope of the criminal prosecution and outside the expertise of either the investigator or the prosecutor.

One principal manifestation of the perceived retreat from criminal law in this area is the focus within civil forfeiture regimes upon *in rem* measures, thus

---

12 A. Moffitt, *A Quarter to Midnight: The Australian Crisis: Organised Crime and the Decline for the Institutions of State* (Sydney: Angus and Robertson, 1985) at 143.

13 See the Prime Ministerial Statement on National Security, December 2008; and the evidence presented to the Parliamentary Joint Committee on the Australian Crime Commission's *Inquiry into the Legislative Arrangements to Outlaw Serious and Organised Crime Groups* (Canberra: Parliamentary Joint Committee on the Australian Crime Commission, 2009).

14 D. Lusty, 'Civil Forfeiture of Proceeds of Crime in Australia' (2002) 5 *Journal of Money Laundering Control* 345 at 351.

removing the requirement of a previous conviction and a link to a particular offence before property can be forfeited.[15] Another manifestation is the move to introducing a so-called *reverse onus* in unexplained wealth proceedings (discussed separately below), which has raised concerns about a retreat from the criminal law principle to an even higher level.[16] The application of this measure still requires considerable preparatory investigative work by police or other investigators into the financial backgrounds of those linked to the assets being targeted before restraining or confiscation proceedings can be launched. In other words, a detailed brief is required first in order then to be able to oblige the respondent to explain how his or her assets were legitimately acquired. If the respondent provides an explanation – no matter how improbable – the onus shifts back to the proceeds of crime authority. As will be discussed further below, the practical challenges of investigating ownership of assets and various money trails are considerable in themselves and represent a major cultural shift within law enforcement that is relatively recent and only partly achieved so far. The resource implications of financial investigations are also significant for law enforcement agencies, given their often lengthy, intensive nature. This point is one discussed further below.

Significantly greater revenue collection from non-conviction based forfeiture proceedings has also played an important role in reshaping agency, government and public expectations about the relative utility of conviction- and non-conviction based procedures. Bartels compiled figures on recovered proceeds of crime under different systems of recovery across a range of Australian jurisdictions. Her analysis of the Commonwealth system shows that in the year 2002/2003, the first year in which non-conviction measures operated alongside conviction-based measures, non-conviction measures collected a mere A$162,826 while the conviction-based scheme recovered A$3,124,789. By 2008/2009, there had been a massive reversal, whereby conviction-based collections realized A$888,003 while the non-conviction collections realized A$18,313,516. A scheme that had delivered around one-twentieth of the dollars of the other scheme six years earlier had now delivered around 20 times the amount of the other scheme.[17] In this way, civil actions have really come into their own in this period, though it is not a zero-sum of effort between the two; each has its own imperatives and inputs, but the civil process is allowing a focus on asset recovery without the distraction of criminal prosecution requirements.

Overall, the total value of proceeds of crime confiscated in Australia between 1995 and 2011 for the states and territories (except Tasmania and Northern

---

15 See e.g. Proceeds of Crime Act 2002 (Cth) ss 47, 49.

16 These concerns are reflected in the discussions and report Parliamentary Joint Committee on the Australian Crime Commission's *Inquiry into the legislative arrangements to outlaw serious and organised crime groups* (Canberra: Commonweath of Australia, 2009) at 111–114.

17 L. Bartels, *A Review of Confiscation Schemes in Australia*, Technical and Background Paper 36 (Canberra: Australian Institute of Criminology, 2010) at 7.

Territory for which data were not available) was A$421,534,962. Federally, confiscated proceeds of crime during this period totalled A$201,280,051. In all, more than A$623 million has been confiscated in Australia since 1995–1996, with 32 per cent federally derived.[18] Although there is clearly considerable effort made to recover the proceeds of crime in Australia, only a relatively small proportion of the estimated A$10 billion that the Australian Crime Commission (ACC) believes organized crime costs the Australian economy each year is confiscated.[19]

The turning point in Australia in policy terms from exclusive reliance upon conviction-based schemes to non-conviction procedures occurred in the late 1990s, when the Australian Law Reform Commission undertook a large reference examination of the confiscation procedures in Australia.[20] In its report, the commission declared that conviction-based forfeiture had failed to achieve its objectives. It advocated the adoption at the national level of civil-forfeiture laws modelled on New South Wales' Criminal Asset Recovery Act 1990. While most states and territories, apart from NSW and Victoria,[21] did not establish civil forfeiture schemes until the early 2000s, the move was not without even more longstanding precedent. The Commonwealth had taken a tentative step in this direction in 1977 in the form of an amendment to the Customs Act 1901 permitting the forfeiture of cash, cheques or goods established, on the balance of probabilities, to have been derived from dealings in prohibited narcotics imported into Australia without the need for a criminal charge or a conviction.[22] This *in rem* procedure, distinct from the criminal *in personam* approach, reminded the law reformers and politicians involved at the time in responding to the challenges of organized crime that the civil law had long played a role in dealing with the instruments and profits associated with criminal activity, drawing upon venerable equitable and common law notions such as tainted property and unjust enrichment.

Federal Machinery for Recovering the Proceeds of Crime

In relation to the Federal machinery for the recovery of the proceeds of crime, there are a number of key government agencies in addition to the spectrum of other agencies and organizations (in particular, financial institutions) that may hold and provide information relating to restraint and confiscation proceedings. Key federal agencies include: the Australian Federal Police (AFP); the Australian Customs and Border Protection Service (ACBPS); the Australian Crime Commission (ACC); the

---

18   Unpublished research by the Australian Institute of Criminology 2013.

19   Australian Crime Commission *Organised Crime in Australia* (Canberra, 2011).

20   Australian Law Reform Commission, *Confiscation that Counts: A Review of the Proceeds of Crime Act 1987* (Sydney: ALRC Report 87, 1999).

21   Ibid., at 6.

22   D. Lusty, 'Civil Forfeiture of Proceeds of Crime in Australia' (2002) 5(4) *Journal of Money Laundering Control* 345 at 345.

Australian Security and Investment Commission (ASIC); the Australian Taxation Office (ATO); the Commonwealth Director of Public Prosecutions (CDPP); and the Insolvency and Trustee Service Australia (ITSA).

In the past the CDPP has assumed the responsibility for conducting the actual proceedings associated with restraint and confiscation. Since 2 April 2012, the Commissioner of the AFP has undertaken all new proceedings where a restraining order is required. This and other recent efforts to improve the performance of inter-agency arrangements are discussed in the penultimate section of this chapter.

The majority of confiscation action at a Commonwealth level is taken under the Proceeds of Crime Act 2002 (Cth), which came into force on 1 January 2003. The main purposes of this act are twofold: to deprive criminals of the proceeds and benefits gained from criminal conduct, and to prevent the reinvestment of those proceeds and benefits in further criminal activities. The Proceeds of Crime Act includes both conviction-based and non-conviction based streams of confiscation. Action can also be taken under the Proceeds of Crime Act based on either the criminal conduct of the person (action *in personam*) or the property being the proceeds or instrument of certain offences (action *in rem*), and is almost always initiated by way of an application for a restraining order, which restrains specified assets.

Under the Proceeds of Crime Act *2002* (Cth), there are five main types of final orders:

- Conviction-based forfeiture;[23]
- non-conviction based forfeiture, which allows confiscation action to be taken independently of the prosecution process, where a court is satisfied that a person has committed a serious offence,[24] or that the property is the proceeds of an indictable offence or the instrument of a serious offence;[25]
- pecuniary penalty orders, which require a person to pay an amount based on the benefits the person has derived from his or her criminal conduct;[26]
- literary proceeds orders, which require a person to pay an amount based on the literary proceeds that he or she has derived from commercial exploitation of his or her criminal notoriety (e.g. through paid media interviews or book deals);[27] and
- unexplained wealth orders, which require a person to pay a proportion of their wealth, where they cannot satisfy a court that their wealth was legitimately acquired.[28]

---

23 Proceeds of Crime Act 2002 (Cth) ss 48 and 92.
24 ss 47.
25 s 49.
26 s 116.
27 s 152.
28 s 179B.

As noted, proceeds of crime actions are civil proceedings.[29] Most orders under the Proceeds of Crime Act are made by a court, which ensures that orders are only made after receiving independent consideration by a judicial officer. Applications for proceeds of crime orders are brought by the Commissioner of the Australian Federal Police (AFP) or the Commonwealth Director of Public Prosecutions.

Like most proceeds of crime regimes, the Proceeds of Crime Act also contains a range of provisions to safeguard the interests of innocent parties, including orders to pay compensation[30] or exclude property from restraint or forfeiture where a person can show that his or her property is not the proceeds of crime or the instrument of an offence.[31] A court can also make an order requiring the Commonwealth to pay money to the dependant of a person who had his or her property forfeited, to ease any hardship to that dependant that would otherwise be caused by the forfeiture order.[32]

Proceeds recovered under the Proceeds of Crime Act are paid into a special account, the Confiscated Assets Account. The majority of the funds in this account are used to support programmes for crime prevention measures, law enforcement measures, measures relating to the treatment of drug addiction, and diversionary measures relating to the illegal use of drugs. Since the introduction of this legislation, over A$95 million has been reinvested in the community through these types of programmes. Some of the funds have gone to the Australian Federal Police to support trials of new initiatives in crime prevention and law enforcement, including the operations of the Criminal Assets Confiscation Taskforce.[33] During 2011–2012, the government provided nearly A$6 million in funding from the proceeds of crime for non-governmental organizations to support a range of crime prevention activities.[34] In this way, the special account has not been visibly linked to notions of incentivization or downturns in police budgets, and it is not recurrent funding, so cannot be relied on.

Recovered proceeds can also be shared with other countries that make a significant contribution to the recovery of the proceeds or to the investigation or prosecution of the relevant unlawful authority. Australia also has a comprehensive mutual assistance regime, under the Mutual Assistance in Criminal Matters Act 1987 (Cth), which allows for assistance to be given in criminal asset confiscation

---

29   s 315.

30   ss 77 and 94A.

31   ss 29, 73 and 94.

32   s 72.

33   Parliament of Australia, *Parliamentary Joint Committee on Law Enforcement, Commonwealth unexplained wealth legislation and arrangements*, Hansard, 7 March 2012, at 4.

34   Attorney-General's Department, *Annual report 2011–12* (Canberra: Commonwealth of Australia, 2012).

matters. Where the relevant criteria are satisfied, Australia can provide a broad range of assistance to other countries, including tracing assets using notices to financial institutions, production orders and monitoring orders; executing search warrants; and registering and enforcing foreign orders with respect to proceeds of crime.

State Machinery for Recovering the Proceeds of Crime

All Australian states and territories have legislation that can be used to recover criminal assets.[35] The original Australian state and territory legislation for recovering assets adopted conviction-based recovery. Most states and territories have since reformed their laws to include the ability to confiscate assets using civil recovery. All Australian states and territories, with the exception of Tasmania, now have legislation allowing for both civil- and conviction-based recovery.

New South Wales

New South Wales currently has two Acts allowing the recovery of criminal assets. The NSW Crime Commission recovers assets under the Criminal Assets Recovery Act 1990 (NSW) and assets associated with indictable drug offences under the Confiscation of Proceeds of Crime Act 1989 (NSW). The Office of the Director of Public Prosecutions recovers assets associated with other offences under the Confiscation of Proceeds of Crime Act 1989 (NSW). The Confiscation of Proceeds of Crime Act 1989 (NSW) is a conviction-based means of recovering assets while the Criminal Assets Recovery Act 1990 (NSW) provides for civil recovery in NSW.

Australian Capital Territory

The Australian Capital Territory's confiscation legislation is currently the Confiscation of Criminal Assets Act 2003 (Act) which has provisions for both conviction-based and civil asset recovery. The Office of the Director of Public Prosecutions applies for orders under this act in the ACT. The Confiscation of Criminal Assets Act 2003 (ACT) repealed the Proceeds of Crime Act 1991 (ACT). The earlier act contained provisions for conviction-based asset recovery only.

Queensland

The Criminal Proceeds Confiscation Act 2002 (Qld) also allows for conviction-based recovery and civil recovery in Queensland. The Office of the Director of Public Prosecution administers the conviction-based recovery scheme under

---

35   Based on unpublished research by the Australian Institute of Criminology 2013.

this act and Queensland's Crime and Misconduct Commission is responsible for administering the civil recovery scheme. The Criminal Proceeds Confiscation Act 2002 (Qld) repealed the Crimes (Confiscation) Act 1989 (Qld) which, like earlier legislation in other states, allowed for conviction-based recovery.

South Australia

The Criminal Assets Confiscation Act 2005 (SA) is the current legislation directing the recovery of criminal assets in South Australia. This is the third asset-recovery act to be enacted in South Australia. The Criminal Assets Confiscation Act 1996 (SA) and the Crimes (Confiscation of Profits) Act 1986 (SA) required a conviction or proof beyond reasonable doubt that an offence took place before an order to recover assets was issued. The South Australian Office of the Director of Public Prosecution issues orders to recover assets under the current legislation.

Western Australia

The Criminal Property Confiscation Act 2000 (WA) is the current asset recovery legislation in Western Australia. This act also contains conviction based asset recovery provisions and non-conviction based asset-recovery provisions. The Criminal Property Confiscation Act 2000 (WA), unlike legislation in other states, uses the concept of unexplained wealth to recover assets without a conviction. The civil recovery available in federal instruments and in other states requires proof of a civil standard demonstrating that the assets in question are tainted. Unexplained wealth differs as it requires the respondent to establish that the wealth was lawfully obtained. The burden of proof lies with the respondent and not the state. The Office of the Director of Public Prosecution for Western Australia applies for each kind of order under the Act.

Victoria

The Confiscation Act 1997 (Vic) repealed the earlier Crimes (Confiscation of Profits) Act 1986 (Vic) and introduced civil recovery in Victoria. The Director of Public Prosecution for Victoria may apply for orders for civil recovery and for conviction-based recovery.

Northern Territory

The Criminal Property Forfeiture Act 2002 (NT) repealed the previous Crimes (Confiscation) Act 1988 (NT). The current legislation contains conviction-based recovery and civil recovery provisions and, like the Western Australian legislation, also contains unexplained wealth provisions. The Office of the Director of Public Prosecutions applies for orders for recovery in the Northern Territory.

Tasmania

Tasmania remains the only Australian jurisdiction that still requires an offender to be convicted of a crime prior to the confiscation of any property. There are no stated reasons for this singular stance, though Tasmania is a relatively small state with relatively small stakes in terms of organized crime. The Crimes (Confiscation of Profits) Act 1993 (Tasmania) does not allow civil forfeiture or challenges of unexplained wealth. The Office of the Director of Public Prosecution for Tasmania is the applicant of recovery orders in Tasmania.

Recent Developments

Over the past three years, there have been significant changes to Australia's proceeds of crime regime to make it more responsive to the threats posed by organized crime. This has included changes to legislation, including the introduction of unexplained wealth provisions, as well as a shift in how criminal assets confiscation matters are investigated and litigated. These developments should be seen in the context of the move away from conviction-based forfeiture to the greater use of the civil (non-conviction based) provisions, and the development of in-house resources specializing in criminal assets which utilize investigators with financial analysis skills and litigators with commercial litigation backgrounds to facilitate this shift.

A major impetus for these changes has been a growing recognition of the need to have a multifaceted approach to combat serious and organized crime, by both prosecuting illegal activity and removing illicitly derived wealth. In February 2010, the Australian Government passed two pieces of legislation specifically designed to target serious and organized crime, namely the Crimes Legislation Amendment (Serious and Organised Crime) Act 2010 and the Crimes Legislation Amendment (Serious and Organised Crime) Act (No. 2) 2010. This legislation introduced new offences targeting those who support or direct the activities of criminal organizations, and also strengthened criminal asset confiscation and anti-money laundering regimes, broadened access to telecommunication interception powers for the investigation of organized crime offences and provided greater protection for undercover law enforcement officers who infiltrate criminal organizations.

Many of these changes to the criminal asset confiscation regime implemented recommendations made in the *Report on the Independent Review of the Operation of the Proceeds of Crime Act 2002* by Mr Tom Sherman AO, which was tabled in Federal Parliament in October 2006.[36] These amendments introduced freezing

---

36   T. Sherman, *Report on the Independent Review of the Operation of the Proceeds of Crime Act 2002* (Canberra: Commonwealth of Australia, 2006): http://parlinfo.aph.gov.au/parlInfo/search/display/display.w3p;adv=yes;orderBy=customrank;page=6;query=tom%2Bsherman%2Bproceeds;rec=13;resCount=Default (accessed 18 April 2013).

orders and unexplained wealth orders, removed the six-year time limitation on non-conviction based orders, provided for the restraint and forfeiture of instruments of serious crime without requiring a conviction, and improved the ability to share information obtained under the act (including with foreign countries). This has markedly improved the Commonwealth's ability to confiscate criminal assets, especially where a conviction has not been obtained.

Unexplained Wealth

One of the most substantial changes made by the Commonwealth's Crimes Legislation Amendment (Serious and Organised Crime) Act 2010 was the introduction of unexplained wealth provisions at the federal level. Western Australia was the first Australian jurisdiction to introduce them in 2000 as part of the Criminal Property Confiscation Act 2000, followed in 2003 by the Northern Territory through its Criminal Property Forfeiture Act 2002. These are a somewhat novel invention in the realm of proceeds of crime orders, and Australia is one of the few countries to have introduced them to date. Since the introduction of Commonwealth unexplained wealth legislation, similar laws have been enacted in Queensland, South Australia and New South Wales. However, there are differences between the laws in each jurisdiction, especially in relation to whether some connection to criminal conduct is required. There is evidence of a growing international interest in unexplained wealth provisions as an innovative approach to addressing concerns about illicit enrichment and as an alternative to the introduction of an illicit enrichment offence.[37]

Broadly speaking, under these provisions, if a court is satisfied that there are reasonable grounds to suspect that a person's total wealth exceeds the value of the person's wealth that was lawfully acquired, the court can make an order compelling the person to attend court and prove, on the balance of probabilities, that their wealth was not derived from offences falling under a Commonwealth head of constitutional power. In their purest form, unexplained wealth provisions do not require a link to an offence. The Western Australian and Northern Territory provisions are examples of these types of provisions. However, the Commonwealth unexplained wealth provisions contain a link to an offence with Commonwealth power to ensure that they fall within the Commonwealth's power to legislate under the Constitution. If a person cannot demonstrate this, the court may make an order

---

37 Booz Allen Hamilton, *Comparative Evaluation of Unexplained Wealth Orders* (Washington, DC: Department of Justice, 2012). See for example, the comments made by the Implementation Review Group in relation to Australia's implementation of the United National Convention against Corruption. Implementation Review Group, *Review of Implementation of the United Nations Convention against Corruption* (18–22 June 2012) (Conference of the State Parties to the United National Convention against Corruption, UN Doc CAC/COSP/IRG/I/2/1).

requiring them to pay to the Commonwealth the difference between their total wealth and their legitimate wealth.

These provisions are specifically aimed at those who remain at arm's length from the commission of offences and who are not always able to be directly linked to specific offences. In particular, unexplained wealth orders are designed to target senior organized crime figures who fund and benefit from organized crime groups, but seldom carry out the physical elements of crimes.

Under the Commonwealth model, there are three types of orders which can be sought in relation to unexplained wealth: unexplained-wealth restraining orders; preliminary unexplained-wealth orders and unexplained-wealth orders.

Unexplained Wealth Restraining Orders

Unexplained wealth restraining orders are interim orders that restrict a person's ability to dispose of or otherwise deal with property. These provisions ensure that property is preserved and cannot be dealt with to defeat an ultimate unexplained-wealth order.

Under section 20A of the Proceeds of Crime Act 2002 (Cth), a court may make an unexplained-wealth order if it is satisfied that there are reasonable grounds to suspect that:

- a person's total wealth exceeds the value of wealth that they have lawfully acquired; and
- that the person has committed an offence against a law of the Commonwealth, a foreign indictable offence or a State offence that has a federal aspect; and/or
- the whole or any part of the person's wealth was derived from an offence against a law of the Commonwealth, a foreign indictable offence or a State offence that has a federal aspect.

Unexplained wealth restraining orders can only be made following an application from the Commissioner of the AFP and must be supported by an affidavit from an authorized officer.[38] A court has discretion in deciding whether to make a restraining order and may also refuse to make an order if it considers that it is not in the public interest to do so.[39] The Commonwealth may also be required to give an appropriate undertaking with respect to the payment of costs and damages prior to an order being made.[40]

---

38 Authorized officers are defined in the Proceeds of Crime Act to be certain employees of the AFP, Australian Commission for Law Enforcement Integrity, Australian Crime Commission, Customs and Border Protection, Australian Securities and Investments Commission (Australia's corporate regulator) and Australian Taxation Office.

39 s 20A(4).

40 s 21.

While an unexplained wealth restraining order is not a pre-requisite for a preliminary unexplained wealth order or unexplained-wealth order, on a practical level it is often necessary to restrain property to prevent it from being dispersed or placed out of the reach of law enforcement agencies.

Preliminary Unexplained Wealth Orders

A preliminary unexplained wealth order is an order requiring a person to appear before a court for the purposes of determining whether or not an unexplained-wealth order should be made. Under section 179B of the Proceeds of Crime Act 2002 (Cth), a court may make a preliminary unexplained-wealth order if it is satisfied that an authorized officer has reasonable grounds to suspect that a person's total wealth exceeds the value of the person's wealth that was lawfully acquired. A preliminary unexplained wealth order can only be made where the Commissioner of the AFP or the Commonwealth Director of Public Prosecutions has applied for an unexplained wealth order.

Unexplained Wealth Orders

If a preliminary unexplained wealth order has been made and the court is not satisfied that the person's wealth was not derived from an offence against a law of the Commonwealth, a foreign indictable offence or a State offence that has a federal aspect, it may make an unexplained wealth order.[41] The burden of showing that wealth was not derived from offences under Commonwealth power falls on the person in relation to whom the preliminary order was issued. The person is required to satisfy the court on the balance of probabilities.

An unexplained wealth order makes payable to the Commonwealth an amount which, in the court's opinion, constitutes the difference between the person's total wealth and the value of the person's property which the court is satisfied did not derive from the commission of one of the above offence. That is, the difference between their total wealth and the wealth that has been legitimately acquired.

As with unexplained wealth restraining orders and preliminary unexplained wealth orders, a court has discretion with respect to whether or not to make an unexplained wealth order. A court making an unexplained-wealth order must also direct the Commonwealth to pay a specified amount to a dependant of the person, if it is satisfied that the unexplained wealth order would cause hardship to that person and the amount is necessary to offset that hardship.[42] There is an additional requirement that if the dependant is over 18 years old, they must not have been aware of the conduct that was the subject of the order.

---

41   s 179E.
42   s 179L.

Unexplained Wealth Provisions – Are They Effective?

While the introduction of unexplained wealth provisions in 2010 was not without criticism, with a number of organizations expressing their concerns that the provisions were a removal of the presumption of innocence and other common law rights;[43] there are also grounds for concern that expectations of these provisions' effectiveness against organized crime are unrealistic and that their implementation is far more difficult than might be expected. Part of the context for assessing the contribution from provisions of this kind comes from the experience in Western Australia and the Northern Territory. Despite these provisions appearing to have very broad application, the practical reality is that their application is narrower than originally envisaged by the legislature. This is not to undermine the usefulness of the unexplained wealth provisions, as without them there are undoubtedly cases that might otherwise be out of the reach of proceeds of crime litigation. However, it is important that these provisions are viewed as just one option in the arsenal of proceeds of crime tools.

As noted earlier, unexplained wealth provisions have existed in Western Australia since 2000 and the Northern Territory since 2003. While opinions differ, and there has been no systematic assessment of their effectiveness relative to other measures, experience in these jurisdictions indicates that their introduction has often not been without difficulty. In the case of Western Australia, a recent inquiry in the state noted that in the first eight years of operation, there had been just 24 unexplained wealth declarations made.[44] In part it would appear the low usage can be explained by reluctance on the part of the Director of Public Prosecution to make applications under its provisions on philosophical as well as practical grounds,[45] to the extent that these provisions have been assessed recently as being 'completely dormant'.[46]

However, a more powerful reason explaining the limited impact of these provisions has been the parallel availability of 'drug-trafficker declarations'. In the Criminal Property Confiscation Act 2000 (WA), section 8 provides that once a person is declared to be a drug trafficker 'as a result of being convicted of a confiscation offence that was committed after the commencement of this Act', all the property owned or effectively controlled at the time of the declaration is automatically forfeited. Property forfeited also includes all property given away at any time before the making of the declaration 'whether the gift was made before

---

43 A. Gray, 'The Compatibility of Unexplained wealth provisions and "civil" forfeiture regimes with Kable' (2012) 12 *QUT Law & Justice Journal* 18 and 'Forfeiture provisions and the criminal/civil divide' (2012) 15 *New Criminal Law Review* 32.

44 Parliamentary Joint Standing Committee on the Corruption and Crime Commission, *Proceeds of Crime and Unexplained Wealth: A Role for the Corruption and Crime Commission?* (Perth: Parliament of Western Australia, 2012) at 3.

45 Ibid., at 4.

46 Ibid., at 6.

or after the commencement of this Act'. In his evidence to an inquiry looking into unexplained wealth in Western Australia, the Director of Public Prosecution, Joseph McGrath, indicated that 'substantial unexplained wealth in [his] state is taken through drug-trafficker declarations' that in states lacking drug-trafficker declarations 'would be pursuing ... through unexplained wealth provisions'.[47] He calculated that of the nearly A\$60 million confiscated over the 11 years of the Act's operation, around two-thirds (A\$40.5 million) had been raised through drug-trafficker declarations. In its assessment of the various WA provisions relating to proceeds of crime and particularly unexplained wealth, the Booz Allen Hamilton report noted that use of the drug-trafficker declaration 'is far simpler for the government than use of UWOs [Unexplained Wealth Orders] or other alternatives under the legislation'.[48]

There have been more favourable assessments of unexplained wealth provisions in the Northern Territory, under its Criminal Property Confiscation Act 2003 (NT).[49] While substantially modelled on the Western Australian law, there are differences in form that possibly partly explain its perceived success relative to the WA experience. One is that the NT law allows the courts to take into consideration an offender's cooperation in forfeiture proceedings at the sentencing stage of criminal proceedings. This may have made the financial investigations required for an application more straightforward and hence less resource intensive. Another is that forfeiture requires a court order on constitutional grounds as well as a declaration; this has possibly vested greater confidence in its exercise by the DPP in contrast to the WA position. However, as we note later in our discussion of 'Next Steps', the evidential basis for measuring effectiveness of different asset recovery provisions in tackling organized crime is presently not strong and could be greatly improved.

At a Commonwealth level, the unexplained wealth provisions are yet to be tested in court, though there are a number of ongoing investigations. At this stage it is unclear how the courts will interpret the provisions. The experience in the two jurisdictions that have commenced proceedings, the Northern Territory and Western Australia, is that the majority of matters are settled prior to a hearing.

On 13 July 2011, the Parliamentary Joint Committee on Law Enforcement commenced an inquiry into Commonwealth unexplained-wealth legislation and arrangements. On 19 March 2012, the committee handed down its Final Report, which makes 18 recommendations to further improve the Commonwealth's unexplained wealth regime.[50] These include reducing a court's discretion to

---

47 Ibid., at 21.

48 Booz Allen Hamilton, *Comparative Evaluation of Unexplained Wealth Orders* at 73.

49 Parliamentary Joint Committee on the Australian Crime Commission, *Inquiry into the Legislative Arrangements to Outlaw Serious and Organised Crime Groups* (Canberra: Commonwealth of Australia, 2009).

50 Parliamentary Joint Committee on Law Enforcement, *Final Report on the Inquiry into Commonwealth Unexplained Wealth Legislation and Arrangements* (Canberra:

make unexplained wealth orders, removing the ability for assets covered by an unexplained wealth restraining order to be used to meet the person's legal costs, enhancing the ability to gather evidence in relation to unexplained wealth, and considering ways to minimize the link to offences within the power of the Commonwealth. If adopted, these recommendations will provide greater certainty in the litigation of matters pertaining to unexplained wealth. The government introduced the Crimes Legislation Amendment (Organised Crime and Other Measures) Bill 2012 in the house of representatives on 28 November 2012. This bill incorporates the majority of the recommendations made by the committee. The bill was referred to the Senate Legal and Constitutional Affairs Legislation Committee, which is due to report back on 13 March 2013.

Summary of Existing Measures

Table 6.1 provides a summary of, and comparison between, current measures.

Table 6.1   Summary of asset recovery measures in Australia

	Conviction-based forfeiture	Civil forfeiture	Unexplained wealth
Test	Beyond reasonable doubt; conviction for criminal offence	On balance of probabilities/more likely than not	On balance of probabilities/more likely than not
Onus of proof	Crown	Crown	Respondent
Types of orders	Restraining, forfeiture	Restraining, forfeiture, pecuniary penalty; literary proceeds	Restraining, unexplained-wealth order; drug-trafficker declaration
Principal agency responsible	DPP	DPP in Victoria, WA, NT, SA, and ACT; CMC (Qu.), NSWCC (NSW); CACTF (Cth)	DPP in WA, SA, NT, CACTF (Cth), NSWCC
Jurisdictions	All	Cth, ACT, NSW, Qld, SA, Vic	WA, NT, Cth, SA, Queensland,* NSW

Note: Adapted from Table 5.11 in Australia (Parliamentary Joint Committee on the Australian Crime Commission), *Inquiry into the Legislative Arrangements to Outlaw Serious and Organised Crime Groups* (Canberra: Commonwealth of Australia, 2009); * In bill form at time of writing (January 2013): Criminal Proceeds Confiscation (Unexplained Wealth and Serious Drug Offender Confiscation Order) Amendment Bill 2012.

Commonwealth of Australia, 2012): http://www.aph.gov.au/Parliamentary_Business/Com mittees/Senate_Committees?url=le_ctte/completed_inquiries/2010-13/unexplained_ wealth/report/index.htm (accessed 18 April 2013).

Joint Task Forces

The establishment of a new multi-agency Criminal Assets Confiscation Taskforce,[51] in early 2011 constitutes a major change to the way that Australia, at the federal level, investigates and litigates matters pertaining to the proceeds of crime. This initiative arises from a commitment made by the government during the 2010 Federal election. The model for the task force was developed following a consideration of other types of institutional arrangements for the investigation and litigation of criminal asset matters that had been adopted domestically and internationally, including criminal asset confiscation arrangements in the United Kingdom, Ireland, Canada, United States and New Zealand.

The task force is led by the AFP and brings together agencies with a key role in the investigation and litigation of proceeds of crime matters, including the ACC and the ATO. Task force investigations teams are located in several cities around Australia and incorporate a mix of specialist skills from the AFP including federal agents (police officers), forensic accountants and financial investigators. The ATO provides financial analysis support through co-located officers, and further support in the form of officers in its Serious Non-Compliance Teams, who take action on matters referred to them by the task force, where the ATO considers it is appropriate. The ACC also contributes co-located officers and provides support in target identification and strategic advice on money-flows that impact on Australia.

The establishment of the task force has also led to changes in the way that proceeds of crime matters are litigated. In December 2011, the parliament passed the Crimes Legislation Amendment Act (No. 2) 2011, which enabled the Commissioner of the AFP to conduct proceeds of crime litigation on behalf of the Criminal Assets Confiscation Taskforce. Prior to the passage of this legislation, the Commonwealth Director of Public Prosecution had been the only Commonwealth agency empowered to undertake proceeds of crime litigation.

Although now both the Commonwealth Director of Public Prosecutions and the AFP are each empowered under the act to undertake proceeds of crime litigation, a working agreement in place between the two agencies has resulted in the effective transfer of this function from the Commonwealth Director of Public Prosecutions to the Commissioner of the AFP. This transfer reflects the fact that proceeds of crime action has shifted away from reliance on a criminal conviction, especially with the expansion of non-conviction based forfeiture provisions and the introduction of unexplained-wealth provisions in 2010.

The Commissioner of the AFP has been responsible for the conduct of litigation for almost all new matters since 2 April 2012 and has also taken over the majority of proceeds of crime matters previously litigated by the Commonwealth Director of Public Prosecution. This work is undertaken by a dedicated group of litigators within the AFP, known as the Proceeds of Crime Litigation Team.

---

51   See http://www.afp.gov.au/policing/proceeds-of-crime.aspx (accessed 18 April 2013).

These litigators have been recruited from a broad range of areas, including from private commercial litigation practice, the bar and the Commonwealth and State Public Prosecutions Offices. Over half have a primarily civil, rather than criminal, litigation background. It is anticipated that this diversity of experience will encourage innovation and support a more proactive approach to criminal-asset confiscation. It also reflects the reality that proceeds of crime litigation is civil in nature, even though it is obviously closely connected with criminal investigation and prosecution, and is primarily a criminal law enforcement weapon.

The Proceeds of Crime Litigation Teams works collaboratively with the task-force investigations teams, and are co-located with the investigators in AFP offices around Australia. However, the litigation function is exercised independently of the investigators, and sits under a different management structure to that of the investigators. The commissioner's powers under the Proceeds of Crime Act have been delegated to the Manager, Proceeds of Crime Litigation.

As for the successes of the Criminal Assets Confiscation Taskforce, the task force has already reinvigorated efforts to target criminal profits. While the success of the task force will not be measured simply in terms of the amount of assets restrained and confiscated (disruptive effects on crime groups and referrals to revenue collection agencies, capacity to handle larger, more complex cases must also be considered), its establishment has already led to a large increase in the amount of assets restrained. In the 2011–2012 financial year, approximately A$97 million of assets were restrained as a result of investigations by the AFP and the task force, compared with almost A$41 million of assets in 2010–2011 and approximately A$18 million in 2009–2010.

The establishment of the Taskforce and Litigation team has also led to larger and more complex cases being pursued. Operation Beaufighter (which concerns a tax evasion and money-laundering scheme) is perhaps one of the best examples of the success of the collaborative approach taken by the task force.[52] It was also the first litigation conducted by the Proceeds of Crime Litigation Team.

The litigation is connected to a seven-month Project Wickenby[53] joint investigation between the AFP and ATO, which is the largest tax fraud investigation identified since Project Wickenby was launched in 2006. Following this investigation, the AFP charged a 67-year-old man with conspiring to dishonestly cause a loss to the Australian Taxation Office and conspiring to deal in the proceeds of crime to the value of $63 million. The task force conducted the proceeds of crime investigation, and luxury assets including prime real estate in Sydney and

---

52   See http://assistant.treasurer.gov.au/DisplayDocs.aspx?doc=pressreleases/2012/0 19.htm&pageID=003&min=djba&Year=&DocType= (accessed 18 April 2013).

53   Project Wickenby is a cross-agency task force, established in 2006, to protect the integrity of Australia's financial and regulatory systems by preventing people from promoting or participating in the abusive use of offshore secrecy havens. See http://www. ato.gov.au/corporate/content.aspx?doc=/content/00220075.htm (accessed 18 April 2013).

the Gold Coast, prestige vehicles and yachts, have been restrained. The criminal prosecution and proceeds of crime matters are still before the courts.

The objective behind the collaborative nature of the task force was to ensure that a coordinated and integrated approach to asset confiscation is adopted. The task force will seek to reduce duplication by allowing the development of the most effective strategy in each particular case, whether via proceeds action, tax remedies, civil debt recovery or recovery through international cooperation with foreign law-enforcement agencies. With the important involvement of the ATO, the task force also aims to protect the public finances of Australia from criminal abuse of the tax system.

The task force works closely with other Commonwealth agencies, and State and Territory law enforcement agencies. For example, one of the first investigations undertaken by the task force in April 2011 related to a joint investigation between the AFP, the Victoria Police, ACC and Customs and Border Protection into an organized crime syndicate that was allegedly trafficking drugs throughout Australia. As part of its investigation, officers from the task force seized approximately A\$4.5 million worth of assets, including two residential properties, a light aircraft and three luxury vehicles.[54]

Other Changes to Australia's Criminal Asset Recovery Regime

Australia has also made a number of changes to improve and expand its international mutual assistance regime. The Extradition and Mutual Assistance in Criminal Matters Legislation Amendment Act 2012 (Cth) received royal assent on 20 March 2012 and came into force on 20 September 2012. The Amendment Act followed a comprehensive review of Australia's international crime cooperation laws, which were first developed more than 20 years ago.

In the proceeds of crime sphere, these amendments will mean that from 20 September 2012, Australia will be able to register non-conviction based proceeds of crime orders from, and seek temporary non-conviction based restraining orders on behalf of, any country following a mutual assistance request. Australia can currently only register foreign non-conviction based proceeds of crime orders made in countries that are listed in regulations: the United States, the United Kingdom, Canada, Ireland and South Africa. Additionally, Australia can only seek temporary non-conviction based restraining orders on behalf of those same countries.

These changes to the mutual assistance regime reflect the more widespread use of non-conviction based proceeds of crime orders around the world. They will enable Australian authorities to act quickly to register these types of orders at the request of any country rather than being limited to countries specified in

---

54 Australian Federal Police, *Annual Report 2010–11* (Commonwealth of Australia, Canberra, 2011) at 50: http://www.afp.gov.au/media-centre/publications/~/media/afp/pdf/a/assumed-identities-annual-report-2010-2011.ashx (accessed 18 April 2013).

regulations. The previous process of having to list countries in the regulations was time consuming and as such could cause unnecessary delay (giving offenders the opportunity to disperse assets). The act also made some more minor amendments which streamline the process through which the Attorney-General can authorize investigative assistance for proceeds of crime related requests from a foreign country.

The Next Steps

Given the significant reform that has occurred in Australia's proceeds of crime regime over the last three years, the coming years are likely to see consolidation of these changes and attempts to ensure that they are implemented in the way that the legislatures intended.

For the Criminal Asset Confiscation Taskforce, the next few years will see it building its litigation capacity to ensure that it can realize the government's goal of a more proactive and integrated asset confiscation regime. This will include building relationships with both domestic and international partners with the aim of improving cooperation and sharing information on best practice approaches to asset confiscation. It will also be important to ensure that procedures are put in place to ensure that the new litigation powers are exercised independently and operate effectively. It is likely that the number and nature of appeals brought by the commissioner will increase, as the legislation is tested through the courts in a more proactive and robust way.

Efforts to continue the harmonization of laws across Australia's various jurisdictions will continue. The recent report of the Parliamentary Joint Committee on Law Enforcement has recommended that the 'issue of harmonization of unexplained wealth laws [be placed] on the agenda of the Standing Committee on Law and Justice',[55] a body on which the various attorneys-general and ministers for justice in Australia and New Zealand are represented. Currently, debates are ongoing about the best way of proceeding in this direction. The peculiarities of Australia's federal system mean that obtaining consensus between the different levels of government on how to harmonize may prove difficult.[56] At the same time, government ministers and senior police have recognized the risk of having gaps between jurisdictions on laws of this kind. There is at least anecdotal evidence that in response to the early adoption of unexplained wealth provisions in the

---

55 Parliamentary Joint Committee on Law Enforcement, *Commonwealth Unexplained Wealth Legislation and Arrangements*, Hansard, 7 March 2012, Recommendation 18, at 84.

56 This has certainly been the experience in the past. The fact that on constitutional grounds most criminal law matters are state and territory responsibilities means that there is an unavoidable structural impediment to coordinating legislative and other policy responses at national and international levels.

Northern Territory some organized crime players have moved out of the territory into adjacent Australian states.[57]

Cooperation between Australia's different agencies involved in this area also, arguably, merits further refinement in terms of sharing of returns from joint operations against organized crime groups with assets or property in different jurisdictions.

Another aspect of cooperation is acknowledging and utilizing the respective capacities of the agencies involved. While there has been considerable focus in policy terms in recent years upon the exercise of powers by police and law-enforcement bodies, there has been less focus upon the less prominent, but often more impressive, functions of taxation authorities, and especially the ATO. As David Lusty noted some years ago:

> The amount collected from criminals under federal income tax laws is around ten times greater than the total recovered under all Australian laws specifically designed for confiscating proceeds of crime, which include some of the broadest civil forfeiture laws in the world.[58]

Improving Australia's capability to cooperate with foreign jurisdictions will greatly enhance its ability to investigate unexplained wealth matters, as well as allowing authorities to respond to claims that wealth has been derived from legitimate sources overseas more effectively. As unexplained-wealth laws are adopted by more countries, there is likely to be greater focus on improved cooperation and relationship-building between those jurisdictions with unexplained wealth provisions. The Australian Government is already working to increase awareness of unexplained wealth laws in its law and justice capacity-building programmes in the Asia-Pacific region.

Showing the effectiveness of these measures, apart from dollars and realizable assets recovered, is an outstanding challenge. Arguably, too much effort currently focuses on *outputs* (e.g. dollars recovered) rather than *outcomes* (e.g. crime reduction). Evidence-based policy in this area remains weak. As Bartels has noted: 'It is not clear that such [confiscation] laws are having their desired, and at times, stated effect in terms of adversely impacting on criminal activity, especially in the context of organised crime.'[59]

Given the limited evidence of their effectiveness in disrupting and dismantling organized crime groups, managing expectations of these schemes will be important.

---

57 Parliamentary Joint Committee on the Australian Crime Commission, *Inquiry into the Legislative Arrangements to Outlaw Serious and Organised Crime Groups* (Commonwealth of Australia, Canberra, 2009) at 107–108, Evidence of Commander Colleen Gwynne, Northern Territory Police.

58 D. Lusty, 'Taxing the untouchables who profit from organised crime' at 214.

59 L. Bartels, *A Review of Confiscation Schemes in Australia*, Technical and Background Paper 36 (Canberra: Australian Institute of Criminology, 2010) at 24.

Further efforts could be made to increase publicity not only of the amounts seized in major cases, but also on the benefits to the community from these seizures and recoveries. As also noted earlier, the forfeiture of criminal assets is one of several key strategic directions in tackling organized crime in Australia. While there is clearly considerable illicitly-acquired wealth that has not yet been successfully restrained or forfeited, achieving greater success will depend in part upon the other components of the strategy also functioning effectively.

It is essential that multi-disciplinary teams capable and resourced to undertake the, often lengthy, financial investigations required are established and maintained. Experience in Australia points to the limitations associated with allowing these matters to remain principally or wholly in the hands of prosecution authorities. While objections of principle have been seen in one or two jurisdictions to partly explain the limited exercise of asset recovery mechanisms, the issue is more practical in nature. Lawyers are not usually trained or encouraged to specialize in the cognate areas required for competent financial investigations. These teams however are expensive undertakings. While they are capable of bringing in considerably more in dollar terms than their actual running expenses,[60] they are still vulnerable to being under-funded in a fiscally-restrained government environment.

Another practice seen in some jurisdictions including Queensland's Crime and Misconduct Commission, and the Commonwealth Crime and Corruption Task Force, is the placing of financial investigators within criminal investigation teams, thus bringing together the skills and legal powers of criminal investigators with those of financial specialists. This trend could be extended across all the Australian jurisdictions where, in many instances, criminal asset recovery remains a by-product or after thought in the context of criminal investigations and prosecutions. As Her Majesty's Inspectorate of Constabulary in the United Kingdom observed: 'Asset recovery must be seen as a crime-fighting tactic rather than [as just] an income generating tool.'[61]

Conclusions

Criminal asset recovery remains highly topical in Australia. At the time of writing (January 2013), the latest Communique from the Standing Council on Law and Justice (a group constituted principally by state, territory and national attorneys-general from Australia and New Zealand) dated 5 October 2012 recorded an agreement that the Council's Senior Officers Group on Organised Crime would develop 'measures to improve asset confiscation laws and the identification and

---

60   See, for example, the New South Wales Crime Commission, *Annual Report 2010–11* (Sydney: 2011).

61   Her Majesty's Inspectorate of Constabulary, *Payback Time: Joint Review of Asset Recovery Since the Proceeds of Crime Act 2002* (London: Home Office, 2004) at 9.

pursuit of unexplained wealth'.[62] After a period of reluctance among Australian jurisdictions to go down the path of unexplained wealth laws, the embrace represented by this approach is now on the cusp of becoming total. One can predict that all jurisdictions will be in line with it within one or two years. Further effort is needed to find ways in which the nine distinct criminal law jurisdictions, eight different police forces, a number of specialist law-enforcement agencies, nine different prosecution authorities, plus associated state, territory and national taxation authorities, not to mention the range of other government and private agencies holding information relevant to financial investigations, can cooperate more effectively in identifying suitable targets and bringing proceedings.

---

62   Standing Committee on Law and Justice, *Communique*, 5 October 2012.

Chapter 7

'Hitting Back' at Organized Crime: The Adoption of Civil Forfeiture in Ireland

Colin King[1]

Introduction

Organized crime is now firmly entrenched at the heart of popular discourse on crime in Ireland. Since the mid 1990s, there has been a raft of legislative measures enacted to combat the threat posed by organized crime, and politicians have been quick to resort to emotive sound bites justifying the need for ever-more draconian legislation that strikes at due process values. Over the past 15 years, there have, for example, been significant changes to anti-money laundering legislation,[2] the rules of surveillance,[3] powers of detention,[4] the law governing bail,[5] the law governing participation in organized crime type activities,[6] the adoption of civil forfeiture,[7] the establishment of the Criminal Assets Bureau,[8] and the establishment of an ad hoc witness protection programme. There has also been considerable academic commentary on how the threat of organized crime has influenced criminal justice reform in Ireland. For example, O'Donnell and O'Sullivan have discussed this in relation to zero-tolerance policing,[9] Campbell has examined how the pre-trial and trial process have been affected,[10] and Conway and Mulqueen have argued that there is now a shift towards the securitization of crime.[11] This chapter contributes to this debate by examining how organized crime was thrust into the heart of popular

1   I thank Prof. Dermot Walsh, Prof. Clive Walker and Dr Eimear Spain for valuable feedback.
2   Criminal Justice (Money Laundering and Terrorist Financing) Act, 2010.
3   Criminal Justice (Surveillance) Act, 2009.
4   Criminal Justice (Drug Trafficking) Act, 1996.
5   Bail Act, 1997; Criminal Justice Act, 2007.
6   Criminal Justice Act, 2006; Criminal Justice (Amendment) Act, 2009.
7   Proceeds of Crime Acts, 1996–2005.
8   Criminal Assets Bureau Act, 1996.
9   I. O'Donnell and E. O'Sullivan, 'The Politics of Intolerance – Irish Style' (2003) 43(1) *British Journal of Criminology* 41.
10   L. Campbell, 'Re-configuring the pretrial and trial processes in Ireland in the fight against organised crime' (2008) 12(3) *International Journal of Evidence and Proof* 208.
11   V. Conway and M. Mulqueen, 'The 2009 Anti-Gangland Package: Ireland's New Security Blanket?' (2009) 19(4) *Irish Criminal Law Journal* 106.

discourse in the law and order debate, and how the subsequent enactment of civil forfeiture legislation represented a radical shift in 'hitting back' at the upper echelons of organized criminal activity. A number of other jurisdictions have followed suit in enacting civil forfeiture legislation to target the illicit gains of organized criminal activities. For example, in the UK, the White Paper, *One Step Ahead*, emphasized that challenges posed by organized crime cannot be dealt with by conventional law-enforcement responses in isolation.[12] In this collection, Gallant demonstrates that the principal objective of civil forfeiture legislation in Canada 'is to scythe organised crime by scything its wealth'[13] while Goldsmith, Gray and Smith demonstrate how organized crime in Australia is now seen as a national security concern, resulting in the enactment of unexplained wealth legislation and the establishment of multi-agency task forces.[14]

This chapter demonstrates how the threat of organized crime has resulted in radical change to the conventional criminal process in Ireland. It examines the political rhetoric surrounding organized crime and argues that, in the wake of particularly sensationalist events, the political clamour to be seen as tough on crime has resulted in a radical new approach to combating organized crime, namely the use of the civil process to target ill-gotten gains. Although it has been argued that the move to the civil process represents a proportionate response to a serious societal problem,[15] namely the growing threat posed by organized crime, it is not, however, possible to sustain such an argument without detailed knowledge as to the nature and extent of organized crime. There is an inadequate knowledge base concerning organized crime in Ireland and, in its absence, there arises instead 'a web of mythical imagery and stereotypes'.[16] These myths enable sweeping political statements to be made about the scale of the problem posed by organized crime. With organized crime policy-making, all too often '"belief statements" exceed fact/observation based statements',[17] which does not bode well for law reform. As Campbell points out: 'Measured consideration and implementation of procedural reform is currently lacking in the Irish context, which is characterised by ad hoc and pragmatic rather than principled reactions to the perceived threat of organised criminality.'[18] This is especially important today, when Irish proceeds

---

12   Home Office, *One Step Ahead: A 21st Century Strategy to Defeat Organised Crime* (London: Stationery Office, 2004).

13   See Chapter 8.

14   See Chapter 6.

15   S. Murphy, 'Tracing the proceeds of crime: Legal and Constitutional Implications' (1999) 9(2) *Irish Criminal Law Journal* 160.

16   K. von Lampe, 'Making the second step before the first: Assessing organized crime: The case of Germany' (2005) 42 *Crime, Law and Social Change* 227 at 253.

17   P.C. van Duyne and T. Vander Beken, 'The incantation of the EU organised crime policy making' (2009) 51(2) *Crime, Law and Social Change* 261 at 278.

18   L. Campbell, 'Re-configuring the pretrial and trial processes in Ireland in the fight against organised crime' (2008) 12(3) *International Journal of Evidence and Proof* 208 at 233.

of crime legislation is being reviewed to ascertain the need for enhanced powers[19] but in the absence of any evaluation as to the effectiveness of the current regime.

Law Reform: The Politics of Organized Crime in Ireland

Indices of Change

While there had been concern in relation to, for example, armed robberies and the heroin epidemic in the Republic of Ireland during the 1980s,[20] it was only in the mid 1990s that the threat of organized crime really gained a foothold in political and popular minds. The context of the political discourse at that time reflects what Garland describes as *indices of change*.[21] These well-known landmarks of transformation in the criminal justice system include: the decline of the rehabilitative ideal; the re-emergence of punitive sanctions and expressive justice; changes in the emotional tone of crime policy; the return of the victim to centre stage; above all else, the public must be protected; issues of crime, law and order now figure prominently in the political world; the reinvention of the prison; the transformation of criminological thought; the expanding infrastructure of crime prevention and community safety; the role of civil society and the commercialization of crime control; new management styles and working practices; and a perpetual sense of crisis.[22] These indices of change are to be widely seen in the discourse surrounding reform of the Irish criminal justice system, particularly since the 1990s when the threat of organized crime gathered momentum as a political tool. Law and order is now high on the political agenda. In line with the changes discussed by Garland, there is a profound sentiment that the police must be afforded greater powers, so that criminals may be caught and punished, and the public protected. Expert research findings are often discarded on a whim in favour of more populist (and repressive) policies. Intuitively appealing strategies are seized upon, often

---

19   Criminal Assets Bureau, *Annual Report 2010* (Dublin: Stationery Office, 2011) para. 7.5.

20   See, for example, D. Bennett, 'Are they always right? Investigation and proof in a citizen anti-heroin movement' in M. Tomlinson, T. Varley and C. McCullagh (eds), *Whose Law and Order? Aspects of Crime and Social Control in Irish Society* (Belfast: Sociological Association of Ireland, 1988).

21   D. Garland, *The Culture of Control: Crime and Social Order in Contemporary Society* (Oxford: Oxford University Press, 2001).

22   See, for example, S. Hallsworth and J. Lea, 'Reconstructing Leviathan: Emerging contours of the security state' (2011) 15(2) *Theoretical Criminology* 141; L. Zedner, 'Securing liberty in the face of terror: Reflections from criminal justice' (2005) 32(4) *Journal of Law and Society* 507; D. Johnson, 'Anger about crime and support for punitive criminal justice policies' (2009) 11(1) *Punishment and Society* 51; S. Kilcommins and B. Vaughan, 'Reconfiguring State-Accused Relations in Ireland' (2006) 41 *Irish Jurist* (n.s.) 90.

without any empirical research to support (or discredit) the potential for success. This is even more so when, in the face of a particularly notorious incident, politicians are quick to seize the opportunity to introduce radical, perhaps even draconian, legislation in the fight against crime, in the interests of 'us'. These factors were illustrated in 1996 when the government reacted to two particularly notorious murders[23] by introducing a radical package of measures, including powers of civil forfeiture[24] and the establishment of the Criminal Assets Bureau,[25] which significantly altered relations between criminal justice authorities and the individual. These murders 'generated the conditions where a harsh response to perceived lawlessness became acceptable'.[26] The result was, what Garland refers to as, significant 'long-term structural transformations'[27] (as opposed to temporary and reversible short-term shifts in policy emphasis), that set the tone for future reform in dealing with the problem of organized crime. Yet, while demands for reform were particularly vociferous in the face of the ever-increasing threat posed by organized crime, it has been suggested that the term 'organized crime' only entered into popular discourse – and immediately took centre stage – in Ireland in 1996 on the back of media-driven and political influence.[28] These events might be seen as the precipitating factors in a long line of folk devils posing a threat to society;[29] organized crime would henceforth be elevated to the status of a security threat equivalent to the threat posed by paramilitaries.[30]

As Fennell emphasizes: 'The tenor of the debate and commentary is *never* without a context, never without a particular crime. Rarely is there a call for a

---

23   The murder of Detective Garda Jerry McCabe on 6 June 1996, during an armed robbery by members of a terrorist organization, followed by the murder of the journalist Veronica Guerin by a criminal gang on 26 June 1996, proved to be catalysts in law and order reform in Ireland.

24   Proceeds of Crime Act, 1996, as amended by the Proceeds of Crime (Amendment) Act, 2005.

25   Criminal Assets Bureau Act, 1996.

26   I. O'Donnell and E. O'Sullivan, 'The Politics of Intolerance – Irish Style' (2003) 43(1) *British Journal of Criminology* 41 at 48.

27   D. Garland, *The Culture of Control: Crime and Social Order in Contemporary Society* (Oxford: Oxford University Press, 2001) 22.

28   J. Meade, 'Organised crime, moral panic and law reform: The Irish adoption of civil forfeiture' (2000) 10(1) *Irish Criminal Law Journal* 11.

29   See S. Cohen, *Folk Devils and Moral Panics: The Creation of the Mods and Rockers* (Oxford: 3rd ed., Blackwell, 1987). For more recent discussion, in the context of organized crime, see M. Woodiwiss and D. Hobbs, 'Organized Evil and the Atlantic Alliance: Moral panics and the rhetoric of organized crime policing in America and Britain' (2009) 49(1) *British Journal of Criminology* 106.

30   S. Kilcommins and B. Vaughan, 'A perpetual State of Emergency: Subverting the rule of law in Ireland' (2004) 35 *Cambrian LR* 55 at 74.

more general debate.'[31] As O'Donnell notes, the origins of criminal justice policy-making is all too often found in the political reaction to a perceived crisis; reform is not 'informed by research findings and seldom tempered by rational debate'.[32] Yet, while certain reforms or policies might well be intuitively appealing, they are rarely evidence-led. The 1996 political response to perceived threats posed by organized crime might be described as 'fear management', all too often based on shaky foundations of knowledge as to the phenomenon of 'organized crime' itself.[33] This is strikingly true in the context of organized crime policy-making in Ireland. In the wake of what were highly emotive standpoints spanning the political spectrum, far-reaching legislation was quickly put on the statute book from which it is now difficult to retreat.

Regressive Policy-Making

The perception of a country embroiled in a crime crisis has been evident in the political arena over the past few decades. Since the 1990s, there has been a demonstrative shift towards repressive policies, designed to swing the pendulum in favour of the State in the criminal process.[34] There has been a marked demonization of those suspected (let alone convicted) of criminal activity, with the battle line firmly drawn between 'us' and 'them'. Politicians have made reference to 'home-grown Mafia',[35] 'godfathers of crime',[36] and 'professional, organised drug pushers'.[37] The system was seen as not working for 'us'. 'Criminals' had all the rights, and it was the innocent who suffered. Inevitably, such political rhetoric would result in a significant overhaul of the criminal justice system. There were vociferous calls to shift the balance of the law to the detriment of the criminal, for a recalibration of the scales of justice. A victim-orientated approach was demanded, backed up by criticism of the judiciary for being out of touch with reality. Conventional criminal procedure was seen as inadequate for combating the threat posed by organized crime and something more was perceived to be needed.

---

31   C. Fennell, *Crime and Crisis in Ireland: Justice by Illusion* (Cork: Cork University Press, 1993) 31.

32   I. O'Donnell, 'Crime and justice in the Republic of Ireland' (2005) 2(1) *European Journal of Criminology* 99 at 101.

33   P.C. van Duyne and T. Vander Beken, 'The incantation of the EU organised crime policy making' at 262.

34   See, for example, L. Campbell, 'Criminal justice and penal populism in Ireland' (2008) 28(4) *Legal Studies* 559.

35   Dáil Éireann, Private Members' Business – Organised Crime (Restraint and Disposal of Illicit Assets) Bill, 1996, Second Stage, 2 July 1996 vol. 467, col. 2442, per Deputy Alan Shatter.

36   Dáil Éireann, Private Members' Business – Measures Against Crime: Motion, 2 July 1996, vol. 467, col. 2396, per Deputy Mary Harney.

37   Seanad Éireann, Bail Bill, 1997, Second Stage, 23 April 1997, vol. 151, col. 277–278, per Senator Dan Neville.

Inevitably, there followed significant substantive and institutional changes, and, alongside changes made to criminal law and procedure,[38] civil forfeiture was adopted as a tool to target the assets of those engaged in criminal activity.

Perceived inadequacies of the criminal process could, so it was assumed, be cured by the use of the civil process to seize criminal assets. As Deputy Liz O'Donnell exclaimed,

> ... given the difficulties experienced in getting convictions, or even gathering evidence, a new power is needed to [restrain] the use of assets outside the context of criminal proceedings ... if we cannot arrest the criminals, why not confiscate their assets?[39]

This new approach, whereby the focus would be on the financial gains stemming from illicit activity, represented a radical change from the conventional criminal process involving investigation, arrest, charge and prosecution. It represented a significant re-calibration of the relationship between the State and the individual.[40] In a liberal democracy, such as Ireland, procedural protections such as the presumption of innocence, the right to silence and the right to trial by jury are often enshrined in the constitution.[41] In criminal proceedings, it is for the State to establish, beyond reasonable doubt, the guilt of an accused. The accused can remain mute and put the State to proof.[42] In civil forfeiture proceedings, however, such procedural protections are conveniently bypassed – for example the standard of proof is the civil standard, the balance of probabilities, and the respondent can be required to cooperate with the authorities (for example, by providing information as to income or sources of income). Before turning to the rationale of, and concern surrounding, civil forfeiture, we first must consider whether organized crime in Ireland represented such a threat as to merit the significant change of focus to targeting 'criminal' assets in the absence of the procedural safeguards of the criminal process.

---

38   For example, the Criminal Justice (Drug Trafficking) Act, 1996.

39   Dáil Éireann, Private Members' Business – Organised Crime (Restraint and Disposal of Illicit Assets) Bill, 1996, Second Stage, 2 July 1996, vol. 467, col. 2435.

40   C. King, 'Using civil processes in pursuit of criminal law objectives: a case study of non-conviction-based asset forfeiture' (2012) 16(4) *International Journal of Evidence and Proof* 337.

41   See generally, D. Walsh, *Criminal Procedure* (Dublin: Thomson Round Hall, 2002). There have, however, been significant encroachments upon these rights, often in response to threats posed by organized crime and terrorist activities.

42   Though, adverse inferences are increasingly permitted where a suspect does remain silent. See, for example, the Criminal Justice Act 2006, s72A, as inserted by s 9 of the Criminal Justice (Amendment) Act 2009.

Crime in Ireland: An Organized Crime Threat?

There can be no doubt that crime levels in Ireland have increased over time, albeit with significant fluctuations. The level of indictable offences consistently increased from 48,387 in 1975 to 102,387 in 1983. This was followed by a period when crime levels steadily declined – by 1987 the level of indictable offences stood at 85,358. This level, however, was followed by another period of growth reaching a peak of 102,484 in 1995. Another period of decline then followed, with the figure in 1999 standing at 81,274.[43] With the exception of 1987, overall crime rates were, at this time, at the lowest level since 1980. These trends are illustrated in Figure 7.1.

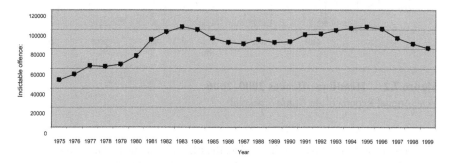

Figure 7.1   Indictable offences 1975–1999
Note: Annual Reports of *An Garda Síochána*.

In 2000, a new classification of offences was introduced to replace the old indictable/non-indictable offences categorization. This new classification distinguished between headline and non-headline offences.[44] In 2000, the number of headline offences began at 73,276 but quickly increased to a peak of 106,415 within two years. This dramatic increase in the official level of crime is, however, at least partly a consequence of procedural changes – for example the introduction of the PULSE (Police Using Leading Systems Effectively) computer system in 1999 and the adoption of the new classification of offences in 2000. Such changes distort any comparison with earlier years and particular caution must be exercised

---

43   These figures are taken from the annual reports of *An Garda Síochána* (Irish police). See also E. O'Sullivan and I. O'Donnell, 'Why is crime decreasing' (2001) 11(1) *Irish Criminal Law Journal* 2.

44   The headline/non-headline classification of offences was itself subsequently jettisoned after the Central Statistics Office assumed responsibility for publication of crime rates in 2006: Central Statistics Office *Irish Crime Classification System (ICCS)* (Dublin: 2008).

when interpreting official crime rates from this period. The level of headline offences remained relatively constant thereafter, hovering around the 100,000 mark.[45] This is illustrated in Figure 7.2.

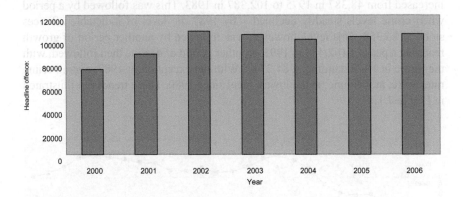

Figure 7.2   Headline offences 2000–2006
Note: Annual Reports of *An Garda Síochána*.

On their own, and taken at face value, the official statistics would suggest that, during the late 1990s and early 2000s, Ireland was a country with a relatively low crime problem,[46] notwithstanding a general perception that crime was a significant problem. Public concern was matched in the political arena, with politicians keen to wrap themselves in the mantle of law and order and calling for increased powers in support of criminal justice agencies. Added to public concern and political posturing was the portrayal of crime in the media, where the focus is often on extreme, atypical and sensational incidents. It is little wonder then that public perceptions of the crime situation do not correspond with the factual situation, at least as measured in the official statistics.[47]

Care must be exercised, however, when considering the official crime statistics. While the public perception of crime does not correspond with the situation reported in the official statistics, it must be recognized that the official statistics

---

45 The ICCS has now shifted emphasis away from a notional 'global figure' of crime: Central Statistics Office, *Irish Crime Classification System (ICCS)* (Dublin, 2008).

46 For an international comparison, see I. O'Donnell, 'Interpreting Crime Trends' (2002) 12(1) *Irish Criminal Law Journal* 10; I. O'Donnell, 'Patterns in crime' (2004) 14(2) *Irish Criminal Law Journal* 2.

47 M. O'Connell, 'Is Irish public opinion towards crime distorted by media bias?' (1999) 14(2) *European Journal of Communication* 191.

themselves do not portray a complete picture.[48] Official crime statistics suffer from a number of inherent and well-known deficiencies, including the fact that they do not include crimes that are not reported to the police or are not recorded if they are reported; traditionally, offences prosecuted by other agencies (such as welfare and revenue frauds and health and safety violations) were excluded; the statistics are susceptible to changes in counting rules or procedural changes; and they are affected by changes in public confidence in the police.[49] The overview presented by the total number of recorded offences is, therefore, somewhat misleading. As the Central Statistics Office has stressed: 'It is impossible to make definitive statements about total crime levels in Ireland by considering Garda recorded offences only.'[50] In relation to organized crime, these deficiencies are even more pronounced. For example, organized crime-type activities are included in broader categories that encompass a wide range of illegal, and more frequently occurring, criminal activities, and there might well be a lower propensity to report organized crime-related offences for fear of retaliation.[51] The ever-changing nature of organized crime[52] also presents its own difficulties for measuring organized criminal activities based solely on official statistics. Clearly, 'only very broad – if any – trends in the nature and extent of organised crime can be expected to find expression in the official crime statistics'.[53] Unlike other jurisdictions, there are few alternative sources of information as to the nature or scale of organized crime in Ireland – 'There remains an excessive dependence on the official picture; when this is unclear, explanation becomes difficult.'[54] Given that Ireland did not participate in the International Crime Victims Survey during the 1990s, there are difficulties with drawing a comparison with the extent of crime, particularly organized crime, in other jurisdictions at that time.

But, whilst official statistics do suffer from a number of limitations, it must be recognized that they remain a useful source of information so long as modest demands are made of the data. Furthermore, when it comes to more serious forms of criminal offences (particularly homicide offences, serious assault

---

48   Z. MacDonald, 'Official Crime statistics: Their use and interpretation' (2002) *The Economic Journal* F85.

49   See, for example, M. Maguire, 'Crime data and statistics' in M. Maguire, R. Morgan and R. Reiner (eds), *The Oxford Handbook of Criminology* (4th ed., Oxford: Oxford University Press, 2007).

50   Central Statistics Office, *Irish Crime Classification System (ICCS)* (Dublin: 2008) para. 2.2.

51   K. von Lampe, 'Making the second step before the first: Assessing organized crime: The case of Germany' (2004) 42 *Crime, Law and Social Change* 227 at 235–236.

52   See, generally, Europol, *EU Organised Crime Threat Assessment 2011* (The Hague: 2011).

53   K. von Lampe, 'Making the second step before the first: Assessing organized crime: The case of Germany' (2004) 42 *Crime, Law and Social Change* 227 at 236.

54   I. O'Donnell, 'Crime and Justice in the Republic of Ireland' (2005) 2(1) *European Journal of Criminology* 99 at 109.

etc.), such offences are more likely to come to the attention of the authorities and consequently be included in official statistics than, say, a minor incident of criminal damage.[55] Reference to official statistics, then, is particularly important in the context of considering political responses to organized crime (albeit not the extent of organized crime itself). While the total number of recorded crimes fell during the 1990s, offences that capture the public attention did increase. For example, the number of Group I offences (encompassing offences against the person, such as murder, manslaughter, dangerous driving causing death, traffic fatalities, possession of firearms with intent to endanger life, assault and other related offences) increased 16.9 per cent over the time period 1990–1998 – from 1,631 to 1,907 offences. Increases in, for example, the number of unlawful killings served to contribute to the perception that the country was engulfed in a crime crisis.[56] The number of murders in 1990 was 16, and 14 of these had been detected. However, by the middle of the decade – in 1995, the year prior to the anti-crime package announced in the summer of 1996, – the number of murders had increased to 41, with 30 of these detected.[57] Similarly, increases can be seen in drug-related offences too. In 1990 the number of persons charged under the Misuse of Drugs Acts, 1977–1984 was 2,071 (which itself represented a 54.1 per cent increase on the previous year).[58] In 1995, the number of persons charged had increased to 3,730.[59] The National Crime Forum, established to gauge comments and suggestions from the general public and relevant experts, stated: 'There is considerable, and understandable, public concern at the damage which the recent growth in drug abuse is doing: the lives wrecked, the attendant crimes and the development of a significant criminal underworld.'[60] Clearly then, it would be wrong to simply dismiss, without more, political reaction to the crime situation – particularly that concerning organized crime – as simply yet another moral panic.

---

55   For consideration of some of the uses of official statistics, see W.G. Skogan, 'The validity of official crime statistics: An empirical investigation' (1974) *Social Science Quarterly* 25.

56   See, for example, E. Dooley, *Homicide in Ireland 1992–1996* (Dublin: Stationery Office, 2001).

57   In 2000 these figures were, respectively, 39 and 32 (and there have been significant increases in subsequent years too).

58   This is the overall figure, as given in the *Garda* Annual Report, which does not distinguish between different forms of drug offence. The Annual Report does state, however, that the increase relates mainly to small amounts of cannabis and cannabis resin for personal use and does not indicate any great increase in trafficking. An Garda Síochána, *Annual Report on Crime 1990* (Dublin: Stationery Office, 1991) 35.

59   The quantities of drugs seized are also significant in this time period; heroin seizures increased from 578.24 g to 6.4 kg, while cocaine seizures increased from 1008.60 g to 21.8 kg.

60   *Report of the National Crime Forum* (Dublin: Institute of Public Administration, 1998) 69.

The concern, though, is whether the subsequent response, the adoption of wide-ranging reforms to the criminal justice system, was a form of reactionary politics that strikes to the heart of respect for human rights and due process values.[61] While it has been suggested that the Proceeds of Crime Act is 'a proportionate response to the dramatic growth in organised crime which has occurred in the past decade',[62] such a sweeping generalized statement withers under scrutiny in the absence of supporting evidence. What, for example, do we know of the nature and/or extent of organized crime in Ireland? The answer is not a lot.[63] There is, inevitably, an element of uncertainty, therefore, when discussing the proportionality, and/or effectiveness, of civil forfeiture as a response to organized criminal activities, not to mention a number of caveats that must constantly be born in mind. Such uncertainty, however, does not prevent politicians and/or law-enforcement officials lauding the benefits of this innovative tool.

Arguments in Favour of Civil Forfeiture

The adoption of civil forfeiture represented a significant change of approach in the fight against organized crime in Ireland, a shift away from the conventional criminal process of investigation, prosecution, conviction, punishment. The Proceeds of Crime Act authorizes seizure, and ultimately forfeiture, of property absent of criminal conviction, often based on hearsay evidence and on the civil standard of proof. One of the main arguments used to justify civil forfeiture concerns the procedural benefits that it carries. As we have seen already, in the mid-1990s, there was a widespread belief that the criminal process alone was inadequate to deal with the threat posed by organized crime. Something more was deemed to be needed, namely the use of the civil process to target those at the upper echelons

---

61   A more cynical perspective might point to the fact that the Private Members' Organised Crime (Restraint and Disposal of Illicit Assets) Bill was introduced in such a short time-frame after the McCabe and Guerin murders which would suggest that politicians were simply waiting for an opportune moment to introduce the proposals to the *Oireachtas* (legislature) after a previous unsuccessful attempt in the early 1990s.

62   S. Murphy, 'Tracing the proceeds of crime: Legal and Constitutional Implications' (1999) 9(2) *Irish Criminal Law Journal* 160. Compare P.A.J. Waddington, 'Mugging as a moral panic: A Question of proportion' (1986) 37(2) *British Journal of Sociology* 245.

63   There are, of course, significant difficulties in gauging the threat of organized crime. See T. Vander Beken, 'Risky business: A risk-based methodology to measure organized crime' (2004) 41 *Crime, Law and Social Change* 471. In the UK, there have been attempts to quantify the threat posed by organized crime activities, for example: S. Brand and R. Price, *The economic and social costs of crime* (London: Home Office, 2000); Performance and Innovation Unit *Recovering the Proceeds of Crime* (London: Cabinet Office, 2000); Home Office, *One Step Ahead: A 21st Century Strategy to Defeat Organised Crime* (London: Stationery Office, 2004).

of criminal activity.[64] In civil forfeiture proceedings to seize 'criminal' assets, the State does not have to establish guilt or, indeed, any wrongdoing on the part of an individual.[65] The State simply has to establish that the property concerned constitutes proceeds of crime. And, of course, given that it purports to be a civil process, the standard of proof is on the balance of probabilities as opposed to the higher standard of beyond reasonable doubt required in criminal proceedings. Further, the presumption of innocence does not apply in such proceedings. Clearly, resort to the civil process is attractive to law-enforcement agencies, not least because it is, for the most part, more efficient and expedient than the more cumbersome criminal process.[66]

Related to such procedural indulgences is the view that civil forfeiture is an ideal (indeed, perhaps the only) method of targeting those at the upper echelons of organized criminal groups. If they cannot be brought to justice in the conventional manner, then at least the financial incentive for engaging in criminal activity can be removed. As has been pointed out by Simser: 'Where organized crime insulates itself from culpability through the use of foot soldiers, civil forfeiture can still effectively get at the lifeblood of the organization – its money.'[67] According to Ashe and Reid: 'The phenomenon of the controllers being able to insulate themselves has long been the major issue in combating organised crime, and the 1996 legislation [*namely, the Proceeds of Crime Act, 1996 and the Criminal Assets Bureau Act, 1996*] in Ireland may be seen as a direct attack on those people by attacking directly the proceeds of crime.'[68] In *M v D*, Moriarty J referred to:

> the international phenomenon, far from peculiar to Ireland, that significant numbers of persons who engage as principals in lucrative professional crime, particularly that referable to the illicit supply of controlled drugs, are alert and effectively able to insulate themselves against the risk of successful criminal prosecution through deployment of intermediaries.[69]

Moriarty J went on to state that the Proceeds of Crime Act 'is designed to enable the lower probative requirements of civil law to be utilised in appropriate cases, not

---

64 Official discourse focuses on a hierarchical idea of 'organised crime', though the reality is often very different. See, for example, Z.J. Alach, 'An incipient taxonomy of organised crime' (2011) 14(1) *Trends in Organized Crime* 56.

65 See, for example, *Murphy v Gilligan* [2011] IEHC 62.

66 T. Jaggar and M. Sutherland Williams, 'Civil recovery: Then and Now' (2010) *Criminal Bar Quarterly* 5; T.P. Farley, 'Asset forfeiture reform: A law enforcement response' (1994) 39 *New York Law School Law Review* 149.

67 J. Simser, 'Perspectives on civil forfeiture' in S. Young (ed.), *Civil Forfeiture of Criminal Property: Legal Measures for Targeting the Proceeds of Crime* (Cheltenham: Edward Elgar, 2009) 20.

68 M. Ashe and P. Reid, 'Ireland: The Celtic Tiger bites – The attack on the proceeds of crime' (2001) 4(3) *Journal of Money Laundering Control* 253 at 256.

69 [1998] 3 IR 175, 178.

to achieve penal sanctions, but to effectively deprive such persons of such illicit financial fruits of their labours as can be shown to be proceeds of crime'.[70] Given that criminal convictions are all too often seen to be beyond reach in relation to the 'organizers', post-conviction confiscation of criminal assets is, of course, also not possible. Even where criminal convictions are secured, deficiencies in post-conviction forfeiture regimes often mean that criminals are in a position to enjoy their ill-gotten gains (and, indeed, to use such gains for further criminal activity) after punishment. It is not surprising then that the non-conviction approach has grown in prominence in recent decades. This approach is increasingly being used across the common-law world (for example, in the USA, Canada, Australia, the UK and South Africa)[71] in the fight against organized crime.

Criticism of Civil Forfeiture

The first criticism of civil forfeiture is that it is not necessary, that the conventional criminal justice system is in fact adequate to tackle organized crime. Police and prosecution authorities have a vast arsenal available to them for tackling criminal behaviour. For example, there are, *inter alia*, powers: to stop and question; to stop and search; of entry, search and seizure; to issue search warrants (including some vested in the police); of arrest, detention and questioning; of surveillance; to restrict the right to bail; to draw adverse inferences and encroach upon the right to silence; to try without a jury; to protect witnesses; to shift the evidential burden of proof onto the accused in certain circumstances; to impose mandatory sentencing; and to use anti-terrorism powers. In recent decades, this array of powers has been further enhanced, and there is a demonstrative shift towards the crime control model at the expense of due process norms.[72] It would certainly appear that the Criminal Assets Bureau itself is focused on pursuing, to the utmost of its powers, those suspected, accused and/or convicted of criminal wrongdoing. For example, the Bureau has targeted a person with a conviction for armed robbery and suspected of being a significant player in drug trafficking,[73] a person with convictions for murder, drugs offences and firearms offences,[74] people suspected of,[75] or convicted

---

70 Ibid.

71 For discussion of developments in Australia and Canada, see chapters 6 and 8 respectively.

72 See, for example, A. Ryan, 'Arrest and detention: A review of the law' (2000) 10(1) *Irish Criminal Law Journal* 2; S. Kilcommins and B. Vaughan, 'Reconfiguring State-accused relations in Ireland' (2006) 41 *Irish Jurist* (n.s) 90.

73 'Hands-on worker has armed raid conviction here' *Irish Times*, 6 March 1998.

74 'Killer made £720,000 in drugs deal' *Irish Times*, 30 July 1999.

75 'Assets bureau seizes €17,360 in cash from drug dealer' *Irish Times*, 9 October 2007.

of,[76] involvement in the drugs trade, those engaged in corruption,[77] and people with convictions for receiving and/or handling stolen property.[78] Given that the Bureau purports to operate outside the conventional criminal process, procedural safeguards that are insisted upon in the criminal process do not apply.

Inevitably, the adoption of civil forfeiture raises serious issues as to the rights of the individual, not least because a person 'charged' with involvement in criminal activity is effectively 'tried' in civil proceedings but stripped of the benefit of criminal process procedural protections such as the presumption of innocence and the higher criminal standard of proof.[79] The adoption of civil forfeiture as a tool of law enforcement has been described as 'a frontal assault on due process'.[80] Another commentator has suggested that States are enacting such procedures for the express purpose of imposing punishment while avoiding the heavy burden of safeguards afforded to an individual in the criminal process.[81] As Piety points out:

> The doctrine of civil forfeiture has turned into a legal juggernaut, crushing every due process claim thrown in its path: the privilege against self-incrimination, the prohibition against cruel and unusual punishment, the right to trial by jury, the right to a verdict rendered only after a finding of guilt beyond a reasonable doubt, the right to be free from being twice charged with the same offense, the right to be free from government seizures of property absent probable cause, and the right to counsel of choice. All of the claims to these rights have been rejected, and their existence limited, or eliminated entirely, in the realm of civil forfeiture ... Because the entire civil forfeiture doctrine is made up of legal fictions that if applied in a logically consistent manner provide no internal check on the government's power to employ forfeiture, its application is virtually unbounded.[82]

It might be suggested that since certain 'civil' sanctions exact punishment as severe as criminal sanctions, they ought to attract enhanced safeguards that are inherent in criminal procedure. Cheh, however, while recognizing that 'this idea is

---

76 'Contest over Gilligan's millions' *Irish Times*, 17 November 2005.

77 'The political fixer who can't hide from the past' *Irish Times*, 29 November 2003.

78 'Couple oppose Cab order to seize house, ring and cash' *Irish Times*, 19 March 2010.

79 A. Ashworth, 'Is the criminal law a lost cause?' (2000) 116 *Law Quarterly Review* 225.

80 J. Lea, 'Hitting criminals where it hurts: Organised crime and the erosion of due process' (2004) 35 *Cambrian Law Review* 81 at 83.

81 S. Klein, 'Civil in rem forfeiture and double jeopardy' (1996–1997) 82 *Iowa Law Review* 183 at 188.

82 T.R. Piety, 'Scorched Earth: How the expansion of civil forfeiture doctrine has laid waste to due process' (1991) 45(4) *University of Miami Law Review* 911 at 921–924.

appealingly straightforward and, sometimes, equitably compelling',[83] rejects this proposition.

> Though the severity of a civil sanction may be an important consideration in applying various constitutional safeguards, the [US] Supreme Court has never adopted this approach. This *sanction equivalency* approach has many serious flaws, not the least of which is the longstanding acceptance of the civil label even as applied to huge punitive damage awards and fabulous forfeitures. Even if one were to confine the argument to only those sanctions that involve losses of liberty equivalent to the quintessential criminal sanctions of incarceration, it is clear that the courts consistently have treated certain deprivations of physical liberty, such as imprisonment for civil contempt and involuntary commitment of the mentally ill, as civil in nature.

> But, mindful of Holmes's admonition that we should have better reasons than just history to support our legal rules, we also should reject the sanction equivalency approach because of practical, common sense concerns. The criminal procedural protections set out in the Constitution are extremely costly and time consuming. In fact, they may add nothing to and even frustrate the goals of fairness, accuracy, and truth-finding. One can view the Bill of Rights itself as a balancing of interests between the costs of procedures and the benefits they confer. Any decision to extend procedural protections beyond those instances where they clearly apply requires a similar calculation.[84]

While Cheh proceeds on the assumption that criminal law safeguards ought not be extended to the imposition of civil sanctions, it is certainly arguable that 'civil' forfeiture is not, de facto, a civil sanction; rather, it is a criminal punishment designed to punish *criminals* for their wrongdoing.[85] It is important to distinguish between *punishment* and *criminal punishment*. As Packer states: 'Not all punishment is criminal punishment but all criminal punishment is punishment.'[86] While civil sanctions, such as punitive damages, imprisonment for contempt and involuntary commitment of the mentally ill can be seen as punitive, they do

---

83   M.M. Cheh, 'Constitutional limits on using civil remedies to achieve criminal law objectives: Understanding and transcending the criminal-civil law distinction' (1991) 42 *Hastings LJ* 1325 at 1350. See further, for the UK Supreme Court's position, *Gale v Serious Organised Crime Agency* [2011] UKSC 49.

84   Ibid., at 1350–1351.

85   See, for example, L. Campbell, 'Theorising asset forfeiture in Ireland' (2007) 71 *Journal of Criminal Law* 441; J. Meade, 'The Disguise of civility: Civil forfeiture of the proceeds of crime and the presumption of innocence in Irish law' (2000) *Hibernian Law Journal* 1.

86   H.L. Packer, *The Limits of the Criminal Sanction* (Palo Alto: Stanford University Press, 1968) 35.

not seek to *criminally* punish a person for wrongdoing. Forfeiture, however, is different, and it is contended that Cheh errs in classifying forfeiture as a civil sanction. Indeed, as has been stressed by Naylor: 'It is impossible to declare a car or house or bank account to be the proceeds of cocaine sales, for example, without simultaneously smearing its owner with the accusation of drug trafficking.'[87]

Cheh further rejects the sanction equivalency approach because of practical, common sense concerns. She regards criminal procedural protections as costly, time-consuming, and an obstacle to the pursuit of fairness, accuracy and truth-finding. As we have seen, a similar viewpoint pervaded political debates in the build-up to the enactment of the Proceeds of Crime Act and the establishment of the Criminal Assets Bureau. Such a focus on the concern for efficiency and expediency at the expense of due process is troubling, not least since it casts to one side the foundational principles of criminal evidence.[88] Demands for harsher, more repressive responses to 'the crime problem' have fed through into significant substantive, institutional and procedural reforms that significantly strengthen the hand of the State in the criminal process. Such reform is, of course, at the expense of individual rights. Rather than balancing the interests of the State in prosecuting criminals against the rights of the individual, the scales of justice are now firmly weighed in favour of the State, at the expense of due process norms. It has been said that 'the delicate equilibrium between freedom from government and public protection is being unsettled by an anxious State determined to show strength by "tooling up" in the fight against crime'.[89] Yet, as Costigan and Thomas point out:

> Due process is not inconsistent with the notion of crime suppression: as a normative model, it prescribes the *procedure* to be employed in the prosecution of offenders. Although the due process model is commonly seen to imply a reduction in the efficiency of the criminal process, this view is predicated on the notion that fact-finding reliability is of secondary importance as a value. But public confidence is not secured simply by high rates of prosecution and conviction, as the reaction to publicised miscarriages of justice has shown; adherence to due process is essential to the very legitimacy of the criminal justice system.[90]

Indeed, it is questionable whether there ought to be any further balancing exercise when criminal matters are at issue. A balance has already been achieved

---

87   R.T. Naylor, 'Wash-out: A critique of follow-the-money methods in crime control policy' (1999) 32(1) *Crime, Law and Social Change* 1 at 41.

88   See, generally, P. Roberts and A. Zuckerman, *Criminal Evidence* (Oxford: Oxford University Press, 2010).

89   S. Kilcommins and B. Vaughan, 'Reconfiguring state-accused relations in Ireland' (2006) 41 *Irish Jurist* (n.s) 90 at 92.

90   R. Costigan and P.A. Thomas, 'Anonymous witnesses' (2000) 51 *Northern Ireland Legal Quarterly* 326 at 357–358.

– requiring, *inter alia*, the presumption of innocence, with the burden of proof upon the State to prove its case beyond reasonable doubt, alongside exclusionary rules of evidence – and, it is submitted, the rights afforded to an individual under the criminal process ought not be jettisoned, in the interests of efficiency and expediency, simply by labelling a process as 'civil'. That, however, is the effect of the Proceeds of Crime Act. By virtue of its placement in the civil realm, it is able to circumvent criminal procedural safeguards. While the government of the day wanted to demonstrate a stance of being tough on crime, it effected a radical shift in the relationship between the State and the individual, enacting legislation with profound long-term implications, and which is, of course, difficult to reverse (at least for any government with aspirations of re-election).

Judicial Reactions

Notwithstanding such criticisms, civil forfeiture has withstood constitutional scrutiny before the Irish courts. The seminal decision on the Proceeds of Crime Act was delivered by the Supreme Court in *Murphy v GM, PB, PC Ltd, GH; Gilligan v CAB*.[91] The central issue there was whether proceedings under the Act are civil or criminal in nature. If they are criminal then they would fall foul of constitutionally protected safeguards. As Keane CJ stated:

> It is almost beyond argument that, if the procedures under ss. 2, 3 and 4 of the Act of 1996 constituted in substance, albeit not in form, the trial of persons on criminal charges, they would be invalid having regard to the provisions of the Constitution. The virtual absence of the presumption of innocence, the provision that the standard of proof is to be on the balance of probabilities and the admissibility of hearsay evidence taken together are inconsistent with the requirement in Article 38.1 of the Constitution that
>
> > "No person shall be tried on any criminal charge save in due course of law."
>
> It is also clear that, if these procedures constitute the trial of a person on a criminal charge, which, depending on the value of the property, might or might not constitute a minor offence, the absence of any provision for a trial by jury of such a charge in the Act would clearly be in violation of Article 38.5 of the Constitution.[92]

---

91   [2001] 4 IR 113.

92   *Murphy v GM, PB, PC Ltd, GH; Gilligan v CAB* [2001] 4 IR 113, 135–136. Compare *FJMcK v AF and JF* [2002] IR 242, 258–259.

After a review of the case law, Keane CJ found that the *indicia* of a 'crime', set out in *Melling v O'Mathghamhna*,[93] are not present in the Act of 1996:

> In contrast, in proceedings under ss. 3 and 4 of the Act of 1996, there is no
> provision for the arrest or detention of any person, for the admission of persons
> to bail, for the imprisonment of a person in default of payment of a penalty, for
> a form of criminal trial initiated by summons or indictment, for the recording of
> a conviction in any form or for the entering of a *nolle prosequi* at any stage.[94]

The Irish Supreme Court, however, focused more on form rather than substance. The Proceeds of Crime Act is, it is contended, punitive. Civil forfeiture was adopted to 'hit back' at those engaged in crime and the underlying punitive sentiment is clear to see. Further, it was felt that targeting illicit assets would act as a deterrent in that it would eliminate the incentive to commit crime and also remove the capital for further criminal activity. Where proceedings are initiated against a specified individual, so too would that individual experience some form of social stigma.

The Irish courts, however, have rejected the contention that the Proceeds of Crime Act is punitive. In *Gilligan v CAB*, McGuinness J, while recognizing that the Proceeds of Crime Act provides 'a method of attacking a certain form of criminality', went on to say that removal of the proceeds of crime 'could well be viewed in the light of reparation rather than punishment or penalty'.[95] In *M v D*, Moriarty J expressed the view that the Act was designed 'not to achieve penal sanctions, but to effectively deprive [*the principals of professional crime*] of such illicit fruits of their labours as can be shown to be proceeds of crime'.[96] Given that the highest courts in Ireland have consistently upheld the civil nature of the Proceeds of Crime Act, there is little prospect of any further constitutional challenge proving successful in this respect. Civil forfeiture legislation is, however, expected to be challenged before the European Court of Human Rights in the not-too-distant future.[97]

---

93   [1962] IR 1.
94   [2001] 4 IR 113, 147.
95   [1998] 3 IR 185, 217–218.
96   [1998] 3 IR 175, 178.
97   In Ireland, it has long been anticipated that the decision in *Gilligan v CAB* [1998] 3 IR 185 (HC), [2001] 4 IR 113 (SC) would be pursued in Strasbourg, while in *Gale v Serious Organised Crime Agency* [2011] UKSC 49 the UK Supreme Court indicated at paras 32 (Lord Phillips), 60 (Lord Clarke), and 117 (Lord Brown) that this area would benefit from consideration by the Grand Chamber of the European Court of Human Rights. For further consideration of civil forfeiture and the ECHR, see C. King, 'Civil forfeiture and Article 6 of the ECHR: Due process implications for England and Wales and Ireland' (2013) *Legal Studies* (forthcoming, DOI: 10.1111/lest.12018).

'Hitting Back' at Organized Crime?

How effective is civil forfeiture at denying criminals the benefit of their ill-gotten gains? Has it had a significant impact on how organized crime groups conduct their activities? Has it acted as a valid deterrent? These, and other, questions are important when examining how effective civil forfeiture has been in hitting back at organized crime. The impact of civil forfeiture is especially relevant today in that the Irish Minister for Justice, Equality and Defence has established a committee to consider the effective implementation of proceeds of crime legislation.[98]

It has been recognized that '[e]valuating the effectiveness of a law, especially the effectiveness of unexplained wealth laws, is a complex and difficult task'.[99] At this point, it is worth briefly reviewing some anecdotal evidence concerning the Proceeds of Crime Act. It is widely believed that the Act has impacted upon the activities of organized crime groups, either in the form of disrupting and/ or dismantling their illicit activities. In the years immediately following the enactment of the Act, there was a concerted focus on persons who were suspected of directing organized-crime type activities and who had accumulated significant wealth, all with no apparent legitimate income to sustain such wealth. For various reasons, even though such individuals were known to the police there was insufficient evidence against them to justify bringing a criminal prosecution. The adoption of civil forfeiture had a significant impact on the Irish crime scene, notably in that many criminal figures moved from Ireland to the continent, often Spain or the Netherlands. In reality, though, these people continued to direct criminal activity from afar. Even where they ceased all involvement in the Irish crime scene the vacuum was quickly filled by new crime groups. Significantly, the Criminal Assets Bureau was in a position to seize at least some of the accumulated assets held by these people before they could be removed from the jurisdiction. While money, for example, was easily transferable it was not always possible for property to be sold before the Bureau came calling. After initial 'success', the Bureau turned to middle- and lower-ranking criminals. While the Bureau has recognized that this 'may not realise extensive funds', it 'illustrates the Bureau's ability to react to local community concern and as such is seen as an effective use of Bureau resources'.[100]

Turning now to the (admittedly limited) statistical evidence that is available. The annual reports of the Criminal Assets Bureau provide some insight into the use of the Proceeds of Crime Act. According to its 2010 Annual Report, the Bureau obtained 12 consent disposal orders (to the value of €2,810,902.52), as well as

---

98   Criminal Assets Bureau, *Annual Report 2010* (Dublin: Stationery Office, 2011) para. 7.5.

99   Booz Allen Hamilton, *Comparative Evaluation of Unexplained Wealth Orders: Prepared for the US Department of Justice, National Institute of Justice* (Washington, DC: 2011) 103.

100   Criminal Assets Bureau, *Annual Report 2007* (Dublin: Stationery Office, 2008) 'Letter to Commissioner from Chief Bureau Officer'.

14 interim orders (€7,019,475.88 and Stg£63,535) and 17 interlocutory orders (€4,526,527.72) during that year. Annual reports regularly proclaim, for example, that the Bureau 'has had another successful year in the context of pursuing its statutory remit'.[101] In the political arena, so too we hear statements such as:

> The Criminal Assets Bureau has been at the forefront of the fight against organised crime, including drug trafficking, in this jurisdiction since its inception in 1996. The significant successes that the Bureau continues to achieve by its operations demonstrates the effectiveness of its approach in pursuing illegally gotten gains.[102]

This statement was accompanied by the figures published in the Annual Reports – see Table 7.1 below. Such self-congratulation rests on the value of assets realized by the Bureau. These figures, though, do not allow any meaningful assessment of the Proceeds of Crime Act. The figures simply demonstrate that the Bureau has successfully utilized the provisions under the Proceeds of Crime Act, but tell us little else. These figures do not, for example, tell us how much an impact the Bureau has had in disrupting and/or deterring organized crime activities.

Table 7.1   Monies secured by CAB from 1996–2007

Year	s.2 Interim Order	s.3 Interlocutory Order	s.4 and 4A Disposal Order
1996	IR£2,101,000	IR£2,048,000	n/a
1997	IR£2,334,680	IR£1,496,180	n/a
1998	IR£1,682,545	IR£1,091,413	n/a
1999	IR£1,500,000	IR£813,659	n/a
2000	IR£838,536 Stg£52,230	IR£1,641,215	n/a
2001	IR£1,872,655 Stg£491,114	IR£1,342,951 Stg£279,635	n/a
Total: 1996–2001	*IR£10,329,416 Stg£543,344*	*IR£8,433,418 Stg£279,635*	*n/a*
Total euro equivalent: 1996–2001	*€13,115,652*	*€10,708,231*	*n/a*

    101   Criminal Assets Bureau, *Annual Report 2010* (Dublin: Stationery Office, 2011) 'Letter to Minister from Commissioner'.

    102   Dáil Éireann Debates, vol. 661, Written Answer – Criminal Assets Bureau, 24 September 2008, Minister Dermot Ahern.

Year	s.2 Interim Order	s.3 Interlocutory Order	s.4 and 4A Disposal Order
2002	€3,709,086 Stg£17,802,004 US$5,558,377	€2,504,669 Stg£1,993,094 US$5,247,821	n/a
2003	€3,045,842 Stg£12,150	€71,699 Stg£557,070	n/a
2004	€1,027,152 Stg£6,115	€1,688,652 Stg£375	€275,875
2005	€5,860,335 US$314,620	€1,200,526 Stg£26,760 US$130,000	€2,002,738
2006	€2,836,480 Stg£ 294, 289	€726,351	€2,459,865
2007	€9,804,193 Stg30,690	€9,848,433	€1,435,341
Total: 2002–2007	*€26,283,088 Stg£18,145,248 US$5,872,997*	*€16,040,330 Stg£2,577,299 US$5,377,821*	*€6,173,819*
Total: 1996– 2007	*€39,398,740 Stg£18,688,592 US$5,872,997*	*€26,748,561 Stg£2,856,934 US$5,377,821*	*€6,173,819*

Note: Adapted from Dáil Éireann Debates, vol. 661, Written Answer – Criminal Assets Bureau, 24 September 2008, Minister Dermot Ahern.

Experience from Australia demonstrates that despite a lack of evidence as to the effectiveness of proceeds of crime legislation such legislation has become progressively more severe.[103] Ireland must be careful not to follow the same route in the absence of evidence that civil forfeiture, and other follow-the-money techniques, are having the desired effect. A rigorous evaluation of the Proceeds of Crime Act is required before any policy decision is made (as is the task of the committee reviewing the Irish legislation) as to 'whether statutory amendments are necessary and, if so, prepare draft heads for a Bill to be considered by the Attorney General'.[104] A 2010 review of similar legislation in Australia emphasized the need for further research on the impact and effectiveness of unexplained wealth

---

103   A. Freiberg and R. Fox, 'Evaluating the effectiveness of Australia's confiscation laws' (2000) 33 *Australian and New Zealand Journal of Criminology* 239. See further Chapter 6.

104   Criminal Assets Bureau, *Annual Report 2010* (Dublin: Stationery Office, 2011) para. 7.5.

legislation.[105] A 2011 report commissioned by the National Institute of Justice in the United States, drawing upon international best practice, concluded

> UWOs [*unexplained wealth orders*] have the potential to be a powerful weapon in the fight against organized and serious crime. If used appropriately they can deprive criminals of their ill-gotten gains, they are especially effective in forfeiting assets that are difficult to be connected to an offense. However it is important to emphasize that their effectiveness is limited. While powerful, expectations about their impact should be moderate and realistic.[106]

Writing in 2000, Freiberg and Fox drew attention to the dearth of empirical research on the effectiveness of unexplained wealth legislation, recognizing that 'Oft-repeated statements by politicians that the legislation has been "successful" in confiscating criminal profits, citing the sums restrained or recovered in specific cases as evidence, confound the particular and the general.'[107] Of course seizure of assets might be seen as 'successful' in the sense that it prevents an offender from benefiting from criminal activity.[108] Freiberg and Fox go on to state, however:

> But occasional success in stripping some offenders of their ill-gotten gains alone is insufficient to justify the ever widening reach of the legislation, and the eroding effect of its departure from generally accepted principles of due process in criminal justice. Since the scope and potency of the confiscatory legislation is defended by reference to its broader deterrent effect on serious crime and criminals, it behoves those who defend its measures to ensure that they are properly targeted against the principals of organised crime, rather than bit players who contribute little to the enterprise in capital or planning. Furthermore, if confiscation legislation has not lived up to its promises because it has not been appropriately exploited, further enlargement of the confiscatory powers should be deferred until weaknesses in the implementation policies and the known operational inefficiencies have been remedied.[109]

The Irish authorities would do well to bear such words of caution in mind as part of the ongoing review of proceeds of crime legislation in Ireland.

---

105   L. Bartels, 'Unexplained wealth laws in Australia' (2010) *Trends and issues in crime and criminal justice (no. 395)* 6.

106   Booz Allen Hamilton, *Comparative Evaluation of Unexplained Wealth Orders* 148.

107   A. Freiberg and R. Fox, 'Evaluating the effectiveness of Australia's confiscation laws'.

108   Ibid.

109   Ibid.

Conclusion

Since the 1990s, the Irish criminal justice system has undergone significant change. The conventional criminal law approach of investigation, prosecution, conviction and punishment is no longer regarded as the sole means of crime control. Faced with increasing criminal activity associated with organized crime, Ireland has turned to the civil process in a bid to supplement perceived weaknesses in the criminal enforcement model. The use of civil processes is personified in the adoption of civil forfeiture to target the financial assets of those engaged in criminal activity, particularly those at the upper echelons of organized criminal activity.[110] Yet, the effectiveness of 'follow-the-money' approaches as a tool of law enforcement – while admittedly intuitively appealing – is largely untested. As Naylor states:

> Everyone agrees with the fundamental principle, that criminals should not profit from their crimes. However, beyond that basic conviction, there is no real consensus on how large the problem of criminal money flows really is, on why society is actually worse off when criminals, rather than legitimate business people, consume, save or invest, or on just what level of "collateral" damage society should be called upon to accept in the name of a war on criminal profits. Despite the fact that so many key questions have remained not merely unanswered, but usually unasked, police forces around the world are being turned loose to find, freeze and forfeit the presumed proceeds of crime on the basis of little more than a vague assurance that this is the most resource-effective way to deal with economically-motivated crime.[111]

The Proceeds of Crime Act was hastily rushed through parliament in the summer of 1996 in the wake of significant concerns surrounding organized crime and little thought was given to the implications, and likely effectiveness, of this legislation. The leitmotif at that time was that demand for legislation, to 'hit back' at the criminal elements of society, had to be satiated. In the absence of detailed understanding and evidence-based research on 'what works',[112] criminal justice policy in Ireland will continue to be driven by this sense of populist punitiveness whereby harsh regimes are introduced for no other reason than that they are intuitively appealing. As one commentator states: 'When facts are unavailable, the argument is often won by the politician who shouts loudest or has the most compelling anecdote. Although this is not a peculiarly Irish situation, neither is

---

110   C. King, 'Using civil processes in pursuit of criminal law objectives: a case study of non-conviction-based asset forfeiture'.

111   R.T. Naylor, 'Wash-out: A critique of follow-the-money methods in crime control policy' at 50.

112   See M. Levi and M. Maguire, 'Reducing and preventing organised crime: An evidence-based critique' (2004) 41(5) *Crime, Law and Social Change* 397 at 404.

it a recipe for considered debate and principled reform.'[113] The adoption of civil forfeiture in 1996 is illustrative of such a populist approach to law reform. A post-conviction regime had only been adopted two years previously,[114] which afforded significant powers to deprive convicted criminals of their ill-gotten gains. Yet, this legislation was not even afforded fair opportunity to have an impact before it was usurped by more radical powers under the Proceeds of Crime Act 1996. Moreover, by going down the 'civil' route, the State circumvents due process norms that would be respected under a post-conviction regime. The Irish legislature has, in the absence of rational and tempered debate, enacted far-reaching measures to counter organized crime even though there is little understanding as to the threat posed by such crime. Moreover, 16 years after the enactment of the Proceeds of Crime Act, it is still not possible to say decisively whether this new approach has significantly impacted upon organized crime type activities in Ireland.

---

113   I. O'Donnell, 'Crime and justice in the Republic of Ireland' (2005) 2(1) *European Journal of Criminology* 99 at 107.
114   Criminal Justice Act 1994.

Chapter 8

Civil Processes and Tainted Assets: Exploring Canadian Models of Forfeiture

Michelle Gallant

Introduction

Frequently trumpeted as the device to sound the death knell of organized crime, civil forfeiture laws arrived in the Canadian provinces of Alberta and Ontario in 2001 and then swiftly spread across the country. By the close of the decade, most provinces had enacted legislative regimes permitting assets tainted by association with crime to be forfeit through civil legal processes. These laws allow property related to an alleged crime to be taken by the province without any accompanying need to prove, in a criminal prosecution, the commission of a crime.[1]

The principal objective of these devices is to scythe organized crime by scything its wealth. Tainted assets are perceived as the temptress, the lifeblood, the foundation of large-scale criminal groups. Civil tools, in contrast to criminal tools, more effectively capture that wealth since a gentle tilting of the probabilities more readily taints valuable property than when pressing that balance beyond a reasonable doubt.

This chapter maps Canada's exploration of the potential of civil forfeiture to disrupt organized crime and criminal wealth. Significant parts of the journey have already been traversed, with Canada's highest court condoning aspects of the strategy in 2009. Other aspects, including compliance with constitutional rights, remain to be explored. Some aspects of the civil legal strategy arguably require serious reconsideration.

---

1 See Civil Forfeiture Act (British Columbia), 2005; Victims Restitution and Compensation Payment Act (Alberta), 2001; Seizure of Criminal Property Act (Saskatchewan), 2005; Criminal Property Forfeiture Act (Manitoba), 2004; Civil Remedies Act (Ontario), 2001; Act Respecting the Forfeiture, Administration and Appropriation of Proceeds and Instruments of Unlawful Activity (Quebec), 2007; Civil Forfeiture Act (New Brunswick), 2010; Civil Forfeiture Act (Nova Scotia), 2007. There is no federal law equivalent. A principal debate underpinning these laws, discussed latterly, is which level of government, federal or provincial, has the constitutional competence to create civil forfeiture laws.

A Brief History of Civil Forfeiture

Modern forfeiture law, sometimes called civil forfeiture, refers to contemporary legal devices developed to facilitate the taking of property tainted by crime together with the vesting of title to that property in the state. Typically, forfeiture connotes the ability of the state, or some agency representing the state, to use civil processes to divest assets, whether money, personal property (such as cars and boats) or real property, based on a suspected link to criminal activity.

Some commentators trace the origins of forfeiture to biblical passages in Exodus and to the ancient deodands doctrine, a phrase meaning 'given up to God'.[2] Broadly, the term referred to the idea that some interest in property was to be surrendered, or 'given up to God' for its connection with some species of wrongful activity. Later, forfeiture came to be applied to things categorized as *malem in se*, things evil in and of themselves. Evil generally meant things whose possession or use was unlawful such as distillery equipment during prohibition, illegal arms, or illegal drugs. In neither of these historical contexts, either in ancient times or more recently, was the forfeiture necessarily preceded by a criminal conviction. Forfeiture happened whether someone was prosecuted for some related offence or not.

A different version, usually described as criminal forfeiture, has long co-existed. Criminal forfeiture refers to the termination of property rights predicated upon conviction for a criminal offence. While the medieval criminal-forfeiture law has long been abolished, its automatic consequences too harsh for a compassionate society to bear, criminal forfeiture continues to have a place in modern law.[3] In the United States, criminal forfeiture refers to the post-conviction access to legal mechanisms that ease the task of securing title to property. In Canada, criminal forfeiture, triggered by a conviction, captures certain categories of property, chiefly any riches derived from crime, commonly known as the proceeds of crime.[4] New forfeiture laws, arguably appropriately characterized as civil forfeiture, also capture the proceeds of crime though they are not precipitated by a criminal conviction.

Ancient and modern admiralty and customs law acknowledge another forfeiture device. Ships involved in wrongdoing occasioned on the high seas were liable to be seized and forfeit upon arrival at a port, as were goods upon which excise duties had not been paid.[5] Unlike criminal forfeiture, these proceeding did not depend upon any parallel or prior prosecution. In fact, in this context, the subject of the

---

2   J. Finklestein, 'The goring ox: Some historical perspectives on deodands, forfeiture, wrongful death and the western notion of sovereignty' (1973) 46 *Temple Law Quarterly* 169 at 182–182; M. Gallant, *Money Laundering and the Proceeds of Crime: Economic Crime and Civil Remedies* (Cheltenham: Edward Elgar, 2005) 58–59.

3   Forfeiture Act 1870 (UK) c. 23.

4   Criminal Code RSC 1985 ss 462.37–462.49.

5   See *Martineau v MNR* (2004) 3 SCR 737.

forfeiture was the ship, not the owner of the ship, or the goods, not the importer of the goods. Not preceded by any conviction, admiralty and custom law takings are sometimes referred to as civil forfeitures.

Modern forfeiture, or civil-forfeiture law, entered the contemporary lexicon through the United States. It was plucked from relative anonymity of customs and admiralty law to become the foundation of new crime control strategies. However, apart from its non-conviction based character, on a substantive level current civil forfeiture laws, whether in the United States, Canada, or elsewhere, share little in common with their historical forebears. Much judicial interpretation of modern forfeiture often begins the inquiry deep in legal history, whether with the forfeiture of ships or the forfeiture of assets whose possession is unlawful.[6] Present-day civil forfeiture emerged as the antidote for the vast accumulations of criminal wealth. Modern devices are starkly different from any ancestors.[7]

In the 1970s, the United States initiated an assault on resources linked to criminal activity. The money component of crime, chiefly the amounts tied to the illegal drugs trade, precipitated the development of strategies focused on criminal resources, whether cash and assets tainted by connections with crime or things used in the commission of crime.[8] Forfeiture was chosen as an integral piece of this strategy, an essential feature of legislative instruments. Both criminal (conviction-based) and civil forfeiture provisions were enacted. This enabled unprecedented seizures of money, assets and real property derived from criminal activity or used in the furtherance of crime.

While US developments influenced the Canadian provinces, the global community also awakened to the problem posed by extraordinary criminal wealth. Wealth supposedly figured as the enticement to crime, the grease that facilitated its commission and the foundation of global criminal enterprises.[9] A series of latter-day international conventions, starting with a drugs trafficking treaty in 1988, encouraged the implementation of laws attentive to criminal finance.[10]

---

6   *The Palmyra* (1827) 25 US 1; *Harmony v United States* (The Brig Malek) (1844) 2 How 210; *AG Coffey v United States* (1886) 116 US 684; *Boyd v US* (1886) 116 US 616.

7   The differences are so stark, the US courts' insistence on interpreting modern laws in light of previous forfeiture jurisprudence proved confusing and contradictory: M. Gallant, 'Ontario (Attorney General) v \$29,020 in Canadian Currency: A Comment on Proceeds of Crime and Provincial Forfeiture Laws' (2006) 52 *Criminal Law Quarterly* 64, 78–79.

8   Racketeer-Influenced and Corrupt Organizations (RICO) Act introduced forfeiture and other civil strategies: 18 USC ss 1961–1968 (1982). See G. Lynch, 'RICO: The crime of being a criminal, Parts I & II' (1987) 87 *Columbia Law Review* 661; N. Abrams, 'A new proposal for limiting private civil RICO' (1989–1990) 37 *University of California Los Angeles Law Review* 1.

9   See Gallant n 2, 7–17.

10   W. Gilmore, *Dirty Money: The Evolution of International Measures to Counter Money Laundering and the Financing of Terrorism* (4th ed., Strasbourg: Council of Europe Publishing, 2008); William Gilmore, *Combating International Drug Trafficking* (London: Commonwealth Secretariat, 1991).

Preventing money laundering, the act of attempting to purge tainted earnings of their unlawful character, captivated global actors throughout the 1990 and generated copious international initiatives. Confiscation, the post-conviction taking of criminal property (also known as criminal forfeiture) was mandated.[11] Although this cascade of norms did not speak specifically to civil forfeiture, it did draw significant attention to the link between money and crime and galvanized a global pursuit of tainted assets.

Prompted by the global action, in the early 1990s Canada introduced proceeds of crime laws.[12] In the main, these consisted of the criminalization of money laundering and the establishment of criminal, though not civil, forfeiture laws. This first brush with forfeiture laws, emanating from the federal government, facilitated the removal of funds tainted by crime upon conviction of an offence. Also established were certain quasi-civil forfeiture laws that applied to the export and import of financial instruments.[13] The export or the import of currency or monetary instruments in excess of CAN$10,000 coupled with a failure to declare that action results in immediate forfeiture. With these forfeitures, the actual seizure and forfeiture operate on the basis of 'reasonable grounds', rather than a balance of probabilities standard.[14] Once forfeit, a claimant's recourse is a direct appeal to the Federal Minister of Public Safety and Emergency Preparedness. Sometimes called 'administrative forfeiture', a criminal conviction does not precede forfeiture of the financial instrument.[15] These are triggered by the failure to declare the export or import of the instruments, and not on the basis of a belief that the instruments represent criminal funds.[16]

With anti-money laundering laws, criminal forfeiture and the new customs' law forfeiture in place, the task fell to the provinces to decide whether to follow the American model and to enact much more comprehensive civil devices. Two

---

11   UN Convention Against Illicit Traffic in Narcotic Drugs and Psychotropic Substances, 1988, art. 5 (requiring confiscation, or criminal forfeiture, of the proceeds of drugs offences); UN Convention Against Transnational Organized Crime, 2000, art. 12 (extending confiscation, and criminal forfeiture, to non-drug offences) (UNTS I-39574).

12   Proceeds of Crime (Money Laundering and Terrorist Financing Act SC 2000 c 17 (which repealed and replaced Canada's first money-laundering legislation, Proceeds of Crime (Money Laundering) Act SC s 26, 1991).

13   Ibid., s 9.

14   Ibid., s 18.

15   See for example, *Hui v Minister of Public Safety* (2008) FCA 281; *Tourki v Canada (Minister of Public Safety and Emergency Preparedness)* (2007) FCA 186; *Sellathurai v Canada (Minister of Public Safety and Emergency Preparedness)* (2008) FCA 255; *Haman v Minister of Public Safety and Emergency Preparedness* (2007) FC 691; *Van Phat Hoang v Minister of National Revenue and Emergency Preparedness* (2006) FC 182.

16   The forfeited instrument, however, can be returned to the claimant upon payment of a penalty unless it is suspected that the instrument represents proceeds of crime or terrorist finance: Proceeds of Crime (Money Laundering and Terrorist Financing Act SC 2000 s 18 (2).

rationales were repeatedly cited for adopting civil instruments. The first, echoing the flavour of US and global developments, was organized crime and the need to tackle its financial underpinnings.[17] Organized crime, gang violence, drugs trafficking and drugs profits, all served to justify laws targeting criminal assets. The second was the interests of the victims of crime, the offering of some mechanism to ensure victims received some measure of compensation:

> ... this new bill that will allow the courts to use wrongfully obtained profits and property to repair harm done to victims of crime and other illegal acts. It will do this by making it easier for Albertans to regain their property or obtain court-ordered restitution for losses suffered as a result of illegal activity.[18]

Seizing assets linked to crime would readily provide a pool of resources from which payments could be made to defray the social costs, individual and collective, of criminal activity.

In the wider global debates, it is lucidly clear that the dominant purpose of the assault on criminal assets is the control of organized crime. In the Canadian provincial context, compensation for victims of crime jostles with control of organized crime as the rationale for civil forfeitures. Much of the jurisprudence arising under provincial forfeiture recognizes twin objectives, fighting crime and the achievement of some kind of compensation for the victims. None of the modern laws, however, emerged from a victim's rights movement or some other ideal traditionally serviced by the canons of the civil justice system.

In 2001, the province of Ontario enacted a civil forfeiture under the rubric of remedies for organized crime.[19] A few weeks later, Alberta enacted a restitution and compensation law.[20] Other provinces followed.

Taking property linked to crime, without any accompanying criminal proceedings, is quite an astonishing proposal. The provinces receive an extraordinary power to interfere with, and divest, interests in property. Ordinarily the principles of criminal law and the panoply of rights that govern the criminal process would regulate the provinces' ability to take property because of the intersection with crime. Civil forfeiture regimes circumvent that process and the accompanying rights. Access to the tainted assets is thereby greatly eased.

---

17 Manitoba Legislative Assembly, Hansard, 4 December 2003 No. 11B 441–446; Ontario Legislative Assembly, Hansard, 1 November 2001, 1850–2130; Saskatchewan Legislative Assembly, Hansard 25 April 2005 No, 98A, 2605–2680; Ontario, *Taking the Profit out of Crime: The Ontario Government's Summit on New Approaches to Fighting Organized Crime* (Queen's Printer, 2002).

18 Alberta Legislative Assembly, Hansard, 19 November 2001, 1101.

19 Civil Remedies Act (Ontario) 2001.

20 Victims Restitution and Compensation Payment Act (Alberta) 2001.

Provincial Forfeiture Models

Over the course of the last decade, eight Canadian provinces have implemented civil regimes that permit the taking of assets tainted by crime, the majority of which rely on forfeiture.[21] Uniquely, the province of Alberta relies on disposal orders and disposal hearings although these processes are not distinctly different in substance from forfeiture.[22]

A series of common architectural features define the provincial laws. First is the creation of two provincial statutory actions, both of which are forms of forfeiture. The province receives the ability to bring an action to forfeit property derived from crime, typically defined as the proceeds of unlawful activity. The second power the province receives is the ability to bring an action to forfeit the instruments of unlawful activity. 'Proceeds of unlawful activity' connotes any property, inclusive of real property, derived from, or intended for use in, unlawful activity. 'Instruments of unlawful activity' refers to things used in, or likely to be used in, the commission of unlawful activity and is intended to, or would be likely to result in the acquisition of property.[23] With the exception of New Brunswick and Quebec, the latter provision extends to property that caused, or might cause, serious bodily harm to a person.[24] In this latter respect, the Canadian models differ from laws forged in other jurisdictions. Creating civil regimes that enable the taking of the proceeds of crime, or the instruments of crime, are somewhat common. Less orthodox are modern devices that permit the forfeiture of property that caused, or is likely to cause, serious bodily harm.

A second shared feature of provincial laws is the explicit incorporation of the trappings of civil legal processes. The most notable civil law characteristic is an explicit reference to the civil standard of proof as the legal norm governing a forfeiture action.[25] This is a rather unusual feature of any legislative device. Direct references to a particular standard of proof, whether civil or criminal, do not ordinarily feature in legislative instruments since the nature of the process and subject matter typically implies the standard. The governing threshold for criminal

---

21   Civil Forfeiture Act (British Columbia) 2005; Seizure of Criminal Property Act (Saskatchewan), 2005; Criminal Property Forfeiture Act (Manitoba) 2004; Act Respecting the Forfeiture, Administration and Appropriation of Proceeds and Instruments of Unlawful Activity (Quebec) 2007; Civil Forfeiture Act (New Brunswick), 2010; Civil Forfeiture Act (Nova Scotia) 2007.

22   Equally anomalous is the fact that the Alberta law is entitled the Victims Restitution and Compensation Act whereas most of the laws feature the word 'forfeiture' in the title.

23   See Civil Remedies Act (Ontario) 2001, s 7 (1) & (2) and Civil Forfeiture Act (British Columbia) 2005, s 1. References are chiefly to the Ontario and British Columbia regimes as representative models.

24   Ibid.

25   Civil Forfeiture Act (British Columbia) 2005, s 16; Civil Remedies Act (Ontario) 2001, s 16; Victims Restitution and Compensation Payment Act (Alberta) 2001, s 51; Seizure of Criminal Property Act (Saskatchewan) 2005, s 13.

prosecutions is the criminal standard of proof beyond a reasonable doubt. The civil standard, normally implicit, regulates all other proceedings in Canada, whether at the provincial or federal level.[26] The provincial forfeiture laws unequivocally provide that the civil standard of proof, in other words, a balance of probabilities standard, regulates forfeitures.

Similarly, the provincial laws contemplate *in rem*, as opposed to *in personam*, liability, another feature that is indicative of a civil process. '*In rem*' typically refers to a thing, with liability attaching to that object. This form of liability is common to admiralty law and the *in rem* liability of ships.[27] '*In personam*' denotes the implicit burden arising from most criminal and civil proceedings, the personal liability of the individual. Consistent with *in rem* liability – a liability that cannot readily be associated with the criminal law since it does not involve any sentient person who stands accused of an offence – the subject of the action is the proceeds of crime or the instrument of crime.[28] It is not the person who possesses, or otherwise enjoys some proprietary interest, in that property. The reliance on *in rem* liability is explicit under Ontario law.[29] Under other regimes, it is palpably obvious given that the property is the defendant named in a forfeiture action.

A third shared attribute of the provincial regulation is the provision of some kind of protection for persons who have interests in property liable to forfeiture but who may not be aware of, or connected to, the unlawful activity that underlies the action. The British Columbia model, for example, offers a measure of protection to 'uninvolved interest holders'. These are defined as individuals who own some interest in property that is an instrument of crime yet did not engage, directly or indirectly, in the crime nor had they knowledge of the crime nor did they receive a financial benefit from the crime.[30] Similarly, the laws afford some protection to owners who acquire property for fair value but did not know, nor could they have known, that the property was the proceeds of crime.[31] Sometimes that protection comes at a price. The interests of owners of the instruments of crime may be protected, but to be sheltered from forfeiture they must have taken measures to prevent the co-optation of the property into criminal ventures.[32] A property owner in receipt of rental payments that exceed fair market value (a financial benefit) who turns a blind eye to illicit uses of premises might lose their property interests.[33]

---

26 *Continental Insurance Co v Dalton Cartage Co* (1982) 1 SCR 164.

27 Liability is limited to the value of the ship, or goods, seized and the owner of the *res* is not personally liable; *Goodwin v AT & B No. 28* [1954] SCR 513.

28 Obscene books may be a close exception, e.g. UK Obscene Publication Act 1959 s 3 and *United States v One Book Entitled Ulysses by James Joyce* 72 F 2d 705 (1934).

29 Civil Remedies Act (Ontario) 2001, s 15.6.

30 Civil Forfeiture Act (British Columbia), 2005, s 12 & 14. Under the Ontario model, the protection applies to responsible owners: Civil Remedies Act (Ontario) 2001, s 7 & 8.

31 Ibid.

32 Ibid.

33 *British Columbia (Director of Civil Forfeiture) v Rai* [2011] BCSC 186.

Fourth, the provincial mechanisms seek to channel forfeited assets to public purposes or other beneficial usages, including financial benefits to the victims of crime. In this way, forfeited property does not flow into general provincial revenues. It remains segregated subject to re-investment into crime control, the alleviation of the costs of crime and assistance to victims. At times, the victims of crime might be well known or easy to identify, such as an individual affected by an investment fraud.[34] At others, the connection between the proceeds and a civil claimant may be less direct such as the use of recovered drug proceeds to fund assistance for drug addicts.

Fifth, under all models, the forfeiture action is triggered by criminal offences. 'Unlawful activity' refers to acts that constitute crimes pursuant to the Canadian criminal code.[35] There is, of course, no need to prove that offence beyond a reasonable doubt. The triggering happens if, on the balance of probabilities, a crime has occurred.

Finally, the provincial regimes acknowledge a residual discretionary power in the courts to refuse to order forfeiture when it is 'in the interests of justice' to do so.[36]

While the precise ingredients of the provincial laws differ, these themes constitute the organizational core of Canadian forfeiture. Some of these components clearly underscore why civil forfeiture has gained prominence as a modern crime control device. Reliance on the civil, as opposed to the criminal, standard of proof greatly eases the province's task of securing its claim to property. The threshold of a balance of probabilities is considerably lower than the criminal norm of beyond a reasonable doubt. At no point in a forfeiture action must the province meet the higher criminal standard. Some regimes categorically reject placing any faith in prior acquittals or stays of proceedings.[37] The unlawful activity may still be proven. Others ease the burden on the province by creating a presumption that proceeds exist if a claimant's legitimate income is significantly disproportionate to his lifestyle.[38] Still other laws countenance the fact that the province need not prove that any unlawful acquisition of property is linked to any specific criminal offence.[39] It need only be proved that the property is linked to *some* offence.

Targeting tainted assets through the reliance on the *in rem* modality is also appreciably more efficient in a global crime control environment. In a setting in

---

34   *Director of Civil Forfeiture v Doe* [2010] BCSC 940.

35   They can also include offences defined under provincial law; Civil Remedies Act (Ontario) 2001, s 2.

36   Civil Forfeiture Act (British Columbia) 2005, s 6; Civil Remedies Act (Ontario) 2001, s 3.

37   Civil Forfeiture Act (British Columbia) 2005, s 18.

38   Act Respecting the Forfeiture, Administration and Appropriation of Proceeds and Instruments of Unlawful Activity (Quebec) 2007, s 11.

39   Seizure of Criminal Property Act (Saskatchewan) 2005, s 7 (2) A & B; Criminal Property Forfeiture Act (Manitoba) 2004, s 14.11 (a) and (b).

which assets readily cross borders, the ability to seize the tainted object and take action against the objects assists enforcement. Individuals do not have to be sought and extradited to the enforcing jurisdiction. Rather, the assets, the proceeds or the instrument tainted by criminal activity, can be immediately seized and subject to forfeiture proceedings.

Though pallid in contrast to the stirring of opposition in the United States,[40] the introduction of provincial civil forfeiture regimes elicited modest resistance in Canada.[41] Only in the Yukon Territory was resistance sufficient to cause a legislative retreat.[42] Nor have constitutional challenges met with much success, as shall next be considered.

Constitutional Constraints

Two constitutional constraints shape legislative action in Canada. Since Canada is a federal state, specific areas of legislative competence are assigned to the federal government and others to the provincial governments. It is unconstitutional for one level of state to pass legislation that comes within the jurisdiction of the other. If it does, the law is *ultra vires* and therefore invalid. The second constraint is the Canadian Charter of Rights and Freedoms (the 'Charter').[43] The validity of a provincial law requires that it both lies within the constitutional competence of a particular state actor and that it complies with constitutional rights.

Civil forfeiture regulation attracts constitutional considerations of both types. The dominant theme animating current constitutional challenges, largely derivative of the common architecture, is whether forfeiture is a criminal or quasi-criminal action or whether it is wholly, or exclusively, a civil proceeding. Classification plays a role in determining the appropriate jurisdictional allocation of the tool, whether federal or provincial. It also plays a significant role in discerning whether

---

40   T. Piety, 'Scorched Earth: How the expansion of the civil forfeiture doctrine has laid waste to due process' (1991) 45 *University of Miami Law Review* 911; M. Schecter, 'Note: Fear and loathing and the forfeiture laws' (1990) 74 *Cornell Law Review* 1151; L. Levy, *A License to Steal: The Forfeiture of Property* (Chapel Hill: University of North Carolina Press, 1996); J. Maxeiner, 'Bane of American forfeiture law: Banished at last?' (1977) 62 *Cornell Law Review* 768.

41   There is virtually no academic commentary in Canada regarding the introduction of civil forfeiture laws. See M. Gallant, 'Alberta and Ontario: Civilizing the money-centered model of crime control' (2004) 4 *Asper Review of International Business and Trade Law* 13.

42   In the Yukon territory, civil forfeiture law was proposed in May 2010 and withdrawn, due to public protest, in October 2010: 'Yukon Shelves Civil Forfeiture Act' (*CBC News*, 26 October 2010): http://www.cbc.ca/news/canada/north/story/2010/10/26/yukon-civil-forfeiture-act.html (accessed 12 November 2011).

43   Part 1 of the Constitution Act 1982 being Schedule B to the Canada Act 1982 (UK) c 11.

the law respects *Charter* rights given that a criminal characterization would necessarily draw into operation more stringent rights-based safeguards. A criminal characterization would also be fatal to the provincial strategy.

Federalism

The jurisdictional question has already been decided by Canada's highest court. *Chatterjee v Attorney General of Ontario* involved a challenge to Ontario's civil forfeiture law, the claim being that the law exceeded provincial constitutional competence.[44] The province contended that the law fell within provincial jurisdiction over property and civil rights.[45] The respondent contended that the law fell into the category of criminal law, a legislative area over which the federal government enjoys exclusive legislative authority.[46]

The Supreme Court determined that the civil forfeiture regime was a law in relation to property and civil rights and, therefore, within provincial competence. While the court concluded that the law touched on powers assigned the federal parliament, namely the criminal law power, it found that provincial forfeiture law did not create new offences, did not seek to impose criminal liability and did not extend, or add to, a criminal sentence. The law's underlying purpose, stated as deterring crime and compensating victims, fell squarely within provincial competence. Any overlap with federal jurisdiction over the criminal law was incidental. Moreover, though the law might have certain punitive effects, a characteristic familiar to the criminal sphere, its dominant objective was to render crime unprofitable, to seize tainted assets and to ensure some measure of compensation to the victims of crime or otherwise remedy the social costs of criminal activity. All of these were valid provincial objects in the constitutional context. Accordingly, the court upheld the constitutionality of Ontario's civil forfeiture law.

In this respect, the aspects of a forfeiture action associated with the realm of the civil law were sufficiently pronounced to secure its location within the ambit of property and civil rights for the purposes of the constitutional inquiry. Criminal features, particularly the fact that provincial actions are intimately tied to breaches of Canadian criminal law, were not sufficient to dislodge the civil character.

Obviously the division of powers question differs from the rights-based analysis. The Canadian Charter applies to federal and provincial legislative actions. A series of rights, generally referred to as Charter rights, govern the relationship

---

44 [2009] SCC 19, [2009] 1 SCR 624. For an excellent critical analysis of this decision, see J. Krane, *Forfeited: Civil Forfeiture and the Canadian Constitution* (Toronto: LLM Thesis, University of Toronto, 2010) (arguing that the provincial civil regimes are clearly not consonant with constitution norms).

45 Constitution Act 1982 being Schedule B to the Canada Act 1982 (UK) c 11, s 92(13). See also R. Hubbard et al., *Money Laundering and the Proceeds of Crime* (Toronto: Irwin Law, 2004) 593–651.

46 Ibid., s 91(27).

between individuals and the state, imposing a constraint on legislative power.[47] A law that is not consonant with particular Charter rights may be held to be invalid. Some violations, however, are tolerable provided that the violation occurs as a reasonable limit within a free and democratic society.[48]

Charter Rights

Although rights-based challenges to provincial laws have begun to percolate through the courts, very little of decisive quality can be distilled from these scatterings. Given that forfeiture affects rights to property, an anticipated challenge would be a violation of property rights, but the Canadian constitution does not protect these.[49]

The Charter confers a series of specific legal rights on individuals charged with an offence. These are referred to as section 11 (d) rights and include the right to be informed of the charge, the right to be tried within a reasonable time, and the right to be presumed innocent until proved guilty in a court of law. The presumption of innocence is intimately tied to the criminal standard of proof beyond a reasonable doubt. It operates in the criminal, and not the civil, context. The *Chatterjee* decision weakens arguments that civil forfeiture attracts the presumption of innocence and therefore that the incorporation of the civil standard into the proceedings violates section 11 (d).

To invoke section 11 (d) rights, an individual must be 'charged with an offence'. In deciding whether to place the provincial forfeiture law in the criminal or the civil justice sphere, *Chatterjee* held that no one risked conviction for a criminal offence. Nor was forfeiture part of a criminal sentence. 'Charged with an offence' does not necessarily require a formal charge, the classic mark of the criminal law. If an individual risks a punitive sanction, section 11 (d) might be invoked.[50] The court in *Chatterjee* recognized that forfeiture might have punitive effects in some cases although the weight of its analysis is more fully supportive of the non-criminal, remedial, civil character of the proceeding. That analysis does not completely preclude the argument that forfeiture attracts the presumption of innocence but the decision certainly moves away from the application of s 11 (d) Charter rights.

The lower standard of proof, the civil standard, might shape Charter challenges emanating from section 7, the right to life, liberty and security of the person, and not to be deprived thereof except in accordance with the principles of fundamental justice. A particular argument is whether the civil standard of proof in the context of allegations of criminal activity coheres with section 7. Since the balance of

---

47   *McKinney v University of Guelph* [1990] 3 SCR 229 at 261.

48   Charter (n 36) s 1.

49   P. Hogg, *Constitutional Law of Canada Volume II* (5th ed., Toronto: Thomson Carswell, 2007) 381–383.

50   *R v Wigglesworth* (1987) 2 SCR 541.

probabilities standard is a central tenet of the civil justice system,[51] it would be odd to conclude that reliance on this standard rankles with principles of fundamental justice.[52] Notably, in *Chatterjee* rights-based challenges were pursued early in the litigation and later abandoned.[53]

Apart from constitutional limits, the legal doctrines of *res judicata*, issue estoppel and abuse of process limit the enforcement of provincial forfeiture laws. Rather than invaliding the legislative apparatus these legal doctrines might offer some relief in individual cases. Where forfeiture sought and refused within the confines of a criminal proceeding is followed by an action to obtain a similar result under provincial forfeiture law, an abuse of process might pre-empt the subsequent action.[54] Aspects of these doctrines have arisen under the civil forfeiture laws, with mixed results.[55] Similar to the rights-based challenges and the division of powers inquiry, the distinction between civil and criminal processes informs the operation of these doctrines.

Prospects and Problems

As challenges filter through the judicial system, facets of the civil forfeiture experiment in Canada should elicit a little unease. The project seems to have become firmly rooted in law without garnering much attention. In species, the provincial laws parallel, in their jurisdictional reach, the entire scope the criminal law. This yields tremendous potential to supplant much of the criminal law since most crime involves assets in one form or another, whether accumulations of property, wrongful appropriations of property or the use of property in connection with an offence. Yet civil forfeiture has failed to generate much analysis.[56] The idea of forfeiting criminal wealth has much merit. There are also reasons to be decidedly cautious.

---

51 *F.H. v McDougall* (2008) 3 SCR 41.

52 *Ontario (Attorney General) v 8477 Darlington Crescent* (2011) ONCA 363.

53 *Ontario (Attorney General) v Chatterjee* (2007) ONCA 406.

54 *Chatterjee*, [2009] SCC 19, [2009] 1 SCR 624 paras 50–52. At para. 40, the Court said there is no 'general bar to a province enacting civil consequences to criminal acts provided the provinces does so for its own purposes in relation to provincial heads of legislative power'.

55 *British Columbia (Director of Civil Forfeiture) v Hyland* (2010) BCCA 148 (in which a prior prosecution did not preclude a subsequent action); *Ontario (Attorney General) v Cole-Watson* [2007] OJ No. 1742 (in which a forfeiture action subsequent to a criminal proceeding was denied on the basis of abuse of process and issue estoppel); *British Columbia (Director of Civil Forfeiture) v Wolff* (2010) BCSC 774.

56 An exception is J. McKeachie and J. Simser, 'Civil asset forfeiture in Canada' in S. Young (ed.), *Civil Forfeiture of Criminal Property: Legal Measures for Targeting the Proceeds of Crime* (Cheltenham: Edward Elgar, 2009).

Many, if not most, of the civil forfeitures actions brought under provincial law occur in the presence of existing or anticipated criminal proceedings. They sometimes follow a failed prosecution or an investigation that has failed to yield sufficient proof to attach criminal liability. Most forfeiture is in connection with offences related to illegal drugs. Many obviously involve alleged drugs proceeds, principally cash. A considerable portion of reported cases concerns real property. Quite often, that property is rental property, commonly identified as a 'grow-op'. Marijuana production, rather than synthetic drugs or cocaine derivatives, are the most frequent.[57]

Regarding the specific struggle with organized crime, the legislation would appear to achieve some of its ambitions. Organized crime's chief illegal business is notoriously the drugs trade. In Canada, the media and the police regularly refer to a group known as 'Hell's Angels' as a criminal organization involved in drug trafficking and other nefarious activities. In 2007, the province of British Columbia brought an action to forfeit a clubhouse owned and operated by Hell's Angels.[58] The province claimed that the clubhouse constituted an instrument of crime because it was used to promote and facilitate both social and criminal activities for the benefit of its members, prospects, frequenters and associates. There appeared to be an unlicensed bar on the premises and possibly illegal weapons. A number of motorcycles were also seized. At trial, an interim order was granted, preserving the clubhouse and assets and denying access.[59] A court later upheld the order, with the exception of the motorcycles, concluding that these were merely incidentally parked at the property.[60] Ultimate disposition of the forfeiture remains to be concluded.

Predictably, forfeiture has been applied to wealth associated with organized crime. Civil forfeiture has also been used in rather unexpected ways. Vehicles, particularly expensive vehicles, linked to racing activity on public roads have been subject to forfeiture.[61] So, too, has the property of individuals allegedly culpable of

---

57 This trend is reflected in British Columbia and Ontario where forfeiture has been more widely used. It is anticipated that other provinces will echo this pattern.

58 *British Columbia (Director of Civil Forfeiture) v Angel Acres Recreation and Festival Property Ltd* [2007] BCSC 1648, [2007] BCJ No. 2475.

59 Ibid.

60 *British Columbia (Director of Civil Forfeiture) v Angel Acres Recreation and Festival Property Ltd* [2009] BCSC 322, [2009] BCJ No. 455. Upheld on appeal, *British Columbia (Director of Civil Forfeiture) v Angel Acres Recreation and Festival Properties Ltd* [2010] BCCA 539, [2010] BCJ No. 2347.

61 Tracy Holmes, 'Forfeiture Office to Assess Street-Racing Luxury Cars' (11 September 2011): http://www.bclocalnews.com/news/129469313.html (accessed 9 December 2011). These forfeitures occurred under British Columbia law. Ontario civil forfeiture law was specifically amended to include provisions that allow vehicles to be forfeit for highway safety infractions: Civil Remedies Act (Ontario) 2001 Part III.I.

assaults been liable to forfeiture.[62] Notions of criminally acquired wealth form no part of the latter. Nor is there any claim of a connection to some broader organized criminal group. To a degree, then, civil forfeiture may be gently drifting from its moorings, the implications of which, as discussed latterly, are worrisome.

Given that the provinces have seized and forfeited considerable amounts of assets tainted by the drugs trade, arguably the strategy is succeeding in undermining criminal activity. Precisely how success is measured is unclear. In the United States, where forfeiture has been increasingly deployed since the late 1980s, there is no particular agreement as to the achievements of this strategy. Much of the American programme, often called 'asset forfeiture', uses the amounts of forfeited revenues as indicia of success.[63] Such a formulation tends to invite the question of whether the civil devices are about crime control or about revenue generation. Some claim that the evidence only shows that vast amounts of property are being seized and that vast intrusions into the rights of Americans are occurring. If judged as a device for dampening criminal activity, these returns are not measures of the success of forfeiture but measures of failure.

Within Canada, it is not clear how the provinces propose to measure the success of the civil forfeiture regime although hints of the American 'revenue' generation model certainly exist. In British Columbia, for example, a government report cites the impressive scope of assets seized and liable to forfeiture as indications of the promise the new laws hold.[64] There is no apparent pretence of offering any other barometer of accomplishment. Of course, bringing tainted assets under provincial control, removing tainted assets from the public domain and re-investing in the social structure can be a gauge of achievement.

A particularly disconcerting piece of the provincial efforts are undercurrents that indicate that civil forfeiture operates on a cost-recovery basis. To handle the attacks on tainted earnings, most provinces have created units or divisions to administer forfeiture laws. Some of these operate on a cost-recovery basis.[65] The provincial agencies aim to recover sufficient tainted assets to covers the costs of their forfeiture operations thus imposing no budgetary costs. The units generate, rather than expend, government funds. This is a rather unusual, and troubling,

---

62   'Lawsuit Over Manitoba House Spurs Rights Concerns' (CBC News online) 30 December 2010: http://www.cbc.ca/news/canada/manitoba/story/2010/12/30/mb-skavins ky-civil-claim-reaction.html (accessed 13 December 2011).

63   Most accounts of asset forfeiture in the US speak of the amounts of property forfeit rather crime levels or effects on the illegal drugs trade. Congressional reports related to asset forfeiture merely delineate amounts forfeit and their geographic origins; United States Department of Justice, *Asset Forfeiture Program*: http://www.justice.gov/jmd/afp/ (accessed 4 December 2011).

64   British Columbia Minister of Public Safety and Solicitor General, *Civil Forfeiture Office: Two Year Status Report* (Victoria: Civil Forfeiture Office, 2008) 2–3. Particularly worrisome is the fact that the report lists as one of the criteria for commencement of a forfeiture action the 'potential return on investment'.

65   Ibid., 3.

feature for state entities dealing with crime.[66] It tends to distort priorities and jeopardize independent objective analysis.[67] On occasion, tying forfeiture revenues to specific budgets can cause corruption or risk instilling a competitive fervour, which, at the very least, would not be a welcome feature of state responses to crime.

The fact that forfeiture may have drifted significantly from its initial mooring is perhaps the most alarming development. Gradually, civil forfeiture has expanded from the idea of targeting the acquisition of criminal wealth to targeting any crime and any element of crime. This occurs through the marching of civil devices into territory that is not, in any manner, allied with organized crime or burgeoning criminal wealth. That expansion happens partly through application of the instrument. More formally, it happens through legislative expansion.

Many countries have devised instruments that enable civil proceedings to be used to seize assets tainted by crime. The ability to seize the proceeds of crime, or the profits of crime, or some other description of revenues derived from criminal activity is common. It is less common to embark on the Canadian path of permitting the forfeiture of the instruments of crime. Much, much less widespread is an action to forfeit an instrument of unlawful activity likely to be used to engage in crime that, in turn, might cause serious bodily harm. The provincial devices, then, cast the broadest net to capture tainted property.

Certain forfeitures might be justified as loose approximations of civil justice, the taking of the proceeds of crime proportionate to the damage caused to individuals as well as the costs to provincial treasuries. The amount of compensation owed equates to the acquired wealth. There is considerable symmetry in this analytical understanding, whereby forfeiture fulfils the role of generic civil actions with the quantity of the proceeds taken constituting the remedy, roughly equivalent to the injury caused. Civil actions usually seek to restore the status, to place the plaintiff in the position they would have occupied prior to the defendant's interference. The defendant surrenders his profit from crime, his gains, and is thereby restored to the position he occupied before the offence. The surrender of the gains helps restore the social equilibrium that existed prior to the offence.

This loose approximation only holds for the forfeiture of the proceeds of crime. The forfeiture of the instruments of crime, this extension of forfeiture beyond the proceeds, does not approximate any sense of civil justice. It is not aimed at the profits of the venture. It is aimed at resources tainted by association with crime. There is no civil law equivalent for the instruments concept. In ancient times, and under current Canadian criminal law, some forfeiture provisions capture assets

---

66   E. Blumenson and E. Nilson, 'Policing for Profit: the drug wars hidden economic agenda' (1998) 65 *University of Chicago Law Review* 35; M. Williams et al., *Policing for Profit: The Abuse of Civil Asset Forfeiture* (Arlington, VA: Institute for Justice, 2010).

67   J. Worrall, 'Addicted to the drug war: The role of civil asset forfeiture as a budgetary necessity in contemporary law enforcement' (2001) 29 *Journal of Criminal Justice Studies* 171.

that are unlawful to possess. That does not apply to a vehicle or to real property. If the quantity of the proceeds of crime is loosely analogous to the amount of compensation, there is in some sense proportionality between the taking and the wrongdoing. Forfeiture of the instruments of crimes offers no such equivalency: the action may be vastly out of proportion with the alleged offences. Expensive vehicles caught engaged in road racing, for example, trigger a far more significant cost than the loss of much cheaper models. Tax evasion, the deceitful failure to declare a few thousand dollars of cash income, could precipitate the forfeiture of an expensive house if the tax returns were completed in a home office.

If the expansion to instruments of crimes presents a strain, the liability to forfeiture of 'instruments likely to cause, or that may have caused, bodily harm' proves much more troubling. What if forfeiture is sought for a house within which an alleged assault occurred – perhaps after much drinking one individual punched another? The house allegedly qualifies at an instrument of crime liable to forfeiture given it was the location of the crime. To a pronounced degree, this progression from serious wealth and profitable crime to the crime of assault deviates starkly from the initial purposes of the introduction of civil forfeiture. The situation would not involve organized crime where wealth creation is an objective. Nor does the idea of tackling the financial dimension of crime have any application. Taking the profits of crime hardly serves as a justification for the forfeiture. Nor does the taking of a house on this basis fit within some even relaxed notion of 'instrument of crime'. It is difficult to conceive of any random physical location somehow facilitating criminal activity. Perhaps a fast sleek aeroplane capable of flying low to avoid detection might facilitate crime if it is specifically designed to conceal the transport of drugs across national boundaries. Or maybe vast tracts of land purchased at the edge of mountain ranges and used to cultivate marijuana plants serve as instruments that facilitate drug trafficking. In these cases, there is some real connection, a meaningful connection, between the instrument and an offence.[68] Yet what is the profit connection, or the facilitative connection, between a house and an assault?

Moreover, civil forfeiture represents a vast extension of state power, replicating the ambit of the criminal law and placing powerful new civil tools at the state's disposal. There may be some reason to suspend concern about the incredible span of this power when the state is confronting organized crime. There may be some parity of arms between the state and organized crime. Perhaps powerful new tools are needed to confront a powerful contemporary phenomenon. But the alleged perpetrator of the assault is not that powerful entity. Rather, the enormous power of the state may be pitted against the powerless, the ill, the addicted, the socially excluded or the marginalized. The residual discretionary power of the courts to

---

68 Some courts have read in a proportionality requirement to forfeitures of the instruments of crime, requiring that an instrument be 'meaningfully' linked to an offence: *Alberta (Minister of Justice and Attorney General) v Sykes* [2011] ABCA 191, [2011] AJ No. 678.

decline forfeiture when it determines it is 'in the interest of justice' offers little comfort for an aggrieved property owner. It is a weak constraint on possible individual enforcement excesses, particularly if it applies sparsely and only in exceptional cases.[69] In any event, to leave these concerns at the altar of judicial discretion may not be prudent strategy.

It is evidently premature to offer a final assessment of the advantages and disadvantages of the arrival of civil forfeiture on Canadian shores. There is much promise, much potential for changing tainted wealth into public benefit. There is also much potential for excesses. Some thought to revising the pernicious aspects of civil forfeiture laws is warranted, in particular, ensuring some proportionality between the taking of property and the underlying alleged criminal offences.

---

69   *Ontario (Attorney General) v 1140 Aubin Road, Windsor and 3142 Halpin Road Windsor (in rem)* [2011] ONCA 363, [2011] OJ No. 2122.

Asset Recovery: Substantive or Symbolic?

Jackie Harvey

Introduction

1986 was significant for would-be financial miscreants across the world as this was the year when money laundering, or more specifically laundering the proceeds of crime, became criminalized within international law.[1] Crime money is an asset, whereas money laundering is a process emanating from an associated criminal activity. It can be argued that there already existed a criminal legal framework appropriate for prosecuting the underlying predicate offence that gives rise to the funds to be laundered. Sharman goes on to point out that since 1986, '170 states have criminalized money laundering, and most ... have set up specialized agencies to combat it'.[2] It is, therefore, salutary to observe the resultant global expansion in the legislative framework together with its attendant agencies of enforcement. Over the 20-year period since the creation of the Financial Action Task Force ('FATF') in 1989, there has been a small explosion in the number of governmental and quasi-government agencies that have added anti-money laundering legislation ('AML') to their existing mandate or, significantly, have come into existence specifically as a result of AML legislation.

The arrival in the UK of the Proceeds of Crime Act 2002 ('POCA'), and specifically sections 327 to 329, as amended by the Serious Organised Crime and Police Act 2005 ('SOCPA'), was widely regarded as contributing a significant weapon to the armoury deployed in the fight against crime. This Act provided a far wider range of powers, beyond AML provisions, covering not only criminal[3] but also civil recovery.[4] For a government focused on proving the adage that 'crime does not pay', it provided the recovery agency with 'powers that were so extensive it could even seize assets from people who had not been convicted of any crime'.[5]

---

1   N. Cribb, 'Tracing and confiscating the proceeds of crime' (2003) 11(2) *Journal of Financial Crime* 168 at 172; J. Sharman, 'Power and discourse in policy diffusion: anti-money laundering in developing states' (2008) 52 *International Studies Quarterly* 635 at 635.

2   Ibid.

3   Proceeds of Crime Act 2002 Parts 2–4.

4   Proceeds of Crime Act 2002 Part 5.

5   BBC, 'Crime assets agency "ill-planned"': http://news.bbe.co.uk/go/pr/-/1/hi/uk_politics/7040680.stm, 11 October 2007 (accessed 15 June 2011).

AML was grounded in the presumption that criminals could be dissuaded from engaging in socially undesirable activity simply by making it unprofitable to pursue. The mantra of the incoming Blair government, set out in the Labour Party Manifesto 1997, promised to be 'tough on crime and tough on the causes of crime', and this mantra became embedded in the philosophy of relevant government departments. The Home Office[6] commented that 'seizing criminals' assets ... is a key tool of law enforcement. It reduces crime, ... and ensures (and shows) that crime does not pay'. Similarly, Gottschalk, writing for the Home Office, asserted that 'The confiscation of criminal assets by the Courts forms a key part of efforts to tackle the criminal economy and crime more generally'.[7] Indeed, as noted by HM Treasury, the purpose of the AML regulation was to 'change the economics of crime by increasing both the costs and the risks of laundering'.[8] This appealingly simple approach relies, however, on the presumption that those bent on law-breaking react to external forces in a predictable and predetermined way. Further, it is assumed that laundering can be separated as an activity, discrete from any predicate offence. Thus, 'They consider criminals rational cost-benefit calculators and presume that money laundering is a profession unto itself.'[9] Such presumptions of rationality[10] sit within the normative framework of law-making, whereby rules are established that reflect the dominant discourse and transgressions dealt with such that the environment is orderly, independent and, importantly, predictable. However, this response ignores the complexity and frequent irrationality of the perpetrator.

> Thus the criminal came to be viewed not as a complex product of psycho-socio-economic conditions but as a simple cost-benefit calculator. It followed that crime could be addressed by merely tilting the likely outcome of such a calculation to reduce the potential profitability of the criminal's actions, and to

---

6 Home Office, *Rebalancing the Criminal Justice System in Favour of the Law-abiding Majority: Cutting Crime, Reducing Re-offending and Protecting the Public* (London: Stationery Office, 2008) 36.

7 E. Gottschalk, *Public Attitudes to Asset Recovery and Awareness of the Community Cashback Scheme – Results from an Opinion Poll* (London: Research and Analysis Unit, Home Office, 2010) at 1: http://www.homeoffice.gov.uk/publications/about-us/public-opinion-polls/community-cashback-poll?view=Binary (accessed 22 June 2011).

8 HM Treasury, *Money Laundering Regulations 2001, Final Regulatory Impact Assessment* (London, 2001) para. 48.

9 T. Blickman, *Countering Illicit and Unregulated Money Flows: Money Laundering, Tax Evasion and Financial Regulation* (2009) Crime & Globalisation Debate Papers TNI Briefing Series December: http://www.tni.org/sites/www.tni.org/files/download/crime3_0.pdf (accessed 2 April 2013) 10.

10 C. Gerner-Beuerle, 'In search of rationality in company law' (2010) 73 *Modern Law Review* 1048 provides an interesting discussion of the differing disciplinary definitions of the term at 1052.

incapacitate (by stripping away economic assets as well as by imprisonment) those who failed to heed the initial warning.[11]

Although it is theoretically valid to consider the sociological context of anti-money laundering legislation, legislators appeared content to make assumptions about the behaviours and responses of those whose action such legislation seeks, a priori, to modify. Thus, consistent with the ideas of sociologist Emile Durkheim: 'A violation incites the non-violators (society as a whole) to cling together in opposition to the violation, reaffirming that society's bond and its adherence to certain norms.'[12]

Despite this argument, there are some individuals[13] who continue to view civil asset recovery as having a beneficial role as a deterrent to money laundering simply because 'profit motivates most criminals'.[14] Cribb goes on to justify asset recovery on the grounds that: reinvestment of such assets perpetuates a cycle of crime; imprisonment is insufficient as criminals either continue to operate their enterprises from prison or re-establish them on release; and lack of fairness to the majority of law-abiding individuals. Such arguments are fairly well rehearsed, and a substantially similar set appear in Gottschalk, although the latter, reporting on a survey of public opinion, does note that awareness of asset recovery was generally low.[15] There can be little doubt, therefore, as to the intentions of the legislation whereby:

> Acquisition, use, possession, disguise, concealment, conversion, transfer or removal from one country to another of the benefit of any criminal conduct can be money laundering. Even an attempt to do any of these things, or becoming involved in an arrangement which facilitates them can constitute a money laundering offence.[16]

and

> Put simply, POCA makes it possible to seize cash from a suspected criminal and places the onus on that individual to prove that the money has been acquired

---

11   R.T. Naylor, 'Towards a general theory of profit-driven crimes' (2003) 43 *British Journal of Criminology* 81 as cited in R. Bosworth-Davies, 'Money Laundering – Chapter Four' (2007) 10(1) *Journal of Money Laundering Control* 66, 88.

12   http://durkheim.itgo.com/crime.html (accessed 23 June 2011).

13   N. Cribb, fn 1; J. Simser, 'Money laundering and asset cloaking techniques' (2008) 11(1) *Journal of Money Laundering Control* 15.

14   N. Cribb, fn 1, 169.

15   E. Gottschalk, fn 7, 1.

16   Crown Prosecution Service, *Money Laundering Offences – Part 7 Proceeds of Crime Act 2002 updated 06/02/2008*, Proceeds of Crime Act Money Laundering Offences: Legal Guidance, at 6: http://cps.gov.uk/legal/p_to_r/proceeds_of_crime_money_laundering/ (accessed 14 May 2011).

legitimately. Confiscation orders, reflecting the value of criminal proceeds, can be made against those who commit any of a wide range of offences or can be shown to engage in a "criminal lifestyle". The Act also creates an all-encompassing web to catch anyone who moves, hides, converts or otherwise has possession of cash or property that represent the proceeds of crime.[17]

Under POCA, a criminal can be subject to a cash seizure, a restraint and may also witness the removal, via a court recovery order, of the proceeds of his crime. If these prove unsuccessful, he can also find himself relieved of any physical assets through civil recovery. It is salutary to observe, as stated by Chamberlain,[18] that 'the criminal route should not be used if the primary aim is to secure return of the assets', arguing that criminal prosecutions, requiring proof beyond reasonable doubt, should be designed to secure conviction rather than recover assets. Civil proceedings, on the other hand, put the evidential onus on defendants, as they should easily be able to prove how they acquired the asset in question. This switch in burden of proof (allied with a lower standard of proof) means that they 'cannot, as in criminal proceedings, sit back in silence and rely on reasonable doubt'.[19]

Agency Bias, Legitimacy and Fact Restructuring

Within an economic paradigm (and social-welfare economics in particular), legislation is justified on the grounds that it addresses negative externalities[20] in such a way as to increase overall social welfare, assuming that government intervention is taken as being cost-neutral. However, as argued by Hantke-Domas,[21] such an assumption frequently does not hold in practice as the legislative framework cannot be extended in the absence of incurring positive transaction costs. These will arise through the necessary creation of new agencies of government tasked with responsibility for enforcement of such legislation. It is perfectly rational that, once created, these sorts of agencies will ensure that they not only justify their existence but that demand for their service is also continued. Hence, Chong and

---

17   Her Majesty's Inspectorate of Court Administration (HMICA), *Payback Time, Joint Review of Asset Recovery since the Proceeds of Crime Act 2002*, 2004: http://www.hmica.gov.uk/files/Full.pdf at 8 (accessed 2 April 2013).

18   K. Chamberlain, 'Recovering the proceeds of corruption' (2002) 6(2) *Journal of Money Laundering Control* 157, 157.

19   D. Lusty, 'Civil Forfeiture of Proceeds of Crime in Australia' (2002) 5(4) *Journal of Money Laundering Control* 345, 345.

20   In classical economics, markets are presumed to be efficient and intervention through legislation takes place to correct market inefficiencies such as information asymmetry.

21   M. Hantke-Domas, 'The Public Interest Theory of Regulation: Non-existence or misinterpretation' (2003) 15 *European Journal of Law and Economics* 165.

López-de-Silanes, quoting Rahn, draw attention to the ludicrous situation of 'the police creating increased demand for their services by inventing new crimes'.[22]

Indeed, 'the definitions of the "headline" laundering offences are now so wide that almost any financial transaction is capable of being laundering, if some of the money or other property in fact has its provenance in crime'.[23] By simply broadening the definition,[24] the problem becomes bigger, attracting greater public attention. Combine with this trend the ascription of the overwhelming importance of function, whereby POCA was feted as combining within a single piece of legislation 'the law governing investigations, money laundering offences and confiscation',[25] and, ingeniously, the result is that a rationale is supplied for yet further resources, such that the entire system become self-reinforcing.[26] Thus, objectivity becomes supplanted by perception 'since decisions are determined by what a decision maker perceives rather than what might objectively be the case'.[27]

In part, such behaviour may be rationalized as legitimacy-seeking activity by the agencies involved.[28] Legitimacy is a construct applied within business and accounting literature. Legitimacy means 'a generalized perception or assumption that the actions of an entity are desirable, proper, or appropriate within some socially constructed system of norms, values, beliefs, and definitions'.[29] This interpretation is reinforced elsewhere; for example, Stanley[30] in a discussion of financial market regulation refers to its role in terms of 'applied legitimation'. Consistent with Boyne,[31] the organizational structures that come into being gain their legitimacy through the wider support of the law-abiding majority.

---

22   A. Chong and F. López-de-Silanes, *Money Laundering and its Regulation* (Washington, DC: Inter-American Development Bank, 2007) at 5 citing R. Rahn, 'The Case against Federalising Airport Security' (Washington, DC: Cato Institute, 2001): www. cato.org/pub_display.php?pub_id=3865 (accessed 12 March 2009).

23   P. Alldridge, 'Money laundering and globalization' (2008) 35(4) *Journal of Law and Society* 437, 442.

24   P. van Duyne, 'Money laundering policy: Fears and facts' in P. van Duyne, K. von Lampe and J. Newell (eds), *Criminal Finances and Organising Crime in Europe* (Nijmegen: Wolf Legal Publishers, 2003).

25   N. Cribb, fn 1, 179.

26   P. Alldridge, fn 23.

27   V. Hoffmann, T. Trautmann and J. Hamprecht, 'Regulatory uncertainty: A reason to postpone investments? Not necessarily' (2009) 46(7) *Journal of Management Studies* 1227, 1229.

28   J. Oliveria, L. Rodrigues and R. Craig, 'Voluntary risk reporting to enhance institutional and organisational legitimacy' (2011) 19(3) *Journal of Financial Regulation and Compliance* 271.

29   M. Suchman, 'Managing legitimacy: Strategic and institutional approaches' (1995) 20(3) *Academy of Management Review* 571, 574.

30   C. Stanley, 'Mavericks at the casino: Legal and ethical indeterminacy in the financial markets' (1994) 2(2) *Journal of Asset Protection and Financial Crime* 137, 137.

31   R. Boyne, *Subject, Society and Culture* (London: Sage, 2001).

Spencer and Broad[32] invoke an interesting dimension to the criminal policy-making framework by reference to the work of Van Duyne and Vander Beken:[33]

> They argue that the fear of organised crime or the articulation of the threat of organised crime interacts with what can be described as "knowledge based policy making", much of which seems to be the restructuring of the "facts" to fit with the articulated fear.

A similar approach can be extrapolated to the field of asset recovery where one can observe a desire to achieve something tangible that can be used as *ex post* justification of such 'threat'; and what better way to demonstrate the 'threat' of organized crime and money laundering than by pointing to the vast perceived wealth that is accumulated and thus available for recovery. Of relevance here is the work of Dubourg and Prichard[34] in which they estimate 'the value of additional criminal assets theoretically available for seizure is about £2bn per year in the UK, with more than £3bn of revenue sent overseas annually'. The authors do note, however, that their calculations are rather more reliant on judgement than on 'hard evidence', arguing that it was better to provide estimates rather than force policy-makers to operate in a vacuum. However, it is equally valid to point out that a 'vacuum' might provide a preferable basis for policy-making than inaccurate guesswork contrarily presented as fact. Sadly too often, the original caveats of the authors are disassociated from subsequent repetition of the apparent 'facts'. Is it coincidental that the derived values are curiously similar to those reported by HM Treasury,[35] whereby unsophisticated extrapolation is used to arrive at a figure for laundered money of £2–3 billion, with the further identification of 'criminal "capital formation" – that is assets invested in a possible seizable form of about £5 billion, £3 billion of which is exported overseas'.[36] From a methodological perspective, it remains unclear how any of these numbers have been derived.

---

32   J. Spencer and R. Broad, 'Lifting the veil on SOCA and the UKHTC: Policymaking responses to organised crime' in P. van Duyne, A. Antonopoulos, J. Harvey, A. Maljevic, T. Vander Beken and K. von Lampe (eds), *Cross-Border Crime Inroads on Integrity in Europe* (Tilburg: Wolf Legal, 2010) 263.

33   P. van Duyne and T. Vander Beken, 'The incantations of EU crime policy making' (2009) 51(2) *Crime, Law and Social Change* 261.

34   R. Dubourg and S. Prichard (eds), *Organised Crime: Revenues, Economic and Social Costs, and Criminal Assets Available for Seizure* (London: Home Office, 2008): http://www.homeoffice.gov.uk/about-us/freedom-of-information/released-information1/foi-archive-crime/9886.pdf?view=Binary (accessed 9 September 2010) 57.

35   HM Treasury, *The Financial Challenge to Crime and Terrorism* (London, 2007): www.hm-treasury.gov.uk (accessed 9 September 2010) 29.

36   HM Treasury, fn 35, 8.

Scattered Evidence

In the light of these estimates, it is no small wonder that the expectations for asset recovery performance were set at unrealistically high levels. Giddy at the thought of such assets ripe for recovery, targets were set for law enforcement agencies to recover £250m in 2009–2010 with, more significantly, a longer-term goal of up to £1 billion.[37] In reality, despite such a lofty aspiration, the practical application of the money-laundering and asset recovery regime proved more modest in achievement, an outcome compounded by the unanticipated costs associated with civil recovery cases.

The result, as calculated by Sproat,[38] was that for the financial year 2005/2006 the estimated cost of recovering every £1 was £3.73, clearly, a far from attractive outcome. Harvey and Lau[39] were equally critical of outcomes. Using data from both the Assets Recovery Agency ('ARA') and the Home Office, they indicated that those criminals apprehended and subjected to POCA were far from financially sophisticated individuals. It remained unproven that they were intent on undermining the integrity of the financial system. They appeared to be more often small-level operators, the recovery of whose assets (through multiple small-level payments) placed a considerable burden onto the legal system. As they reported, across the range of agencies with asset-recovery powers, the median value of amounts remitted onto JARD (the Joint Assets Recovery Database) over the period 2003–2006 fell in the range of between £300 and £500. They were, however, somewhat sympathetic to the challenges faced by the ARA in working with what appeared to the dregs of prior failed criminal cases.

> The Agency commented at the start that the referring law enforcement agencies referred old criminal cases which had either been "thrown out" by the criminal courts or for which there was insufficient evidence to bring a criminal prosecution. They are handed over to the ARA to pursue a new civil case but are often so old that effectively the ARA had to re-start the investigation.[40]

---

37   Home Office, *Rebalancing the Criminal Justice System in Favour of the Law-abiding Majority: Cutting Crime, Reducing Re-offending and Protecting the Public'* (London: Home Office, 2008) 36.

38   P. Sproat, 'The new policing of assets and the new assets of policing: A tentative financial cost-benefit analysis of the UK's anti-money laundering and asset recovery regime' (2007) 10(3) *Journal of Money Laundering Control* 277.

39   J. Harvey and S. Lau, 'Crime-money records, recovery and their meaning' in P. van Duyne, J. Harvey, A. Maljevic, K. von Lampe and S. Miroslav (eds), *European Crime-markets at Cross-roads: Extended and Extending Criminal Europe* (Tilburg: Wolf Legal, 2008).

40   J. Harvey and S. Lau, fn 39, 298–299.

With the government stung into action and wishing to be seen to respond to subsequent criticism of the work of the ARA,[41] it was inevitable that there would be changes, given that the 'ARA had cost £65m over four years but seized assets worth £23m'.[42] The result was that, in April 2008, its civil recovery activity was absorbed into the Serious Organised Crime Agency ('SOCA'). SOCA (created in April 2006) had been given the heady mandate to recover the proceeds of crime alongside tackling drug, immigration and other organized crime.

The 2008/2009 SOCA Annual Report refers to the opinion expressed by the SARs Committee[43] that 'SOCA continued to perform well and that the model and approach taken was now recognized internationally as an example of global best practice'.[44] Despite this positive spin and given that SOCA was the product of a merger between multiple agencies, there was little indication that time had been taken to address pre-identified operational problems within its constituent organizations. An interview carried out by the author in 2008 with an officer from SOCA indicated that NCIS (the previous UK Financial Intelligence Unit) was a poorly-run organization with a large number of staff seconded from law-enforcement agencies as well as from Customs. Further, the interviewee indicated that the latter organization had been subject to criticism over crime investigation, thus it was 'three poor organisations creating one big one'.[45] Potential inefficiencies arising from political solutions are perhaps illustrated through looking at the operational cost structure of the regime which indicated a 48 per cent jump in funding from £282.8m to £419.4m between 2005/2006 and 2006/2007 following the creation of the merged entity.[46]

Compounding the problem of the higher running costs, Rider indicated that the poor performance of the old ARA continued into the new SOCA: 'it was

---

41 M. Fleming, 'UK law enforcement agency use and management of suspicious activity reports: Towards determining the value of the regime' (London: University College London, 30 June 2005); S. Lander, *Review of the Suspicious Activity Reports Regime (the SARs Review)* (London: SOCA, 2006); A. Kennedy, 'An Evaluation of the recovery of criminal proceeds in the United Kingdom' (2007) 10(1) *Journal of Money Laundering Control* 33.

42 BBC 'Crime assets agency "ill-planned"': http://news.bbe.co.uk/go/pr/-/1/hi/uk_politics/7040680.stm, 11 October 2007 (accessed 9 September 2010).

43 The SARs Regime Committee produces an annual review of the operation and performance of the SARs Regime. Membership of this Committee consists of: SOCA; Association of Chief Police Officers; British Bankers' Association; Financial Services Authority; Her Majesty's (HM) Revenue & Customs; HM Treasury; Home Office; Institute of Chartered Accountants in England and Wales; Law Society of England and Wales; Metropolitan Police Service; and National Terrorist Financial Investigation Unit.

44 Serious Organised Crime Agency, *Annual Report 2008/9*: http://www.soca.gov.uk/about-soca/library (accessed 9 September 2010) 31.

45 J. Harvey and S. Lau, fn 39, 193.

46 Calculated from the statement of accounts for the component agencies for 2005/2006 and from the SOCA *Annual Report for 2006/7*.

revealed that SOCA has seized only £1 from organised crime for every £15 in its budget. Indeed on this basis the abolished Asset Recovery Agency (ARA) looks like a good investment!'[47] He does, however, defend the ARA, arguing that asset recovery provides only one part of the story (presumably having in mind the value of 'disruption') and that the extreme caution within the Agency to opening itself to inspection (as illustrated later in this chapter) could be seen as compromising to its integrity.

Public data from SOCA, shown in Table 9.1, provides details of funds recovered since its inception. Assuming the figures relate to funds remitted into government accounts, the data provided indicate the total amounts recovered via criminal and civil proceedings from 2006/2007 to 2008/2009. It is important to note that restraints can be placed for any hypothetical value of assets 'frozen' in advance of investigation, so the important information refers to the eventual confiscation orders imposed by the courts. As explained by SOCA, restraint orders precede confiscation orders and are put in place to prevent disposal of assets prior to trial and all these figures are, therefore, only estimates. Within POCA there is a 'benefit test' used to determine 'benefit' received from a criminal lifestyle. However it is the courts that decide the amount available to be subject to such order, based on their assessment of presented evidence. It is recognized that not all orders granted may be recovered in reality. However, court judgments are now viewed as being 'sharper' as prosecutors have more experience of investigation such that data presented to the court is more accurate, hence it is suggested that the proportion of recovery is now much higher than at the inception of POCA.[48]

Table 9.1   Asset recovery

	2006/7 (£m)	2007/8 (£m)	2008/9 (£m)
Cash seizure	3.3	8.0	9.2
Restraint orders	27.2	46.8	128.8
Confiscation orders	14.5	11.6	29.7
Civil recovery	n/a	n/a	16.7

Note: SOCA, fn 44 at 32.

As with the comparison of costs pre- and post- agency creation, it is interesting to compare this information to the data previously obtained from the Home Office that provided totals for asset recovery receipts remitted into the consolidated fund

47   B. Rider, 'Cost Effectiveness – a two edged sword!' (2009) 12(4) *Journal of Money Laundering Control*, Editorial, i.

48   Information provided to the author by SOCA.

from all authorities with asset recovery powers.[49] This calculation indicates that for the fiscal year prior to the inception of SOCA, cash seizures totalled £20.2m with confiscation orders of £25.5m. While allowing for the existence of data anomalies and differences in recording it is interesting to consider this in light of the cost data in Table 9.1, apparently providing support for the comments of Rider.

A Peek Through the Door

Heeding Rider's call for accessibility, several attempts were made by the author to gain access through the doors of SOCA. The most recent of these commenced during 2008 when an initial e-mail request to SOCA was simply ignored. Granted this may have been due to the complexity of the data that had been requested (designed to mirror information that, in 2004, had previously been made available to the author from the ARA).

A subsequent request in February 2009, through a named contact met with greater success and was forwarded within the organization to a person 'who remembered the original request'. However, the eventual response received was: 'We cannot provide this information. If you require further information on asset recovery performance (in general) you will need to submit a FOI request to the Home Office.'[50] A second attempt through a different source was made in October 2009 which enabled contact with a different operational part of the organization. This person had apparently been copied into the original request and responded to the author that the direction to pursue the FOI route (to which there had been no response) had been incorrect. This response prompted a subsequent exchange of e-mails over a two-month period between December 2009 and February 2010. While there was an evident willingness to assist, the major problem that the request had posed for the organization derived from their perceived responsibilities under data-protection laws. The respondent reported that previously-sought legal interpretation led the agency to conclude that the data requested by the author could not be released without the individual permission of all relevant organizations with joint responsibility for the content of the Joint Asset Recovery Database ('JARD'). Given the numbers involved, the adoption of this interpretation essentially removes the possibility of any download of data from this crucial database to a third party.

Eventually, after requiring greater specificity around both the data required and its proposed application, SOCA agreed that more generic aggregate data could be made available. This was sent to the author in the form of a number of

---

49   This compilation includes: the Asset Recovery Agency including all Regional Asset Recovery Teams; HMRC enforcement and compliance; the National Crime Squad (formed in 1998 and merged into SOCA in 2006); the National Criminal Intelligence Service (NCIS) (formed in 1992 and merged into SOCA in 2006); and SOCA.

50   E-mail correspondence with author dated 31 March 2009.

data tables supported by an underlying explanation, however there was, perhaps not unreasonably, concern expressed to ensure that the information was fully explained and thus correctly interpreted. Thus, the sender also requested that the author contacted them for further discussion upon receipt.

The data provided was in fact generic data produced for the Asset Recovery Working Group ('ARWG'). As pointed out by the SOCA correspondent:

> This group is a collection of "senior practitioners" and policy people from SOCA, HMRC, NPIA, ACPO, Home Office, DWP and others. Its purpose is "To deliver HMG's asset recovery vision by mainstreaming asset recovery activities" – in essence it is the main forum for organisations involved in asset recovery work to share problems and best practice.[51]

The data provided had been extracted from their internal Management Information System end of year report for 2008/2009, and the receipts data in relation to England, Wales and Northern Ireland had been checked (and presumably reconciled) with Home Office data as at February 2010. It remains a source of confusion that the information supplied by SOCA with respect to asset recovery receipts could not be reconciled with that reported in Table 9.1 taken from published SOCA sources.

There was interest to see if this information could be reconciled with, and thus be used to update, an earlier asset recovery study undertaken by the author.[52] This study had looked at databases held by both the Home Office (in respect of cash seizure, forfeiture and asset recovery arising from the criminal recovery processes) and by the UK ARA for civil recovery only. Unfortunately, the information available from SOCA lacked the rich detail of the ARA data, so for the time being such information remains beyond the scrutiny of academics. It should, however, have been possible to revisit and update the information from the Home Office with that supplied through SOCA as both are drawing from the same JARD database. The original study covered a three-year period from 2003/2004 to 2005/2006. It was therefore considered valuable to extract from this, data that would be comparable with the content of the tables provided by SOCA, one of which is presented in Table 9.2 below.

As explained by the respondent, Table 9.2 shows both cash seizures made together with their actual cash forfeiture orders granted. There is known to be attrition between actual seizures and orders granted reflecting two dimensions: (i) that the value of cash seized might well be estimated, when entered onto the database, rather than actually counted; and (ii) some of the cash may *ex post* have to be returned to the owner. It was stated that users of these figures are aware of the potential inaccuracy of the value of cash seizures and thus do not generalize from them.

---

51   E-mail to author dated 1 February 2010.

52   J. Harvey and S. Lau, fn 39. It should be noted that the majority of the information reported here was not published as part of the original paper.

Table 9.2   POCA cash seizure and forfeiture breakdown, 2004–2009

	2004/05	2005/06	2006/07	2007/08	2008/09
Cash Seizure (volume)	1,318	1,295	2,274	5,103	6,108
Cash Seizure (value £m)	39.4	62.8	52.5	68.4	106.7
Cash Forfeiture orders granted (volume)	590	790	1,152	2,598	3,223
Cash Forfeiture orders granted* (value £m)	21.7	30.7	31.2	33.8	39.4
Cash Receipts (value £m)	19.8	30.4	31.8	31.5	39.8

Note: SOCA data; * As provided by SOCA, the time-lag between order and remittance and the occasional variation resulting from the appeals process means that there is a discrepancy between the value of orders obtained in a year and the value of receipts (indicated as cash receipts on the next line) 'banked' in the same time-frame.

The comparable information extracted from the earlier Home Office data is produced in Table 9.3 below. Focusing, for example, on the cash forfeiture orders granted, frustratingly, there is no consistency between these two sets of data.

Table 9.3   Cash seizure and forfeiture orders granted and entered on JARD, 2003–2006

	2003/04	2004/05	2005/06
Cash Seizure (volume)	242	666	546
Cash Seizure (value £m)	12.9	28.1	75.3
Cash Forfeiture orders granted (volume)	302	407	884
Cash Forfeiture orders (value £m)	19.0	17.7	33.2

Note: Home Office data.

Table 9.4 illustrates the magnitude of the errors between the two data sets. It is assumed that the information provided by SOCA is likely to be the more accurate since they are custodians of the database. It was hypothesized that prior years might also include orders made under a wider range of legislation, although this does not appear to aid interpretation. Alternatively, figures for prior years might have been updated and hence subsequently revised or there might have been error in download and transcription in the original data.

Table 9.4   Cash seizure data discrepancy between SOCA and Home Office

Difference between the two sources	2004/05	2005/06
Cash Seizure (volume)	652	749
Cash Seizure (value £m)	11.3	(12.5)
Cash Forfeiture orders granted (volume)	183	(94)
Cash Forfeiture orders (value £m)	4.0	(2.5)

Note: Values expressed as SOCA data less Home Office.

As noted, in addition to cash seizure and forfeiture, SOCA is also able to make use of confiscation orders. An interpretation of the information supplied by SOCA and contained in Table 9.5 was supplied to the author. Confiscation orders granted by the courts will remain open until they have been fully paid and can be then closed. Thus, they can remain open for some time either because the court has agreed to payment by instalments or because sums do not exist to be recovered. The latter was said to have occurred as a result of: the criminal having transferred ownership; or holding assets with third party interest; or having assets held offshore. Presumably, however, it might also arise as a result of the order applied for from the courts having been over-estimated in the first place. Therefore, there is expected to be a discrepancy between orders obtained and receipts recovered because in addition the flows recorded may well arise from different cases.

This information was also obtained as part of the earlier data provided by the Home Office work and this is presented in Table 9.5, for comparison with the data provided directly by SOCA shown in Table 9.6. Once again and as illustrated in Table 9.7, for the two years of overlapping data, there is inconsistency between the two data sets that frustrates the efforts made to interpret the accuracy and reliability of the information.

Table 9.5   Volume and value of confiscation orders granted and entered on JARD, 2003–2006

	2003/04	2004/05	2005/06
Confiscation orders obtained (volume)	1,554	2,596	3,935
Confiscation orders obtained (value £m)	105.1	130.3	143.0
Confiscation receipts entered onto JARD (value £m)	22.4	66.8	61.4

Note: Home Office data.

Table 9.6   POCA confiscation orders obtained 2004–2009

	2004/05	2005/06	2006/07	2007/08	2008/09
Confiscation orders obtained (volume)	2,425	3,703	4,062	5,065	5,790
Value of confiscation orders obtained* (value £m net of compensation payments to victim)	129.3	126.9	152.1	202.9	216.0
Confiscation receipts (value £m)**	54.0	61.3	77.8	96.3	89.1

Note: SOCA data; * This is the value of the order at the point it is granted by the court; ** The confiscation receipts are not directly comparable with the confiscation orders for reasons explained above.

Table 9.7   Confiscation data discrepancy between SOCA and Home Office

Difference between the two sources	2004/05	2005/06
Confiscation orders obtained (volume)	(171)	(232)
Confiscation orders obtained (value £m)	(1.0)	(16.1)
Confiscation receipts (value £m)	(12.8)	(0.1)

Note: Values expressed as SOCA data less Home Office.

Irrespective of attempts to reconcile data sets, focusing on the information provided by SOCA indicates that there has been a significant increase in the volumes of cash seizures and in the volume of confiscation orders in recent years (Tables 9.2 and 9.6). It is interesting, however, to consider the average value of seizure (as shown in Table 9.8). Despite the apparent increase in activity, the average size of each seizure is tending to decrease, and consistent with earlier findings, this trend might suggest that those being apprehended under the legislation are the less sophisticated operators.

Table 9.8   Average asset recovery for cash seizures and confiscation orders

	2004/05	2005/06	2006/07	2007/08	2008/09
Cash Seizure (volume)	1,318	1,295	2,274	5,103	6,108
Cash Seizure (value £m)	39.4	62.8	52.5	68.4	106.7
Mean value (£)	29,894	48,494	23,087	13,404	17,469
Cash forfeiture orders (volume)	590	790	1,152	2,598	3,223
Cash forfeiture orders (value £m)	21.7	30.7	31.2	33.8	39.4
Mean value (£)	36,780	38,861	27,083	13,010	12,225
Confiscation orders (volume)	2,425	3,703	4,062	5,065	5,790
Confiscation orders (value £m)	129.3	126.9	152.1	202.9	216.0
Mean value (£)	53,320	34,270	37,445	40,059	37,306

Note: SOCA data supplied to author.

A further area of interest is the source of generation for the assets recovered, that is, the predicate offence. It was possible to interrogate the recovery data by offence type and severity, something that had been missing from the original analysis of Harvey and Lau.[53] This provides an indication of cash forfeiture and confiscation orders volume and value for the year 2008/2009. The data from SOCA is presented according to the NIM (the National Intelligence Model) classification.[54] As explained by the respondent, the NIM classification is used across law enforcement and thus more widely than just the JARD database as it is a recognized way of grouping work at different levels of significance. Mostly, the NIM classification used in asset recovery will have been determined by the existing operational investigation underway in relation to the predicate offence. To a certain extent the classification could be 'subjective' to the officer entering the data, but decisions will be made in the light of this NIM classification. Of course there could still be definitional inconsistency over classification of the predicate crime which is determined by the reporting agency, especially since there are some 4,000 users of JARD over a range of organizations. For example, it is unclear as to the precise difference (if any) between 'drug trafficking' and 'money laundering drugs'.

From the data presented in tables 9.9 to 9.11, the greatest number of orders emanate from drug trafficking with the major source of orders (54 per cent) being at the lower classification NIM level 1, that is local level issues. This finding again indicates something of an absence of sophistication and is consistent with the data included in Table 9.8. Although it must be acknowledged that there remain a significant number of cases that are unallocated and simply left as 'others', it would be reasonable to expect that the average size of each recovery would increase through the various NIM levels, with larger recoveries being made at NIM level 3 ('Serious and organized crime – usually operating on a national and international scale') than at NIM 1 and, for the most part, this outcome is found to be the case. It is evident that a significant proportion of assets are recovered from drug-related crime. Recovery from fraud is on a low scale and could well arise

---

53   J. Harvey and S. Lau, fn 39.

54   As published by NCIS in 2000 (http://www.intelligenceanalysis.net/National%20 Intelligence%20Model.pdf, accessed 20 April 2013), it makes the following distinctions: Level 1: Local issues – usually the crimes, criminals, and other problems affecting a basic command unit or small force area. The scope of the crimes will be wide ranging from low-value thefts to great seriousness such as murder; Level 2: Cross-border issues – usually the actions of a criminal or other specific problems affecting more than one basic command unit. Problems may affect a group of basic command units, neighbouring forces or a group of forces. Issues will be capable of resolution by forces, perhaps with support from national agencies; Level 3: Serious and organised crime – usually operating on a national and international scale, requiring identification by proactive means and response primarily through targeting operations by dedicated units and a preventative response on a national basis. See now Association of Chief Police Officers, *Guidance on the Management of Police Information* (2nd ed., London: National Police Improvement Agency, 2010).

from welfare benefit rather than sophisticated financial fraud. There appears little recovered from other areas of criminal activity.

Table 9.9   POCA volume of cash forfeiture by NIM level and offence type financial year 2008/2009

	Drug trafficking	ML drugs	ML other	Fraud/tax evasion	Counterfeit and handling stolen goods	Burglary robbery	Terrorism arms	Prostitution and people trafficking	Others	Total
NIM Level 1	707	315	243	109	63	95	6	39	161	1,738
NIM Level 2	172	69	78	25	13	40	4	14	33	448
NIM Level 3	37	47	103	7	4	4	2	18	11	233
Others	203	73	223	67	30	35	2	14	157	804
Total	1,119	504	647	208	110	174	14	85	362	3,223

Note: Data for this and all subsequent tables supplied to the author by SOCA (tables 9.9 to 9.14).

Table 9.10   POCA value of cash forfeiture (£m) by NIM level and offence type financial year 2008/2009

£ millions	Drug trafficking	ML drugs	ML other	Fraud/tax evasion	Counterfeit and handling stolen goods	Burglary robbery	Terrorism arms	Prostitution and people trafficking	Others	Total
NIM Level 1	3.4	1.3	1.8	0.5	0.3	0.5	0.0	0.2	1.0	9.15
NIM Level 2	2.3	1.3	3.0	0.1	0.0	0.1	0.0	0.1	0.4	7.25
NIM Level 3	1.9	2.8	3.0	0.1	0.0	0.0	0.0	0.1	0.1	8.04
Others	2.1	1.1	7.5	0.8	0.6	0.1	0.1	0.1	2.6	14.96
Total	9.67	6.50	15.26	1.50	0.97	0.76	0.13	0.51	4.11	39.40

Table 9.11 **Average size (£) of forfeiture by NIM level**

£	Drug trafficking	ML drugs	ML other	Fraud/tax evasion	Counterfeit and handling stolen goods	Burglary robbery	Terrorism arms	Prostitution and people trafficking	Others	Total
NIM Level 1	4,809	4,127	7,407	4,587	4,767	5,263	–	5,128	6,211	4,809
NIM Level 2	13,372	18,841	38,461	4,000	–	2,500	–	7,143	12,121	13,372
NIM Level 3	51,551	59,574	29,126	14,286	–	–	–	5,555	9,091	51,551
Others	13,345	15,068	33,632	11,940	20,000	2,857	50,000	7,143	16,561	13,345
Total	4,809	4,127	7,407	4,587	4,767	5,263	–	5,128	6,211	4,809

In addition to more detailed information in relation to cash forfeiture, SOCA also supplied data on confiscation orders granted, although these do not necessarily imply funds have been recovered. Details of the volume of these orders are presented in Table 9.12, with corresponding values shown in Table 9.13, and average recoveries in Table 9.14. There is greater evidence of a progression in average value here than in the case of cash seizures. However, it is to be borne in mind that the amounts relate to court orders, and there is no concrete evidence that these sums either existed or were indeed collected. It is interesting to observe the activity around tax evasion/fraud, although as the majority of cases appear to be at NIM level 1, it could be that the emphasis is on tax recovery rather than fraud.

Table 9.12 **Volume of confiscation orders obtained by NIM level and offence type financial year 2008/2009**

	Drug trafficking	ML drugs	ML other	Fraud/tax evasion	Counterfeit and handling stolen goods	Burglary robbery	Terrorism arms	Prostitution and people trafficking	Others	Total
NIM Level 1	1979	71	74	494	115	403	2	25	34	3,197
NIM Level 2	485	57	102	172	51	112	4	39	27	1,049
NIM Level 3	420	26	27	150	14	24	1	20	50	732
Others	357	17	53	196	38	97	1	11	42	812
Total	3,241	171	256	1,012	218	636	8	95	153	5,790

Table 9.13 **Value of confiscation orders obtained (inclusive of compensation) by NIM level and offence type financial year 2008/2009**

	Drug trafficking	ML drugs	ML other	Fraud/tax evasion	Counterfeit and handling stolen goods	Burglary robbery	Terrorism arms	Prostitution and people trafficking	Others	Total
NIM Level 1	11.8	1.3	3.2	15.5	2.2	4.6	0.1	0.9	1.4	41.1
NIM Level 2	11.9	3.2	10.2	19.5	2.0	4.4	0.0	1.2	2.2	54.6
NIM Level 3	23.9	14.1	7.3	43.1	0.4	0.4	0.0	2.5	4.2	95.8
Others	6.3	1.3	3.0	38.5	1.0	1.3	0.0	0.4	1.3	53.1
Total	53.9	19.9	23.8	116.6	5.5	10.7	0.1	4.9	9.2	244.7

Table 9.14 **Average size of confiscation order by NIM level (£) 2008/2009**

£	Drug trafficking	ML drugs	ML other	Fraud/tax evasion	Counterfeit and handling stolen goods	Burglary robbery	Terrorism arms	Prostitution and people trafficking	Others	Total
NIM Level 1	5,963	18,310	43,243	3,036	19,130	11,414	50,000	36,000	41,176	5,963
NIM Level 2	24,563	56,140	100,000	113,372	39,216	39,286	–	30,769	81,481	24,563
NIM Level 3	56,905	542,308	270,370	287,333	28,571	16,667	–	125,000	84,000	56,905
Others	17,647	76,471	56,604	196,429	26,316	13,402	–	36,364	30,952	17,647
Total	5,963	18,310	43,243	3,036	19,130	11,414	50,000	36,000	41,176	5,963

Although appreciative of the fact that this data has been shared, it does not really enable interrogation by the author of the asset recovery database to the extent that had been hoped. One issue for academics working in this field is undoubtedly around the fact that JARD may have been originally constituted to serve a different purpose. Thus, much of the data is for operational issues that have a different objective to understanding asset recovery. It is also to be assumed that the size of the database must now be significant, making it difficult to extract meaningful information.

Discussion

The logical reasoning for asset recovery laws is that depriving criminals of the proceeds of crime will makes crime less attractive to commit whilst at the same time providing signals to deter other would-be criminal entrepreneurs. However, there is a growing body of evidence[55] that has suggested that although this tactic makes sense in theory it does not necessarily hold up in practice. The original analysis of ARA data by Harvey and Lau[56] concluded that the evidence on the sums recovered suggested criminal activity on a somewhat modest financial scale. Levi[57] supported this view of a complete lack of sophistication evident amongst techniques of laundering. Clearly, crime reduction involves a focus different to that of asset recovery, and we should endorse wholeheartedly Levi's call for an evaluation within this context. No one enquires about the 'vast annual gap between estimated proceeds of crime (both stocks and flows) and asset forfeitures/ taxes on crime'.[58] Does the evidence supplied by SOCA indicate that their activity in relation to asset recovery is indeed substantive? It would be valuable for SOCA to open wider the door on asset recovery to shed greater light not only on this area but also on their wider activities.

Harvey[59] noted the view of police that prosecutions brought under POCA would have been, and could be, far higher – they are expensive to pursue and are merely capped by the resources put into the investigations. There is evidence to suggest, however, that anti-money laundering legislation is not quite as effective and easy to implement as may have been suggested by the government in some of its earlier policy papers. While there are clear gaps in the knowledge of the current academic literature by virtue of lack of access, it is suggested that the amounts

---

55   P. Alldridge, *Money Laundering Law: Forfeiture, confiscation, civil recovery, criminal laundering and taxation of the proceeds of crime* (Oxford: Hart Publishing, 2003); P. Reuter and E. Truman, 'Anti-money laundering overkill? It's time to ask how well the system is working' (2005) *The International Economy* 55; J. Harvey, 'Just how effective is money laundering legislation' (2008) 21(3) *Security Journal* 189.

56   J. Harvey and S. Lau, fn 39.

57   M. Levi, 'New frontiers of criminal liability: Money laundering and proceeds of crime' (2000) 3(3) *Journal of Money Laundering Control* 223.

58   M. Levi, '*Pecunia non olet*? The control of money-laundering revisited' in F. Bovenkerk and M. Levi (eds), *The Organised Crime Community* (New York: Springer, 2007) 161, 177.

59   J. Harvey, 'Policing criminal money flows: the role of law enforcement – paragons or pariahs?' in P. van Duyne, J. Harvey, A. Maljevic, et al. (eds), *Crime, Money and Criminal Mobility in Europe* (Tilburg: Wolf Legal, 2009).

available for recovery are less than accurate, skewing performance expectations placed upon those with the task of its recovery.

As a final point, it is worth revisiting the words of Fleming[60] who suggested 'a more effective and informing approach to the data held would be to enable interrogation of the data with specific policy informing questions'. How very true.

---

60   M. Fleming, 'UK Law Enforcement Agency Use and Management of Suspicious Activity Reports: Towards determining the value of the regime' (London: University College, London, 30 June, 2005) 15.

Chapter 10

Corruption, the United Nations Convention against Corruption ('UNCAC') and Asset Recovery

Indira Carr and Robert Jago

Introduction

Soon after the civil uprising in Egypt and other North African states ('the Arab Spring'), there were widespread calls to return the assets of the deposed and departing political elites that had been obtained through corrupt activities and which were located in foreign jurisdictions. The demand for the return of these assets to the state of origin, the victim of the illicit activities of the political elites, is neither shocking nor surprising. It is in keeping with a fundamental legal principle that 'no man shall profit from his wrongdoing'.[1] And the victims of such large scale corruption and embezzlement of a state's wealth are the countless citizens of the state who live in abject poverty and eke out a miserable existence in inhumane conditions. As the US Attorney General Eric Holder observed: 'When kleptocrats loot their nations' treasuries, steal natural resources, and embezzle development aid, they condemn their nations' children to starvation and disease. In the face of this manifest injustice, asset recovery is a global imperative.'[2]

In response to the asset recovery calls from civil society in Egypt, Switzerland, a country well known for the secrecy of its banking laws, took the first step in the process of asset recovery by freezing the former President Mubarak's assets of £500 million soon after his overthrow. The UK response, however, was not so accommodating, as indicated by a recent investigation conducted by BBC Arabic

---

1 In *Riggs v. Palmer* 115 N.Y. 506 (1889), a probate case, the court found for the plaintiffs on the basis there would be a violation of universal law by allowing Elmer Palmer to profit from his wrongdoing. See A.C. Hutchinson, *It's All in the Game: A Nonfoundationalist Account of Law and Adjudication* (Durham: Duke University Press, 2000) for criticisms of this principle.

2 Speech at Global forum IV, Doha, November 2009, available at: http://www.justice.gov/ag/speeches/2009/ag-speech-091107.html (accessed 1 January 2011).

and released by *Al-Hayat* and *The Guardian*.[3] Mubarak's assets, including luxury houses in Chelsea and Kensington, are yet to be frozen. This news has not come as a surprise to asset recovery specialists. According to Professor Mark Pieth:

> [I]t doesn't astonish me that much because I'm not sure that the rules on so-called PEPs [Politically Exposed People] are really fully implemented in the UK. The state is not bending over backwards yet to help. … Egypt had a strong relationship to the west, and quite a strong relationship to the UK for that matter. … [For the British government] Egypt's military generals are probably still a guarantor for safety whereas the new parliament and the new president are probably looked on with reservation … I would expect Britain is careful not to squarely go against the remnants of the old regime.[4]

Asset recovery has always been a complex area of the law, especially where the assets are located in a foreign jurisdiction. The complexity is caused by a number of factors: inability of a requesting state to provide evidence to link the assets to corruption, confidence in the level of cooperation between the requesting state and the state where the assets are located, the robustness of the laws of the state where the assets are located to act upon the request and to apply suitable legal measures such as freezing, and the lack of legal and forensic expertise in the requesting state in respect of asset recovery. Added to these is the difficult issue of political will. The BBC Arabic investigation, for instance, seems to point to a lack of political will on the part of the UK. International relations experts may well be able to justify this reluctance on the part of the UK by pointing to the constant changes and shifts in a highly sensitive part of the world. Whatever the political machinations may be and however strong the justifications for not making asset recovery possible, we must not lose sight of the fact that it is the citizens who are being ignored and their rights to life, education and health that are being trampled upon.

Given the complexities and the link between corruption and the flight of assets to other jurisdictions, the United Nations Convention against Corruption 2003 ('UNCAC')[5] has devoted a whole chapter to asset recovery, also the focus of this chapter. The aim of this chapter is to assess the framework of asset recovery as provided in the UNCAC against the axes of corruption and money laundering. This chapter argues that the facilitation of asset recovery through the adoption of common standards and mutual cooperation is of limited use in an environment where anti-money laundering mechanisms such as 'know your customer' rules are

---

3   J. Shenker, 'Scandal of Mubarak's regime millions in UK', *The Guardian*, 2 September 2012 available at: http://www.guardian.co.uk/world/2012/sep/02/scandal-mub arak-regime-millions-assets-uk (accessed 10 October 2012).

4   Ibid.

5   UNGA resolution 58/4 of 31 October 2003. The convention entered into force on 14 December 2005. See http://www.unodc.org/unodc/en/treaties/CAC/.

ignored by banks[6] and legal mechanisms such as shell companies are used to hide illicitly obtained assets.

The chapter consists of two parts. The first provides a broad picture of the evolution of the international anti-corruption framework and UNCAC's place within this framework. The second part focuses on asset recovery and the use of legal mechanisms such as shell companies and shelf companies to hide the ownership of assets. Where relevant, cases are used for illustrative purposes.

Corruption and the International Anti-Corruption Framework

Corruption in Modern Times

Corruption perhaps is as old as humanity. There is no doubt that it existed in ancient kingdoms, since it features in a number of ancient Indian, Greek and Chinese texts.[7] Corruption in modern times has seen abuse of power by public officials for private gain.[8] Officials solicit bribes, be it at a petty level when providing basic services to citizens such as passports and electricity connections or at a grand level when states engage in transactions with businesses such as public procurement contracts and infrastructure projects. These demands of the public officials and the political elites were accommodated by the private sector after the Second World War through a variety of mechanisms, ranging from high levels of agent commissions to overpricing of the project. Most states turned a blind eye when the private sector supplied bribes to public officials in foreign jurisdictions. The reason was a self-seeking one. It meant that their companies gained a competitive advantage in obtaining business abroad, thereby contributing to jobs at home and to national economic growth. However, this tolerance towards the activities of the private sector shifted dramatically in the United States, when a Securities & Exchange Commission survey in the 1970s found that more than 400 US-based companies had made illegal payments of well over US$ 300 million to foreign government officials, politicians and political parties to facilitate trade. The US soon after passed the Foreign Corrupt Practices Act 1977 ('FCPA)' to prevent bribery by making it an offence to give bribes to foreign public officials. It took

---

6   See the recent scandal surrounding HSBC at: http://www.telegraph.co.uk/finance/newsbysector/banksandfinance/9496361/HSBC-in-talks-to-settle-US-money-laundering-claims.html (accessed 1 November 2012).

7   See for instance, S. Ni and P.H. Van, 'High Corruption in Ming and Qing China' available at: http://web.missouri.edu/~nix/calibration_china_02.pdf (accessed 12 November 2012); Kautilya *Arthshastra* Book II, Chapter IX 'Examination of the Conduct of Government Servants' available at: http://www.sdstate.edu/projectsouthasia/upload/Book-II-The-Duties-of-Government-Superintendents.pdf (accessed 1 September 2012).

8   This is a commonly accepted definition by the World Bank and Transparency International, a Civil Society Organisation (CSO) devoted to fighting corruption.

20 years for the standard set by the US to take root globally. Thereafter, the mid 1990s saw a flurry of activity, both on the part of the international community and economists. Suddenly the tables were turned. An activity seen as a functional tool for speeding up economic development in the third world as well as giving a competitive advantage to the private sector located in the first world[9] was now viewed as causing economic harm to a nation's wealth and the prosperity of its citizens. Corruption was seen as depriving millions of the poor from access to basic welfare needs. In the face of the gathering anti-corruption voices, the World Bank, which had hitherto remained silent on corruption despite being aware of substantial losses to corruption in the infrastructure projects funded by it, added its support to calls for taking action against corruption. Thus, in 1996, the World Bank's then President (James D. Wolfensohn) gave his famous speech on the 'cancer of corruption' and its debilitating effects on the poor and development that needed to be tackled urgently. This point was made again in 1999 at the Ninth International Anti-Corruption Conference, when he said that 'there [was] nothing more important than the issue of corruption [since] at the fore the incidence of poverty is the issue of equity, and at the core of the issue of equity is the issue of corruption'.[10] Corruption was no longer a political issue but an economic one.

Alongside these developments, a spate of conventions emerged from international law-making organizations. In the following paragraphs, we provide a brief account of some of these conventions. Among the conventions in force, the UNCAC received an extremely favourable response in the form of ratifications from over 150 states. This overwhelming response has the potential to improve legislation in many countries during the process of implementation by the ratifying state.

The International Regulatory Approach: Anti-Corruption Conventions

Inter-governmental institutions, such as the Organisation of Economic Co-operation and Development ('OECD') and the United Nations ('UN'), saw regulation as the

---

9   This functional view of corruption can be supported to some extent. For instance, corruption did ease the way for entry of foreign businesses in to India, which with its highly bureaucratic system of licences and permits, made entry of the foreign private sector near impossible. For more on the positive effects of corruption, see J. Heidenheimer and V.T. Le Vine (eds) *Political Corruption: A Handbook* (London: Transaction Publishers, 1989). However, the initial successes of corruption in creating entry may have had a long-term effect on India. It has become a highly corrupt country where corruption seems to have become de rigueur. This suggests that the functionalist view may have been short sighted in viewing corruption as a contributor to economic development.

10   Address available at: http://worldbank.org./WEBSITE/EXTERNAL/NEWS/0,,contentMDK,20023463-menuPK:34474-pagePK:34370-pIPK:34424-theSitePK:467,00.html (accessed 1 September 2012).

best initial step to tackling corruption.[11] The justification for adopting regulation was first and foremost to bring about harmonization across jurisdictions since many of them did not have corruption specific legislation or, if they did, it was outdated. Amongst the common-law jurisdictions, whilst there was legislation based on, or derived from, English law on bribery, they were not sufficiently broad in scope for instance to address the bribery of foreign public officials.

The first two conventions, the Organisation of American State Inter-American Convention against Corruption 1996 ('IACAC') and the OECD Convention on the Bribery of Foreign Public Officials in International Business Transactions ('OECD Anti-bribery Convention') were influenced by the FCPA. However, there are differences between the two conventions. The IACAC creates corruption offences both where there is a mutual exchange between the offeror and the offeree (as in a bribe) and where there is no mutual exchange (such as embezzlement).[12] Within bribery, it includes both solicitation of a bribe (passive bribery) by a public official and offer of a bribe (active bribery) to a public official. Influenced by the FCPA, it includes a provision on transnational bribery of foreign public officials.[13] A unique feature of this convention is the creation of the offence of illicit enrichment, where a government official cannot reasonably explain the increase in his assets in relation to official earnings.[14] The IACAC also tries to include comprehensive provisions on mutual cooperation between states, regarding measures such as freezing and confiscation of property, extradition and bank secrecy.[15]

The OECD Anti-bribery Convention concentrates on the supply of bribes to foreign public officials in specific circumstances, namely international business transactions.[16] It does not address the demand side (solicitation) of bribes and

---

11   There are also a number of voluntary measures for tackling corruption but these centre round the concept of corporate social responsibility (CSR) and are aimed at companies. An example of this is the OECD Guidelines for Multinational Corporations, 2011 edition: http://www.oecd.org/mne/48004323.pdf (accessed on 1 September 2012).

12   Arts VI(1)(a) and (b).

13   Art VIII. There is no definition of the term 'foreign public official', but there is a definition of 'public official' in Art I which includes any official or employee of the state or its agencies, including those who have been selected, appointed, or elected to perform activities in the name of the state or in the services of the state, at any level or its hierarchy. Presumably this will help in interpreting the term 'foreign public official'.

14   Art IX. This article is controversial since it places the burden of proof on the accused to show that the assets were obtained in a lawful manner. See D.A. Gantz, 'Globalising sanction against foreign bribery: The emergence of an international legal consensus (1998)18(2) *North Western Journal of International Law and Business* 457; R.H. Sutton, 'Controlling corruption through collective means: Advocating the Inter-American Convention against corruption' (1997) 20 *Fordham International Law Journal* 1427.

15   See Arts XIV, XV and XVI.

16   See Art 1(1). The phrase 'international business transactions' is not defined though in the Preamble it states it includes 'trade and investment'. This means that it will include not only sale of goods but also services and also investment transactions, such

understandably so, since it would create circumstances in which a state would have jurisdiction over a foreign public official. To combat accounting practices used to hide bribery, the OECD Anti-bribery Convention includes provisions that focus on the maintenance of books and records and their disclosure.[17] Better financial management reflects one of the basic supports for anti-corruption action also advanced by the World Bank in its multi-pronged approach to fighting corruption.[18] As with IACAC, there are provisions on mutual cooperation and extradition.[19] While the OECD Anti-bribery Convention does not touch upon asset recovery, the convention requires the contracting states that have made bribery of a domestic public official a predicate offence for the purposes of the application of its money-laundering legislation to extend it to include bribery of a foreign public official irrespective of the location where the bribery occurred.[20] Making bribery a predicate offence in money-laundering legislation is an important step since money laundering is closely linked with the flight of assets from a state.

These two conventions were followed by the Council of Europe Criminal Law Convention on Corruption 1999 ('COE Convention')[21] and the African Union Convention on Corruption 2003 ('AU Convention').[22] Of these the COE Convention, whilst covering the ground set by the IACAC, took the innovative step of including bribery in the private sector. Given the ambiguities that could result from generic definitions of 'public official', it also included specific provisions of the services that fall within the public sector such that any doubts about whether judges, arbitrators, members of assemblies, officials of international organizations, international courts officials, arbitrators and jurors fall within the class of 'public officials' are dispelled.[23] The concept of corruption, however, is construed restrictively to include bribery and trading in influence. It also creates a

---

as the opening of overseas campuses by universities. For more on this specific issue see I. Carr and O. Outhwaite, 'The OECD Anti-Bribery Convention: Ten Years On' (2009) 5(1) *Manchester Journal of International Economic Law* 3. In the UK Bribery Act 2010 the phrase 'relevant commercial organisation' is widely defined to include the activities of educational institutions (such as Oxford Publishing Ltd who had to pay £1.9m to the Serious Fraud Office as a result of having secured lucrative contracts in different African countries: A. Spence, 'Oxford University Press learns an expensive lesson', *The Times*, 4 July 2012.

17   Art 8.

18   See 'A Multi-pronged Strategy for Combating Corruption' available at: http://siteresources.worldbank.org/ECAEXT/Resources/Anticorruption/chapter4.pdf (accessed 1 January 2010).

19   See Arts 9 and 10.

20   Art 7.

21   CETS 173. There is also a Council of Europe Civil Law Convention (CETS 174).

22   Text available at: http://www.africa-union.org/official_documents/Treaties_%20Conventions_%20Protocols/Convention%20on%20Combating%20Corruption.pdf (accessed 21 April 2013).

23   See Arts –6, Arts 12 and 20.

specific accounting offence with the intention of improving financial management such that practices of creating or using of an invoice or other accounting documents containing false or incomplete information, and unlawfully omitting to make a record of payment, are not engaged in.[24] The convention also includes provisions on mutual cooperation and extradition.[25]

By comparison, the AU Convention expands the concept of corruption extensively and provides a list of offences which include active and passive bribery, trading in influence, embezzlement[26] and the controversial illicit enrichment offence that was created in the IACAC. A novel provision is the one on political funding, which expects states to proscribe the use of funds acquired through illegal and corrupt practices to finance political parties and incorporate the principle of transparency in such funding.[27] It is notable that the AU Convention is the only convention that raises the issue of funding of political parties. It is not unknown in developing countries for illicitly obtained funds to be channelled into the funding of political parties, and these contributions are returned by way of favours (e.g. special taxation arrangements, public procurement contracts, sale of land) to the donors once the parties come into power. The issue of party funding, however, is extremely sensitive, though in developed countries it is not normally addressed in anti-corruption legislation. Next, the AU Convention makes the use and laundering of, or the concealment of, proceeds from corrupt activities into criminal offences.[28] This is consolidated further through provisions on procedure that require states to trace, freeze and seize and confiscate the instrumentalities and proceeds of corruption.[29] As we shall ascertain when considering the UNCAC asset recovery framework, the AU provisions make only a slight dent into the issue of asset recovery and does not go far enough in involving financial institutions in the fight against corruption. Recognizing the link between money laundering and corruption and the difficulties caused by banking secrecy in the investigation process, the AU Convention expects states parties to enter into bilateral agreements to waive banking secrecy on dubious accounts together and to impart powers to competent authorities, subject to judicial oversight, to obtain evidence that is in the possession of banks and financial institutions.

As the title of the AU Convention makes explicit, it also focuses on prevention. Relevant provisions range from raising public awareness and protection of informants to raising the integrity of public officials through asset declaration and

---

24   Art 14.

25   Arts 26 and 27.

26   Embezzlement was specifically made an offence, since in many civil law countries the offence of embezzlement is regarded as distinct from corruption which normally refers to bribery. See A. Muna, *Understanding the African Union Convention on Preventing and Combating Corruption and Related Offences* (Berlin: Transparency International, 2005).

27   Art 10.

28   Arts 4 and 6.

29   Art 16.

codes of conduct. As with the other conventions, there are provisions on mutual cooperation and extradition.

Soon after the AU Convention, the UNCAC was adopted.[30] While the AU Convention set the scene for a comprehensive approach, the UNCAC went further. The two areas that are relevant for the purposes of this chapter – asset recovery and money laundering – are discussed at some length in the second part of this chapter. The UNCAC is much wider in scope than the conventions drafted by the OAS and the OECD since it includes a list of offences covering both private and public sector corruption, active and passive bribery, trading in influence, illicit enrichment, abuse of function, and laundering and concealing the proceeds of corruption.[31] In taking this comprehensive approach, it also covers aspects that may hinder enforcement, such as use of force, threats or the offer of bribes in order to induce false testimony or interfere in the giving of testimony or production of evidence or the intimidation of officials in order to interfere with the exercise of their official duties in respect of the offices covered by the convention. Protection of whistle-blowers and witnesses is also addressed.[32]

Preventive measures, a matter addressed to some extent by the AU Convention, are also addressed in the UNCAC. These range from provisions on banking secrecy, prevention and detection of transfers of proceeds of crime, creation of financial intelligence units, participation of society, improving accounting procedures and introducing codes of conduct both in the private and public sectors. Unlike the other conventions, the UNCAC takes a more expansive approach to mutual cooperation by including various provisions detailing cooperation between national authorities, between national authorities and the private sector, international cooperation, mutual legal assistance, law enforcement cooperation and extradition.[33] After all, mutual cooperation is an important cornerstone for facilitating and enabling asset recovery.

Asset Recovery

Before engaging with UNCAC's asset-recovery framework, it makes sense to discuss briefly the justification of asset recovery since much of the literature on this subject does not explore this issue, there being an assumption that asset recovery is a desirable form of punishment.[34] In justifying the recovery of assets,

---

30   Text available at: http://www.unodc.org/documents/treaties/UNCAC/Publications/Convention/08-50026_E.pdf (accessed 18 January 2013).

31   Arts 15–24.

32   Art 32.

33   Arts 38–40, 43–46.

34   The importance of asset recovery from a functional perspective is highlighted in the *Legislative Guide for the Implementation of the United Nations Convention against*

we draw upon the arguments put forward generally in relation to punishment by penologists and consider their application here.

Justifying Asset Recovery

The justifications for asset recovery are multi-faceted. The recovery of assets from a wayward company, a rogue official or a straightforward embezzler demonstrates a variety of functions. Initially there is a willingness to punish; there is an opportunity to deter others along with an opportunity for symbolic denunciation of an action; there can be a commitment to recover and finally there should be an opportunity for rehabilitation, which can involve reparation. In this section we explore each of these functions with a view to understanding why the recovery of assets is important and what theoretical justifications there are for this recovery. Finally, we shall ask if there needs to be a primary function from which all others follow.

One of the important functions of asset recovery is to punish those who have unlawfully dissipated assets. We have referred to the company which has become 'wayward', the official who is labelled 'rogue', and the 'straightforward' embezzler. These entities must be punished for their activities. Traditional justifications for punishment adopt a retributive tone and require explanation. Walker[35] explores a range of justifications for retribution, and considering two of them here will assist with the task in hand.

Firstly, those who have dissipated assets arguably owe a 'debt to society'. The offender has generated a debt as a result of his actions and the state now requires that debt to be repaid. Walker is suspicious of the label 'debt', preferring it to be considered in the context of reparation. Using the punishment of attempts to illustrate his argument, it is understood that if someone tries to dissipate assets they owe no debt to society but we would still punish them.[36]

Secondly, it can be argued that punishment can rectify an 'unfair advantage'. The offender has taken something which does not belong to them, and this is to their advantage. Walker is concerned about this justification and relies on the work of Duff to explain his concern:

> What kind of attitude is expressed in the thought that the immoral or criminal agent has gained an unfair profit? That thought is most familiar when we ourselves are tempted by the wrongdoer's actions; we think that someone who has profited by trickery or deceit could do so only because others restrain themselves from such immoral methods – and that we could do as well as him if we did not thus restrain ourselves; we watch a dishonest entrepreneur,

---

Corruption (New York: United Nations) para. 667.

35   N. Walker, *Why Punish?* (Oxford: Oxford University Press, 1991).
36   Ibid., 73.

or a colleague on the fiddle, or an adulterous spouse, with envious and self-righteously disapproving eyes. Surely, however, we do not think of the murderer or rapist in such terms as these or, if our condemnation of them does reflect such thoughts, we should surely feel ashamed of ourselves for being thus tempted by what we do. This suggests that the idea that the wicked profit unfairly by their wrong-doing reflects a grudging and less than whole-hearted commitment to the values which they flout ...[37]

The message here is clear. If we label the purpose of punishment as the rectifying of an unfair advantage, we are supporting the idea that the 'treatment' of the assets is no more than a 'taking advantage' of an existing position. Such labels minimize the impact of the activity and reduce it to a cursory disapproval. This should not be a justification for recovery.

One condition for punishment is deserts.[38] To ensure just deserts, any punishment has to be commensurate with the offence committed. This is the proportionality principle, and it is as relevant for those who dissipate assets as any other offender. Von Hirsch and Ashworth explain the fundamental tenets of the proportionality principle.[39] First, offences need to be ranked according to the ordinal level of seriousness. This is where offences are compared to each other and ranked according to seriousness.[40] Depending on the level of dissipation, it is assumed that these offences will not be punished more harshly than those which involve a significant violation of physical integrity. Secondly, the offence needs to be fixed within the type of offence, and this is cardinal proportionality.[41] Here, the amount of assets taken and factors such as abuse of trust are considered. This enables the individual offender to receive their just deserts and is the preferred rationale for punishment of the individual.

Deterrence is arguably a key justification for asset recovery, especially where assets are recovered as a result of corruption. Deterrence takes two forms, general and individual. The chief proponent of general deterrence was Bentham who argued that punishment was a form of pain to be avoided.[42] Punishment could be justified if it benefits society as a whole by deterring offenders. This idea then lost popularity until Andenaes resurrected it during the 1960s.[43] General deterrence

---

37   R.A. Duff, *Trials and Punishments* (Cambridge: Cambridge University Press, 1986) quoted in N. Walker, *Why Punish?* (Oxford: Oxford University Press, 1991) 76.

38   See further L. Alexander, K. Kessler Ferzan with S. Morse, *Crime and Culpability: A Theory of Criminal Law* (Cambridge: Cambridge University Press, 2009) 7.

39   A. von Hirsch and A. Ashworth, *Proportionate Sentencing* (Oxford: Oxford University Press, 2004) 131.

40   Ibid., 137.

41   Ibid., 141.

42   J. Bentham, *Introduction to the Principles of Morals and Legislation* (London: Payne, 1789).

43   J. Andenaes, 'The general preventative effects of punishment' (1966) 114 *University of Pennsylvania Law Review*, 949.

refers to the effect that a threat of punishment has in convincing people to refrain from prohibited conduct.[44] It would appear that the easiest measure of general deterrence is an examination of the reoffending rates in any one particular type of offence. There are clear limits to this form of deterrence. First, it is empirically very difficult to measure the effectiveness of any one deterrent upon those who refrain from engaging in the prohibited conduct. Secondly, it is objectionable for any one person to be disproportionately punished with the aim of deterring society as a whole.[45] In the context of financial crimes, the case of Bernard Madoff[46] illustrates general deterrence in practice. The nature of his fraudulent offending was extensive, but his sentence of 150 years in prison was arguably disproportionate on the ordinal scale and certainly contrary to the totality principle. This principle requires those who sentence to add up the number of offences to be sentenced and then consider the overall penalty to ensure a proportionate sentence. In the Madoff case, general deterrence required a message to deter others who thought such schemes would ensure profiteering through illegal means.[47] And yet a 2009 poll suggested that only 19 per cent feel deterred as a result of Madoff's sentence.[48]

Individual deterrence is charged with ensuring that offenders do not reoffend once their punishment is over. In the case of Madoff, this may not be possible due to his extensive prison sentence. However, in less alarming examples the purpose is to deter the actor from engaging in the prohibited conduct again. Once again, this concept has been criticized. It has been suggested that there is little evidence to suggest that if an offender is punished more harshly for the sake of deterrence they will then be deterred from offending again.[49] It has also been argued that whilst desistance may be the desired path for offenders, it is sadly not the case that they will always be able to stick to that path.[50]

Does deterrence therefore assist us when justifying asset recovery? It is submitted cautiously that it does. Firstly those who have dissipated assets tend, although not exclusively, to include people who have previously been in positions

---

44   A. von Hirsch, *Doing Justice: The Choice of Punishments* (New York: Hill and Wang, 1976) 38.

45   A. Ashworth, *Sentencing and Criminal Justice* (Cambridge: Cambridge University Press, 2010) 78–84.

46   See D. Rushe, 'Bernard Madoff says banks and funds were "complicit" in $90bn fraud', available at: http://www.guardian.co.uk/business/2011/feb/16/bernard-madoff-says-banks-complicit-in-fraud?intcmp=239 (accessed 1 November 2012).

47   See http://www.guardian.co.uk/business/2009/jun/29/bernard-madoff-sentence (accessed 18 January 2013)

48   See http://mycrains.crainsnewyork.com/blogs/polls/2009/06/will-madoffs-150ye ar-sentence/ (accessed 18 January 2013)

49   L. Zedner, *Criminal Justice* (Oxford: Oxford University Press, 2004) 93–95.

50   R. Burnett and S. Maruna, 'So prison works, does it?' (2004) 43 *Howard Journal of Criminal Justice* 390.

of power. Had Sani Abacha[51] and Ferdinand Marcos[52] been sent to prison, they would have found conditions in those prisons rather less opulent than the living conditions, to which they had become accustomed. Secondly, the international community has an obligation to prevent, for the reasons outlined above, widespread dissipation, and therefore penalties are needed to deter those who would otherwise consider this course of action. However, this stance may offend any principle of proportionality, and a clearer research base, demonstrating empirically the efficacy of this principle, is required to defend its application.

Closely linked to deterrence is the idea of denunciation. Denunciation involves the prevention of crime through the prohibited activity being denounced. Like deterrence, it has a social value and it requires society, through the courts, to express condemnation of the activity with a view to educating people as to the consequences of offending. Denunciation also requires a symbolic blaming which is linked with excessive treatment as a way of urging people to desist from the temptation to engage in the prohibited conduct. This arguably provides social cohesion, as society sees that those who break the law are punished for doing so.[53] Although 'making an example' of an offender is potentially attractive because of its communicative function, the concerns surrounding deterrence equally apply here that any punishment needs to be proportionate.

A key justification for asset recovery involves incapacitation. By placing the offender in prison, by freezing their assets and by preventing companies from trading, the idea is to stop the prohibited activity. The most reliable form of incapacitation is the death penalty.[54] However, the nature of these financial offences means that the death penalty can never be justified. Even in light of Madoff's excessive activities, it was never seriously thought that such frauds should result in the death penalty.[55] Most offenders will receive determinate sentences. The length of their sentence will depend on the nature of the offending, and only if the public requires protection will the offender be subject to an extended sentence. The offences here, in spite of their extensive collateral societal consequences, would rarely demand a penalty for public protection. This suggests that incapacitation can only ever be limited in its effectiveness. If people have been sophisticated in their methods of dissipating assets it is naive to think they would be unable to continue this activity if incarcerated. A company can be prevented from trading, but it can simply acquire another name and set up its stall elsewhere. The physical

---

51 Sani Abacha was the President of Nigeria from 1993 to 1998 and is said to have embezzled £5 billion during this period from Nigeria.

52 The Marcos Case is discussed below.

53 M. Moore, *Placing Blame: A Theory of Criminal Law* (Oxford: Oxford University Press, 1997) 84–85.

54 N. Walker, *Why Punish?* (Oxford: Oxford University Press, 1991) 34.

55 It has been suggested that China would have executed such an extensive fraudster. See http://www.law.com/jsp/law/international/LawArticleIntl.jsp?id=1202427517680&Is_Chinas_WhiteCollar_Death_Penalty_Fair (accessed 1 November 2012).

restraints of incapacitation do not directly apply in the case of asset recovery. Incapacitation does deprive the offender of their previously acquired lifestyle but the means of continued offending are arguably still within their grasp.

The final justification for asset recovery is rehabilitation. From an individual offender perspective compulsory measures can be justified on the basis that they will 'cure' or at least enable the offender's 'recovery'. This means that an individual can be treated in an attempt to divert them from patterns of offending behaviour. The concept of corporate rehabilitation has also emerged. In 2006, it was discovered that Siemens, a German engineering company, had been dissipating assets as a way of offering substantial bribes to win lucrative contracts. Siemens then had to go through a period of corporate rehabilitation. Siemens paid over €2bn in fines and has been required to pay US$100m to non-profit organizations fighting corruption. This form of rehabilitation has seen Siemens 'atone for its sins' in an attempt to restore the trust of both the business community and society at large.[56] Rehabilitation, however, is not without its critics and concerns have often been raised about disproportionate penalties being imposed in the name of 'treating' an offender.[57] Yet the Siemens example would suggest that there is room for this justification in the case of companies.

Alongside the justification for rehabilitation, there is the role of reparation. Closely linked with rehabilitation, it requires some form of community participation. Zedner has argued that reparation is 'a rebellion against law's dominion and the reassertion of populist rights of participation'.[58] This is important in the context of asset recovery because sometimes punishing the individual or company offender whether to deter, denounce or incapacitate is not enough. In this context, reparation has much to offer. We return to the looting of Nigeria by Sani Abacha. Whilst Abacha was dead by the time his appropriation of funds (between US$3 and 5 billion) had been discovered, the response by the international community demonstrated a commitment to a form of 'state reparation'. Abacha had been able to carry out this looting by utilizing a variety of complex transactions around the world. By 2004, US$505.5 million, which had been hidden in Swiss banks, was sent back to Nigeria. Rather than being dissipated once more, it was decided that these funds could be divested back into the community via pro-poor projects as a form of reparation. The success of these projects has been discussed elsewhere, but the commitment to some form of reparation is clear.[59]

---

56   See http://www.guardian.co.uk/sustainable-business/recovering-business-trust-sie mens (accessed 1 November 2012).

57   A. Ashworth, *Sentencing and Criminal Justice* 86–87.

58   L. Zedner, 'Reparation and Retribution: Are they reconcilable? (1994) 57 *Modern Law Review* 228 at 232.

59   I. Jimu, 'Managing proceeds of asset recovery: The case of Nigeria, Peru, the Philippines and Kazakhstan' *International Centre for Asset Recovery Working Paper Series No 06* (Basel: Basel Institute of Governance, 2009).

Having explored the different justifications for asset recovery, it would appear that declaring a primary justification is context specific. We must guard against polarizing these justifications in an attempt to make them presumptively incompatible,[60] but it is clear that in the case of individuals there is a strong impulse for all sentences to punish but to do so proportionately. This is more difficult in the case of corporations, and so it has been argued that in these instances rehabilitation is preferred. According to Braithwaite and Geis:

> [r]ehabilitation is a more workable strategy with corporate crime than with traditional crime because criminogenic organizational structures are more malleable than are criminogenic human perspectives. A new internal compliance group can be put in place much more readily than a new superego.[61]

The approach taken towards Siemens, which was involved in corruption globally, is illustrative of this view.[62] When it comes to individual offenders dissipating assets in abuse of their position, then there is much to be said for the reparative model. The example of Nigeria[63] provides a practical and potentially effective response to the problem when assets have been dissipated and substantial sums of state money recovered. There is little point endowing another individual with such large sums, and the pro-poor projects offer some opportunity for reparation.[64]

The UNCAC

Asset Recovery and Money Laundering in the UNCAC

Until the design of the UNCAC asset recovery framework, there was no internationally agreed framework on asset recovery. Instead, asset recovery was dependent on the national laws and the goodwill of the state to which a request was made. The Marcos case illustrates some of the difficulties associated with investigation and the challenges faced in foreign jurisdictions by the requesting state, though only an outline can be provided here.[65]

---

60   L. Zedner, *Criminal Justice* 107.

61   J. Braithwaite and G. Geis, 'On theory and action for corporate crime control' (1982) 28 *Crime and Delinquency* 292 at 310.

62   Dietz and Gillespie view this as 'penance', suggestive of remorse and renewed 'benevolence' see G. Dietz and G. Gillespie, *The Recovery of Trust: Case Studies of Organisation Failure and Trust Repair* (London: Institute of Business Ethics, 2012) 10.

63   I. Jimu, 'Managing proceeds of asset recovery: The case of Nigeria, Peru, the Philippines and Kazakhstan' 11–15.

64   See http://siteresources.worldbank.org/INTNIGERIA/Resources/Abacha_Funds_ Monitoring_1221.pdf (accessed 1 November 2012).

65   For more details see Chronology (draft 1): Efforts to Recover Assets Looted by Ferdinand Marcos of the Philippines (August 2007), available at: http://www.assetrecovery.

The Marcos Case

Ferdinand Marcos was the President of the Philippines from 1965 to 1986. In 1983 his government was accused of assassinating his opponent, Benigno Aquino Jr. The resulting public outrage eventually manifested itself as the 'People Power Revolution', and he was eventually removed from power in 1986. It was discovered that, during his tenure, he had moved funds accumulated through kickbacks, bribes and withdrawals from the treasury, and had diverted international aid to a number of foreign jurisdictions including Switzerland.[66] The successor government immediately set up the Philippines Presidential Commission of Good Government ('PCGG') to recover the assets. They had a difficult task, but the Malacanang documents[67] helped in tracing part of the appropriated assets to Switzerland. However, there remained problems since the Philippines did not have a treaty with Switzerland on mutual legal assistance ('MLA') in criminal matters. Nevertheless, the Swiss authorities (the Swiss Federal Council) imposed a unilateral freeze order on Marcos's assets. They also instructed the Swiss Banking Commission to find out in which banks the Marcos's assets were located. This was an unprecedented act on the part of the Swiss authorities, but, according to the Swiss Federal Council, it had expected a request from the Philippines. When the MLA request eventually arrived, the Swiss authorities found that the request was generic and indeterminate.[68] In December 1990 the Swiss Federal Supreme Court agreed to the transfer of bank documents subject to certain conditions.[69] In the absence of a mutual treaty between the two countries on mutual assistance, Switzerland relied on its Federal Act on International Mutual Assistance in Criminal Matters.[70]

---

org/kc/resources/org.apache.wicket.Application/repo?nid=62506d95-a33e-11dc-bf1b-335d0754ba85 (accessed 1 November 2012).

66   T.S. Greenberg et al., *Stolen Asset Recovery (StAR) Initiative Challenges, Opportunities and Action Plan* (Washington, DC: The World Bank, 2007); C. de Quiros, *Dead Aim: How Marcos Ambushed Philippine Democracy* (Pasig City: Foundation for Worldwide People's Power, 1997).

67   These were documents found in the Malacanang Palace which had yet not been shredded by the fleeing Marcoses. See D. Chaikin, 'Tracking the proceeds of organised crime – The Marcos Case' Paper presented at the Transnational Crime Conference convened by the Institute of Criminology in association with the Australian Federal Police and Australian Customs Service, Canberra, 9–10 March 2000.

68   This deficiency could perhaps be attributed to the lack of expertise of the PCGG.

69   See the conditions in 'Chronology (draft 1): Efforts to Recover Assets Looted by Ferdinand Marcos of the Philippines (August 2007)', available at: http://www.asset recovery.org/kc/resource/org.apache.wicket.Application/repo?nid=62506d95-a33e-11dc-bf1b-335d0754ba85 (accessed 1 November 2012).

70   Bundesgesetz über internationale Rechtshilfe in Strafsachen (Rechtshilfegesetz, IRSG), adopted 20 March 1981.

After many twists and turns, they agreed to a transfer of the frozen assets. On the basis of this a new request was made by the Philippines authorities to transfer the assets to the Philippine National Bank ('PNB'). As expected there was an appeal against the order from Marcos, other parties, banks and the foundations that Marcos had established. The Superior Court quashed the District Attorney's decision. The case went to the Federal Supreme Court which stated that in exceptional circumstances 'anticipatory restitution' was possible in the absence of a valid and enforceable decision on the part of the requesting state.[71] The Supreme Court also examined whether the proceedings against Marcos satisfied human-rights standards including the right to a fair trial but found that the Philippines met these standards by virtue of their constitution being a party to the International Covenant on Civil and Political Rights and the fact that Switzerland had recently entered into an extradition treaty with the Philippines.

As a result, funds to the value of approximately US$ 567,200,000 were transferred to a PNB escrow account in 1998, but these funds were not freely available to the Philippines government. The District Attorney of Zurich retained control over the funds according to the guidelines set by the Attorney General.[72] In 2003 the Philippines Supreme Court decided that the funds held in the escrow account had been illegitimately obtained by Marcos and that these funds should be transferred to the government and be used to buy land to support poor farmers.[73] The funds held in the PNB escrow account were finally transferred to the Philippines treasury in 2004. The delay in the transfer to the treasury was in part due to the demand for compensation following successful proceedings by the Society of Ex-Detainees for the Liberation of Detainees and for Amnesty invoking the US Alien Tort Claims Act[74] against Marcos for torture.[75]

This case study highlights the problems encountered in asset recovery. The lack of evidence hinders the tracing of funds. It was purely fortuitous that some of the crucial documentation had not been destroyed by the departing president which meant that the investigating authorities were able to trace these funds to accounts in Swiss banks. The absence of a bilateral treaty for mutual assistance between the two states could have caused problems had not Switzerland's national legislation enabled this process to occur. Also the multiplicity of actions in different jurisdictions, initiated not only by the authorities but also by the torture victims,

---

71   See D. Chaikin, 'Tracking the proceeds of organised crime – The Marcos Case' at 13–14.

72   Ibid.

73   Chronology (draft 1): Efforts to Recover Assets Looted by Ferdinand Marcos of the Philippines (August 2007)', available at: http://www.assetrecovery.org/kc/resources/org. apache.wicket.Application/repo?nid=62506d95-a33e-11dc-bf1b-335d0754ba85 (accessed 1 November 2012) 13.

74   28 USC s 1789

75   See M. Mendoza, 'Is closure still possible for the Marcos human rights victims' (2012) 1 *Social Transformations* 115.

added a further dimension to how the repatriated funds were to be used. A further issue is whether the incoming regime in the requesting state will follow the rule of law and respect human-rights standards when prosecuting deposed leaders accused of embezzling state funds. An examination of the chronology of the Marcos case also indicates that the authorities in the requesting state were inexperienced, as for instance where they sent a request which was generic and indeterminate. A further issue is the nagging doubt even where assets are recovered as to whether all of the assets have been traced. It is commonly believed that the assets recovered by the Philippines were just a fraction of the assets embezzled by Marcos.

The UNCAC Asset Recovery Framework

Against some of the complexities described above, it makes perfect sense to have a common framework that facilitates the recovery of assets. For the UNCAC, the return of assets is a fundamental principle of the convention as expressed in Article 51. Cooperation, assistance and strengthening of procedures within financial institutions and state parties are seen as the cornerstones for facilitating the recovery of the assets. The approach enshrined in Chapter V of the UNCAC includes preventative mechanisms,[76] measures for direct recovery of property,[77] procedures for asset recovery that include taking action on foreign confiscation orders,[78] and the return of the property to the requesting states, or legitimate owners and compensating victims.[79]

Article 52 focuses on prevention by requiring states to put in place procedures to ensure that relevant gatekeepers such as banks are aware of the sources of their funds and the names of beneficiaries and to plug any gaps that may facilitate the use of financial institutions for hiding illicitly obtained funds. This article therefore requires states parties to adopt the following: issuing advisories requiring financial institutions to 'verify identity of customers, take reasonable steps to determine the identity of beneficial owners of funds deposited into high-value accounts and to conduct enhanced scrutiny of accounts sought or maintained by or on behalf of individuals who are, or have been, entrusted with prominent public functions and their family members and close associates'.[80] The intention behind this provision is to stop looted assets from getting into the system and emerging as legitimate funds. The states parties are required to draw on the initiatives of regional, interregional and multilateral organizations[81] on money laundering, for

---

76   Article 52.
77   Article 53.
78   Articles 54–55.
79   Article 57.
80   Article 52(1).
81   According to the interpretation of Art 14 on money laundering in the UNCAC, it is clear that this refers to the Recommendations from the Financial Action Task Force on Money Laundering, and other initiatives from, for example, the Caribbean Financial Action

the purposes of identifying: (1) the types of persons for whose accounts enhanced scrutiny will be expected; (2) the types of accounts to which particular attention should be paid; and (3) to notify the financial institutions of the identity of particular persons whose accounts will require enhanced scrutiny.[82] There is no doubt that such guidance from the state will help the financial institutions to take a harmonized and effective approach in exercising their due diligence and customer identification activities.[83] As part of exercising diligence financial institutions are expected to maintain adequate records of the accounts including the identity of the customer and the beneficial owner.[84] There is however no indication of period of time for maintaining these records, but, given that corruption-related prosecutions can take a long time, it would make sense to keep these records for a reasonably long period. After all, the requirement for keeping records serves an evidentiary purpose and hence an essential component in the investigation and identification processes of assets. While it is left to states parties to decide the period for which the records should be maintained, the lack of physical space for keeping these records is unlikely to pose a problem in most countries with sophisticated IT infrastructures. However, in some developing countries, banks still continue to use handwritten ledgers, and these states may have to face these issues when determining the length of time for which the records are kept. There may be other factors that states parties will have to consider in implementing these provisions. These relate to data management and include issues of confidentiality, banking secrecy, privacy and data protection.

The UNCAC also requires states parties to prohibit the establishment of banks that do not have a physical presence and that are not affiliated with a regulated financial authority.[85] This provision lacks clarity since it does not indicate what the meaning of the phrase 'physical presence' is. The interpretative notes, however, state that the phrase is to be understood as having 'meaningful mind and management' located within the jurisdiction.[86] This suggests that low-level staff would not meet the requirement of physical presence. It seems similar to the 'directing mind' principle used for finding the liability of legal persons in common

---

Task Force, the Commonwealth, the Council of Europe and the European Union, amongst others.

    82   Article 52(2)(a)-(b).
    83   See UN General Assembly A/A58/422/Add.1.para.52, 7 October 2003: http://www.unodc.org/pdf/crime/convention_corruption/session_7/422add1.pdf (accessed 1 November 2012).
    84   Article 52(3).
    85   Article 52(4).
    86   Ibid.

law.[87] Another note refers to such banks as shell banks,[88] but it is not possible to state with any clarity how these entities are organized or operated.

Article 52(5) and (6) continues the preventative mechanisms by requiring states parties to consider financial disclosure on the part of the public officials and to maintain appropriate records. However, these provisions are optional, and states parties are only required to 'consider' these paragraphs when implementing the convention. It must be added that many states do have asset declaration laws, but their effectiveness is highly questionable. The approaches adopted are not uniform, and there does not seem to be any formal process for verifying the declarations. To illustrate, in Ghana asset declaration is voluntary and the information given by the public official is not verified, whilst in Uganda filing is required every two years though there does not seem to be a process of checking.[89] If the purpose of asset declaration is to identify illicit activities, making it optional is questionable.

A problem that could be faced by the requesting state is that the mutual legal assistance afforded by the state in which the assets are located may only make reference to assistance in criminal cases. In some circumstances, the requesting state may wish to take civil action – this could be due to the death of the offender or the inability to meet the higher burden of proof required in criminal cases.[90] Civil action is then more viable, and the convention makes room for alternative options. Article 53(a) requires states parties to permit another state party to initiate civil action in their courts to establish title to or ownership of property acquired through the offences of corruption established by the UNCAC. The other provisions within Article 53 when implemented will also enable the courts to pay compensation or damages to another state party for the harm caused by the corruption offences,[91] and to recognize another state party's claim as a legitimate owner of property acquired through the commission of corruption offences.[92]

The mechanisms for recovery are addressed in Article 54. Confiscation of property is addressed in Article 54(1). By virtue of Article 54(1)(a) states parties are required to permit its competent authorities to give effect to a confiscation

---

87   *Tesco Supermarkets Ltd v Nattrass* [1972] AC 153; see also E. Ferran, 'Corporate Attribution and the Directing Mind and Will' (2001) 127 *Law Quarterly Review* 239.

88   The Financial Action Task Force Recommendations' Glossary defines shell bank as 'a bank that has no physical presence in the country in which it is incorporated and licensed, and which is unaffiliated with a regulated financial group that is subject to effective consolidated supervision. *Physical presence* means meaningful mind and management located within a country. The existence simply of a local agent or low level staff does not constitute physical presence': http://www.fatf-gafi.org/pages/glossary/s-t/ (accessed 1 November 2012)

89   Ghana Public Office Holders (Declaration of Assets and Disqualification) Act 1998 and Uganda Leadership Code Act 2002.

90   In the UK it is possible to take both civil and criminal action for recovery of assets. See Chapter 3.

91   Article 53(b).

92   Article 53(c).

order from another state party. They are also required to take measures that would permit its competent authorities to order the confiscation of property of foreign origin on the basis of money-laundering convictions. These provisions obviously are geared to ease the process of confiscation, and when implemented should bring about a harmonization in the laws of states parties. Article 54(1) also has another (optional) solution to ease confiscation of property. Paragraph (c) requests states parties to consider the confiscation of property without a criminal conviction in cases in which the 'offender cannot be prosecuted by reason of death, flight or absence or in other appropriate cases'. While death, flight or absence are easy to interpret, it is not very clear what 'appropriate cases' would cover, and the Legislative Guide is unhelpful. Not being mandatory, it will be interesting to see how many states implement Article 54(1)(c). Article 54(2) provides details on the measures to be taken by the state parties for freezing and seizure of property which will be confiscated eventually.

Article 55 focuses on mutual assistance and international legal cooperation and in brief requires states parties to provide 'assistance to the greatest extent possible'. The importance of legal assistance is vital to the success of any attempt to recover assets. Article 55 provides details on how requests for confiscation are to be made and the details that are to be included. As we saw in the Marcos case, the request for MLA from the authorities in the Philippines was criticized for being indeterminate and generic. Such an issue should not arise when the UNCAC is fully implemented by the states parties.

The issue of the return of the assets is covered by Article 57, and it is a mandatory requirement that states parties ensure that property they have confiscated can be returned to the requesting state whilst taking into account the bona fide rights of third parties who may be the legitimate owners. The illustration provided in the Legislative Guide is helpful. While it may be possible to argue where the funds have been embezzled from the state treasury (as in the Marcos case) they belong to the state and should be returned to it, the same cannot be said where the funds have been acquired through a bribe from a private party or a company. The state here has no legal ownership, though it could argue that it was harmed by the bribe that was given. The UNCAC addresses these competing interests in Article 57(3) by setting rules that take into account a number of factors, such as the type of corruption offence and the strength of evidence of ownership.

A feature that stands out in Chapter V is the provision of special cooperation[93] which could be described as a proactive measure to disclose information to another state party if they think that the information might be useful to them for the purposes of investigation, prosecution or judicial proceeding. How far this provision will be acted upon by the states parties during the implementation stage is debatable, since it seems to place an onerous burden on the relevant state authorities not only to maintain a watchful eye but to inform other states parties who may be affected by the information gathered, thus becoming an offshore investigative arm.

---

93   Article 56.

The preventative theme in the context of asset recovery as introduced by Article 52 is strengthened in Article 57, which requires states parties to cooperate with one another so that the illicit transfer of proceeds can be prevented and fought effectively. States are also expected to cooperate in promoting ways and means of recovering these proceeds. For this purpose, states are required to consider the establishing of a financial intelligence unit ('FIU') with responsibility for receiving, analysing and disseminating reports of suspicious activities to competent authorities. The suggestion for specialized units is a theme that occurs in other parts of the convention as well, for instance the setting up of specialized anti-corruption agencies to deal solely with corruption related offences. However, the effectiveness of such specialized units is debatable. Many developing countries have anti-corruption agencies (including Zambia, Tanzania, Uganda and Ethiopia), but so far these have had limited success in prosecuting corruption cases successfully or curbing corruption.[94] The reasons often provided for their lack of success is lack of funding and/or specialist expertise, and political interference. To some extent, the UK Serious Fraud Office has faced similar problems, illustrated by the lack of funding as well as political interference when the investigation of BAE Systems was dropped.[95]

Money Laundering and the UNCAC

In taking a comprehensive approach to fighting corruption, the UNCAC does not restrict itself solely to what may be seen as obvious candidates (e.g. bribery and trading in influence). It also includes in its mandatory list an offence of laundering of the proceeds of crime in Article 23.

Provided the knowledge and intentionality requirements are met, Article 23(1) (a)(i) covers both the person converting or transferring property in illicitly obtained goods for the purposes of disguising the illicit origin of the goods and the person assisting the person who is involved in the commission of a predicate offence. Article 23(1)(a)(ii) focuses on the concealment or disguise of the true nature, sources, location, disposition or ownership with respect to property, again with the knowledge that the property is the proceeds of crime. This provision would

94 Based on an initial study on corruption and bribery laws in sub-Saharan African countries prepared by I. Carr for the OECD.

95 Charter House, 'Secret documents reveal that Blair urged end to BAE investigation': http://www.thecornerhouse.org.uk/resource/secret-documents-reveal-blair-urged-end-bae-investigation (accessed 1 November 2012); *R (Corner House Research) v Serious Fraud Office* [2008] UKHL 60. Problems in the handling of cases by the SFO, include the use by the SFO of inadequate and unfair information to obtain warrants (see *Rawlinson & Hunter Trustees, Vincent Tchenghuiz and Robert Tchenghuiz v SFO* [2012] EWHC 2254 (Admin); HM CPS Inspectorate *Report to the Attorney General on the Inspection of the Serious Fraud Office November 2012* (London: HMCPSI Publication No CP001:71) available at: http://www.hmcpsi.gov.uk/documents/reports/THM/SFO/SFO_Nov12_rpt.pdf (accessed 1 January 2013).

cover situations where companies such as shell companies are used to disguise the ownership of the assets.

Article 23(1)(b) creates two further offences. The first is the acquisition, use or possession of property that is known at the time of receipt to be the proceeds of crime. So a banker who receives the use of an expensive yacht over the weekend from one of the bank's customers knowing that the property has been obtained with illicit funds would be caught by this provision. The second covers participation in, association with, or conspiracy to commit, aiding, abetting and facilitating any of the offences established in Article 23. The extensive reach of Article 23 will therefore cover the activities of gate keepers such as lawyers, financial advisers and consultants who offer advice on how to disguise or conceal the proceeds of crime.

Again with money laundering in mind, the UNCAC in Article 14 requires states parties to put in place a 'comprehensive domestic regulatory and supervisory regime' that governs banks and non-bank financial institutions that are involved in formal or informal services for the transmission of money or value. This applies to both natural and legal persons. This article also expects states parties to ensure that the regulatory and supervisory regime includes the use of due diligence mechanisms such as customer identification and beneficial owner identification, maintenance of records and the reporting of suspicious transactions. These add to a number of anti-money laundering standards in place, such as the FATF Recommendations, and the framework devised by the UNCAC seem to reflect the current best practices.[96]

The facilitation of the recovery of assets is the cure, but by including laundering of the proceeds within its framework, the UNCAC is also focusing on prevention. Given the difficulties surrounding evidence-gathering, it makes sense to promote prevention vigorously. As stated in the previous paragraph, anti-money laundering ('AML') standards have been around for some time, and many, including EU member states, have regulations on money laundering.[97] Yet it seems many are ignoring the rules. Where bankers and other gatekeepers ignore the AML standards and regulations, serious doubts about the strength of these mechanisms are raised.[98] And where there is lack of political will, as is the case in many countries,[99] fighting the axes of corruption and money laundering will continue to be difficult. It seems therefore that the prevention mechanisms formulated by the

---

96   See further I. Carr and M. Goldby, 'Recovering the Proceeds of Corruption: UNCAC and Anti-Money Laundering Standards' [2011] *Journal of Business Law* 170.

97   See for instance the UK Money Laundering Regulations 2007.

98   See 'Senate report HSBC "allowed drug money laundering"': http://www.bbc.co.uk/news/business-18866018 (accessed 1 November 2012); Jill Treanor, 'HSBC warns money-laundering fines could top $1.5bn', available at: http://www.guardian.co.uk/business/2012/nov/05/hsbc-warns-money-laundering-fines (accessed 10 November 2012);

99   See especially Chapter 5.

UNCAC may be of limited use. As to whether asset declaration will be facilitated as a result of implementing Chapter V remains to be seen.

Corporate Vehicles

This chapter would be incomplete without highlighting the difficulties created by the use of corporate vehicles ('CVs') in the asset recovery process. CVs are often used to hide or distance individuals involved in corrupt activities from their assets, especially in the context of grand corruption. Typical CVs that seem to be widely used include shell companies and off-the-shelf companies, also called shelf companies. According to the 'StAR' (Stolen Asset Recovery) Initiative Report, a shell company is 'a non-operational company – that is a legal entity that has no independent operations, significant assets, ongoing business activities, or employees'.[100] According to this report, shell companies are also used for legitimate purposes as in the course of a merger, joint venture or for protecting assets from creditors. However, since a shell company does not follow the types of activities that a company would normally undertake (e.g. shareholders meetings, keeping minutes, sponsorships) or have employees and engage in any economic activity it makes investigation into the affairs of a shell company difficult.

Another format is the shelf company. These companies are incorporated like companies, but the shareholders are inactive and the company is left dormant. Upon sale, the shares of the shareholders are transferred to the purchaser and so are its tax history and credit. The directors of the company may resign upon sale or may continue as nominees. The outside world is aware of the change in ownership only if the new ownership is registered. Where the change is not registered investigations are difficult to pursue and are therefore useful vehicles in obscuring the ownership of illicitly obtained assets. It must however be noted that shelf companies also have legitimate uses especially in jurisdictions where the setting up of a company may take a long time due to bureaucratic requirements.

Foundations used for charitable purposes are another useful form for hiding assets. Where foundations are used normally the contributors do not have rights of ownership since they are ceded to the foundation though the contributors may well sit on the foundation's council thus giving them some form of control over its affairs. Marcos used foundations for the purposes of concealing assets and so did another former president of the Philippines, Joseph Estrada. He set up the Erap Muslim Youth Foundation which carried on legitimate activities helping poor Muslim youth. However in 2007 the Sandigbayan held that US$ 4.3 million of the

---

100   E. Van de Does de Willebois, E.H. Halter, R.A. Harrison, et al., *The Puppet Master* (Washington, DC: The World Bank, 2011) 34. See also OECD, *Behind the Corporate Veil: Using Corporate Entities for Illicit Purposes* (Paris: OECD, 2001).

protection money that Estrada had collected from illegal gambling operations had been deposited in the foundation's bank accounts.[101]

The above provides a flavour of the difficulties for investigative authorities when CVs are used. While the UNCAC has facilitated asset recovery, it has not addressed the misuse of legitimate entities such as foundations and shelf companies by corrupt individuals or groups. Further effort would require visiting the corporate law of each jurisdiction to harmonize it and strengthen it sufficiently to reveal ownership. And where parties act on behalf of another, a declaration giving details of whose behalf they are acting on should be imposed as a minimum requirement. According to the StAR Report, investigating authorities are not sufficiently conversant with corporate law or with how CVs can be gainfully used by fraudsters, which suggests that there is room for putting in place mechanisms that impart better understanding. It may be also useful to arrive at common definitions for CVs, thus paving the way towards easy identification.

Conclusion

The UNCAC has made tremendous effort to both prevent laundering of assets and to facilitate their recovery. The effectiveness of these provisions will depend eventually on their implementation in the ratifying states and the extent to which these states are willing to enforce their anti-corruption laws. The lack of prosecution should not be taken to indicate that there is no corruption at all. It is just that there is no political will. Where there is political will, a problem which remains is the use of CVs such as shell companies that make investigations difficult. The time has now come for policymakers to develop legislation that will address this gap.

---

101 *People of the Philippines v Joseph Ejercito Estrada*, Sandigbayan Criminal case No. 26558 (for Plunder) 12 September 2007, http://jlp-law.com/blog/people-philippines-vs-joseph-estrada-sandiganbayan-criminal-case-26558-plunder/ (accessed 1 November 2012). See further Chapter 11.

PART III:
Responses to the Financing of Terrorist Activity

Chapter 11

Terrorism Financing and the Policing of Charities: Who Pays the Price?

Clive Walker

Background

The attention given to the financing of terrorism has intensified since the attacks on September 11, 2001 for two reasons. First, international terrorism outruns local neighbourhoods both for recruits and targets and so garners its resources through dispersed and sophisticated channels. The second reason is that the impact of *jihadi* terrorism on 9/11 and thereafter has energized international condemnation and the universal demand for action, in contrast to earlier times when international endorsement of counter-terrorism measures was often lukewarm and hobbled by political support for national liberationist and anti-imperialist movements.

The shifting international psyche was signalled, *inter alia*, by the United Nations International Convention for the Suppression of the Financing of Terrorism 1999,[1] though it is notable that just four ratifications, including by the United Kingdom, were lodged before 9/11.[2] The United Nations Security Council also passed resolutions against support for individuals and groups associated with the Taliban and Al-Qa'ida from 1999, starting with Resolution 1267. These policies became universal peremptory edicts with the United Nations Security Council Resolution 1373 of 28 September 2001.[3] There was subsequent endorsement and enforcement by the European Union.[4]

One important aspect of the intensification of *jihadi* terrorism, and the focus on countering terrorism finances since 9/11, is that charities have fallen under closer scrutiny as potential, if not prime, channels of terrorism finance. Underlying

---

1   A/RES/54/109 of 9 December 1999.

2   See M. Lehto, *Indirect Responsibility for Terrorist Acts* (Leiden: Nijhoff, 2010) ch. 6.

3   See P.C. Szasz, 'The Security Council starts legislating' (2002) 96 *American Journal of International Law* 901; Counter-Terrorism Committee Executive Directorate, *Technical Guide to the Implementation of Security Council Resolution 1373 (2001)* (New York, 2009).

4   Council Regulation (EC) 2580/2001 of 27 December 2001; Council Regulation (EC) 881/2002 of 27 May 2002. See further Commission Communication, *The Prevention of and Fight Against Terrorism Financing through Enhanced National Level Coordination and Greater Transparency of the Non-profit Sector* (COM(2005) 620 final).

characteristics within charities which give rise to vulnerability include enhanced public trust through the embodying of ideals of civic volunteerism,[5] diversity of financial activities, cash intensiveness, a lighter regulatory regime than for financial institutions, complex multiple donor patterns and the involvement of politically committed individuals. The United Kingdom government's current commitment to fostering the 'Big Society' also signals greater prominence for the roles undertaken by charities.[6]

The potential link between charities and terrorism finance was signalled internationally as an innate risk by the Financial Action Task Force ('FATF') in October 2001 when it issued its Special Recommendation VIII on Terrorism Financing.[7] The FATF identifies three categories of charity abuse.[8] The first concerns the use of bogus charities as fronts for terrorists. The second, more widespread, is the fraudulent (or at least furtive) diversion of properly raised funds which are subverted to terrorist purposes. The third example involves broader exploitation of a charitable umbrella, such as through the recruitment and payment of extremists or for the propagation or glorification of a militant ideology. It is difficult to find clear examples in the United Kingdom experience within the first category, though serious allegations have been sustained elsewhere.[9] The second category will typically arouse suspicions about the humanitarian work abroad of cultural associations based within ethnic minority communities, especially if they distribute funds through overseas associates.

---

5   See T. Barkay, 'Regulation and voluntarism' (2009) 3 *Regulation & Governance* 360. The ideal is damaged by evidence of abuses: M. Gibbelman and S. Gelman, 'A loss of credibility' (2004) 15 *Voluntas* 355.

6   Cabinet Office, *Giving Green Paper* (London, 2010) 18. See also K. O'Halloran, 'Government-charity boundaries' in M. McGregor-Lowndes and K. O'Halloran (eds), *Modernising Charity Law* (Cheltenham: Edward Elgar Publishing, 2010).

7   These rules were revised in 2012: http://www.fatf-gafi.org/topics/fatfrecomm endations/documents/ixspecialrecommendations.html (accessed 27 February 2013). See further FATF, *International Best Practices: Combating the Abuse of Non-profit Organisations – Special Recommendation VIII* (Paris, 2002); Home Office and HM Treasury, *Review of Safeguards to Protect the Charitable Sector (England and Wales) from Terrorist Abuse* (London, 2007) Annex B.

8   FATF, *Terrorist Financing* (Paris, 2008) 10, 11.

9   See V.B. Bjorkalnd, J.I. Reynoso and A. Hazlett, 'Terrorism and Money Laundering' (2005) 25 *Pace Law Review* 233, 245, 300; V. Comras, 'Al Qaeda finances and funding to affiliate groups' in J.K. Giraldo and H.A. Trinkunas (eds), *Terrorism Financing and State Responses* (Stanford, CA: Stanford University Press, 2007) 118. The leading US example is the Holy Land Foundation, the financial activities of which were forbidden as an instrument of HAMAS by Executive Order 12947 (25 January 1995) and Executive Order 13224 (4 December 2001) and officials of which were found guilty of supporting terrorism in 2008, following which the charitable funds have been applied to satisfying the judgments of victims of HAMAS (*US v Holy Land Foundation* (2011) US Dist. LEXIS 46155 (USDC ND Texas)).

The risk of charitable funding of jihadi terrorism is viewed as enhanced by two further factors.[10] One is the Islamic canonical tax, of *zakat* – which is the religious duty to donate a proportion of one's wealth for charitable purposes. The second factor relates to those charities which are active in regions of conflict (such as Afghanistan, Pakistan, Palestine, Somalia and, hitherto, Sri Lanka) and are thereby especially vulnerable to being compromised by the unavoidability of working alongside protagonists within the conflict.

These depictions of the political and legal salience of contemporary terrorism finance and the centrality of charities in its gathering and transmission generally underplay the personal (non-financial) commitment which drives terrorism and the personal integrity of charity workers who view their independence from terrorism and government as crucial to their work.[11] Reliance upon charities as sources of finance may also compromise the independence of terrorist groups from public sentiment and thereby affect their freedom to undertake militant action.[12] The allegations of complicity in terrorism also overplay the analogy to criminal racketeering or more generally to rational choice theory.[13] Thus, while the worldwide outlay of Al-Qa'ida has been estimated to incur costs of up to $30m per annum,[14] individual operations may involve modest costs, much of

---

10　A further factor often mentioned is the use of informal remittance systems, such as *hawala*. This issue will not be tackled here since it is more associated with émigré workers than charities, but see N. Passas, *Informal Value Transfer Systems, Terrorism and Money Laundering* (Washington, DC: Report to the National Institute of Justice, 2003); M. de Goede, 'Hawala Discourses and the war on terrorist finance' (2003) 21 *Environment Planning D: Society and Space* 513; S. Keene, *Hawala and related Informal Value Transfer Systems* (Shrivenham: Defence Academy Journal, 2007); E.A. Thompson, 'Misplaced Blame: Islam, Terrorism and the Origins of Hawala' (2007) 11 *Yearbook of UN Law* 279; M. Vaccini, *Alternative remittance Systems and Terrorist Finance* (Washington, DC: Paper No. 180, World Bank, 2009); C.B. Bowers, 'Hawala, money lending, and terrorist financing' (2009) 37 *Denver Journal of International Law and Policy* 379.

11　The independence from government is emphasized by A. Zwitter, *Human Security, Law and the Prevention of Terrorism* (Abingdon: Routledge, 2012) 88–90.

12　See M. Freeman, 'The sources of terrorist financing' (2011) 34 *Studies in Conflict & Terrorism* 461, 471.

13　See A. Valino, et al., 'The economics of terrorism' in M. Buesa and T. Baumert (eds), *The Economic Repercussions of Terrorism* (Oxford: Oxford University Press, 2010) 13.

14　House of Lords European Union Committee, *Money Laundering and the Financing of Terrorism* HL 132 (2008–09) para. 9. See also R. Ehrenfeld, *Funding Evil* (Santa Monica, CA: Bonus Books, 2003); J.M. Burr and R.O. Collins, *Alms for Jihad* (New York: Cambridge University Press, 2006); R.T. Naylor, *Satanic Purses* (Montreal: McGill-Queen's University Press, 2006); N. Passas, 'Terrorism financing mechanisms and policy dilemmas' in J. Giraldo and H. Trinkunas (eds), *Terrorism Financing and State Responses* (Stanford CA: Stanford University Press, 2007); J. Gurulé, *Unfunding Terrorism* (Cheltenham: Edward Elgar, 2008); M. Pieth, 'Financing of terrorism' in M. Pieth (ed.), *Financing Terrorism* (Heidelberg: Springer, 2010).

which may be derived and defrayed by individual protagonists reliant on lawful sources and with the availability of state sponsorship much diminished.[15] The very ambitious attacks on 11 September 2001, did consume up to $500,000 in travel and accommodation expenses.[16] However, the 11 March 2003 Madrid bombers incurred costs of just €8,315,[17] while the 7 July 2005 London bombers left an equally light financial footprint of around £8,000.[18] There is even some evidence from Iraq that incoming would-be foreign *mujahideen* rendered funds to Al-Qa'ida rather than the reverse.[19] The contention that concentration upon terrorism financing is important because of underlying organizational costs and that citation of trivial operational costs misses this factor[20] has truth in some situations, especially for hierarchical, geographically situated terrorist groups. However, the late modern (dis)organization of many *jihadi* groups should be taken into account, and their distinct operational formation displays contrasts with more nationalist-oriented terror groups and also from organized criminal gangs.

Consequently, the qualitative prominence of the anti-terrorism financing activities and legislation is not evidently correlated with quantitative impact. For example, terrorism asset forfeitures in 2008/2009 in England and Wales were around £839,000, with a larger sum probably emanating from Northern Ireland; cash seizures of terrorism assets totalled £494,699 between 2001 and 2007.[21] By comparison 'SOCA', the Serious Organised Crime Agency (whose efforts against criminal assets amount to around 60 per cent of police totals), reported in 2008/2009 cash seizures of £9.2m, confiscation of £29.7m and civil recovery of £16.7m,[22]

---

15   An exception is Hizbollah: M. Levitt, 'Hezbollah finances' in J.K. Giraldo and H.A. Trinkunas, *Terrorism Financing and State Responses* (Stanford, CA: Stanford University Press, 2007) 148.

16   National Commission on Terrorist Attacks upon the United States, *Final Report* (Washington, DC: USGPO, 2004) 172.

17   T. Baumert, 'The impact of terrorist attacks on stock markets' in M. Buesa and T. Baumert (eds), *The Economic Repercussions of Terrorism* (Oxford: Oxford University Press, 2010) 181.

18   Home Office, *Report of the Official Account of the Bombings in London on the 7th July 2005* HC 1087 (2005–06) paras 63, 64.

19   See B. Bahney et al., *An Economic Analysis of the Financial Records of Al-Qa'ida in Iraq* (Santa Monica: RAND, 2010).

20   See M. Freeman, 'The sources of terrorist financing' (2011) 34 *Studies in Conflict & Terrorism* 461, 462.

21   C. Walker, *Terrorism and the Law* (Oxford: Oxford University Press, 2011) paras 9.45, 9.64.

22   Serious Organised Crime Agency, *Annual Report 2008/09* (London: Home Office, 2009) 32. The recoveries recorded in the *Annual Report 2011/12* (London: Home Office, 2012) 15 are even lower with cash seizures at £8m, confiscation £14m and civil recovery £11.5. See further chapters 3 and 9.

totals which are seen as relatively low compared to targets[23] and therefore form part of the reason for the establishment of a National Crime Agency.[24]

In the light of such indicia, it has been suggested that 'publicity – far more than financial resources – is as essential for terrorists as the air they breathe'.[25] Nevertheless, the policy of attacking terrorism finance persists. More cynical explanations are that it is less contentious to curtail property rights than expressive rights, and that the focus is more a state ploy to assert control over the voluntary sector or even to add to the discomforts of unwelcome diasporas.[26] Conversely, it is rightly asserted that tight financial regulation embodies the sound preventive purpose of stemming even larger flow of resources to terrorism.[27]

So far as the United Kingdom law is concerned, it has become a constant refrain that 'money is a crucial factor in the continuance of terrorism'.[28] Legislation against the funding of Irish and international terrorism has burgeoned over the past two decades, with attention to *jihadi* terrorism merely reinforcing well-established tactics. The current code is executed by the Terrorism Act 2000, Pt III, comprising several offences, extensive powers of seizure and forfeiture, and civil forfeiture through cash seizures. These measures were supplemented by Anti-Terrorism, Crime and Security Act 2001. Part I replaced and extended beyond internal or external borders the cash seizure powers in the Terrorism Act 2000. There were also new measures to extend the scope of investigative and freezing powers, including account monitoring and customer information orders. Freezing powers are further regulated by the Counter-Terrorism Act 2008, Part V. More recently, litigation about international sanctions has produced the Al-Qa'ida and Taliban (Asset Freezing) Regulations 2010[29] and the Terrorist Asset-Freezing etc. Act 2010. This legislation is to be applied in ways which reflect the strategy set out

---

23 See Serious Organised Crime Agency, *Annual Report 2009/10* (London: Home Office, 2010) 88.

24 Home Office, *Policing in the 21st Century: Reconnecting Police and the People* Cm 7925 (2010) para. 4.32; Home Office, *The National Crime Agency: A plan for the creation of a national crime-fighting capability* Cm 8097 (London, 2011). See further the criticisms in Criminal Justice Joint Inspection, *Joint Thematic Review of Asset Recovery* (London, 2010).

25 B.L. Nacos, *Mass-Mediated Terrorism* (Lanham, MD: Rowman & Littlefield, 2002) 193.

26 See M. Sidel, 'The Third Sector, human security, and anti-terrorism' (2006) 17 *Voluntas* 199, 203.

27 See M. Levi, 'Combating the financing of terrorism' (2010) 50 *British Journal of Criminology* 650, 663–665.

28 *Report of the Operation of the Prevention of Terrorism (Temporary Provisions) Act 1976* Cmnd 8803 (1983) para. 213.

29 SI 2010/1197.

originally in the *Action Plan on Terrorist Financing* of 2001[30] and now contained in the 'CONTEST' documentation.[31]

The mechanisms for the policing of charities in regard to terrorism financing are manifest, but, beyond a brief exposition of these instruments, the key question to be tackled in this chapter is 'who pays the price' for that policing? It will be found that the impact of policing is very uneven, an outcome which raises doubts about the strategies being deployed and whether different tactics might be more suitable. In pursuance of this theme, this chapter will first explain the policing mechanisms which are being deployed. Some take the form of expectations placed on charities themselves, while others are imposed from without, mainly by the Charity Commission. The findings will lead into analysis of where the policing burden falls and then an exploration of possible alternative approaches.

Policing and Regulatory Mechanisms Applied to Charities

'Policing' is invoked here in the sense of a broad concept.[32] Formal police interventions do affect charities, but a range of other regulatory bodies are more often closer to the front line of 'policing', as are the charities themselves. 'Policing' is selected as the primary framing term for this chapter rather than 'regulation' because of the closer relationship than is normal in civil administrative processes to the potential intervention of the formal police and the coercive criminal law. At the same time, it must be recognized that many of the forms of discipline and oversight to be discussed could fall within a broad conception of 'regulation'.[33] In particular, an escalatory compliance pyramid model, as articulated by Ayres and Braithwaite,[34] envisages increasingly severe tiers of regulation on the part of administrators. Yet even this more sophisticated regulatory model is still not a neat fit for counter-terrorism financing. First, the official policies around countering terrorism finances do not readily associate themselves with an entry point of

---

30   HC Deb vol 372, col 940 15 October 2001, Gordon Brown.

31   See Home Office, *Countering International Terrorism* (London: Cm 6888, 2006), as updated by (London: Cm 7547, 2009; Cm 7833, 2010; Cm 8123, 2011; Cm 8583, 2013. In the 2013 version, the vulnerabilities of charities are mentioned as part of the 'Pursue' element of CONTEST: Ibid., para. 2.26).

32   See L. Zedner, 'Policing before and after the police' (2006) 46 *British Journal of Criminology* 78; T. Jones and T. Newburn, *Plural Policing* (London: Routledge, 2006).

33   See C. Hood, H. Rothstein and R. Baldwin, *The Government of Risk: Understanding Risk Regulation Regimes* (Oxford: Oxford University Press, 2001); J. Black, 'Enrolling actors in regulatory systems' [2003] *Public Law* 63; P. Vincent-Jones, *The New Public Contracting* (Oxford: Oxford University Press, 2006) ch. 3; N. Gunningham, 'Enforcement and compliance strategies' in R. Baldwin, M. Lodge and M. Cave, *Oxford Handbook of Regulation* (Oxford: Oxford University Press, 2010).

34   I. Ayres and J. Braithwaite, *Responsive Regulation* (New York: Oxford University Press, 1992) 35.

indulgence or responsiveness.[35] Even 'self-regulation' is immediately underlined by insistent criminal law duties. Thus, a relevant distinction between 'policing' and 'regulation' being applied here is that, within the latter concept, coercion and sanction are variable features within regulation rather than performing as primary features as within policing. Second, there exists some 'fragmentation of authority within the regulatory space' which blurs the neat contours of any supposed pyramid.[36]

Whether within 'policing' or 'regulation', there are the following essential elements of activity: the specification of rules or standards; the monitoring of compliance; and the establishment of enforcement devices.[37] These elements will be reflected at two policing levels: 'internal' and 'external'.

Internal Policing

Private policing beyond the state apparatus, including self-policing, is a growing phenomenon.[38] Internal policing applied to charities demands that each organization should monitor its own business and procedures to ensure that terrorism financing does not take place. Of course, there are also 'external' laws to set and enforce the standards, but the charity must police itself, in the same way that money-laundering counteraction depends primarily on high standards of vigilance by financial institutions themselves.

A number of specialist measures form the vehicles for this watchfulness in the field of terrorism financing. First, there is a general duty not to withhold information about terrorism, breach of which is a criminal offence. The offence is committed under section 38B(2) of the Terrorism Act 2000. An offence occurs where a person, without reasonable excuse, does not disclose information which:

... he knows or believes might be of material assistance

(a) in preventing the commission by another person of an act of terrorism; or
(b) in securing the apprehension, prosecution or conviction of another person,
in the United Kingdom, for an offence involving the commission, preparation or instigation of an act of terrorism.

---

35   But there is responsiveness in policy making: E.A. Bloodgood and J. Tremblay-Boire, 'NGO responses to counter terrorism regulations after September 11th' (2010) 12(4) *International Journal of Not-for-Profit Law* 5, 14.

36   C. Scott, 'Analysing regulatory space' [2001] *Public Law* 329, 346.

37   P. Vincent-Jones, *The New Public Contracting* 69.

38   See L. Johnston and C.D. Shearing, *Governing Security* (London: Routledge, 2002); M. Button, *Private Policing* (Cullompton: Willan, 2002).

This extraordinary measure[39] applies to the trustees of charities. While there is no record of any trustee being prosecuted, the offence is applied by the police across a broad spectrum as a reminder and even a threat.

A more onerous duty along the same lines is imposed by section 19(1) of the Terrorism Act 2000. When a person believes or suspects that another person has committed an offence under either of sections 15 to 18 on the basis of information accruing in the course of a trade, profession, business or employment, an offence is committed if the information is not disclosed to a police officer or member of the Serious Organised Crime Agency or even the Charity Commission[40] as soon as reasonably practicable. The width of the duty is striking. It is sufficient to have a subjective belief or suspicion which can only be safely suppressed if the intermediary has a 'reasonable excuse' under sub-section (3). This defence is not subject to the interpretive rule in section 118 which ensures that only an evidential burden is imposed. It is arguable that this switch is fair only in the context of professionals who are trained and keep records; the extension to voluntary enterprises is more dubious.[41] Under section 19(7), the duty has a global reach to equivalent transactions overseas.

In the drafting of the Terrorism Act 2000, the government emphasized the confinement of the onerous duty under section 19 to professionals handling finance, though it recognized that family and business relations may overlap in the situation of small enterprises. However, the reach of section 19 has been significantly supplemented by the Counter-Terrorism Act 2008, section 77, arising from allegations that charities are being misused as vehicles for raising or transferring money to terrorists.[42] Section 77 inserts, as section 22A of the Terrorism Act 2000, a new definition of 'employment' which encompasses both paid and unpaid employment and can even include voluntary work. In this way, unpaid volunteers who are the trustees of a charity must act with the same insight as professional forensic accountants. The Home Office misleadingly describes the amendment as 'a very minor change to close a possible gap in the current provisions'.[43] The result might be to deter community-spirited individuals, though the burden placed on charities to lodge Suspicious Activity Reports ('SARs')[44]

---

39   See further C. Walker, 'Conscripting the public in terrorism policing' [2010] *Criminal Law Review* 441.

40   *OG96: Charities and Terrorism* (London, 2007) para. 4.3.

41   See also I. Smith, T. Owen and A. Bodnar, *Asset Recovery, Criminal Confiscation, and Civil Recovery* (2nd ed., Oxford: Oxford University Press, 2007) para. I.3.634.

42   See HM Treasury, *The Financial Challenge to Crime and Terrorism* (London, 2007); Home Office and HM Treasury, *Review of Safeguards to Protect the Charitable Sector (England and Wales) from Terrorist Abuse*.

43   Home Office, *Possible Measures for Inclusion into a Future Counter-Terrorism Bill* (London, 2007) para. 22. See E.A. Bloodgood and J. Tremblay-Boire, 'International NGOs and National Regulation in an Age of Terrorism' 167.

44   See https://www.ukciu.gov.uk/%28sct3dnqovty1ocisb5hzfy45%29/saronline.aspx (accessed 27 February 2013). The impact of SARs is debated: S. Lander, *Review of the*

may be stricter in law than is recognized in practice. In 2006, just 48 SARs were issued from the charitable sector, a dearth of suspicion which officialdom finds 'hard to explain',[45] especially as defensive reporting is commonplace in most other sectors.[46]

An even stricter duty to disclose is imposed on the 'regulated sector'[47] by Schedule 2, Part III, of the Anti-Terrorism, Crime and Security Act 2001. This duty is applied instead of, and not additional to, section 19 to most businesses handling substantial financial activity. Under section 21A (inserted into the Terrorism Act 2000), a person in that sector commits an offence by knowing or suspecting or having reasonable grounds for knowing or suspecting, that another person has attempted or committed an offence under either of sections 15 to 18 (including with extra-territorial effect), unless that information is disclosed to a constable, officer of SOCA, or the employer's nominated officer as soon as practicable. The duty is subject to a reasonable excuse not to disclose and to exceptions for privileged legal advice.[48] The objective standard of liability, which can arise without subjective awareness of any suspicion, is justified by the '[g]reater awareness and higher standards of reporting in the financial sector'.[49] Given that objective standard, the court must consider whether there was compliance with guidance by the relevant supervisory authority or professional body. That guidance has to be approved by the Treasury and be published in a manner approved by the Treasury. Guidance is issued via the Joint Money Laundering Steering Group.[50]

Charities do not generally fall within the 'regulated sector', but the financial institutions which handle their transactions certainly do so. Because charities cannot operate without financial services, the stricter duties thereby affect charities indirectly. One United Kingdom based financial institution has been subject to domestic regulatory sanction on account of not being sufficiently attentive to the potential terrorism links of their charity customers. The Royal Bank of Scotland was fined £5.6m (including a 30 per cent discount for early settlement) by the Financial

---

Suspicious Activity Reports Regime (London: Home Office, 2006); HM Treasury, *The Financial Challenge to Crime and Terrorism* paras 2.39, 2.60; House of Lords European Union Committee, *Money Laundering and the Financing of Terrorism* HL 132 (2008–09) and HL 11 (2010–11).

45   Home Office and HM Treasury, *Review of Safeguards to Protect the Charitable Sector (England and Wales) from Terrorist Abuse* paras 3.3, 3.6.

46   See C. Walker, *Terrorism and the Law* para. 9.76.

47   Terrorism Act 2000, Sch 3A, as substituted by: Terrorism Act 2000 (Business in the Regulated Sector and Supervisory Authorities) Order 2007, SI 2007/3288; Terrorism Act 2000 and Proceeds of Crime Act 2002 (Amendment) Regulations 2007, SI 2007/3398.

48   Terrorism Act 2000 and Proceeds of Crime Act 2002 (Amendment) Regulations 2007, SI 2007/3398, Sch 1, para. 3, as required by 2005/60/EC, art. 23.2.

49   Home Office, *Regulatory Impact Assessment: Terrorist Property* (London, 2001) para. 8.

50   British Bankers' Association, *Guidance on the Prevention of Money Laundering and the Financing of Terrorism for the Financial Services Industry.*

Services Authority in 2010 for failing to ensure funds were not transferred to people or organizations on sanctions lists, leading to an 'unacceptable risk' of facilitating terrorist financing.[51] More serious criticisms[52] and regulatory penalties[53] and civil litigation have also been encountered by financial institutions in the United States, sometimes arising from the alleged defaults of United Kingdom banks.[54]

External Policing

External policing is principally exerted by the Charity Commission, now operating under Part II of the Charities Act 2011.[55] Some of its regulatory decisions are subject, under Part XVII, to consideration by the Charity Tribunal.[56]

In the context of alleged links to terrorism, there may be two triggers for investigation.[57] One is that the charity may be overstepping the boundaries of its charitable status by supporting political purposes or activities sympathetic to those of terrorist groups. The demarcation line between 'political' and 'charitable' is often difficult to draw, but the continued disqualification of political involvement has support in principle from government and the courts.[58] For its part, the Charity Commission warns against the adoption of any political purpose and against any political activities as a core business, though political campaigns in support of

---

51   http://www.fsa.gov.uk/pubs/other/rbs_group.pdf (accessed 27 July 2011). The RBS was fined £750,000 in 2002 for breaches of money-laundering regulations. See further Financial Services Authority, *Banks' Management of High Money-laundering Risk Situations* (London: 2011).

52   See US Senate Permanent Sub-Committee on Investigations, *US Vulnerability to Money Laundering, Drugs and Terrorist Financing* (Washington, DC, 2012). HSBC paid a fine of $1.92bn. Following the report of the New York Department of Financial Service, *In the Matter of Standard Chartered Bank New York Branch* (New York, 2012), that bank paid a settlement of $327m.

53   See *In re Federal Branch of the Arab Bank plc New York* (US Department of Treasury Financial Crimes Enforcement Network, 2005–2) (fine of $24m).

54   See *Linde v Arab Bank, PLC* 353 F. Supp 2d 327 (EDNY, 2004), 463 F. Supp 2d 310 (EDNY, 2006), 269 FRD 186 (EDNY, 2010); *Weiss v National Westminster Bank* 2008 US Dist LEXIS 99443, 2013 U.S. Dist. LEXIS 52628 (EDNY); *Strauss v Credit Lyonnais* 242 FRD 199 (EDNY 2007), 249 FRD 429 (EDNY, 2008), 2013 U.S. Dist. LEXIS 28451; *Goldberg v UBS AG* 660 F. Supp 2d 410 (EDNY, 2009). A full list of both criminal and civil litigation in the US may be found at: http://www.investigativeproject.org/cases.php (accessed 4 June 2011).

55   See H. Picarda, *The Law and Practice Relating to Charities* (4th ed., Haywards Heath: Bloomsbury, 2011) ch. 46.

56   See ibid., ch. 52.

57   See A.C. Burgess, *Charity Investigations* (2nd ed., Haywards Heath: Tottel, 2006).

58   See E. Burt, 'Charities and Political Activity: Time to Rethink the Rules' (1998) 69 *Political Quarterly* 23; A. Dunn, 'To foster or to temper? Regulating the political activities of the voluntary and community sector' (2006) 26 *Legal Studies* 500; K. Atkinson, 'Obstacles to political campaigning by charities' (2009) 12 *Charity Law and Practice Review* 36.

charitable purposes may be acceptable.[59] This first potential problem has not been the prime issue in the context of links to terrorism, either in terms of the extent of political activism or the content of the cause being espoused. On the latter point, it should be noted that not all banned groups champion political programmes which must inevitably be viewed as illegal or even as extreme. Proposals about national separatism are often to be tolerated,[60] though the imposition of *sharia* law may be viewed as beyond the pale.[61] Instead, the allegation is of a second kind – that money is being used to fund activities which are, in part, political or social but also are in part violent.

The enforcement powers of the Charity Commission are indicated in sections 76 to 87 of the Charities Act 2011. The powers arise at any time after an inquiry has been instituted under section 46 either for general or particular purposes. Information-gathering and inquiry powers then arise under sections 46 to 49. The commission may respond to problems by suspending or removing any trustee, officer, agent or employee of the charity, divest or restrain property, restrict transactions, appoint managers and receivers, or establish a scheme for the administration of the charity. Most drastic of all, by section 34(1)(a), the commission 'must remove from the register ... any institution which it no longer considers is a charity ...'.

These powers sound sweeping and are claimed to be 'far in advance of the requirements imposed on charities in most of the rest of the world'.[62] But they are not often used[63] and are in practice circumscribed by two limitations.

The first is that while charities with a turnover above a specified amount (of £5,000) must register under section 30 of the Charities Act 2011, there is no obligation to adopt the form of a charity in the first place by not-for-profit bodies. Charitable status brings evident tax advantages through gift aid[64] and also business

---

59 See Charity Commission, *Speaking Out – Campaigning and Political Activity by Charities* (London: CC9, 2008).

60 See for example, *Castells v Spain*, App no. 11798/85, Ser A 336 (1992); *Arslan v Turkey*, App no. 23462/94, 8 July 1999; *Ceylan v Turkey*, App no. 23556/94, 1999-IV; *Erdoğdu v Turkey*, App no. 25723/94, 2000-VI; *Association Ekin v France*, App no. 39288/98, 2001-VIII; *Isak Tepe v Turkey*, App no. 17129/02, 21 October 2008.

61 *Refah Partisi v Turkey*, App nos 41340/98, 41342/98, 41343/98, 41344/98, 2003-II; *Hizb ut Tahrir v Germany*, App no. 31098/08, 12 June 2012.

62 Home Office and HM Treasury, *Review of Safeguards to Protect the Charitable Sector (England and Wales) from Terrorist Abuse*, para. 3.

63 The number of statutory inquiries opened in 2007–2008 , 2008–2009, 2009–2010, 2010–2011 and 2011–2012 was respectively 19, 19, 9, 3 and 12 (*Charities Back on Track 2011–12: Themes and Lessons from the Charity Commission's Investigations and Regulatory Casework* (London, 2012) 32). A minority of these relate to terrorism: for example, one out of 7 completed inquiries in 2011–2012 see at 34) and 5 out of 85 investigations (see at 37).

64 See Finance Act 1990, s 25, and now the Income Tax Act 2007, s 413 et seq.

rate relief.[65] It also garners social approbation and fosters social capital.[66] But the status of charity also triggers unwelcome oversight and potential interference, a criticism frequently mounted in recent times by independent schools (82 per cent of which are charities) which view themselves as forced by the Charity Commission into concessions (such as scholarships or public access to facilities) to counteract the social exclusivity of high fees.[67] Some groups are suspicious of this meddling and prefer not to register as charities (including by the insertion of non-charitable objects in their constitutions).[68] That course may be taken by minorities who are less conversant with British norms and structures, with mosques providing a case in point. It is reckoned there are up to 1,629 mosques in the United Kingdom.[69] The Charity Commission exercises jurisdiction over a minority and records in its *Annual Report 2009/10* that:[70]

> Through outreach work undertaken by the Faith and Social Cohesion Unit set up in 2007, the Commission has also successfully identified and increased the number of mosques registered with us to 593, a 79% increase from the previous figure of 331.

The second limitation is that policing and enforcement are secondary in the constitution and culture of the Charity Commission. Thus, the *Annual Report 2009/10* states that the Mission of the Charity Commission involves:[71]

> Increasing public trust and confidence in charities by
>
> • enabling charities to maximise their impact
> • enabling compliance with legal obligations
> • encouraging innovation and effectiveness
> • promoting the public interest in charity

---

65   See Local Government Act 1988, s 43 et seq. See K. Parry, *Business Rates: Relief for Charity Shops* (London: SN/PC/00639, House of Commons Library, 2009).

66   See B.E. Dollery and J.L. Wallis, *The Political Economy of the Voluntary Sector* (Cheltenham: Edward Elgar, 2003).

67   See *R (Independent Schools Council) v Charity Commission* [2010] EWHC 2604 (Admin); *Independent Schools Council v Charity Commission for England and Wales* [2011] UKUT 421 (TCC).

68   See B. Lucas and A. Robinson, 'Religion as a head of charity' in M. McGregor-Lowndes and K. O'Halloran (eds), *Modernising Charity Law* (Cheltenham: Edward Elgar Publishing, 2010).

69   http://www.muslimsinbritain.org/resources/masjid_report.pdf (accessed 4 June 2011). The Charity Commission, *Survey of Mosques in England and Wales* (London, 2009) 5 suggests a total of 1102.

70   HC 77 (2010-11) 7.

71   Ibid., 22.

Likewise, the statutory objectives in section 14 of the Charities Act 2011 comprise legal compliance by charity trustees with their legal obligations in exercising control and management of the administration of their charities as just one objective amongst several as follows:

1. The public confidence objective ...
2. The public benefit objective ...
3. The compliance objective ...
4. The charitable resources objective ...
5. The accountability objective ...

In this way, the commission constitutes a 'green-light' regulator rather than a 'red-light' regulator.[72] Its working environment may have become more juridified under the influence of the Human Rights Act 1998,[73] but its mission and approach is based around the facilitation of charities to adapt to their legal environment,[74] as is reflected in words such as 'enabling' and 'promoting'. Even in connection with its work in the legal sphere, its mission statement does not communicate a punitive role but is depicted as 'enabling' legal compliance rather than 'enforcing' or 'imposing' it. Because of this approach, more formal policing agencies find it hard to take over investigations started by the Charity Commission since it pursues a distinct culture and does not aim to collect 'evidence'.[75] Others have referred to the predilection of the Charity Commission and indeed the government for 'soft power', especially through the exercise of financial inducements or threats, a policy which has been most evidently applied to the handling of mosques.[76]

The general stance of the commission is further underlined by the backing of the statutory compliance requirement with one of the statutory 'general functions' of the commission in section 15(1)(3), which, without mention of any punitive or prohibitory sanction, refers to: 'Identifying and investigating apparent misconduct or mismanagement in the administration of charities and taking remedial or

---

72   The terms are adapted from C. Harlow and R. Rawlings, *Law and Administration* (3rd ed., Cambridge: Cambridge University Press, 2009) ch. 1. See further R. Baldwin and J. Black, 'Really Responsive Regulation' (2008) 71 *Modern Law Review* 59; D. Morris, 'The case of England and Wales: Striking the right balance of "hard" law and "soft" law' in S. Phillips and S. Rathgeb Smith (eds), *Governance and Regulation in the Third Sector* (London: Routledge, 2010).

73   See P. Edge and J.M. Loughrey, 'Religious charities and the juridification of the Charity Commission' (2001) 21 *Legal Studies* 36.

74   See E.A. Bloodgood and J. Tremblay-Boire, 'International NGOs and National Regulation in an Age of Terrorism' (2011) 22 *Voluntas* 142, 156.

75   Home Office and HM Treasury, *Review of Safeguards to Protect the Charitable Sector (England and Wales) from Terrorist Abuse* para. 3.20.

76   See P.W. Edge, 'Hard law and soft power' (2010) 12 *Rutgers Journal of Law & Religion* 358.

protective action in connection with misconduct or mismanagement in the administration of charities.'

The 'green-light' approach of the Charity Commission can be further evidenced by its six general duties as set forth in section 16 of the Charities Act 2011. General Duty 2 states that: 'So far as is reasonably practicable, the Charity Commission must, in performing its functions, act in a way which is compatible with the encouragement of (a) all forms of charitable giving, and (b) voluntary participation in charity work.' Furthermore, in performing all its functions, the commission is required by General Duty 4 to 'have regard to the principles of best regulatory practice (including the principles under which regulatory activities should be proportionate, accountable, consistent, transparent and targeted only at cases in which action is needed)'.

The claim that the Charity Commission is hobbled, in part as a matter of framing by law and in part as a self-induced restraining organizational culture, may be next tested by an examination of the application of its powers.

The Application of External Policing

Designated Charities

A distinction may be drawn between those charities which have become designated under the international sanctions regime pursuant to United Nations Security Council Resolutions 1267 and 1373 and other targeted charities. The UN sanctions mechanisms,[77] which are further backed by European Union sanctions,[78] amount to a remarkable new form of international financial outlawry against specified persons and organizations which are not dependent on criminal conviction.[79] They

---

77   See Legal Department of the IMF, *Suppressing the Financing of Terrorism: A Handbook for Legislative Drafting* (Washington, DC: 2003); C. Walker, *Terrorism and the Law* para. 9.127; C. Eckes, 'EU counter-terrorism sanctions against individuals' (2012) 17 *European Foreign Affairs Review* 113; Special Rapporteur on the promotion and protection of human rights and fundamental freedoms while countering terrorism, *Promotion and protection of human rights and fundamental freedoms while countering terrorism* (New York: A/67/396, 2012).

78   See J. Almqvist, 'A human rights critique of European judicial review: counter-terrorism sanctions' (2008) 57 *International & Comparative Law Quarterly* 303; C. Eckes, *EU Counter-Terrorist Policies and Fundamental Rights: The Case of Individual Sanctions* (Oxford: Oxford University Press, 2009); C.C. Murphy, *EU Counter-Terrorism Law: Pre-Emption and the Rule of Law* (Oxford: Hart Publishing, 2012); I. Cameron (ed.), *EU Sanctions: Law and Policy Issues Concerning Restrictive Measures* (Cambridge: Intersentia, 2013).

79   See *Third Report of the Monitoring Group* (S/2002/1338, 17 December 2002) para. 17.

are currently enforced in the United Kingdom by a combination of the Al-Qaida (Asset-Freezing) Regulations 2011[80] and the Terrorist Asset-Freezing etc. Act 2010.[81]

By and large, cases involving designation are straightforward but are not very significant for the purposes of this chapter. Designation will prevent any operation by a charity since it cannot be allowed to hold money or engage in transactions. Most of the charities listed in the targeted financial sanctions lists[82] have not been openly active in any United Kingdom jurisdiction.

One exception is the Sanabel Relief Agency. This charity, whose purpose was to provide relief to Muslims in destitute parts of the world, had registered in 2000 and maintained branches in Birmingham, London, Manchester and Middlesbrough. It was effectively closed in 2006 following international sanctions listing by the United Nations because of links to the Libyan Islamic Fighting Group.[83]

Next, the Islamic Foundation, founded in 1973 and based in Leicester,[84] was subject to action when the Charity Commission detected in 2003 through routine monitoring that two trustees appeared to be individuals named on the international sanctions listings. The commission opened an inquiry and immediately suspended the named trustees. It was discovered that the two trustees did not reside in the United Kingdom and had not been active in the administration of the charity since 1999 and 2000. Nevertheless, they subsequently resigned. At the same time, the Charity Commission sounded a note of futile defiance in the face of international listings:[85]

> The Charity Commission is alert to the possibilities of charities being used to further or support terrorist activities. It will deal with any allegation of potential links between a charity and terrorist activity as an immediate priority. As an independent statutory regulator, the Commission will make its own decisions on the law and facts of the case.

---

80 SI 2011/2742.

81 See Independent Reviewer of the Terrorism Legislation (D. Anderson), *First and Second Reports on the Operation of the Terrorist Asset Freezing etc Act 2010* (London, 2011 and 2012) and HM Treasury, *Responses* (London: Cm 8287 and 8553, 2012 and 2013).

82 See http://www.hm-treasury.gov.uk/fin_sanctions_index.htm (accessed 4 June 2011). It has been estimated that only 24 charities are listed – 'the tip of the iceberg': V. Comras, 'Al Qaeda finances and funding to affiliate groups' in J.K. Giraldo and H.A. Trinkunas (eds), *Terrorism Financing and State Responses* (Stanford, CA: Stanford University Press, 2007) 132.

83 See http://www.un.org/sc/committees/1267/NSQE12406E.shtml (accessed 27 February 2013); D. Lombard, '"Al-Qaida" charity on register for six years' *Third Sector* 19 February 2013, 4.

84 http://www.islamic-foundation.org.uk/User/Home.aspx (accessed 4 June 2011).

85 Charity Commission, *Inquiry: The Islamic Foundation* (London, 2004) para. 8.

Non-Designated Registered Charities

Assuming a charity is registered under the Charities Act but is not internationally designated, then regulatory action is much less straightforward.

The version of 'green-light' regulation adopted here is not that the Charity Commission wholly ignores allegations of terrorism. Its caseload of 180 investigations in 2009–2010 included 11 which related to allegations or suspicions of terrorist-related activities.[86] Rather, the question is what happens during, and as a result of, those investigations. By way of evidence, the Charity Commission was reported in 2007 to have investigated 16 charities as a result of which trustees were removed from several.[87] Four cases should be highlighted.

One concerned the Ikhlas Foundation, which was registered in 1997 and whose main work was reflected in its adopted working title of the 'Muslim Prisoner Support Group' and especially related to prisoners impugned for involvement in terrorism. The group has been of serial concern to the Charity Commission because of the activities of various trustees.[88] In 2007, Mohammed al-Ghabra, a trustee, was removed after he was accused of facilitating terrorism training in Pakistan and was designated by the UN and by the HM Treasury in December 2006.[89] The Charity Commission was apparently unaware of this designation until informed in July 2007. The other trustees resisted any disciplinary action, taking the view that they would be 'considered as hypocrites' if they shunned a colleague because of this official condemnation while at the same time seeking to aid prisoners.[90] The Charity Commission removed him as a trustee in October 2007 and prevented his further participation. However, it imposed no sanction on the remaining trustees even though it viewed them as inadequately recognizing or managing the risks involved with their work. Instead, the inquiry was closed on the commitment by remaining trustees to strengthen their governance within three months.

That undertaking by the trustees did not seem to bear much fruit. A second inquiry began in 2008, when another trustee, Abbas Taj, was suspended by the commission (and later resigned) following his arrest in 2008 and conviction in 2009 for conspiring in an arson attack.[91] The attack was made on the home of Martin

---

86   Home Office, *Prevent Strategy* Cm 8092 (2011) para. 10.196.

87   See Home Office and HM Treasury, *Review of Safeguards to Protect the Charitable Sector (England and Wales) from Terrorist Abuse* para. 3.11.

88   Charity Commission, *Inquiry Reports: The Ikhlas Foundation* (London, 2008 and 2010).

89   See *HM Treasury v al-Ghabra* [2010] UKSC 2 at [1]. Even association with him is cited as prejudicial intelligence against others in control order cases: *Secretary of State for the Home Department v AM* [2009] EWHC 572 (Admin) and [2009] EWHC 3053 (Admin); *Secretary of State for the Home Department v al-Saadi* [2009] EWHC 3390 (Admin); *Secretary of State for the Home Department v AY* [2010] EWHC 1860 (Admin).

90   Charity Commission, *Inquiry Report: The Ikhlas Foundation* para. 16.

91   Croydon Crown Court, 7 July 2009: http://www.thelawpages.com/court-cases/Abbas-Taj-3497-1.law (accessed 4 June 2011).

Rynja, owner of Gibson Square Books which published *The Jewel of Medina*, a novel by US author Shelley Jones which controversially tackles the subject of the Prophet Mohamed's third wife Aisha, who is said to have been married at the age of nine. Taj had helped two other men to go to the publisher's house, where they poured diesel through the letterbox and lit a fire. Two other trustees were also disciplined on unconnected, less serious grounds (for bankruptcy and failing to attend meetings with the commission). The commission recorded that the trustees had failed to deliver on their previous commitments.[92] Despite this recurrently woeful record, the commission concluded its second inquiry by issuing a direction under section 19A by which the trustees were set a further few months after December 2009 to regularize their meetings and membership and to conduct a risk assessment and take action to mitigate risks. Given that the charity had a very modest income of around £5,000 per annum, the risk of terrorism financing should not be exaggerated. Nevertheless, the patience of the Charity Commission accorded to this serially delinquent charity was astonishing, though the Ikhlas Foundation has since been removed from the Register of Charities.

More prominently reported, policing action in regard to a trustee next relates to the removal of Abu Hamza, from the North London Central Mosque (Finsbury Park) in 2004.[93] This mosque became notorious in the late 1990s as a site for 'extremists', many of them foreign émigrés, who were accused of infiltrating the mosque, intimidating moderate locals, and preaching hatred and violence. For a while, the Charity Commission sought to work with all shades of trustees, including Abu Hamza, whose candid assessment of their threat to him was that they were 'nagging nobodies'.[94] However, the commission eventually reached the view that Abu Hamza was the ring-leader of the extremists and must be removed from office, perhaps under media pressure.[95] However, the decisive turning point came when the mosque premises were raided by police on 20 January 2003, whereupon the commission suspended and later removed Abu Hamza as trustee of the charity and also closed a bank account which he secretly operated. Abu Hamza was later convicted of solicitation to murder.[96] Following completion of his sentence, he has been extradited to the USA in respect of terrorism offences, including raising money for fighters in Afghanistan from 1999 to 2001, allegations which have been

---

92   Charity Commission, *Inquiry Report: The Ikhlas Foundation* paras 38, 39.

93   J. Gunning, 'Terrorism, charities and diasporas'; P.W. Edge, 'Hard law and soft power' 366–368. Note also the problems experienced by the Brixton Mosque: A.H. Baker, 'A view from the inside' (2008) 73 *Criminal Justice Matters* 24.

94   D. McGrory, 'They will not gag me, vows London mosque militant', *The Times*, 18 January 2003, 11.

95   D. Turnbull, N. Mahmood and A. Gardner, '9/11: One year on: Sick fanatics meet to "celebrate" Twin Towers terror attacks', *The Sunday Mirror*, 8 September 2002, 4, 5.

96   [2006] EWCA Crim 2918; *Mustapha v United Kingdom*, App no. 31411/07, 18 January 2011.

current for many years.[97] It might be argued that this treatment represents a 'red-light' approach or 'hard law'.[98] However, while it represents the most extreme example imaginable it took several years for decisive action to be implemented. Even then, such action was impelled by police intervention and boosted by very prominent media hostility.

The third case, Iqra, involved arguably the most notorious trustees of all.[99] Iqra, a bookshop and learning centre in the Beeston, Leeds, registered as a charity in 2003. It received grants amounting to £94,000 mainly from local government agencies. However, its activities came to an abrupt halt in 2005, when it was confirmed that two of the July 7 bombers, Mohammed Siddique Khan and Shehzad Tanweer, had acted as trustees. The police raided its premises, as a result of which the remaining trustees claimed that the charity had become inoperative. Another trustee, Khalid Kaliq was subsequently convicted of terrorist-related offences not directly related to Iqra.[100] Yet, not until 2009 did the Charity Commission decide to launch a formal inquiry, and even that step seems to have been prompted by media concerns.[101] In the event, the commission found no evidence that Iqra's finances or premises had been used for the preparation of the July 7 attacks, and it can hardly be blamed for not detecting more astutely than the police or security agencies that some of its trustees were developing into active terrorists.[102] However, the commission found that extremist materials had been possessed and also admitted that no action had been taken over the fact that no reports or accounts had ever been filed by the trustees. Awakening from this stupor, the commission took steps to seize the remaining trust money (£12,500).

Trustee links to Rashid Rauf, who was implicated in the Transatlantic airline liquid bomb plot in 2006 (Operation Overt), was the reason for another inquiry into the Crescent Relief charity which was involved in relief work in Kashmir and Indonesia.[103] The inquiry began in 2006 but was held up until 2011 not only because of the various prosecutions but also because of the failure to keep records and the difficulties of obtaining evidence from abroad. The outcome of the inquiry

---

97   *Mustafa v Government of the United States of America* [2008] EWHC 1357 (Admin); *Babar Ahmad and others v United Kingdom*, App nos 24027/07, 11949/08, 36742/08, 66911/09 and 67354/09, 10 April 2012; *Hamza v Secretary of State for the Home Department* [2012] EWHC 2736 (Admin).

98   P.W. Edge, 'Hard law and soft power' 368 (fn 76).

99   Charity Commission, *Inquiry Report: Iqra* (London, 2011).

100   See *R v K* [2008] EWCA Crim 185.

101   An article in *The Times*, A. Norfolk, 'The backstreet bookshop that taught frontline war' (2009) *The Times*, 29 April 18, 19), is cited: Charity Commission, *Inquiry Report: Iqra* (London, 2011) para. 10.

102   There is concurrence in this finding from the *Coroner's Inquests into the London Bombings of 7 July 2005* (London, 2011) para. 21.

103   Charity Commission, *Inquiry Report: Crescent Relief* (London, 2011). Two trustees are Abdul Rauf (father) and Mohammad Mumtaz (uncle). Rashid Rauf escaped from custody in Pakistan in 2007 and was allegedly killed by a US drone attack in 2008.

was inconclusive, but it was sustained that financial controls had been inadequate and that there had been an ongoing lack of candour and effective management by the trustees. Despite all these serious shortcomings, the commission concluded that the future good intentions of the trustees should be recognized by ordering them to take action within a set time-frame and to submit regular reports. Compliance was confirmed in a *Supplementary Report* later in 2011.

Moving from a focus on trustees to more general allegations, several other charities have been the subject of investigations because of suspicions of links to terrorism. The most persistent allegations have concerned Interpal, the Palestinian Relief and Development Fund, which was established in Britain in 1994 to provide relief to Palestinians in the Occupied Territories, Lebanon and Jordan. Allegations of connections with HAMAS have been made, but not sustained, on several distinct occasions.[104] HAMAS is not proscribed in the United Kingdom (though the closely related HAMAS-Izz al-Din al-Qassem Brigades are proscribed). The charity faced an acute threat to its existence when it was listed as linked to HAMAS by the US Treasury on 22 August 2003,[105] whereupon its activities were investigated by the Charity Commission. The BBC Panorama programme, *Faith, Hate and Charity*, issued fresh allegations in 2006[106] and thereby prompted another Charity Commission investigation in 2007. Its report in 2009 was critical of the due diligence and monitoring procedures then in place, but Interpal was again cleared of promoting terrorist ideology or activities. The Charity Commission appreciated the 'challenging' environment in which Palestinian charities must work and even recognized that:[107]

> Humanitarian assistance cannot be denied to people because they support, actively or otherwise, or are sympathetic towards the work or aims of a political body, such as Hamas. However, assistance cannot be given solely on the basis of a person's support for Hamas.

The sufficiency of cooperation in these inquiries from the American authorities was a matter of some speculation.[108]

---

104   See *Hewitt and others v Grunwald and others* [2004] EWHC 2959 (QB) (the litigation ended with an apology); M. Levitt, *Hamas, Politics, and Charity* (New Haven: Yale University Press, 2006).

105   See http://www.treasury.gov/press-center/press-releases/Pages/js672.aspx (accessed 4 June 2011).

106   The BBC admitted libel for implicating Waseem Yaqub in the allegations, *Press Gazette* 24 May 2007: http://www.pressgazette.co.uk/story.asp?storycode=37734 (accessed 4 June 2011).

107   Charity Commission, *Inquiry Report: Palestinian Relief and Development Fund (Interpal)* (London, 2009) paras 176, 183.

108   See HC Deb vol 492 col 677wa 12 May 2009, Ian Pearson and vol 496 col 182wa 9 September 2009, Ivan Lewis.

Another strand of the attack on Interpal has taken the form of a legal action brought against its bankers in the US District Court (Eastern District of New York). The essence of the complaint, on behalf of families of Americans killed or wounded in attacks in Israel, is the provision of material support to terrorism.[109] Interpal's bank accounts with National Westminster were closed by the bank in 2007. The Islamic Bank of Britain also ended its links with Interpal in 2008 because of pressure from Lloyds TSB which acted as its clearing bank. Another charity to face adverse action through the intercession of a financial institution is the Ummah Welfare Trust, which experienced the withdrawal of its account with Barclays Bank in 2008.[110]

Linkage with HAMAS, via the Al-Ihsan Charitable Society, was the charge levelled against Muslim Aid, founded in 1985 and with operations in 70 countries. Money was set aside for Al-Ihsan in 2005, but there was no transfer because Al-Ihsan became designated within the UK only on 27 June 2005.[111] The commission's reaction was to provide regulatory advice and guidance to the trustees.

Another set of allegations regarding HAMAS arose in connection with the group, Viva Palestina, a project which responded to the Israeli incursion into Gaza in December 2008 and seeks to provide aid convoys.[112] The two founding trustees were George Galloway, at the time a member of parliament, and Sabah Al-Mukhtar, president of the Arab Lawyers Association in the UK. The Charity Commission opened an inquiry in March 2009[113] because of alarm about its non-registration as a charity as well as uncertainty around the control and ultimate application of funds. Its bank (the Islamic Bank of Britain) had frozen its funds because of these concerns and then terminated its relationship, as a result of which monies received after the freeze had to be returned to donors. Charitable registration was imposed in April 2009 on the instructions of the commission, subsequent to which the founding trustees resigned since the categorization was contrary to their wishes.[114] The attempt by the trustees to add two additional and explicitly political (and thereby non-charitable) purposes to the constitution of the body in March 2009[115] was viewed as *ultra vires* by the commission as well as not divesting the funding held of its charitable status. It was also sustained that George

---

109   *Weiss v National Westminster Bank* 2008 US Dist. LEXIS 99443 (USDC, EDNY).

110   T. Jeory, 'Muslims boycott bank over closed accounts' *Sunday Express* 28 December 2008, 15.

111   Charity Commission, *Regulatory Case Report: Muslim Aid* (London, 2010).

112   See http://www.vivapalestina.org/home.htm (accessed 4 June 2011).

113   Charity Commission, *Inquiry Report: Viva Palestina* (London, 2010).

114   See http://www.vivapalestina.org/alerts/GGCC_140409.htm (accessed 4 June 2011).

115   Charity Commission, *Inquiry Report: Viva Palestina* (London, 2010) para. 38: 'Expose crimes committed by Israel against the Palestinian people' and 'Support the rights of the Palestinian people to resist Israeli occupation of their land'.

Galloway had personally donated £25,000 in cash to HAMAS in March 2009, accompanied by the following message:[116]

> To the Prime Minister Ismail Haniyeh: Here is the money. This is not charity. This is politics. The government of Palestine is the best people to decide where this money is needed. And if I could, I would give them 10 times, 100 times more.

In summary, there was an unusually quick and robust response in this case, even though the main problems related to the proper handling of funds rather than the financing of terrorism. Perhaps the publicity attached from the outset of the controversy, magnified by the involvement of George Galloway, made the commission unusually sensitive to being depicted as inactive or supine.

Several other investigations have concerned Tamil charities accused of involvement with the Liberation Tigers of Tamil Eelam ('LTTE' – the Tamil Tigers), a proscribed organization under the Terrorism Act 2000. The Charity Commission began in 2000 investigating the Tamils Rehabilitation Organisation ('TRO') which was founded in 1985 in Tamil Nadu, India, to provide relief to Tamil refugees, and then moved in 1987 to Jaffna.[117] The investigation found that the charity exerted little control once its relief money had been transmitted to Sri Lanka, where local representatives had liaised with LTTE representatives to allocate funding. So serious was the situation that it organized for an interim manager to be appointed to take over the administration of the charity and then agreed for a new charity, the Tamil Support Foundation to be registered in 2005 and for assets and activities to be transferred to it under much tighter control.[118] The Tamils Rehabilitation Organisation was then struck off the register, though on the basis that it was defunct rather than because of abusive practices. Another charity, White Pigeon, was registered in 2005 and involved as a trustee, a former director of the TRO, Navasivayam Sathiyamoorthy.[119]

Another Tamil charity has been treated with greater apparent indulgence. The charity, Sivayogam,[120] was registered in 1995 as an organization which worked with Tamils both in London and in northern Sri Lanka. Concerns surfaced in 2005

---

116   Ibid., para. 26.

117   See Charity Commission, *Inquiry Report: Tamils Rehabilitation Organisation* (London, 2006); Home Office and HM Treasury, *Review of Safeguards to Protect the Charitable Sector (England and Wales) from Terrorist Abuse* Annex C.

118   The Tamils Rehabilitation Organisation was designated as a Specially Designated Global Terrorist in the US under Executive Order 13224, 15 November 2007. A full list of US designated charities is at: http://www.treasury.gov/resource-center/terrorist-illicit-finance/Terrorist-Finance-Tracking/Pages/fto.aspx (accessed 4 June 2011).

119   T. Whipple, 'British Tamils are intimidated into giving money to terrorists', *The Times* 5 February 2007, 8.

120   Charity Commission, *Inquiry Report: Sivayogam* (London, 2010).

when it became apparent that the leading trustee, Nagendram Seevaratnam, had professed LTTE sympathies going back some decades, including an admission of membership before 1991. The inquiry instigated by the Charity Commission found problems with the selection and monitoring of local partners in Sri Lanka, that the financial accounting involved interest-free loans and cash transactions which increased risks,[121] and that the said trustee remained a dominant figure who admitted supporting the LTTE in 2006 and 2007.[122] In another example of its 'green-light' style, the Charity Commission imposed the sanction of removal as a trustee but otherwise sought to work with the impugned charity to improve its standards. Even the attempted removal was reversed by the First-Tier Tribunal (Charity), which viewed the trustee's statements as merely 'unwise and unguarded' in circumstances where he had not been 'warned that his own statements might be used against him or advised of his right to obtain legal advice'.[123] The tribunal did still accept that he had maintained contact with the LTTE,[124] though that fact did not make it necessary or desirable to remove him,[125] and it also found that the investigation had not properly translated all relevant evidence regarding due diligence. Furthermore, the tribunal endorsed a 'green-light' regulatory approach, stating that:[126]

> If there had remained any legitimate regulatory concerns following a proper examination of the evidence originally provided to it, the Tribunal concludes that it would have been appropriate for the Respondent to work with the charity to improve its processes before considering exercising its regulatory powers. As it was, the Respondent exercised its regulatory powers without considering the evidence with which it had been provided.

Seevaratnam later chose to resign from the charity.[127]

Some other statutory inquiries are ongoing. One followed the discovery of munitions allegedly linked to Jamaat-ul-Mujahideen and the arrest of Faisal Mostafa, who had opened and directed an orphanage and madrasa in Bangladesh for Green Crescent, a charity based in Stockport.[128] In June 2012, the Charity

---

121   Ibid., paras 74, 107, 115.
122   Ibid., para. 127.
123   *Nagendram Seevaratnam v Charity Commission for England and Wales and Her Majesty's Attorney General* (CA/2008/0001, 13 October 2009) para. 6.52.
124   Ibid., para. 6.92.
125   Ibid., paras 6.93, 6.117.
126   Ibid., para. 6.75.
127   Charity Commission, *Inquiry Report: Sivayogam* (London, 2010) para. 180.
128   See J. Page, R. Jenkins and M. Evans, 'Terror training in British-run orphanage', *The Times* 26 March 2009, 3.

Commission announced a statutory inquiry to investigate complaints about Masjid Al Tawhid, including accusations of extremism and links to terrorism.[129]

Assessment of Policing Responses

A rather harsh assessment of this track record of the Charity Commission, made in June 2006 via US diplomatic channels, was revealed by Wikileaks in 2011:[130]

> ... a Home Office official, allegedly told US diplomats that the Charity Commission was "completely out of its depth" in how it dealt with groups suspected of funding terrorists. Its officials would have "already trampled over the crime scene" by the time they contacted police, he was reported to have said.

The US diplomats were also highly critical of the failure to police the North Finsbury Park mosque and stated that 'the British Government was aware of "profound shortcomings" in the regulation of charities with links to terrorist groups overseas'.[131] That verdict is now subject to two provisos. One is that further efforts have been instituted since 2006 to tighten the regulations covering charity financing. The second point is that there are competing public interests which may legitimately affect the degree and manner of intervention by the regulators. These two points will now be considered.

In response to the evident perils of terrorist abuse and infiltration of charities, the Home Office and HM Treasury reviewed the policing regime in their 2007 report, *Review of Safeguards to Protect the Charitable Sector (England and Wales) from Terrorist Abuse*.[132] The channelling of funds by charities to terrorists is assessed to be 'extremely rare'. Nevertheless, the government departments urge the Charity Commission to reinforce awareness of risk factors, an approach which chimes with the broader trend towards 'new public risk management'.[133]

The Charity Commission responded in 2008 by publishing its *Counter-Terrorism Strategy*. It is reiterated that the instances of infiltration or abuse remain 'extremely rare' but, when detected, are subject to 'zero tolerance' which will apply

---

129   http://www.masjidtawhid.org/news/56-press-release-denial-of-charges-of-extre mism (accessed 28 February 2013).

130   M. Moore, 'US feared British "sharia banks" would finance terrorist groups', *The Daily Telegraph* 15 March 2011, 8.

131   R. Winnett et al., 'London: Hub of Al-Qaeda's global terrorism network', *The Daily Telegraph* 26 April 2011, 1, 2.

132   (London, 2007) para. 2.10.

133   J. Black, 'The emergence of risk based regulation and the new public risk management in the United Kingdom' [2005] *Public Law* 512. See further P. O'Malley, *Risk, Uncertainty and Government* (London: Glasshouse, 2004); J. Black, 'The role of risk in regulatory processes' in R. Baldwin, M. Lodge and M. Cave, *Oxford Handbook of Regulation* (Oxford: Oxford University Press, 2010).

to any connections to proscribed organizations, support for terrorist activity, or the fostering of 'criminal extremism'.[134] The commission recognizes that, despite the difficulties, there is a need for a 'strong and vibrant sector' since otherwise less regulated mechanisms will prevail in seeking to provide humanitarian relief.[135]

In pursuance of its strategy, various actions have been undertaken to improve trustee awareness, including oversight through a Proactive Monitoring Unit, cooperation between enforcement agencies, and greater intervention. Published advice has been elaborated through the issuance of an *Operational Guidance* and a *Compliance Toolkit*, setting out the commission's approach, and underlining the duties of vigilance and disclosure of trustees, illustrating the possible threats, and giving advice about the work of the Counter Terrorism Team which forms part of the Intensive Casework Unit in Compliance and Support.[136] The documentation was impressively expanded in 2013, when the commission issued several much fuller versions of the *Compliance Toolkits*, including, *Chapter 1: Protecting Charities from Harm, Chapter 2: Due Diligence, Monitoring and Verification of End Use of Charitable Funds*, and *Chapter 5: Protecting Charities from Abuse for Extremist Purposes and Managing the Risk at Events and in Activities – Guidance for Trustees*.[137] Exposed charities (for example, in conflict zones) are encouraged to implement risk management in respect of the choice and work of foreign partners, of specific projects before they are funded, and of funding arrangements and delivery so as to ensure transparency. They are also reminded that they may seek advice from the commission under section 110 of the Charities Act. A subvention of £1m in 2007 also allowed the commission to establish a Faith and Social Cohesion Unit with the objective of engaging with faith communities (primarily Muslim) to identify and encourage registration as a charity and then to assist faith-based charities in their management standards.

Despite these extra initiatives, there has been no discernible change in the 'green-light' approach.[138] The general stance remains one of considerate encouragement rather than hard policing. It is furthermore an approach in which the political implications of potential criticism of the charitable sector remain of vital importance, even during investigations of terrorism links. The prominence of

---

134   (London, 2008) 4, 10; R. Baldwin and J. Black, 'Really responsive risk-based regulation' (2010) 32 *Law and Policy* 181.

135   Ibid., 2, 7.

136   Charity Commission, *OG96: Charities and Terrorism* (London, 2007); Charity Commission, *Compliance Toolkit: Protecting Charities from Harm* (London, 2011).

137   http://www.charitycommission.gov.uk/detailed-guidance/protecting-your-charity/protecting-charities-from-harm-compliance-toolkit/ (accessed 28 September 2013).

138   For the latest condemnation that enforcement by the Charity Commission 'lacks rigour', see House of Commons Committee of Public Accounts, *Charity Commission: The Cup Trust and Tax Avoidance* (2013–14 HC 138 4).

political sensitivity may be evidenced by the statement in the commission's *MP Factsheet 7: Charities and Terrorism* that:[139]

> It is our usual policy to inform the MP or [Welsh] AM when we open a statutory inquiry into a particular charity so you may have a contact point with the Commission to address any concerns or queries which you may have. We are not generally able to give detailed information on the nature of our concerns, although we can confirm the general nature of the complaint or concerns being looked at. We will also inform you when the inquiry is completed and send you a copy of the completed report.

This relationship with politicians goes significantly further than required by the duty under Schedule 1, paragraph 11 of the Charities Act 2011 to make an annual report to parliament. The practice applies even though the local MP has no particular standing or intercessionary role in mediation or in bringing a complaint to the attention of the commission's Independent Complaint Reviewer,[140] though subsequent complaints against the commission may fall within the remit of the Parliamentary and Health Service Ombudsman, whose intervention must be predicated on referral from an MP.[141] One might compare the reticence of the commission about publishing all inquiry reports as a matter of course. According to its website:[142]

> Our intention is to report the outcome of every formal inquiry. However, there will be a small number of exceptions where this is not appropriate. We will not publish an inquiry report where in the Commission's judgement it would have a detrimental impact on the effective regulation of the sector and public trust and confidence in charities.

While this author's multiple requests for access to inquiry reports under Freedom of Information legislation have been successful in every case, the commission's default sensitivity towards wrongdoing contrasts with the predilection of the Home Office for 'naming and shaming'.[143]

This analysis of the overall attitude and approach of the Charity Commission tallies with some recommendations in the report by Lord Hodgson in 2012, *Trusted*

---

139   (London, 2010) 3.

140   See http://www.charity-commission.gov.uk/About_us/Complaining/Complaint_ about_a_charity_index.aspx (accessed 27 February 2013).

141   Parliamentary Commissioner Act 1967, s 6(3).

142   http://www.charity-commission.gov.uk/Our_regulatory_activity/Compliance_ reports/inquiry_reports/default.aspx (accessed 27 February 2013).

143   See for example the introduction of orange high-visibility vests bearing the inscription, 'Community Payback' for all adult offenders carrying out Community Payback: *Engaging Communities in Criminal Justice* Cm 7583 (2009) para. 137.

and Independent: Giving Charity Back to Charities – Review of the Charities Act 2006.[144] Lord Hodgson not only calls for automatic trustee disqualification following any conviction of a terrorism offence[145] (which would not make much difference) but also and more tellingly that the Charity Commission should take 'a more robust approach to potentially failing organisations' and 'proactive as well as reactive steps' in cases of abuse.[146] However, the recommendation that the general threshold for compulsory registration should be raised to £25,000 (subject to voluntary registration under section 30(3) of the Charities Act 2011) drastically undermines tighter enforcement, as a result of which the government has expressed doubts.[147]

Moving next to the competing public goods which might properly retard the sanctioning of charities for terrorism financing, countervailing considerations are that British society should not appear to be stone-hearted in the face of the most difficult humanitarian crises in conflict zones, such as in Palestine, Somalia and Sri Lanka. Such a stance might even aggravate the situation by encouraging less regulated and less cooperative activities, even resulting in a strategic defeat: 'In that event, the government ironically would have exacerbated, not reduced, one ultimate goal of fundamentalist and radical terrorists: the disruption of globalism.'[148] An illustration of such upheaval arises from the United Nations listing of Al Barakaat group in Somalia from 2001 to 2009[149] which some claim to have deepened the crisis in that country and to have encouraged hostility to Western values.[150]

Other oversight agencies, including the police, may not be as tolerant in their relationships or as internationally humanitarian in attitude. Another public good which they promote is the punishment of wrongdoing. There have been 71 prosecutions for offences under section 15 to 18 of the Terrorism Act 2000

---

144   London: Cabinet Office, 2012. See also *Response to the Charities Act Review from the Minister for Civil Society* (Cabinet Office, 2012). A further inquiry by the House of Commons Public Accounts Committee, *Regulation of the Charitable Sector and the Charities Act 2006*, is ongoing.

145   Ibid., para. 4.53.

146   Ibid., para. 4.29, 5.28.

147   Ibid., para. 6.29; *Response to the Charities Act Review from the Minister for Civil Society* (Cabinet Office, 2012) 5.

148   N.J. Crimm, 'High Alert: The government's war on the financing of terrorism and its implications for donors, domestic charitable organizations, and global philanthropy' (2004) 45 *William & Mary Law Review* 1341, 1450–1.

149   The ban was challenged in *Kadi and Al Barakaat International Foundation v Council of the EU* Cases T-315/01, 21 September 2005, C-402/05, 415/05, 3 September 2008, [2008] ECR I-6351. The attempt to reimpose listing was struck down in T-85/09, 30 September 2010.

150   M. Scheinin, *Reports of the Special Rapporteur on the promotion and protection of human rights and fundamental freedoms while countering terrorism* (A/HRC/6/17, 2007) para. 48.

between 2001 and 2007 in Britain. Many offenders have received substantial sentences, including several who would regard themselves as charitable workers, though there is limited evidence that charities have been discouraged overall by this threat.[151] An example is Arunachalam Chrishanthakumar, who became President of the British Tamil Association, a voluntary (non-charitable) group which was set up after proscription of the LTTE in 2001. He was charged with receiving money for terrorism purposes and the collection and supply of army gear and weapons manuals and sentenced to two years imprisonment – it would have been longer but for his humanitarian work. Chrishanthakumar regularly met Special Branch officers, and Clare Short, the former International Development Secretary, appeared as a defence witness. Even the trial judge described him as 'a thoroughly decent man who deliberately broke the law in support of a cause he fervently believed in'.[152]

Conclusions and Future Policing

The United Kingdom approach to those charities assailed by the taint of terrorism funding has been one of considerate understanding if not, at times, downright indulgence. There has been a charitable treatment of charities which is often too 'responsive'.[153] It may appear on paper to amount to 'a strong regulatory model',[154] and even one which is 'sophisticated',[155] but the application of that model to allegations of terrorism links has often proved in practice to be weak and facile and notably feebler than the Charity Commission's attention to the public benefit credentials of independent schools.[156] Despite the re-evaluations and restatements of policy in 2007, there has been scant evidence of any enforcement policy change. Thus, the guidance from the Charity Commission is far from becoming a form of rigid 'stealth law'.[157] More realistically, the Home Office comments

151   See P.A. Sproat, 'The social impact of counter-terrorist finance policies in the UK' (2006) 44 *Crime, Law and Social Change* 441.

152   J.-P. Ford Rojas, 'Tamil jailed for supplying rebel tigers', *Press Association* 12 June 2009.

153   The term is adapted from R. Baldwin and J. Black, 'Really responsive regulation'.

154   M. Levi, 'Combating the financing of terrorism' (2010) 50 *British Journal of Criminology* 650, 650.

155   M. Sidel, 'Counter-Terrorism and the enabling legal and political environment for civil society' (2008) 10(3) *International Journal of Not-for-Profit Law* 7, 39.

156   A. Gilligan, 'Britain's charity watchdog has lost its bite' (2010) *Sunday Telegraph* 16.

157   The phrase was used in criticisms of the US Treasury Department's *Anti-terrorist Financing Guidelines* and *Revised Anti-terrorist Financing Guidelines* (Washington, DC, 2002 and 2005) by the Treasury Guidelines Working Group of Charitable Sector Organizations and Advisors, *Principles of International Charity*: http://www.usig.org/

in its 2011 paper on *Prevent Strategy*[158] that 'The Charity Commission must be seen to be capable of taking robust and vigorous action against charities that are involved in terrorist activity or have links to terrorist organisations.' Notably, this statement is presented as part of the 'Next Steps' agenda (alongside the priority of more emphasis on 'Prevent' work)[159] and therefore does not represent a ringing endorsement of action taken to date. The accompanying independent survey by Lord Carlile is more candidly critical of the commission:[160]

> It has lost a significant proportion of its staff, and as constituted has little prospect of carrying out the fullest inquiries where there are allegations of sophisticated money laundering which channels charitable funds to terrorist groups abroad ...

> The Charity Commission has a very important role as guardian of the governance of charities. They must be seen to take robust and vigorous action against charities involved in terrorism and extremism. Trustees must be left in no doubt of their responsibilities. Further discussion and work between central government and charities is needed to secure the reputation of the Commission as a valuable participant in this area of work.

As well as the 'green-light' approach to charitable trusts, their bankers are seemingly rarely at risk beyond the legal shark pools of the US civil courts. However, the official stance becomes markedly less benevolent when individual volunteers within the tainted charities are identified as sympathizers of extremist groups or as well-meaning couriers. Thus, it is usually worthy individuals who must pay the price for relief work at the margins of legality and not those voluntary or financial institutions which have failed to manage risk or have even turned a blind eye. In short, the Charity Commission is wholly correct to be highly suspicious of self-serving allegations from the opponents of Palestinians, Tamils and other oppressed peoples, and to adopt a stance which is primarily encouraging of compliance with high standards of governance rather than a condemnatory approach. There are also difficulties in regulating small organizations where there are no identifiable salient stakeholders beyond a few trustees.[161] But its serial indulgence of abuses does no favours to charities seeking to engage public support for oppressed people.

The partial misfiring of charities policing should not mean that the potential problems caused by terrorism financing can just be ignored. Aside from the

---

PDFs/Principles_Final.pdf, 2005 (accessed 4 June 2011). See M. Sidel, 'The Third Sector, human security, and anti-terrorism' 206.

158　Home Office, *Prevent Strategy* Cm 8092 (2011) para. 10.203.

159　Ibid., para. 10.204.

160　Lord Carlile, *Report to the Home Secretary of Independent Oversight of Prevent Review and Strategy* (London: Home Office, 2011) paras 58, 60.

161　Compare C.J. Cordery and R.F. Baskerville, 'Charity transgressions, trust and accountability' (2011) 22 *Voluntas* 197.

obvious and most shocking costs of personal harm and family tragedy, terrorism does inflict a host of costs on the state, affecting not only the health of its democracy but also of its economy.[162] However, two obvious reactions should be avoided. One would be to swing entirely towards criminal prosecution and asset forfeiture, a stance which would unduly ignore competing public goods and would create conflict with the voluntary sector and its many public sympathizers.[163] The second mistake would be to reinforce the resolve of the Charity Commission to act in a more punitive fashion. The data from this chapter suggests that it would be difficult to overcome the commission's statutory remit and entrenched 'partnership' culture which contends against punishing charities,[164] a reticence which is shared by overseas and international charity overseers.[165] In any event, it would again be potentially counter-productive for the overall public good to dilute the commission's 'distinctive contribution to the creation of an enabling environment for charities'.[166]

A promising third way is to apply a different set of matrices to the policing of counter-terrorism financing in charities. Prime amongst these[167] should be the value of financial investigation to facilitate intelligence-gathering. Prosecution and confiscation remain ultimate possible outcomes but should be less pressing than objectives such as disruption and the gathering of leads about terrorism activities rather than just financing. The concentration on financial investigation was championed a decade ago by the Cabinet Office's Performance and Innovation Unit's *Recovering the Proceeds of Crime*, which reported that:[168]

---

162   See T. Brück (ed.), *The Economic Analysis of Terrorism* (London: Routledge, 2007); M. Buesa and T. Baumert (eds), *The Economic Repercussions of Terrorism* (Oxford: Oxford University Press, 2010).

163   Compare the approach in the US and elsewhere: M. Sidel, 'Counter-Terrorism and the Enabling Legal and Political Environment for Civil Society'; K. O'Halloran, M. McGregor-Lowndes and K.W. Simon, *Charity Law and Social Policy* (Dordrecht: Springer, 2008) chs 8–10.

164   K. O'Halloran, *The Politics of Charity* (London: Routledge, 2011) 141.

165   See UN Monitoring Group, *Second report of the Monitoring Group established pursuant to resolution 1363 (2001) and extended by resolutions 1390 (2002) and 1455 (2003), on sanctions against Al-Qaida, the Taliban and individuals and entities associated with them* (S/2003/1070, 2 December 2003) para. 39.

166   K. O'Halloran, M. McGregor-Lowndes and K.W. Simon, *Charity Law and Social Policy* 559.

167   Other ideas include the 'whitelisting' of approved charities and greater incentives for disclosure: V. Fitzgerald, 'Global financial information, compliance incentives and terrorist funding' in T. Brück (ed.), *The Economic Analysis of Terrorism* (London: Routledge, 2007); J.M. Winer, 'Globalisation, terrorist finance and global conflict' in M. Pieth (ed.), *Financing Terrorism* (Heidelberg: Springer, 2010).

168   (London, 2000) paras 7.4, 7.5. See also P.C. van Duyne, 'Money laundering' (1998) 37 *Howard Journal* 359, 371; M. Pieth, 'Terrorism financing mechanisms and policy dilemmas' in J.K. Giraldo and H.A. Trinkunas (eds), *Terrorism Financing and State*

... financial investigation is an important tool in the fight against crime. In addition to being the gateway to effective asset identification and recovery, it can provide new avenues for traditional law enforcement investigations.

The PIU surveys found that:

- financial investigation is underused and undervalued;
- it is also underresourced in the UK, with a shortage of people with the right skills; and
- there is little cross-agency co-operation or sharing of best practice.

The 9/11 Commission pointed in the same direction for US policy.[169]

A financial investigation approach may produce fairer treatment between organizations and individuals involved in charitable work and may be easier to square with such desirable objectives as building the 'big (civil) society' and harmonious community relations. It also takes account of the public interest in encouraging the functioning of charities, including their rights to expression and association as well as rights to property. Rights to property could be treated more proportionately if the sanction element of the legal framework is played down.[170] As for rights to expression, there could be advantage to terrorism investigations from the evidence which might be provided by the encouragement of greater openness, a point repeatedly emphasized by Lord Macdonald in his review of counter-terrorism laws.[171] At the same time, limits would remain on direct espousal of militant causes.[172]

A financial investigation approach could have produced an outcome of greater utility to counter-terrorism in many of the inquiries described in this paper. Thus, it would have been more likely to have delivered information about terrorism networks and to close off the facilitation of militancy, including by disinterested players such as financial institutions, but without hurting worthy causes being pursued by humanitarian activists. This financial investigation approach is not best placed in the hands of the Charity Commission but should primarily be conducted by a formal police body. The roles left for the Charity Commission would be as standard-setter by continuing to promulgate operational guidance, as

---

Responses (Stanford, CA: Stanford University Press, 2007) 22; Home Office, *Extending Our Reach: A Comprehensive Approach to Tackling Serious Organized Crime* Cm 7665 (2009) 50.

169   *Executive Summary* (Washington, DC: 2004) 18–19.

170   For an example not in the field of charities, see *Mohunram v National Director of Public Prosecutions* [2007] ZACC 4.

171   *Review of Counter Terrorism and Security Powers* Cm 8803 (2011).

172   Compare the decision of the US Supreme Court in *Holder v Humanitarian Law Project* 561 US (2010) which arguably failed to distinguish the legitimacy of humanitarian activities from their setting.

standard-monitor (with alerts back to the police financial investigators if alarms are sounded), and as standard-applier once the police financial investigators find no criminal wrongdoing but grounds for concern about practices and risk. In this way, the heaviest price for terrorism financing should be paid by professional profit-takers and recipient perpetrators of terrorism.

Chapter 12

US Efforts to Stem the Flow of Funds to Terrorist Organizations: Export Controls, Financial Sanctions and Material Support

Laura K. Donohue[1]

Introduction

The United States' efforts to interrupt the provision of resources to non-state terrorist organizations began in the 1980s, as a number of international terrorist incidents brought the issue to the fore. The Hizbollah bombing of the US Embassy in Beirut, Lebanon in April 1983 and the US Marine barracks six months later demonstrated that non-state actors threatened American interests abroad. Paired with state-sponsored attacks, such as the destruction of Pan Am flight 103 over Lockerbie, Scotland in December 1988 (for which a Scottish court convicted a Libyan intelligence officer),[2] the attacks prompted the United States to pursue three avenues: the first was to make greater use of border restrictions to prevent the shipment of material overseas; the second centred on using economic sanctions and the freezing of foreign assets to go after the state sponsors; and the third focused on interrupting the flow of materials and funds to terrorist organizations at home and abroad via punitive measures.

Reflecting this tripartite approach, three legal instruments emerged: export controls, financial sanctions and material support provisions. It is in the latter two areas that the United States focused its counterterrorist regime following the attacks of 9/11. Financial sanctions and material support proved easier to establish than export controls. They allowed the government to ban all exports to designated entities, enabling the government to bypass the more specific arms export regime. They gave the Executive Branch a significant amount of latitude. And they carried serious criminal penalties. The use of these instruments to interrupt the flow of resources to terrorist organizations, however, is not without concern.

Within the first year of the 9/11 attacks, the rush to list individuals and entities served to discredit the financial sanctions regime in the United States and

---

1   Special thanks to David Cole, Colin King and Clive Walker for their thoughtful comments on an earlier version of this chapter.

2   See *HM Advocate v Megrahi (No 4)* 2002 JC 99. See also *HM Advocate v Megrahi* 2002 JC 38.

overseas. It was not clear whether many of those on the lists had any involvement in terrorism. The US refused to release information supporting their allegations. Designated people and organizations were given no notice and had no opportunity to contest their inclusion, resulting in a lack of due process. First Amendment concerns related to freedom of speech and freedom of association kept step with Fourth Amendment issues. Despite these significant weaknesses, however, the government continued to make use of the sanctions regime.

Over the past five years, the United States has placed the most emphasis on material support. Three factors appear to be behind this shift: first, a steadily expanded definition of what constitutes 'material support'; second, the inclusion of attempt, conspiracy, aiding and abetting in relation to material support; and third, an increased number of entities designated as 'foreign terrorist organizations' in regard to which material support is banned.

As a result of these changes, the related portions of the US criminal code have become integral to almost every terrorism prosecution. Nevertheless, material support instruments are fraught with constitutional and legal questions, ranging from due process and the Fourth Amendment, to First Amendment free speech and free association issues. Perhaps of greatest concern is the attenuated nature of the crime. No actual involvement in terrorism need be demonstrated in a court of law for a defendant to incur penalties. The government contends, for instance, and the Supreme Court agrees, that the Constitution does not preclude the criminalization of speech and other forms of advocacy in support of designated groups, even where the clear intent is to support the group's peaceful or humanitarian aims.[3]

Export Controls

Since the 1980s, the US has pursued three routes to stem the flow of resources to terrorist organizations. The first of these lies in the realm of export controls. Despite recent government rhetoric, however, the extent to which this instrument is either relied upon or, indeed, reliable stands in question.

Legal Framework

The 1976 Arms Export Control Act (AECA) provides the president with the authority to control the export of defense articles and services.[4] This legislation regulates the transfer of both hardware and technology.[5] Under the AECA, the decision of whether to grant export licenses turns in part on whether such shipments

---

3   Holder v Humanitarian Law Project, 561 US ____ (2010).

4   Arms Export Control Act (AECA), Title II of PL 94-329, 90 Stat. President's authority to the secretary of state.

5   Ibid. and see also Executive Order 11958, Administration of Arms Export Controls, 18 January 1977, 42 FR 4311, 3 CFR 1977 Comp., p. 79.

'would contribute to an arms race, aid in the development of weapons of mass destruction, support international terrorism, increase the possibility of outbreak or escalation of conflict, or prejudice the development of bilateral or multilateral arms control or non-proliferation agreements or other arrangements'.[6] A complex web of legislation now governs this area.[7]

Anti-terrorism in particular falls under sections 6(a) and 6(j) of the Export Administration Act of 1979 (as amended). Consistent with these authorities, the secretary of state has designated five countries – Cuba, Iran, North Korea, Sudan and Syria – as state sponsors of international terrorism.[8] In its 1999 Foreign Policy Report the Bureau of Industry and Security (BIS) explained the country-specific rationale. With regard to Iran, for instance:[9]

> The purposes of the controls are to restrict equipment that would be useful in enhancing Iran's military or terrorist-supporting capabilities, and to address other US foreign policy concerns ... The controls also allow the US to prevent shipments of U.S.-origin equipment for uses that could pose a direct threat to US interests. Iran continues to support groups that practice terrorism, including terrorism to disrupt the Middle East Peace Process, and it continues to kill Iranian dissidents abroad.

Syria presents similar concerns: 'Although there is no evidence of direct Syrian Government involvement in the planning or implementing of terrorist acts since 1986, Syria continues to provide support and safe haven to groups that engage in terrorism.'[10] Sudan, in turn, 'allows the use of its territory as sanctuary for terrorists including the Abu Nidal Organization, Hizbollah, Hamas and Palestinian Islamic Jihad'.[11] Counter terrorism concerns thus form part of a broader geopolitical

---

6   Ibid.

7   See, e.g., Arms Export Control Act, 22 USC ss 2751-2799aa-2 and Export Administration Act, 50 USC app 2401-2420. Note that the Export Administration Act is not permanent. 50 USC app 2419. In August 2001 the statute lapsed; however, Executive Order 13222: Continuation of Export Control Regulations 2001 under the IEEPA (50 USC 1701-1707) continued the export controls. This instrument requires annual extension.

8   See Export Administration Regulations, Bureau of Industry and Security, 2 July 2012, Part 742 at 2, available at: http://www.bis.doc.gov/policiesandregulations/ear/742. pdf (accessed 21 January 2013). Note that North Korea, formerly included in this list, was removed on 11 October 2008; however, the export regulations have not, as of the time of writing, been altered to remove the antiterrorism controls placed on the country. A partial explanation for this may be found in an alternative source of authority: namely, under UN Security Council Resolution 1718.

9   Analysis of Control as Required by Section 6(f) of The Act, BIS, pp. 194–195, available at: http://www.bis.doc.gov/pdf/fp8terro.pdf (accessed 21 January 2013).

10   Ibid., 195.

11   Ibid.

picture, in which the countries themselves present a military threat to US national security interests.

Since 1993, five categories of dual-use items destined for military, police, intelligence and other entities in the target countries have come under scrutiny within the anti-terrorist regime: i.e., items related to (1) national security; (2) chemical and biological weapons proliferation; (3) missile proliferation; (4) nuclear weapons proliferation; and (5) the military.[12] Any export of items in these areas falls subject to a 30-day Congressional notification period prior to approval.[13]

Despite the emphasis in the statute on state sponsors of terrorism, for decades export controls have been directed to preventing materials from finding their way to non-state actors as well. As early as 1989, for instance, the US Government used the instrument to stem the flow of weapons to terrorist organizations. That year, two US citizens and one Irish citizen were indicted for conspiracy to violate the AECA and conspiracy to injure and destroy foreign property, related to their research and development of a surface-to-air missile system for the Provisional Irish Republican Army ('IRA') to use in Northern Ireland.[14] According to the Secretary of Commerce, the purpose of these controls is 'to prevent acts of terrorism and to distance the US from nations that have repeatedly supported acts of international terrorism and from individuals and organizations that commit terrorist acts'.[15]

Just as other provisions apply to the entities listed as state sponsors, so, too are other substantive areas seen as a complement to the anti-terrorist regime. A number of export control categories thus reinforce US counter-terrorist efforts, such as measures introduced under the rubric of crime control/human rights, regional stability, embargoes/sanctions/other special controls, toxic chemicals/ chemical precursors/associated equipment, technology and software, biological agents and associated equipment and technology, and missile technology.[16]

These categories work together to provide a framework for limiting the flow of resources to terrorist entities. On 13 July 2011, for instance, the Department of Commerce released a final rule amending the Export Act Regulations (EAR) consistent with the Obama administration's recognition of South Sudan.[17] The fledgling country immediately became eligible for certain export and re-

---

12   Export Administration Act, Section 6(j)(1)(B). Iraq also was previously on the list. See Anti-terrorism Controls, Section 742.8, 742.9, 742.10, 744.10, available at: http://www. bis.doc.gov/pdf/fp8terro.pdf (accessed 21 January 2013).

13   See US Department of Commerce Bureau of Industry and Security, 2012 Report on Foreign Policy-Based Export Controls (Washington, DC: 2012) 36–37 (hereinafter '2012 Report').

14   Federal Bureau of Investigation, *Terrorism 2002–2005* (Washington, DC: US Department of Justice, 2005) 39.

15   *2012 Report*, 38.

16   See ibid., 2–6.

17   76 FR 41046, 13 July 2011. References to the Export Administration Regulations relate to 15 CRF Chapter VII, subchapter C.

export license exceptions, even as some anti-terrorist measures were lifted.[18] Simultaneously, changes adopted in other areas underscored the anti-terrorist agenda: the secretary of commerce, for instance, noted in 2011 that provisions related to the control of aircraft would have an impact on regional stability, national security, antiterrorism and missile technology.[19]

For a country or entity to become subject to anti-terrorist or other export control provisions, the Secretary of Commerce must find that the controls are likely to achieve the intended foreign policy purpose and that such purpose cannot be achieved via negotiations or alternative means. In addition, the Secretary of Commerce must determine that such controls are compatible with US foreign policy objectives and will not, in turn, carry any significant adverse foreign policy consequences.

It is important to recognize here the presentational aspect of anti-terrorism measures as reflecting the rhetorical battle that accompanies the anti-terrorist discourse. The Secretary of Commerce notes, for instance, that: 'Although widespread availability of comparable goods from foreign sources limits the effectiveness of [export controls], the controls restrict access to US-origin commodities, technology, and software, and demonstrate US determination to oppose and distance the US from international terrorism.'[20] Export controls, 'affirm the US commitment to restrict the flow of items and other forms of material support to countries, individuals, or groups for terrorist purposes'.[21] Such concerns may outweigh even the consequent negative economic impact on US industry.[22]

Non-Compliance

Export controls maintained in the interests of US foreign policy require the executive annually to extend such provisions under section 6 of the Export Administration Act of 1979, as amended.[23] To monitor non-compliance, a number of federal entities have inspection and investigatory authorities, such as the Department of Commerce's Office of Export Enforcement, the Department for Homeland Security's ('DHS') US Immigration and Customs Enforcement, and

---

18 See *2012 Report* 4. Export controls have been extended from 21 January 2013, to 20 January 2014: *2013 Report on Foreign Policy-Based Export Controls* 1, available at: http://www.bis.doc.gov/news/2013/2013_foreign_policy_report.pdf (accessed 16 April 2013). Special strictures continued to mark chemical and biological agents, nuclear technologies and hardware, and missile technology. Ibid.

19 *2012 Report*, at 26–27.

20 Ibid., 39.

21 Ibid.

22 See ibid., 29.

23 50 USC app ss 2401–2420 (2000). The president must submit a report to congress for the controls to be extended; such authority has been delegated to the secretary of commerce. See also Executive Order 12002 (7 July 1977); Executive Order 13222 (17 August 2001) and Notice of 12 August 2011, 76 FR 50661 (16 August 2011).

the Department of Justice's Federal Bureau of Investigation. Tools available range from undercover operations, searches without warrants at the borders (for immigration and customs only), wiretaps, overseas investigations, and access and use of forfeiture funds.

Punitive actions, in turn, (whether criminal or administrative) can be taken by a wide range of entities: the Department of Commerce's Bureau of Industry and Security Office of Chief Counsel, the Department of Homeland Security's US Customs and Border Protection, the Department of Justice's US Attorneys' Offices, the Department of State's Directorate of Defense's Trade Controls and Office of Legal Adviser for Political-Military Affairs, and Department of Treasury's Office of Foreign Assets Control.

Current Trends

Despite the existence of the export control regime, the US government does not rely heavily on the measures to stem the flow of goods to international terrorist threats. Furthermore, rhetoric notwithstanding, precious little has been done in the post-9/11 environment to strengthen the legal underpinnings of the regime.

Just over a year after the 9/11 attacks, for instance, the White House announced that it would be undertaking a 'comprehensive assessment of the effectiveness of US defense trade policies, to identify changes necessary to ensure that those policies continue to support US national security and foreign policy goals'.[24] The review, however, resulted neither in any concrete legislative proposals nor in any major revisions of the EAR. Accordingly, in February 2005 the Government Accountability Office ('GAO') determined that the 9/11 attacks had not generated any significant changes to the US arms export control system.[25] If anything, the system had become even more cumbersome.[26]

In 2006 GAO identified several challenges faced by the export control system and made recommendations to improve coordination between the multiple agencies involved.[27] Like the earlier initiatives, these proposals appear to have made little ground. It was not until 2010 that the president announced that he would be seeking significant reforms to the US export control system. The Department of Commerce published notice in the federal register inviting comments on a broad range of issues from industry and the public on the effectiveness of US

---

24 NSPD 19: *Review of Defense Trade Export Policy and National Security*, 21 November 2001.

25 US GAO, *Report to the Chairman, Committee on International Relations, House of Representatives, Defense Trade, Arms Export Control System in the Post-9/11 Environment* (Washington, DC: GAO-05-234, 2005).

26 Ibid.

27 GAO, *Export Controls: Challenges Exist in Enforcement of an Inherently Complex System* (Washington, DC: GAO-07-265, 2006); GAO, *2011 High-Risk Series, An Update* (Washington, DC: GAO-11-278, 2011).

foreign policy-based export controls.[28] The comment period was only open for a month, closing on 3 October 2011.[29] In the end, the department only received two comments – one from an individual (William Root) and one from a university (Massachusetts Institute of Technology).[30] Neither comment specifically addressed the anti-terrorist regime.

It is unclear precisely what the current status is of the anti-terrorism export control regime. The presentational nature of the system appears to be of greater importance than the application of stringent controls. The framework is unwieldy at best and appears to conflate geopolitical concerns and threats to US national security from certain countries with counter-terrorist concerns. The range of items on the anti-terrorism control list is, moreover, broad. It includes, for instance, tractors, large diesel engines, scuba gear and related equipment, and semi-conductor manufacturing equipment.[31] If anything, the Obama administration appears to be looking for ways to reduce the burdens imposed on industry by the current system.[32]

Financial Sanctions Levied on States and Non-State Entities

In contrast to the failure of successive administrations' rigorously to apply the export control regime to counter-terrorism, the post-9/11 environment saw a sudden flurry of activity with regard to financial sanctions. As an instrument of international influence, however, such measures appear to have had limited effect. Fault lies, in part, with the rather haphazard way in which the list was first constructed. Executive Order 13224 also raises constitutional and legal concerns related to due process, the Fourth Amendment and the First Amendment, and it carries significant negative economic and political consequences. Its primary target appears to be Islamic, Arabic, or Middle Eastern individuals and entities. Despite the myriad difficulties associated with the order, it continues to be used,

---

28   76 FR 54426, 1 September 2011.

29   Ibid.

30   2012 BIS Report, 114.

31   Export Administration Regulations, Bureau of Industry and Security, 2 July 2012, Supplement No. 2 to Part 742 – Anti-terrorism controls: North Korea, Syria and Sudan contract Sanctity Dates and Related Policies, 1–13, available at: http://www.bis.doc.gov/policiesandregulations/ear/742.pdf (accessed 21 January 2013).

32   See, e.g., Skadden, Arps, Slate, Meagher and Flom, *Export Control Reform Initiative: The Obama Administration Proposes New Transition Rules for Companies Affected by Recently-Proposed Changes to the Current Export Control System* (New York: 2012), available at: http://www.jdsupra.com/legalnews/export-control-reform-initiative-the-98998/ (accessed 21 January 2013).

with an average of three people and one entity added per month to the hundreds of names currently on the list.[33]

Executive Order 13224

The use of sanctions to prevent the funding of terrorist threats originated with the Trading with the Enemy Act of 1917 (and its subsequent amendments), which provided the Executive with the authority to 'investigate, regulate ... prevent or prohibit ... transactions' during either war or times of national emergency.[34] Abuses during the Nixon administration led to the statute's revocation and replacement with the International Emergency Economic Powers Act of 1977 ('IEEPA').[35] This legislation focuses on threats wholly (or mostly) outside the US. Upon declaration of a national emergency, the president can designate countries, individuals or entities considered a threat to national security, freeze their assets, and block transactions between them and US persons by making it illegal to make or receive any contribution of funds, goods, or services to or from those included on the list.[36] The president delivers any Executive Order listing such targets to the Treasury's Office of Foreign Assets Control ('OFAC'), which then informs banks. Refusal to comply carries criminal and civil penalties.

Initially, the Executive Branch applied IEEPA only to states, with the first orders targeting Libya and Cuba.[37] The US continues to apply the IEEPA to states as a way to interrupt the flow of funding to terrorist organizations. Libya, for instance, was one of the original countries listed 29 December 1979 as a state sponsor of terrorism.[38] In 2006 the State Department lifted its restrictions. In February 2011, however, the President issued Executive Order 13566 under the IEEPA, declaring a national emergency with regard to Muammar Qadhafi's regime.[39] On 1 July 2011, Mohammed El-Gamal, the president and CEO of a company located in North Carolina, agreed to pay a civil penalty of $340,000 for violations of the Export Administration Regulations focused on anti-terrorism restrictions limiting the export of networking equipment to Libya.[40] According to the government's

---

33   Author-maintained database (accessed 16 April 2013). See also Individuals and Entities Designated by the State Department Under E.O. 13224, Bureau of Counterterrorism, last updated 17 December 2012, available at: http://www.state.gov/j/ct/rls/other/des/143210.htm (accessed 16 April 2013).

34   50 USCS appendix s 3.

35   Trading with the Enemy Act, 50 USC s 1702(a)(1)(1977).

36   50 USC s 1702(a)(I)(B)(2001).

37   For Cuba, see http://www.treasury.gov/resource-center/sanctions/Programs/Documents/cuba.pdf (accessed 1 October 2013).

38   22 U.S.C. §2656(f).

39   Executive Order 13566, 25 February 2011, available at: http://www.treasury.gov/resource-center/sanctions/Programs/Documents/2011_libya_eo.pdf (accessed 1 October 2013).

40   Bureau of Industry and Security US Department of Commerce, North Carolina CEO Fined for Export Violations Involving Libya, 1 July 2011, available at: http://www.bis.

allegations, the company, Applied Technology Inc., had transferred equipment to the General Electric Company of Libya without the required licenses from the Department of Commerce.[41] That same month Treasury's Office of Foreign Assets control issued abbreviated regulations to implement the Executive Order.[42]

States, however, are not the only target of executive orders under the IEEPA. In the 1990s, the Clinton administration began including non-state actors, such as Palestinian organizations and the Cali drug cartel. In January 1995, President Clinton issued Executive Order 12947, which froze the US assets of specified terrorists or groups threatening to use force to disrupt the Middle East peace process and prohibited any transfer of 'funds, goods, or services' to the same – a shift which, it could be argued, is effectively *ultra vires* the governing legislation. The Annex to Executive Order 12947 established a 'Specially Designated Terrorist' ('SDT') list, naming a dozen organizations and 18 individuals as targets.[43] Following the Egyptian Islamic Jihad attacks in 1998 on the US embassies in Nairobi and Dar es Salaam, Clinton added Osama bin Laden and a number of his key aides to the SDT list via Executive Order 13099.[44] In 1999 the administration authorized OFAC to expand sanctions to the Taliban in retaliation for their protection of bin Laden.[45] Further additions to the list included, *inter alia*, Hamas and Hizbollah in January 1995, Mousa Mohammed Abu Marzook in August 1995, and the Holy Land Foundation in December 2001.

---

doc.gov/news/2011/bis_press07012011.htm (accessed 21 January 2013). On 14 February 2011, El-Gamal had pleaded guilty to one count of making material false statements and was later sentenced to a fine of $5,000, 100 hours of community service, and two years of supervised probation. Ibid.

41   Ibid., see also *2012 Report* 40.

42   76 Fed. Reg. 38562, 1 July 2011.

43   Executive Order No. 12947, 60 Fed. Reg. 5,079 (23 January 1995), reprinted as amended in 50 USCA. s 1701 (2003). The definition of specially designated terrorist as found in 31 CFR 595.311 reads: '(1) Persons listed in the Annex to Executive Order 12947; (2) Foreign persons designated by the Secretary of State, in coordination with the Secretary of the Treasury and the Attorney General, because they are found: (i) to have committed, or to pose a significant risk of committing, acts of violence that have the purpose or effect of disrupting the Middle East peace process; or (ii) To assist in, sponsor, or provide financial, material, or technological support for, or services in support of, such acts of violence; and (3) Persons determined by they Secretary of the Treasury, in coordination with the Secretary of State and the Attorney General, to be owned or controlled by, or to act for or on behalf of, any other specially designated terrorist.'

44   Executive Order No. 13099, 63 Fed. Reg. 45,167 (20 August 1998).

45   Executive Order No. 13129, 64 Fed. Reg. 36759, 4 July 1999. For continued actions taken against the Taliban see, e.g., Taliban (Afghanistan) Sanctions Regulations, 31 CFR part 545, 66 Fed. Reg. 2726, 11 January 2001. Further amendment to the original order went into place with Executive Order No. 13224, 66 Fed. Reg. 49079, 25 September 2001. The emergency was terminated with respect to the Taliban and Amendment of Executive Order 13224 of 23 September 2001 by Executive Order No. 13268, 67 Fed. Reg. 44751, 3 July 2002.

Within a fortnight of the 9/11 attacks, President Bush issued Executive Order 13224 under the IEEPA, creating a new 'Specially Designated Global Terrorist' ('SDGT') list.[46] This instrument blocked 'all property and interests in property' of not just foreign persons listed in the annex to the order who were determined 'to have committed, or to pose a significant risk of committing, acts of terrorism that threaten the security of US nationals or the national security, foreign policy, or economy of the US', but all persons determined 'to assist in, sponsor, or provide financial, material, or technological support for, or financial or other services to or in support of, such acts of terrorism or those persons listed in the Annex' to the order or determined to be subject to the order, or 'to be otherwise associated with those persons listed in the Annex' to the order.[47]

In practical terms, this language means that any business that has not ceased to interact with the listed entities can itself be listed and have its assets frozen. As originally written, mere 'association' was sufficient for the confiscation of property. The treasury, however, has since narrowed the ground to require an element of control or active engagement with the listed entity.[48] Once such assets are blocked, it becomes illegal to deal in the blocked assets or for any US entity to try to avoid or conspire to avoid the prohibitions or to make donations to relieve human suffering to persons listed under the order or determined to be subject to it.[49]

The Executive Order defines terrorism as an activity that '(i) involves a violent act or an act dangerous to human life, property, or infrastructure; and (ii) appears to be intended – (A) to intimidate or coerce a civilian population; (B) to influence the policy of a government by intimidation or coercion; or (C) to affect the conduct of a government by mass destruction, assassination, kidnapping, or hostage-taking.'[50]

Two points about this aspect of the instrument deserve notice. First, the definition relates to executive determinations, not to a statutory standard that is subsequently subjected to scrutiny in a court of law. Second, once the president names an initial set of designees, most of the subsequent designations are based not on independent findings of terrorism, but on some claim or connection, or executive branch determination, that the group assisted another designated entity.

---

46   Executive Order No. 13224, 23 September 2001, 3 CFR 786, 790.

47   Ibid., s 1.

48   The Humanitarian Law Project and others challenged the 'otherwise associated' provision as unconstitutionally vague and overbroad: *Humanitarian Law Project v US Department of Treasury*, 07-55893, cv-05-08047-abc, 24 August 2009. The treasury responded by issuing a regulation narrowly constructing 'to be otherwise associated with' to mean '(a) to own or control; or (b) to attempt, or to conspire with one or more persons, to act for or on behalf of or to provide financial, material, or technological support, or financial or other services'. 31 CFR s 594.316.

49   For discussion of the administration's launch of the order, see L.K. Donohue, *The Cost of Counterterrorism* (Cambridge: Cambridge University Press, 2008) 166–167.

50   Executive Order No. 13224 (23 September 2001), 3 CFR 786, 790, s 3.

This makes the definition of terrorism somewhat immaterial. Designations are not necessarily predicated on any direct involvement in the act of terrorism itself.

Protections that might otherwise accompany use of the governing statute have been weakened in the post-9/11 environment. The USA PATRIOT Act made three important changes.[51] First, it allowed the executive to submit classified evidence challenging designation under the IEEPA *in camera* and *ex parte*. This means that individuals subject to the order are neither allowed to see the information on which such designation is based, nor be represented by counsel at such hearings.

Second, the USA PATRIOT Act authorized the executive to block assets during the course of an investigation. This provision allowed for assets to be frozen without any actual finding of wrongdoing. Congress did not include exceptions for either humanitarian assistance or for the release of funds to bring suit.[52] Notably, as a practical matter, this means that treasury can indefinitely freeze an individual or entity's assets, without any finding of wrongdoing.[53]

Third, the statute amended the IEEPA to allow the president 'to confiscate any property, subject to the jurisdiction of the US, of any foreign person, foreign organization, or foreign country that he determines has planned, authorized, aided, or engaged in' 'hostilities or attacks against the US', in the process severing any nexus between the assets and any particular act of violence as well as any proportionality between the amount of property seized and the crime.[54] The language removed the judiciary from the process 'when the US is engaged in armed hostilities or has been attacked by a foreign country or foreign nationals'.[55] Taken in conjunction with the Authorization for the Use of Military Force issued by Congress in 2001, the order's language suggests the indefinite suspension of access to the courts at least as the blocking of such assets may relate to 'those nations, organizations, or persons' determined by the president to have 'planned, authorized, committed, or aided the terrorist attacks that occurred on September

---

51   Uniting and Strengthening America by Providing Appropriate Tools Required to Intercept and Obstruct Terrorism (USA PATRIOT) Act of 2001, s 186, 24 October 2001, codified in 50 USC 1861.

52   While the IEEPA itself provides an exception to the embargo on humanitarian aid, the statute also allows the president in his Executive Order to override it. President Clinton did so in Executive Order 12947, with President Bush following course in Executive Order 13224.

53   See *KindHearts for Charitable and Educational Development v Geithner*, US District Court for the Northern District of Ohio Western Division, 3:08-cv-2400, 26 August 2009 (finding treasury's statement that the charity was 'under investigation' constitutionally insufficient absent a warrant based upon probable cause, adequate notice of the basis for the freeze, or a meaningful opportunity for the charity to defend itself).

54   Ibid.

55   Ibid.

11, 2001, or harbored such organizations or persons, in order to prevent any future acts of international terrorism against the US'.[56]

Upon release of Executive Order 13224, the president froze the assets of a dozen individuals and 15 organizations.[57] Within a month, another 39 names had been added to the list.[58] Approximately two weeks later another 22 names issued, with 62 more individuals and entities added within five days. The numbers continued to grow, albeit at a slightly diminished pace, with some 210 people and groups listed by May 2002. On average, the executive added six people per month thereafter, bringing the total to 397 by January 2005.[59]

In the rush to add names and entities to the designation list, the evidence for actual involvement in terrorist activity often left something to be desired. The 9/11 Commission later explained:[60]

> The goal set at the policy levels of the White House and Treasury was to conduct a public and aggressive series of designations to show the world community and our allies that the US was serious about pursuing the financial targets. It entailed a major designation every four weeks, accompanied by derivative designations throughout the month. As a result, Treasury officials acknowledged that some of the evidentiary foundations for the early designations were quite weak. One participant (an advocate of the designation process generally) stated that "we were so forward leaning we almost fell on our face".

Approximately 80 per cent of the money blocked within the first year came under government control within the first three months.[61] In the end, such haste undermined the system as predictions that false designations 'would ultimately jeopardize the US' ability to persuade other countries to designate groups as terrorist organizations' came true.[62] Such 'early missteps', the 9/11 Commission concluded, 'have made other countries unwilling to freeze assets or otherwise act

---

56 Authorization for the Use of Military Force, PL 107-40, 115 Stat. 224, 18 September 2001.

57 Executive Order 13224, 66 Fed. Reg. 49,079 (25 September 2001). See also M. Allen and S. Mufson, 'US Seizes Assets of Three Islamic Groups', *Washington Post*, 5 December 2001 at A1.

58 US Department of the Treasury, Office of Foreign Assets Control, *Terrorism: What You Need to Know about US Sanctions* (Washington, DC, 2005).

59 US Department of the Treasury, *Treasury Designates Individual Financially Fueling Iraqi Insurgency, al Qaida* (Washington, DC: JS-2206, 2005).

60 Terrorist Financing Staff Monograph, *Chapter 5: Al-Barakaat Case Study: The Somali Community and al-Barakaat, National Commission on Terrorist Attacks Upon the United States*, p. 79, available at: http://govinfo.library.unt.edu/911/staff_statements/911_TerrFin_Ch5.pdf (accessed 21 January 2013).

61 R. Lee, *Terrorist Financing: The US and International Response* (Washington, DC: Congressional Research Service, RL 31658, 2002) 12, 27.

62 Ibid.

merely on the basis of a US action. Multilateral freezing mechanisms now require waiting periods before money can be frozen, a change that has eliminated the element of surprise and virtually ensured that little money is actually frozen'.[63]

A United Nations monitoring panel established in January 2004 concluded that al-Qa'ida had successfully evaded sanctions even as the financial sanctions regime had lost 'credibility and operational value'.[64] Countries began to refuse to cooperate with the United States.[65] In March 2006, a UN Security Council report expressed similar concern about the effectiveness of the international financial sanctions regime which had largely been constructed to be consistent with the US measures. The Council of Europe issued a scathing report, saying that the UN list violated the European Convention on Human Rights by omitting protections against arbitrary decisions as well as devices to ensure the accuracy of allegations made by governments or to provide any recourse to the targets of sanctions.[66] In 2008, a decision by the European Court of Justice essentially nullified the parallel European sanctions regime.[67] The court held that because the Security Council system failed to provide an opportunity for a party to defend itself, it violated the European Constitution's implied guarantee of fundamental fairness and, therefore, could not be enforced in Europe.

These failures did not end the regime. Instead, the listing of designated individuals under Executive Order 13224 continues, albeit at a slower pace. Over the first 10 months of 2012, for instance, an average of just over three people per month was added to the list. During the same time period, the list expanded to include nine new entities. Despite the expansion of the list from 2001 onward, it was not until June of 2008 that the US government removed either an individual or an entity from the list. Since that time, fewer than 20 people have been removed. During the same time-frame, only 16 entities appear to have been withdrawn, most of which have been related to Al-Barakaat.

---

63   National Commission on Terrorist Attacks Upon the United States, Nov 27, 2002, Chapter 3: Government Efforts Before and After the September 11 Attacks, at 48, available at: http://govinfo.library.unt.edu/911/staff_statements/911_TerrFin_Ch3.pdf (accessed 15 April 2013).

64   L.K. Donohue, *The Cost of Counterterrorism* (Cambridge: Cambridge University Press, 2008) 176.

65   In 2005 Aqeel al-Aqeel, the former director of al-Haramain filed a lawsuit against four US officials for his inclusion in Executive Order 13224. When the US refused to release any evidence supporting their claim, the Dutch government unfroze his assets. P.K. Abdul Ghafour, 'Aqeel Sues US Officials', Arabnews.com, 14 May 2005, http://www4.arabnews.com/node/266915 (accessed 28 April 2013).

66   D. Crawford, 'The Black Hole of a UN Blacklist' *Wall Street Journal*, 2 October 2006.

67   Joined Cases C-402/05 P & C-415/05 P, *Kadi & AlBarakaat v Council of the European Union and EC Commission* [2008] 3 CMLR 41.

Al-Barakaat

Al-Barakaat presents a strong example of how the listing process progressed and what went wrong. By way of contextual background, the growth of the Somali community in the US stemmed from the 1991 civil war in East Africa.[68] An important question for the community became how to send money back to family members in a region with no banking system and no central bank for handling foreign exchange.[69] Al-Barakaat was designed to fulfil this function. By 9/11, the network had more than 180 offices in 40 countries, with the express intent of sending money to Somalia.[70] In 1998 the network attracted FBI attention as a potential source of terrorist funding.[71]

About two weeks after the attacks, OFAC began to focus on the designation of Al-Barakaat under Executive Order 13224.[72] The 9/11 Commission later described the environment at OFAC as being in 'chaos'.[73] On 7 November 2001 raids commenced on eight Al-Barakaat offices in the US, resulting in the freezing of approximately \$65 million.[74] OFAC turned the event into a public relations spectacle, bringing President Bush to Treasury's Financial Crimes Enforcement Network ('FinCEN'), where he announced, with the Secretary of the Treasury and the Attorney General, that the head of the network was a 'friend and supporter of Usama Bin Ladin'.[75] Secretary of the Treasury Paul O'Neill similarly described the offices as '… a principal source of funding, intelligence and money transfers for Bin Ladin', estimating that some \$25 million per annum was funnelled to terrorism from the network.[76]

The immediate effect of the freezing on the owners of the businesses was severe. Yet the designations were made without sufficient evidence to demonstrate a connection to al-Qa'ida or bin Laden.[77] Despite subsequent investigations at home and abroad, the FBI teams assigned to the project 'could find no evidence at all of any real link between al-Barakaat and terrorism of any type'.[78] O'Neill's claim that some \$25 million per year had been directed towards terrorism proved hyperbole: the entire profits of the network ended up being only \$700,000, none of

68   Terrorist Financing Staff Monograph, supra note 61, Chapter 5: Al-Barakaat Case Study: The Somali Community and al-Barakaat, National Commission on Terrorist Attacks Upon the United States, 67, available at: http://govinfo.library.unt.edu/911/staff_ statements/911_TerrFin_Ch5.pdf (accessed 21 January 2013).
69   Ibid.
70   Ibid.
71   Ibid., at 68–75.
72   Ibid., at 78.
73   Ibid., at 79.
74   Ibid., at 80.
75   Ibid.
76   Ibid.
77   Ibid., at 83.
78   Ibid., at 82–83.

which could be shown to have been terrorist-related, despite detailed and thorough financial records.[79]

The listing of Al-Barakaat caused international consternation, especially when the United States used its powerful international position to include Al-Barakaat on the UN list of financial sanctions. By early 2002 US allies like Sweden and Canada demanded proof of a connection between individuals listed and terrorist activity.[80] There was no mechanism at the time, however, for delisting. It was not until 27 August 2002 that OFAC removed the US-based money remitters in Minneapolis and Columbus, as well as two of three Somali Swedes it had added to its designated entities. The 9/11 Commission concluded:[81]

> The federal agents working on the al-Barakaat criminal investigation in Minneapolis spent hundreds of hours reviewing financial records and interviewing witnesses. Despite this effort, their attempt to make a criminal case simply had no traction. Ultimately, prosecutors were unable to file charges against any of the al-Barakaat participants, with the exception of one of the customers in Minneapolis who was charged with low-level welfare fraud. The FBI supervisor on the criminal case, deciding that their efforts could be better spent elsewhere, closed their investigation.

Legal Concerns and Economic and Political Consequences

The *mens rea* required for criminal sanctions – which carry a similar effect in divesting individuals of access to personal property – is absent when it comes to Executive Order 13224. The instrument does not require that the individual or entity targeted knowingly assist terrorist activity. Instead, it is possible to rely almost entirely on associational links. Mere accusations may therefore prove a sufficient basis for designation.

Al-Barakaat is not the only example of rather over-zealous application of financial sanctions. On 19 November 2002, for instance, OFAC designated the Benevolence International Foundation, claiming that its founder, Enaam Arnaout, had had links to bin Laden in the 1980s. Treasury froze Arnaout's funds under Executive Order 13224, until it could prosecute him under different charges.[82] Another entity, al-Taqwa, a financial network based in Switzerland and the Bahamas, was designated the same day as Al-Barakaat and subject to the same claim that the organization funded terrorist activity. The Bush Administration asserted at the time that Hamas maintained accounts at the financial institution,

---

79 Ibid., at 83. OFAC strongly objected to the FBI's conclusions but failed to provide sufficient evidence to back their claims. See ibid., at 84.

80 Ibid., at 84–85.

81 Ibid., at 86.

82 L.K. Donohue, *The Cost of Counterterrorism* 171.

that in October 2000 al-Taqwa had extended a clandestine line of credit to 'a close associate' of bin Laden, and that the chairman of the bank had given al-Qa'ida and bin Laden financial assistance in late September 2001.[83] When the Swiss Banking Commission looked more carefully, however, it found neither evidence of the bank being used as a front company nor proof that the financial institution engaged in money laundering.[84]

Reliance on association carries a number of real economic and political costs. In 2001, for example, Somalia was in a particularly precarious position. For many households and businesses, remittances were the only source of funding, with up to 50 per cent of the country's GDP coming from such sources.[85] Following US actions against al-Barakaat, the UN estimated that about half of the remittances flowing to Somalia halted.[86] Levels of violence in the region soared, continuing with devastating effect for years afterward.[87] While much of the violence can be attributed to conflict between increasingly hostile parties, economic conditions also played an important role.

Arab Bank, the third largest Arab lender, provides another example. The organization first established a presence in New York in 1982. Citing the 'current operation environment in the United States', however, in February 2005, the bank announced that it would begin closing its US operations.[88] It claimed to have been unaware that payments from a Saudi charity in the West Bank and Gaza strip to families of suicide bombers were being conducted under its auspices. 'We have zero role in determining who receives the payments and why that beneficiary received the payments', commented Shukry Bishara, the chief banking officer.[89] The issue of culpability had both public and private aspects: not only was the government pursuing sanctions against Arab individuals and entities, but, as noted

83   *The USA PATRIOT Act: Investigating Patterns of Terrorist Financing: Hearing before the Subcomm. on Oversight and Instigations of the H. Comm. On Fin. Serv*, 107th Cong. 10 (2002) (statement of Juan C. Zarate, Dep. Ass't Secretary for Terrorism & Violent Crime).

84   D.G. McNeill, Jr., 'Italian Arab is Perplexed by Swiss Raid' *New York Times*, 8 November 2001, at B8.

85   C. Chalmers and M.A. Hassan, *UK Somali Remittances Survey*, Department for International Development (May 2008), available at: http://www.diaspora-centre.org/DOCS/UK_Somali_Remittan.pdf (accessed 21 January 2013).

86   Terrorist Financing Staff Monograph, supra note 61 at 81.

87   Somalia's violence 'catastrophic', BBC News, 22 August 2005, available at: http://news.bbc.co.uk/2/hi/africa/4173230.stm (accessed 21 January 2013).

88   Abdul Jalil Mustafa, Arab Bank to Shut NY Branch, *Arab News*, 10 February 2005, available at: http://www.arabnews.com/node/262196 (accessed 15 April 2013).

89   J. Cordahi, 'Arab Bank Says it Didn't Know of Payments to Bombers' Families' *Bloomberg*, 10 February 2005, available at: http://www.bloomberg.com/apps/news?pid=newsarchive&sid=a_0CRqtqmut0&refer=europe- (accessed 15 April 2013).

by Bloomberg, the families of victims of the September 11, 2001 attacks had begun to use the legal system 'to target Arab individuals, banks, and governments'.[90]

The lack of *mens rea* otherwise required in criminal law did not cause the administration concern. President Bush explained in November 2001: 'We fight the terrorists and we fight all of those who give them aid. America has a message for the nations of the world: ... If you feed a terrorist or fund a terrorist, you're a terrorist, and you will be held accountable by the Untied States and our friends.'[91] While such an approach may make effective political rhetoric, as a legal doctrine it leaves much to be desired.

There is little doubt that the primary targets of Executive Order 13224 are individuals and institutions of Islamic, Arabic and/or Middle Eastern origin. There are but a handful of exceptions to this pattern. In December 2001, for instance, OFAC added Northern Ireland's Continuity IRA, the Loyalist Volunteer Force, the Red Hand Defenders, and the Ulster Defense Association to the list at the same time that it included the First of October Antifascist Resistance Group ('GRAPO' – an armed wing of the Communist Party of Spain (Reconstituted), which is strongly anti-capitalist and anti-American).[92] More recently, in October 2011 the Conspiracy of Fire Nuclei, known as ELA in English (in Greek: *Synomosía Pyrínon Tis Fotiás* – 'SPF'), a radical anarchist organization was added to the list.[93] The listing of non-Arab, or non-Islamic groups under the order, however, is few and far between.

There are a number of other organizations constituted by different ethnic groups and/or non-religious political motivations, moreover, that have been designated terrorist organizations by the US State Department, and which are not included in Executive Order 13224. Omissions include groups such as Basque Fatherland and Liberty (ETA – considered a terrorist organization since 1997), Kach or Kahane Chai (violent, far-right Jewish nationalist organizations), the Kurdistan Workers Party ('PKK' – although the Followers of Islam in Kurdistan or Jund al-Islam is), the Revolutionary Armed Forces of Colombia (in Spanish: *Fuerzas Armadas Revolucionarias de Colombia—Ejército del Pueblo*, 'FARC–EP' and 'FARC'), and the Marxist group Revolutionary Organization 17 November ('17N'). Yet all

---

90   Ibid., in November 2012 the US District Court for the Eastern District of New York (Brooklyn) acquitted the Arab Bank of charges of aiding and abetting Hamas: *Gill v Arab Bank Plc*, 1:11-cv-03706.

91   President George W. Bush, *Remarks to Troops and Families at Fort Campbell* (21 November 2001) http://georgewbush-whitehouse.archives.gov/president/forthosewho serve/07.html (accessed 28 April 2013).

92   In October 2003 the Communist Party of Nepal, a Maoist organization, made the list, but it was removed in September 2012.

93   US Department of the Treasury Office of Foreign Assets Control, Executive Order 13224 – Blocking Property and Prohibiting Transactions with Persons who commit, threaten to commit, or support terrorism, 53, available at: http://www.thepoliticalguide. com/Items/BarackObama/Syria/13224.pdf (accessed 15 April 2013).

of these organizations, as well as others similarly excluded from Executive Order 13224, currently are considered terrorist organizations by the US Department of State.[94]

In summary, while the US has put more emphasis on Executive Order 13224 under the IEEPA over the past decade than on its export control system, its reliance on this instrument has slowed. In part this may be due to the ill-conceived nature of the initial listings and the consequent undermining of the instrument's legitimacy in the US and overseas. Simultaneously, serious constitutional questions persist. Cases such as *KindHearts* and *Al Haramain Islamic Foundation*, for instance, suggest that the designation process under 13224 violates due process and the Fourth Amendment and, in the latter case, that the restrictions imposed on speech domestically violate the First Amendment as well.[95] Critics argue that the criminalization of such activities substitute for guilt by association and verge into the 'preventative paradigm,' as coined by Attorney General John Ashcroft in the wake of 9/11.[96] This paradigm runs directly contrary to some of the basic precepts of the rule of law.

Domestic Material Support Provisions

Domestic material support provisions represent the third way via which the US addresses the flow of funds to terrorist organizations. They are the most frequently used and, in many ways, the most effective instruments. What makes the shift towards material support particularly notable is that, beyond the due process, Fourth Amendment and First Amendment concerns thereby raised, these provisions appear to be substituting for a definition of terrorism in US code – despite the (at most) attenuated connection between the crime and actual terrorist activity.

Early material support initiatives first emerged in 1984, as the Reagan administration sent a bill to Congress to outlaw 'support' of terrorism.[97] In 1990 the term 'material support' took root when the language was folded into the Immigration Act of 1990 as grounds for deportation.[98] It took until the 1993 bombing of the World Trade Center, however, and the 1995 attack on the

---

94   See *KindHearts*, supra note 55, and *Al Haramain Islamic Foundation v US Department of Treasury*, 10-35032, 9th Cir. (23 August 2011).

95   Kach and Kahane Chai, however, may not be on the Executive Order 13224 list because they are already designated under Executive Order 12947.

96   See, e.g., D. Cole, 'Terror Financing, Guilt by Association and the Paradigm of Prevention in the "War on Terror"' in A. Bianchi and A. Keller (eds), *Counterterrorism: Democracy's Challenge* (Oxford: Hart Publishing, 2008).

97   D. Cole and J.X. Dempsey, *Terrorism and the Constitution: Sacrificing Civil Liberties in the Name of National Security* (3rd ed., New York: New Press, 2006) 109.

98   For a discussion of the evolution of material support provisions see D. Cole, *Enemy Aliens* (New York: New Press, 2005).

Murrah Federal Building in Oklahoma City, for criminal law initiatives aimed at preventing individuals from providing material support to terrorist organizations to gain traction.

The first instrument, embedded in the omnibus Violent Crime Control and Law Enforcement Act of 1994, introduced 18 USC section 2339A.[99] Soon afterwards, the Anti-Terrorism and Effective Death Penalty Act of 1996 ('AEDPA') amended section 2339A and added a second provision, located at 18 United States Code ('USC') section 2339B.[100] The purpose of this section was to recognize 'the fungibility of financial resources and other types of material support'.[101] The House Committee Report explained:[102]

> Allowing an individual to supply funds, goods, or services to an organization, or to any of its subgroups, that draw significant funding from the main organization's treasury, helps defray the costs to the terrorist organization of running the ostensibly legitimate activities. This in turn frees an equal sum that can then be spent on terrorist activities.

The USA PATRIOT Act made further alterations to sections 2339A and 2339B, increasing the maximum terms of imprisonment from 10 to 15 years (and up to life imprisonment when death resulted from the offence); adding 'expert advice or assistance' to the criminal offence of material support; and making attempts or conspiracies to provide material support subject to the same maximum penalties as substantive violations of section 2339A.[103] Additional changes came in the Intelligence Reform and Terrorism Prevention Act of 2004, which temporarily amended and broadened the definition of 'material support or resources' in both sections.[104] Soon afterwards, congress made these changes permanent.[105] In June 2002, congress passed a new statute introducing section 2339C, the purpose of which was to implement the International Convention for the Suppression of Terrorist Bombings and to strengthen criminal laws relating to public places, to

---

99   Violent Crime Control and Law Enforcement Act of 1994, PL No. 103-322, Title XII, s 120005, 108 Stat. 2022.

100   Antiterrorism and Effective Death Penalty Act of 1996, PL No. 104-132, Title III, ss 323, 303, 110 Stat. 1255, 1250.

101   H.R. Rept. 104-383, 81 (1995).

102   Ibid.

103   USA PATRIOT Act, PL 107-56, ss 810(c), (d), 811(d), 115 Stat. 380, 381 (2001).

104   Intelligence Reform and Terrorism Prevention Act, PL 108-458, s 6603, 118 Stat. 3762 (2004) (adopting a more general definition that incorporated 'any property, tangible or intangible, or service' in s 2339A, clarifying definitions of the examples of 'training' and 'expert advice or assistance', as well as 'personnel' in s 2339B, and expanding the list of predicate offences in s 2339A).

105   USA PATRIOT Act Improvement and Reauthorization Act, PL 109-177, permanently enshrined these changes through the USA PATRIOT Act Improvement and Reauthorization Act. 104, 120 Stat. 195 (2006).

implement the International Convention of the Suppression of the Financing of Terrorism, and to defend the US against acts of terrorism.[106] In 2004 Congress added yet a fourth provision, section 2339D, aimed at addressing military training.[107]

None of these sections offers a definition of terrorism. Instead, sections 2339A and 2339B have grounded their authorities in a common definition of material support, supplanting the broader concept of terrorism with one premised on assistance and association. To the extent that a definition of terrorism shapes the broader context, the understanding is so broad as to be meaningless. Section 2339A, for instance, limits the statute's reach to certain specified crimes that may (or may not) be of a terrorist nature. Section 2339B, in turn, incorporates by reference the Immigration Act's definition of terrorism by requiring that the Secretary of State has to find that a group has engaged in terrorism in order to designate it as a terrorist organization. It is hard to conceive of any act of violence, however, which does not fall within the Immigration Act's definition: the action must be unlawful in the place where it was committed and involve at least one of a number of actions – including the use of any firearm or other weapon or dangerous device (other than for mere personal monetary gain), with intent to endanger, directly or indirectly, the safety of one or more individuals or to cause substantial damage to property.[108] This means that everything from a man picking up a knife in self-defense to a woman wielding a beer bottle in a bar fight could be considered to be engaged in 'terrorism'. While a brief discussion of all four sections is warranted, it is particularly sections 2339A and 2339B that have become amongst the Department of Justice's most important tools in its counter-terrorist arsenal.[109]

The Contours of 18 USC Section 2339

18 USC section 2339 includes five sections that focus on different aspects of material support. The initial provision, section 2339, outlaws harbouring or concealing any person who is known, or for whom there are reasonable grounds to believe, has committed, or is about to commit one of a number of predicate offences: namely, in outline, acts related to the destruction of aircraft or aircraft facilities, biological weapons, chemical weapons, nuclear materials, arson and bombing of government property, destruction of an energy facility, violence against maritime navigation,

---

106   PL 107-197, title II, s 202(a), 25 June 2002, 116 Stat. 724; amended by PL 107-273, div B., title IV, s 4006, 2 November 2002, 116 Stat. 18913; PL 108-458, title VI, s 6604, 17 December 2004, 118 Stat. 3764; PL 109-177, title IV, s 408, 9 March 2006, 120 Stat. 245.

107   Intelligence Reform and Terrorism Prevention Act, PL 108-458, title VI, s 6602, 17 December 2004, 118 Stat. 3761.

108   Immigration and Nationality Act, section 212(a)(3)(B).

109   See, e.g., C. Doyle, *Terrorist Material Support: An Overview of 18 USC 2339A and 2339B* (Washington, DC: Congressional Research Service CRS 7-5700, 2010).

weapons of mass destruction, or aircraft piracy. The law includes violations of section 2332b relating to acts of terrorism transcending national boundaries as a predicate offence. Under section 2332b, the term 'Federal crime of terrorism' means an offence that 'is calculated to influence or affect the conduct of government by intimidation or coercion, or to retaliate against government conduct; and is a violation of numerous additional predicate offences which include – but go beyond – those incorporated into section 2339. The predicate offences for section 2339 have steadily expanded over time, and no predicate offences, once added, have ever been removed. The amendments implemented by the 1996 Antiterrorism and Effective Death Penalty Act, for instance, expanded the number of predicate offences to include violence at international airports, arson, biological weapons, nuclear weapons, plastic explosives, the destruction of communications facilities, the destruction or defective production of war materials, terrorist violence against Americans overseas, weapons of mass destruction and multi-national terrorism.[110] Less than six months later, congress added three more crimes to the predicate offences, including in the process the use of a firearm during a murderous attack on a federal facility, train wrecking and the use of chemical weapons.[111] Further changes followed the attacks of 9/11.[112]

Having addressed *harbouring or concealing* any person known to engage in the predicate offences, the next section, 18 USC section 2339A, goes on to outlaw *providing material support or resources* or concealing or disguising 'the nature, location, source, or ownership of material support or resources, knowing or intending that they are to be used in preparation for, or in carrying out, a violation of the predicate offences.[113] Penalties for a violation of the statute carry imprisonment from 15 years to life, plus a fine. As used in the statute, the term 'material support or resources' means[114]

> [A]ny property, tangible or intangible, or service, including currency or monetary instruments or financial securities, financial services, lodging, training,

---

110   PL 104-132 (bringing s 232 amendments within the predicate offenses 18 USC ss 37, 81, 175, 831, 842(m) and (n), 1362, 2155 and 2156, 2332, 2332a, and 2332b).

111   PL 104-294, Title VI, s 601(b)(2), (s)(2) and (3), 604(b)(5), 11 October 1996, 110 Stat. 3502, 3506 (adding 18 USC ss 903(c), 1992, and 2332c to the list of predicate offenses).

112   See PL 107-56, title VIII, Sec. 803(a), Oct. 26, 2001, 115 Stat. 376; amended PL 107-273, div B, title IV, Sec. 4005(d)(2), 2 November 2002, 116 Stat. 1813.

113   Added PL 103-322, title XII, Sec. 120005(a), 13 September 1994,108 Stat. 2022; amended PL 104-132, title III, Sec. 323, 24 April 1996, 110 Stat. 1255; PL 104-294, title VI, Secs 601(b)(2), (s)(2), (3), 604(b)(5), 11 October 1996, 110 Stat. 3498,3502, 3506; PL 107-56, title VIII, ss 805(a), 810(c),811(f), 26 October 2001, 115 Stat. 377, 380, 381; PL 107-197,title III, Sec. 301(c), 25 June 2002, 116 Stat. 728; PL 107-273, div B, title IV, Sec. 4002(a)(7), (c)(1), (e)(11), 2 November 2002, 116 Stat. 1807, 1808, 1811; PL 108-458, title VI, Sec. 6603(a)(2), (b), 17 December 2004, 118 Stat. 3762.

114   Ibid.

expert advice or assistance, safehouses, false documentation or identification, communications equipment, facilities, weapons, lethal substances, explosives, personnel (1 or more individuals who may be or include oneself), and transportation, except medicine or religious materials ...

'Training', in turn, means 'instruction or teaching designed to impart a specific skill, as opposed to general knowledge', while the term 'expert advice or assistance' is defined as 'advice or assistance derived from scientific, technical or other specialized knowledge'.[115]

Next, 18 USC section 2339B, outlaws the provision of material support or resources to a foreign terrorist organization.[116] Similar penalties to those noted in 2339A apply. The statute requires that the individual have knowledge (a) that the organization is a designated terrorist organization (as defined by section 219 of the Immigration and Nationality Act), or (b) that the organization has engaged or engages in terrorist activity (as defined by section 212(a)(3)(B) of the Immigration and Nationality Act or section 140(d)(2) of the Foreign Relations Authorization Act, Fiscal Years 1988 and 1989). Section 2339B uses the same definition of 'material support' employed in section 2339A. It adds, with regard to provision of personnel, that prosecution may only follow where an individual 'has knowingly provided, attempted to provide, or conspired to provide a foreign terrorist organization with 1 or more individuals (who may be or include himself) to work under that terrorist organization's direction or control or to organize, manage, supervise, or otherwise direct the operation of that organization'. In addition, 'Individuals who act entirely independently of the foreign terrorist organization to advance its goals or objectives shall not be considered to be working under the foreign terrorist organization's direction and control.' Civil penalties of $50,000 or more per infraction can be exacted from financial institutions that fail to inform the secretary of the treasury about the existence of funds that fall subject to the statute. Extraterritorial jurisdiction broadly applies: namely, where the offender is a US person, a stateless person resident in the US, an individual who has entered the US subsequent to his or her actions, or where the offence occurs in or affects interstate or foreign commerce.

For civil proceedings, at the request of the US government and upon *ex parte* showing, a court may authorize the redaction of classified information, a substitution of a summary of the information, or the substitution of a statement

---

115 Language Current through PL 112-113.

116 Added PL 104-132, title III, Sec. 303(a), 24 April 1996, 110 Stat. 1250; amended PL 107-56, title VIII, Sec. 810(d), 26 October 2001, 115 Stat. 380; PL 108-458, title VI, Sec. 6603(c)-(f), 17 December 2004, 118 Stat. 3762, 3763. The term 'material support' is given the same meaning as in s 2339A. It is worth noting in this context that violations of IEEPA are also criminal. John Walker Lindh, for example, is currently serving 20 years for violating IEEPA by providing assistance to the Taliban: *US v Lindh*, 212 F. Supp 2d 541 (E.D. Va. 2002).

admitting relevant facts that the classified information would tend to prove. In such an event, the documents are sealed. Similar procedures accompany criminal prosecution. The burden of proof lies on the defendant to establish the relevance and materiality of any classified information sought. The court only has four days to consider an expedited appeal. The legislation specifically notes that the government may further invoke military and state secrets privilege to guard classified material.

As a rule of construction, the legislation requires that nothing under its auspices be construed or applied so as to violate the First Amendment. Nor may any person be prosecuted in connection with the terms 'personnel', 'training', or 'expert advice or assistance' where such action was approved by the secretary of state with the concurrence of the attorney general.

In addition to attempting to prevent individuals from harbouring those engaged in terrorism or providing material support to the same, the law in section 2339C outlaws any provision or collection of funds with the intention that they be used (or the knowledge that they are to be used), in full or in part, to carry out:[117]

(A) an act which constitutes an offense within the scope of a treaty specified in subsection (e)(7), as implemented by the US, or

(B) any other act intended to cause death or serious bodily injury to a civilian, or to any other person not taking an active part in the hostilities in a situation of armed conflict, when the purpose of such act, by its nature or context, is to intimidate a population, or to compel a government or an international organization to do or to abstain from doing any act ...

As with section 2339B, extraterritorial jurisdiction applies.[118] The statute makes it illegal to knowingly conceal or disguise the nature, location, source, ownership or control of any material support or resources. Penalties range up to 20 years imprisonment and $10,000 in fines for violations of the statute.

The final relevant section, 18 USC section 2339D, makes it an offence to knowingly *receive military-type training* from or on behalf of a *designated foreign terrorist organization* (as defined by section 219(a)(1) of the Immigration and Nationality Act).[119] Penalties include fines and imprisonment for up to 10 years.

---

117   Nine treaties are specified under 18 USC s 2339C. Armed conflict 'does not include internal disturbances and tensions, such as riots, isolated and sporadic acts of violence, and other acts of a similar nature'. Ibid.

118   See s 2339B(b).

119   The term 'military-type training' is broadly defined to include 'training in means or methods that can cause death or serious bodily injury, destroy or damage property, or disrupt services to critical infrastructure, or training on the use, storage, production, or assembly of any explosive, firearm or other weapon, including any weapon of mass destruction' s 2339D(c)(1). The legislation is similarly broad with regard to what constitutes

In order to be in violation of the statute, the same requirements that accompany section 2339B apply: the individual must have knowledge (a) that the organization is a designated terrorist organization, or (b) that the organization has engaged or engages in terrorist activity (as defined in section 212 of the Immigration and Nationality Act or section 140(d)(2) of the Foreign Relations Authorization Act, Fiscal Years 1988 and 1989). As with the other sections, the federal government exercises extraterritorial jurisdiction over any alleged offences.

Use of Material Support Provisions

Sections 2339A (support of terrorism) and 2339B (support of Designated Terrorist Organizations) have become the keystone of US efforts to stem the flow of funds to terrorist organizations.[120] The number of individuals charged under their auspices has steadily increased from just a few in the five years prior to 9/11, to more than 150 over the subsequent decade.[121] The number of individuals prosecuted

---

the critical infrastructure, including in its remit 'systems and assets vital to national defense, national security, economic security, public health or safety including both regional and national infrastructure.' Such systems may be publicly or privately owned, ranging from gas and oil production, water supply, telecommunications, and electrical power generation, to banking systems, emergency services and transportation (s 2339D(c)(3)).

120   *Review of the Material Support to Terrorism Prohibition Improvements Act: Hearing Before the Subcomm. on Terrorism, Technology and Homeland Security*, 109th Cong., 1st Sess. 45 (2005) (statement of Barry Sabin, Chief, Counterterrorism Section, US Dept. of Justice); *Implementation of the USA PATRIOT Act: Prohibition of Material Support Under Sections 805 of the USA PATRIOT Act and 6603 of the Intelligence Reform and Terrorism Prevention Act of 2004*, 109th Cong., 1st SEss. 18 (2005) (statement of Barry Sabin, Chief, Counterterrorism Section, US Dept. of Justice); D. Cole, 'Out of the Shadows: Preventive Detention, Suspected Terrorists, and War' (2009) 97 *California Law Review* 693, 723 ('The most important of these statutes is 18 USC s 2339B … [R]arely enforced before 9/11, it has since become a principal tool in the Justice Department's "terrorism" prosecutions'); C. Doyle, *Terrorist Material Support: An Overview of 18 USC 2339A and 2339B* (Washington, DC: Congressional Research Service, 7-5700, 2010).

121   Prior to 9/11, for instance, *US v Haouari* No. S1:00-cr-15 (JFK), 2000 WL 1593345 (S.D.N.Y. 25 October 2000) and *US v Afshari* 426 F.3d 1150 (2d Cir. 2005) appear to be some of the few cases underway. But material support cases have steadily increased in number. See, e.g., Indictment, *US v Bout* 1:09-cr-1002 (S.D.N.Y. 24 April 2008); Indictment, *US v Al-Arian* 1:08-cr-00131-LMB (E.D. Va. 26 June 2008); Superseding Indictment, *US v Mehanna et al* No. 1:09-cr-10017 (D. Mass. 15 January 2009), Court Docket (01/15/2009); Indictment, *US v Mosquera-Renteria et al* No. 1:09-cr-00498 (S.D.N.Y. 14 May 2009); Indictment, *US v Boyd* No. 5:09-cr-216-1-FL (E.D.N.C. 22 July 2009); Indictment, *US v Zazi* No. 09-cr-663-RJD (E.D.N.Y. 24 September 2009; Indictment, *US v Patrick Nayyar et al* No. 09-crim-1037 (S.D.N.Y. 26 October 2009); Indictment, *US v Issa et al* No. 1:09-CR-01244 (S.D.N.Y. 30 December 2009); Indictment, *US v Ahmed* 1:10-CR-00131 (S.D.N.Y. 22 February 2010); Indictment, *US v LaRose* No. 2:10-cr-00123 (E.D. Pa. 4 March 2010); Indictment, *US v Khan* No. 10-cr-00240 (N.D. Ill. 1 April 2010); Indictment, *US v Bujol*

annually continues to increase. Three factors have played a primary role in driving such prosecutions: first, the expanded understanding of 'material support'; second, the addition of attempt, conspiracy, aiding and abetting as crimes; and third, an expansion in the number of entities considered 'foreign terrorist organizations'.

Despite repeated constitutional challenges, the definition of what constitutes 'material support' has steadily expanded over the past decade. The USA PATRIOT Act proved the first step along this path, adding 'expert advice or assistance' to the definition of actions outlawed with regard to designated foreign terrorist organizations.[122] The Intelligence Reform and Terrorism Prevention Act of 2004 ('IRTPA'), in turn, even as it added a knowledge requirement to section 2339B, further clarified 'service', 'training, expert advice or assistance' and 'personnel'.[123]

Efforts to challenge this ever-wider understanding of material support through the judiciary have only had limited success. In litigation concerning the Humanitarian Law Project ('HLP'), a non-profit organization dedicated to promoting the peaceful resolution of violent conflict, wanted 'to provide support to the humanitarian and political activities of' the Tamil Tigers ('LTTE') and the Kurdistan Workers' Party.[124] Both the non-profit organization and Judge Fertig had been working with the organizations prior to their designation in 1997, with the aim of supporting their legal and humanitarian work, their international advocacy, and the evolution of their legal and political strategy, as well as 'other forms of advocacy, support and cooperation'.[125] The lower court rejected plaintiff's First Amendment claim, suggesting that the AEDPA only limited potential ways in which HLP could associate with the two organizations but not all forms of association.[126] The statute was within the government's power and furthered the executive branch's 'substantial interest in national security and foreign relations' in a manner unrelated to suppressing the plaintiffs' right to free speech and in a way that would be essential to further a compelling interest in national security and foreign policy.[127] Simultaneously, the court considered the terms 'personnel' and

---

Crim. 4:10-CR-368 (S.D. Tex. 3 June 2010); Superseding Indictment, *US v El-Hanafi et al* No. 1:10-CR-00162 (S.D.N.Y. 14 September 2010).

122   18 USC ss 2339A(b), 2339B(g)(4). See *also Humanitarian Law Project v Mukasey*, 509 F.3d 1122, 1128 (9th Cir. 2007) (discussing the alteration).

123   Intelligence Reform and Terrorism Prevention Act of 2004, PL 108-488, codified as amended at 18 USC s 2339A(b). Note that the 9th Circuit subsequently found the term 'service' unconstitutionally vague. *Humanitarian Law Project v Mukasey*, 552 F.3d 916 (9th Cir. 2009), cert. granted sub nom., *Humanitarian L. Project v Holder*, 130 S.Ct. 48 (2009).

124   *Humanitarian Law Project v Reno*, 9 F. Supp 2d 1205, 1207-08 (C.D. Cal. 1998). See *also Holder v Humanitarian Law Project*, 130 S. Ct. 2705, 2708 (2010).

125   *Humanitarian Law Project v Reno*, 9 F. Supp 2d 1205, 1209 (C.D. Cal. 1998).

126   Ibid., at 1212.

127   Ibid.

'training' to be impermissibly vague.[128] In March 2000 the Ninth Circuit affirmed the lower court's holding.

As aforementioned, congress responded by adding 'expert advice and assistance' to the prohibitions on material support, prompting further challenge by HLP. The Ninth Circuit again determined that the term was impermissibly vague.[129] The court went on to read a *mens rea* requirement into the statute, saying that 'to sustain a conviction under 2339B, the government must prove beyond a reasonable doubt that the donor had knowledge that the organization was designated ... as a foreign terrorist organization or that the donor had knowledge of the organization's unlawful activities that caused it to be so designated'.[130] IRTPA's refinement of 'personnel' and 'training' led the Ninth Circuit to vacate its earlier decision. But IRTPA also added more actions to what would constitute material support. The case finally reached the Supreme Court, which ultimately upheld the expanded understanding of material support.[131] Thus, congress's efforts to clarify the statute's terms brought them within constitutional requirements – even as the number and type of activities falling within the definition of 'material support' expanded.

Many of the activities in question are not themselves violent. The judiciary has justified having such actions fall within the statute on the grounds that 'foreign organizations that engage in terrorist activity are so tainted by their criminal conduct that any contribution to such an organization facilitates that conduct'.[132] Such support 'frees up other resources within the organization that may be put to violent ends. It also importantly helps lend legitimacy to foreign terrorist groups – legitimacy that makes it easier for those groups to persist, to recruit members, and to raise funds – all of which facilitate more terrorist attacks'.[133] This understanding goes well beyond definitions of terrorist activity, which are traditionally tied to the actual or threatened use of violence in support of political aims. Instead, almost any activity that helps an organization that may engage in violence has become criminalized. It includes everything from the construction of web sites to teaching organizations how to engage in the political process.[134] The only exceptions

---

128   Ibid., at 1213–15.

129   *Humanitarian Law Project v Ashcroft*, 309 F. Supp 2d 1185, 1201 (C.D. Cal. 2004). (But note that it rejected the suggestion that the term was overbroad because it incorporated activity otherwise protected by the First Amendment 'such as training in human rights advocacy, giving advice on how to improve medical care and education, and distributing human right literature'. Ibid.)

130   *Humanitarian Law Project v US Department of Justice*, 352 F.3d 382, 405(9th Cir. 2003), vacated, 393 F.3d 902 (9th Cir. 2004).

131   *Holder v Humanitarian Law Project*, 130 S.Ct. 2705, 2708, 2712–16 (2010).

132   Ibid., at 2735 (emphasis in the original).

133   Ibid., at 2735.

134   See, e.g., Second Superseding Indictment at 1-13, *US v Al-Hussayen*, No. CR03-048-C-EJL (D. Idaho, 2004).

provided in the statute are for 'medicine and religious materials'.[135] Everything else is essentially equated with terrorist activity.

It is not just the expansion of what constitutes 'material support' that has contributed to an increasing reliance on these provisions. As aforementioned, following the attacks of 9/11, congress expanded the penalties associated with attempt, conspiracy, and aiding and abetting designated Foreign Terrorist Organizations ('FTOs'). These changes also have had an impact on the expanded use of material support provisions as an instrument in prosecution.

Attempt, consistent with criminal law, is comprised of two parts: first, the intent to commit the underlying offence; and second, a substantial step towards its completion (mere preparation is insufficient).[136] As the Ninth Circuit has explained: 'To constitute a substantial step, a defendant's actions must cross the line between preparation and attempt by unequivocally demonstrating that the crime will take place unless interrupted by independent circumstances.'[137] Thus, even if a defendant is unaware that the underlying offence is not possible – either as a practical matter or because the interlocutors with whom he is dealing are undercover agents, he can nonetheless be found guilty of an attempt to provide material support.

Conspiracy, in turn, relates to the agreement to provide such support.[138] Therefore, as soon as an individual agrees to assist a listed entity, the offence is complete. No actual support must ever be provided. Every person taking part is liable both for conspiring to provide material support and for any foreseeable offence committed by any of the other co-conspirators in furtherance of the overall plan of action.[139]

Under the changes made by the USA PATRIOT Act, attempt and conspiracy are now both punishable by imprisonment of not more than 15 years (or up to life, where the offence results in a death), and/or a fine of not more than $250,000 for

---

135   18 USC 2339A(b)(1).

136   See *Braxton v United States*, 500 US 344, 349 (1991); *US v Bristol-Martir*, 570 F.3d 29, 39 (1st Cir. 2009); *US v Barlow*, 568 F.3d 215, 219 (5th Cir. 2009); *US v DeMarce*, 564 F.3d 989, 998 (8th Cir. 2009). See also discussion on attempt, conspiracy, and aiding and abetting in C. Doyle, *Terrorist Material Support: An Overview of 18 USC 2339A and 2339B* (following analysis in footnotes 150 to 157).

137   *US v Mincoff*, 574 F.3d 1186, 1195 (9th Cir. 2009).

138   *United States v Jimenez Recio*, 537 US 270, 274 (2003) ('the essence of a conspiracy is an agreement to commit an unlawful act); *US v Lockett*, 601 F.3d 837 (8th Cir. 2010) ('In order to convict a defendant of conspiracy, the government must prove: (1) the existence of an agreement to achieve an illegal purpose; (2) the defendant's knowledge of the agreement; and (3) the defendant's knowing participation in the agreement. The agreement does not have to be a formal, explicit agreement; a tacit understanding will suffice.') See also C. Doyle, *Terrorist Material Support: An Overview of 18 USC 2339A and 2339B*.

139   *Pinkerton v United States*, 328 US 640, 647 (1946).

an individual or $500,000 for an organization.[140] Where an attempt is successful, the defendant cannot be punished both for attempt and for the underlying offence; however, for conspiracy, a defendant can be punished both for conspiracy and for the commission of the underlying offence.[141]

Aiding and abetting a violation of section 2339B is punishable under 18 USC section 2. Because of its similarity to conspiracy, the same evidence may support both charges, but, unlike conspiracy, liability can only attach to a crime under 18 USC section 2 where someone actually engages in the underlying offence.[142]

Because of the inclusion of these inchoate offences in the material support provisions, an increasing number of cases are turning on conspiracy and attempt.[143] The fact patterns that are emerging suggest that law enforcement is increasingly approaching individuals who may be inclined to support terrorist organizations and setting up scenarios in which they may be willing to assist these organizations in any number of nonviolent ways. The practice has begun to raise concern about the extent to which entrapment may be entering the picture.[144]

A third factor in the expanded use of these sections has been the increased number of FTOs to which providing material support is a crime. In order for an organization to be considered an FTO under section 2339B, it must (a) be a foreign organization; and (b) engage in terrorist activity.[145] In order to be removed from the list, one of three conditions must hold. The first two conditions require the secretary of state to remove the group where either (a) the secretary finds that the circumstances that were the basis of the designation have changed in such a manner as to warrant a revocation; or (b) where the secretary finds that the national

---

140   18 USC s 2339B(a), 3571.

141   *US v Rivera-Relle*, 333 F.3d 914, 921 n.11 (9th Cir. 2003); *Iannelli v US*, 420 US 770, 777-778 (1975).

142   *US v Liera*, 585 F.3d 1320, 1324 (11th Cir. 2009). See also C. Doyle, *Terrorist Material Support: An Overview of 18 USC 2339A and 2339B* (Washington, DC: Congressional Research Service CRS 7-5700, 2010) at 4.

143   See, e.g., *United States v Ilyas Kashmiri et al*, Second Superseding Indictment, 09-CR-830, N.D.I.L., 25 April 2011; *United States v Ali Charaf Damache and Mohammad Hassan Khalid*, 11-cr-420, E.D.P.A., 20 October 2011; *United States v Mohanad Shareef Hammadi*, 1:11-CR-13-R, W.D.K.Y., 14 August 2012.

144   Recently, for instance, an individual arrested in New York for allegedly trying to blow up the Federal Reserve with an FBI-supplied (fake) device, made public the efforts of undercover FBI agents to pose as al Qaeda facilitators. A Gabbatt, 'New York Federal Reserve "bomb" plotter ensnared in FBI Sting', *The Guardian*, 17 October 2012, available at: http://www.guardian.co.uk/world/2012/oct/17/fbi-federal-reserve-bomb-plot (accessed 21 January 2013).

145   The organization must 'engage in terrorist activity' as defined in s 212(a)(3)(B) of the Immigration and Nationality Act (8 USC s 1182(a)(3)(B), or 'terrorism', as defined in 140(d)(2) of the Foreign Relations Authorization Act, Fiscal Years 1988 and 1989 (22 USC s 2656f(d)(2), or maintain the capability and intent to engage in terrorist activity or terrorism. See Immigration and Nationality Act s 219 (as amended).

security of the US warrants a revocation. The third circumstance merely allows the secretary of state to revoke a designation at any time.

Although section 2339B was enacted in 1996, it was not until October of 1997 that the Secretary of State designated the first group of FTOs. More than two dozen organizations appeared on the first list. Although the initial focus of the designations was rather broad, over the past decade emphasis has moved to Islamist organizations. The list, for instance, includes both al-Qa'ida-related organizations such as al-Qa'ida Iraq and al-Qa'ida in the Arabian Peninsula, as well as other entities, such as the Pakistani Taliban, Columbia's AUC and the LTTE.[146] There have been a total now of some 59 organizations listed as FTOs; 8 of these have been removed, leaving 51 currently designated FTOs. The increase in the number of organizations for which material support is outlawed has further contributed to an increase in the number of prosecutions.

Concluding Remarks

Three legal instruments constitute the US' principal framework for interrupting the flow of funds and resources to terrorist organizations: restrictions placed on export controls, financial sanctions levied on non-state entities, and domestic material support provisions. The last two areas have experienced the greatest movement post-9/11. Early missteps with regard to financial sanctions, however, greatly discredited the subsequent regime. The standards applied in this realm also raise serious questions related to due process, the Fourth Amendment, and the First Amendment.

It is in the third area, domestic material support, that the US government is placing the greatest emphasis. The most important factors in this shift appear to be the expanded definition of what constitutes material support; the inclusion of attempt, conspiracy, and aiding and abetting as aspects of the same; and the increased number of organizations incorporated within the FTO designation system. What makes this shift remarkable is that significantly attenuated relationships appear to be playing a key role in place of creating a crime of terrorism.

This phenomenon is not unique to material support. For example, property associated with 'terrorism' may be subject to broader rules regarding confiscation.[147] Offences labelled as 'terrorist' may similarly serve as predicate offences for certain types of prosecution, such as money laundering and RICO.[148] *Pari passu*, statutes of limitations may be extended for 'terrorist' offences.[149]

---

146   See, e.g., *US v Khan et al*, 11-cr-20331; *United States v McField-Bent, S.D.F.L.*; *USA v Lnu et al*, Docket No. 1:06-mj-00887 (E.D.N.Y. 18 August 2006), Court Docket (08/18/2006).

147   18 USC 981(a)(1)(G).

148   18 USC 1956 (7)(D), 1961(1)(G).

149   18 USC 3286(a), 3282.

Terms of pre-trial detention also may be altered for 'terrorist' crimes, as may the terms of supervised release.[150]

What raises concern, though, with regard to material support, is the increasingly attenuated connection between being a terrorist and, for instance, attempting to engage in material support (such as by providing political advice) to someone known by the individual (or labelled by the secretary of state) to be engaged in acts of terrorism – the definition of which is broad enough to include basic self-defense. Significantly more work needs to be done to look at this growing phenomenon and, as with Executive Order 13224, to consider the due process, Fourth Amendment, and First Amendment implications of using material support provisions in this vein.

---

150   18 USC 3142(f)(1)(A), (g)(1); 18 USC 3583(j), (b). See also C. Doyle, *Terrorist Material Support: An Overview of 18 USC 2339A and 2339B* 9–12.

Chapter 13

Dismantling Terrorist Economics: The Spanish Experience

Thomas Baumert and Mikel Buesa

Introduction[1]

Although the economics of terrorism have gained broad attention from scholars and policymakers, especially after the attacks of 9/11[2] both from the input (terrorist financing) and the output side (economic consequences of terrorism), the financing of the Basque terrorist group Euskadi Ta Askatasuna ('ETA') seems relatively neglected in international studies.[3] However, the ETA announcement (in January 2011) declaring a 'permanent and internationally verifiable' ceasefire,[4] might provide a good opportunity to take a look back over 50 years of Basque terror financing.

The starting point for this study is our definition of terrorism as part of an economic war that aims to economically and psychologically erode its opponent,[5] in the context of terrorism as a 'predatory war model'.[6] Thus, we define, for the

---

1 For a shorter version of this research (with a different timespan of analysis) see M. Buesa and T. Baumert, 'Untangling ETA's finance: An in-depth analysis of the Basque terrorists' economic network and the money it handles' (2013) 24 *Defence and Peace Economics* 1.

2 E. Neumayer, 'The impact of political violence on tourism. Dynamic econometric estimation in a cross national panel' (2004) 48(2) *Journal of Conflict Resolution* 259 at 262.

3 Previous studies about the economic impact of ETA on the Basque Country, include: A. Abadie and J. Gardeazabal, 'The economic cost of conflict: A case study of the Basque Country' (2003) 93(1) *American Economic Review* 113; M. Buesa (ed.), *Economía de la Secesión. El proyecto nacionalista y el País Vasco* (Madrid: Instituto de Estudios Fiscales, 2004).

4 http://www.guardian.co.uk/world/2011/jan/10/eta-declares-permanent-ceasefire (accessed 10 April 2013).

5 M. Buesa, 'Guerra y Terrorismo: el modelo de la economía depredadora de guerra' (IAIF Working Paper, 2005) 50; T. Baumert, 'Do terrorists play the market?' (2008) *Policing. A Journal of Policy and Practice* 434; T. Baumert, 'The impact of terrorist attacks on the stock markets' in M. Buesa and T. Baumert (eds), *The Economic Repercussions of Terrorism* (Oxford: Oxford University Press, 2010).

6 M. Buesa, 'War and terrorism' in M. Buesa and T. Baumert (eds), *The Economic Repercussions of Terrorism* (Oxford: Oxford University Press, 2010).

purpose of this study, terrorism as a form of political action based on the exercise of systematic violence, on the part of organizations which adopt it, against people and property, as a means of achieving public support for their cause, not by ideological persuasion, but through fear, until they undermine the will of citizens and state and force them to accept their demands. It is, to a certain extent, a singular type of war whose armed actions are planned and executed with a view to making society capitulate in the face of the aims of these organizations to dominate or hold power. Actually, this type of war is the opposite of those waged as a consequence of the establishment of the modern developed state, in that it, that is the terrorist organization does not aim to hold on to its own territory in order to settle and establish modes of production intended to sustain its war effort, rather it is willing to destroy the territory in order to make it easier to extract from it the material and financial resources required for its maintenance.

It is in this context that ETA's shift from political and military targets towards economically relevant objectives might be understood.[7] Thus, for example, in September 2002 the Spanish police seized a letter allegedly written by a member of ETA, Henri Parot, in which he urged the leadership of the band to attack, as well as the Interior Ministry and the Supreme Court, 'vital targets such as the Bank of Spain [Central Bank] and the Madrid and Barcelona Stock Exchanges', adding 'I'm convinced that if you do that they'll sit down and negotiate'.[8] Consequently, and as we shall see later on, banking targets have been attacked frequently by ETA, especially with so-called 'low-level terrorism' or *kale borroka* (as explained below).

As we assume that not all international readers might be familiar with the course of ETA and the circumstances surrounding its activities, we shall preface our study with a brief overview of the history of this terrorist group.

---

7   Between 1998 and 2003, the main targets of worldwide terrorist attacks, much more than diplomatic, government and military targets, were assets belonging to the business sector: US Department of State, *Patterns of Global Terrorism* (Washington, DC, 2003) appendix; W. Enders and T. Sandler, *The Political Economy of Terrorism* (Cambridge: Cambridge University Press, 2006) predict that future attacks will centre on economic targets even more. Nearly twice as many companies bought terrorist insurance coverage in 2007 than in 2001: Lloyd's, *Under Attack? Global Business and the Threat of Political Violence* (London, 2007) 18–19 at: http://www.lloyds.com/~/media/lloyds/reports/360/360%20terrorism%20reports/globalbusinessunderattack.pdf (accessed 21 April 2013).

8   Europa Press: 'Prisión para Henri Parot por una carta dirigida a ETA en la que señalaba objetivos', *El Mundo*, 18 November 2005.

ETA's Terrorist Activity

Euskadi ta Askatasuna (ETA)[9] is a terrorist group proscribed as such by the Spanish and French authorities, the UK, the European Union and the United States. ETA was started by a number of middle-class Basque nationalists, many of them university students, in response to what they considered to be the insufficient opposition of the Basque Nationalist Party ('PNV') towards the Franco regime. On 30 July 1959, the day of the Saint Ignatius (patron saint of the Basques), the group was set up with the aim of achieving 'an independent Euskadi through a Basque state, and of free men inside Euskadi'.[10] Although during the 1960s ETA was heavily influenced by Marxism, and ETA still claims to stand for an 'independent, socialist Euskalerria', the main ideology of the group has been radical nationalism, loosely interspersed with racist elements.[11] ETA committed its first assassination in 1968, executing its most significant attack five years later, killing Franco's Prime Minister Luis Carrero Blanco. These were the first of many attacks perpetrated under the 'action-repression-action spiral theory' adopted by the group in 1965.

After the introduction of democracy to Spain, the Basque Country progressively obtained more and more autonomy, not only in the political, but also economic, fiscal, educational and cultural spheres, and to such a degree, that some argue that the 'Basque separatists' goal have been achieved by all but in name',[12] thus rendering ETA's justifications void. Nevertheless, as can be seen in Figure 13.1, they continued and even intensified their activity, which reached a peak of violence in the late 1970s and early 1980s, at the same time developing their economic and political network, hence contradicting those who considered them primarily anti-authoritarian rather than pro-Basque. This led the Spanish government to start the so-called 'dirty war' against terrorism, using secret hit squads named GAL (Grupos Antiterrorista de Liberación).[13] From 1985 onwards, ETA's terrorist activity started to decline, and in 1992 the leaders of the group were arrested in the French town of Bidart. ETA tried to compensate for this tendency by boosting the so-called *kale borroka* (literally 'street fight') actions of low-level street violence against public and private facilities, which might be considered a sort of 'low-

---

9   Nevertheless, many false myths regarding ETA, the Basque Nationalism, and its relation to the rest of Spain still persist, most of which are corrected in Y. Basta, *Euskadi, from Dream to Shame. A Useful Guide to the Basque Tragedy* (Barcelona: Ediciones B, 2005).

10   Although the Basques have a distinctive language and, to some extent, even culture and identity, they have not had an 'independent' state for over a millennium.

11   M. Buesa, *ETA S.A. El dinero que mueve el terrorismo y los costes que genera* (Barcelona: Planeta, 2011) 66.

12   R. Law, *Terrorism: A History* (Cambridge: Polity, 2009) 251.

13   The GAL committed 27 killings and several kidnappings, not only of ETA members but of civilians, some of whom turned out to have nothing to do with the terrorist group. See P. Woodworth, *Dirty War, Clean Hands: ETA, the GAL and Spanish Democracy* (Cork: Cork University Press, 2001).

intensity terrorism'. Again, this trend was turned back in 2003. The proscription in 2002 of ETA's political arm, Batasuna, initiated the latest period in the history of ETA, characterized by a continuous decrease of the number of terrorist attack and victims, and a new increase of street terrorism.

Two factors have been critical in the decline of what was already marginal Basque support for ETA terrorism. The first was the popular reaction against the 1997 ETA kidnapping and murder of the local conservative Basque politician, Miguel Angel Blanco. Several millions of Spaniards, among them 100,000 Basques, marched and publically condemned his murder. Thus, ETA terrorists found themselves on the defensive, realizing they even lacked the support of the communities which hitherto they had believed were 'theirs'. The other event that contributed to the decline of ETA effectiveness was 9/11, a terrorist act of such carnage and magnitude that it undermined in Spain, as it did in much of the West, the justification of terrorism on the part of any organization.[14] As an immediate result of 9/11, the US froze bank accounts associated with ETA members,[15] and the police forces across the world sought a better level of coordination. José María Aznar's conservative government, in conjunction with the French government, launched an all-out police offensive against the group, and several of its key

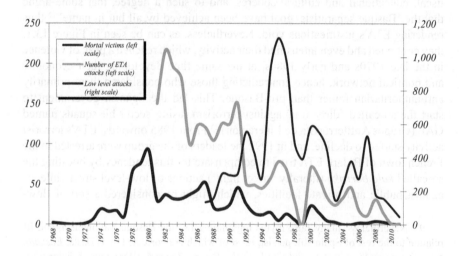

Figure 13.1   ETA's terrorist activity: Number of attacks and victims

Note: Constructed by the authors using data of the Spanish Home Office, Vasco Press and Department for the study of the Economics of Terrorism (UCM).

---

14   In addition, it also meant 'raised the bar' of terrorist attacks in Spain, as 'conventional' ETA attacks now seemed relatively less significant.

15   President George W. Bush: Executive Order 13224 Blocking Property and Prohibiting Transactions with Persons Who Commit, Threaten or Support Terrorism (23 September 2001).

leaders were arrested over the following years. In addition, and as we explain below, Aznar's government also passed a new law that allowed the courts to outlaw any political party that refused to condemn terrorist acts, thus banning Batasuna from any (legal) political activity. Five decades of ETA activity leaves an overall balance of more than 800 mortal victims – roughly one third of them civilians – and thousands injured.[16]

ETA's Economic Network

In 1986, the Spanish and French police dismantled what turned out to be the nerve-centre of ETA's operations in the town of Sokoa on the French Basque coast: an innocent-looking workshop belonging to a cooperative that served as a front for a vast business empire.[17] Among other things, they managed to seize the terrorists' account books. These 'Sokoa papers' clearly showed that, between 1979 and 1986, the terrorist organization had taken in a significant amount of money through racketeering, particularly from the collection of the so-called 'Revolutionary Tax', and from various robberies, of banks and businesses, and from other sources. In fact, the Sokoa accounting ledgers showed that ETA not only financed its terrorist cells but also invested in a political network. In 1979, it paid €120,000 into the coffers of Orain, the publisher of the daily newspaper *Egin*, so that it could buy out the magazine *Punto y Hora* and, from 1979 on, it also provided capital for the group Gestoras Pro-Amnistía, the trade union, Langile Abertzaleen Batzordeak ('LAB'), as well as their political party, Herri Batasuna ('HB').

At the beginning of the 1990s, the network was made up of ETA, the coordinating arm for grassroots and popular organizations, Koordinadora Abertzale Sozialista ('KAS'), the political coalition, HB, the trade union, LAB, the youth organization, Jarrai, the coordinating arm, KAS, the Gestoras Pro-Amnistía, the organization for promoting the Basque language called Euskal Herrian Euskaraz (in Basque in the Basque Country), the student organization Ikasle Abertzaleak (Patriotic Students) and other groups that were supposedly feminist, ecological and cultural. However, not only was ETA dedicated to financing its own shadowy web, but it also invested in legitimate businesses in order to obtain supplementary profits and to launder its ill-gotten gains. Likewise, it set up its own business which employed sympathizers, while it obtained money to finance illegal activities. The operating the business involved a growing number of individuals so that the shadowy web had a widening network of accomplices. And it did so to such an extent that, by the middle of the 1980s, the existence of ETA had become a purely economic necessity: what was important was no longer just political strategy but the business

---

16   For an excellent overview of the victims of ETA see R. Alonso and F. Domínguez, *Vidas rotas. Las víctimas de ETA* (Madrid: Espasa, 2009).

17   The following paragraphs were first published in BastaYa, *Euskadi, from Dream to Shame. A Useful Guide to the Basque Tragedy* (Barcelona: Ediciones B, 2005) 136–138.

it generated, upon which thousands of '*liberados*' (released prisoners) depended. In 1976, ETA set up the Lluis Orain which published the newspaper *Egin* whose operating deficit was subsidized because of its role as the indispensable organ of its communication and propaganda. In the same year, another, more lucrative business was set up: the Herriko Tabernak (literally Town Taverns), a chain of bars and restaurants that spread out across towns and districts and which served as meeting places for sympathizers of the 'Basque National Liberation Movement' from which they could control their immediate surroundings and where they could plan acts of violence or launder illicit money from ETA-KAS-HB.[18]

The business maze set up with shares and privately-owned businesses became so complex that, in 1992, ETA launched the Udaletxe (Town Hall) Project. It was a question of streamlining the overall management and distributing the profits from the 100 businesses making up the terrorist network. In order to run it, they set up the company, Banaka (literally 'One by One'). Thus, one investigating magistrate established in 1997 the legal doctrine – since ratified by numerous sentences handed down by the National Court and Supreme Court – that ETA and its web of satellite organizations are 'one and the same'.[19] This shift in conceptualization made way for *Egin*, KAS, HB, Jarrai and Gestoras Pro-Amnistía, as well as the successive reincarnations and clones of the whole edifice, all to be charged and outlawed, once the courts could prove their connection to ETA.

This fact, together with the relentless pursuit of the terrorists undertaken by the Conservative government of President Aznar, dealt a heavy blow to the economics of ETA, which started to suffer from a lack of liquidity. It meant a turning point in the economic history of the terrorist network, as ETA now suddenly had to rely on its satellites to cover all its costs.

Consequently, in order to keep their terrorist activities going, and to impose their secessionist aim, ETA redesigned this complex network of entities. It was ETA who, besides committing attacks, extortions, armed raids and other crimes, took control of the entire network. Until 1999 its authority over the rest of organizations of the network was exercised through KAS, and from then on through Ekin ('Engage').

At the same time, the exercise of violence required strong logistics and, especially, the systematic collection of information about potential objectives. This was entrusted to three information services, one from ETA itself, the other two from KAS and the newspaper *Egin* until the disappearance of both of them. Of course, ETA also needed to recruit militants willing to perpetrate armed attacks. In the early days of the group and up to the mid 1990s, this was achieved by attracting members from the political organizations related to ETA, mostly single men, 'slightly older than twenty years, with a background of middle class,

---

18   In the 1990s the peak of their activity, the *Herriko Tabernak* showed an annual profit of €12 million.

19   The most recent is the Sentencia Tribunal Supremo (Sala de lo Sala especial del art. 61 de la LOPJ), de 27 March 2003.

autochthonous families, living in small and medium-sized villages in which the use of Euskera (the Basque language) was widespread'.[20]

From then on, ETA recruited its militants from the groups of young 'street fighters' related to Jarrai, Haika and Segi. These 'street fights' were considered to be a sort of low-level or low-intensity terrorism, which nevertheless had an important economic impact, due to their repetition (mainly on weekends).[21] It might be worth pointing out that this new generation of terrorists were of urban origin, with a limited use of Euskera, and who had often grown up in families whose origins lay outside the Basque country and were thus very similar to other groups of European radicals from their same generation, sharing an anti-establishment system ideology.

Due to its intrinsic political core, ETA has needed to organize its activities on the institutional field through its own political party which was under its control. This job was undertaken during two and a half decades by Herri Batasuna, which in 1998 changed its name to Euskal Herritarok and, three years later, to Batasuna. As this party was declared illegal in 2002,[22] ETA was forced to create a new party: first the Communist Party of the Basque Land ('PCTV'), which participated in the elections of 2005, and later the Basque Nationalist Action ('ANV') party, which sought to join in the regional elections of 2007. In February 2011, Sortu, a party described as 'the new Batasuna', was launched. Unlike predecessor parties, Sortu more or less explicitly rejected politically motivated violence, including that of ETA. However on 23 March 2011, the Spanish Supreme Court endorsed the ban on Sortu registering as a political party on the grounds that it was linked to ETA.[23] As a consequence, the radical and more peripheral members of the leftist *abertxale* (Basque nationalist movement) found entry first into the new party, Bildu (which participated in the Basque regional and municipal elections, winning seats for 1,138 deputies) and later Amaiur, which in the November 2011 National elections secured seven seats in the lower house and similarly three in the upper house of the Spanish parliament. The institutional aims obtained by these parties through their municipal, regional and national representatives have been very significant, not only in controlling a huge part of the Basque region, thereby impairing the

---

20   F. Reinares, *Patriotas de la muerte. Quiénes han militado en ETA y por qué* (Madrid: Taurus, 2001) 19.

21   The *kale borroka* campaign suffered a severe setback and came nearly to a halt after the Conservative government of José María Aznar changed the law so that the responsibility for the economic damage caused by the 'street fighters' – mostly youngsters with no own income – shifted from them to their parents (Ley Orgánica 5/2000, de 12 de enero – Boletín Oficial del Estado).

22   According to the Ley Orgánica 672002, de 27 junio, de Partidos Políticos, Boletín Oficial del Estado, núm. 154 de 28 de junio de 2002, 23600–23607.

23   For an overview of the Laws and judicial sentences banning organizations related to ETA, see A. Bourne, 'Terrorism and Party Politics: The illegalization of Sinn Féin and Batasuna', paper presented at 'Elections, Public Opinion and Parties' conference, University of Oxford 7 to 9 September 2012.

exercise of constitutional liberties and the authority of the government but, most importantly, in obtaining and channelling economic resources to ETA.

ETA's Income

Criminal Activities for Raising Funds

Kidnapping and extortion
Extortion was one of the main sources of income for ETA from the 1970s onwards, thus substituting for previously more important activities, like bank robbery and theft generally. Blackmail, which has been mostly practiced against businessmen and self-employed professionals, can adopt two forms of execution: kidnapping and letters of extortion. And in order to make clear their intentions ETA has not hesitated to assassinate or otherwise harm some of the victims, as well as attacking their business facilities[24] and even starting boycott campaigns against their products.[25]

Altogether, ETA benefitted from extortion to the tune of more than €115 million during the three decades between 1978 and 2008. This amount has to be considered a minimum, as the information available, mostly obtained from documents seized from the terrorist group, is incomplete. As seen in Table 13.1 two-thirds of this amount (which in order to make comparisons easier is expressed in terms of 2002 purchase-power parity) came from kidnapping and one-third from extortion.

The kidnapping of businessmen by ETA started in 1972 and reached its peak in the second half of the 1970s and the first of the 1980s. Of the 95 kidnappings perpetrated by ETA, 70 took place between 1976 and 1986. Later this criminal activity declined until it stopped in 1996, mainly due to the fact that kidnapping demands a costly infrastructure, with well-trained militants, and there is a very great risk of detection. Therefore, once ETA had developed less risky forms of obtaining income, it tended to put kidnapping aside. Nevertheless, between 2000 and 2004 ETA once again made use of this tactic, although now in its 'express' version.[26] In fact, 17 cases of 'express kidnapping' were recorded during this period.

---

24   From 2000 onwards, around 45 terrorist attacks (15 per cent of the total), were perpetrated against business interests. ETA started to make use of the *kale borroka* (or street fight), the strategy of low-level terrorism explained above, to damage the properties of the victims. Thus, between 1999 and 2011 nearly a thousand such attacks targeted business facilities (roughly a quarter of *kale borroka* activities).

25   See, for example, the pamphlet *Boikota!* distributed in 2004, which gave the logos of 70 businesses unwilling to cede to ETA's extortion. See. A. Escrivá, 'ETA amenaza ahora a las empresas vascas con boicotear la venta de sus productos', *El Mundo*, 13 June 2004, 18.

26   Express kidnapping is a method of abduction used in some countries, mainly in Latin America, where a small ransom, that a company or family can easily pay, is requested. Often, these kidnappings last only a few days or even hours.

Table 13.1   ETA's income from kidnapping and extortion 1978–2010 (€1000s in 2002 ppp)

Year	Kidnapping (ransom)	Extortion letters	Total
1978	614.5		614.5
1979	69.1		69.1
1980	7,584.3	2,475.2	10,059.5
1981	6,821.0	1,354.2	8,175.2
1982	3,893.3	1,282.0	5,175.3
1983	12,505.9	664.4	13,170.2
1984		574.5	574.5
1985	5,163.9	2,938.3	8,102.2
1986	7,415.0	5,338.8	12,753.8
1987	2,255.0		2,255.0
1988	14,515.3		14,515.3
1989	3,020.1		3,020.1
1990			
1991	222.7	196.0	418.6
1992			
1993	4,020.8	120.6	4,141.4
1994			
1995		5,870.7	5,870.7
1996	885,7		885.7
1997	10,421.5		10,421.5
1998			
1999			
2000		1,073.0	1,073.0
2001	217.8	1,768.6	1,986.4
2002	700.0	1,435.7	2,135.7
2003		1,209.8	1,209.8
2004	38.7	719.5	758.2
2005			
2006		1,149.5	1,149.5
2007		3,843.7	3,843.7
2008		4,045.9	4,045.9
2009		2,758.0	2,758.0
2010		3,927.0	3,927.0
Total	80,364.6	42,745.3	123,109.9

Note: Table constructed using estimations of F. Domínguez, *ETA: Estrategia organizativa y actuaciones, 1978–1992* (Bilbao: Universidad del País Vasco, 1998). The data for extortion in 1995 have been estimated by the *Ertzaintza* (*Capital*, February 2001); for 2000, *ABC*, 17 January and 8 April 2004; from 2001 to 2004, the papers seized from Soledad Iparraguirre (Á. Escrivá, 'ETA aceptó en febrero de 2004 mantener reuniones con el PSOE', *El Mundo*, 2 July 2006); and from 2006 to 2010, authors' own estimations. The data referring to kidnappings between 2001 and 2004 came from the Papeles de Susper (F. Iturribarría, 'ETA ha trasladado a Las Landas las citas para el cobro del impuesto revolucionario', *El Correo*, 17 February 2008).

The amounts demanded by ETA for setting free their hostages varied a lot, ranging from a couple of thousand to several million euros. In most cases, the ransoms were illegally paid by the relatives of the hostage through intermediaries. There have been several exceptions of non-payment, some of them due to the impossibility of raising the amount demanded.

The letters of extortion sent to businessmen requiring them to pay in order to avoid becoming a victim, although less profitable than kidnapping, were a more regular enactment. For this purpose, ETA developed a specific infrastructure charged with contacting and transferring the funds through a complex network. The letters are usually written in an anonymous and formal administrative style which euphemistically dresses up a blatant form of extortion which was called 'revolutionary tax' or 'compulsory contribution'. ETA threatened those who refuse to pay up with death. Once the letter was received, the extortion victim was supposed to contact the blackmailers through certain lawyers or well-known activists from the radical Basque nationalist camp. At one time, the businessmen would receive the order to hand the money over to certain HB offices. The businessman usually received up to four or five letters of extortion. The amount to be paid in the first letter is usually between €120,000 and €300,000. ETA writes: 'In light of the information on your financial situation at our disposal, the set amount [here there is a blank for the sum], the payment of which you will have to make as of [blank for the number of days tafter the date of reception of this notification]. The payment will have to be made in cash with used banknotes. The usual Basque means will have to be used in order to contact our organization.' The letter ends with this threat to the businessman: 'You are solemnly warned that should you refuse to pay the amount stipulated, our organization shall be obliged to take reprisal measures against your property and life as it deems fit. There is no need to remind you that any attempt by you to contact the police will result in dire consequences.' A second letter, identical to the previous one, is sent not only to the businessman but also to his relatives in order to increase the fear factor. After seven months, if the victim has still not paid, a third letter is sent which contains a two-month ultimatum, and informs the victim that he is now a direct objective of ETA. Ten months on, a fourth letter is sent, now stating that the victim will have to pay a 5 per cent surcharge as 'default interest'. The remittance of 150 to 200 letters in October 2003 in which amounts ranging between €20,000 and €200,000 were demanded, was preceded by an attack on the trucks of a transport company that had refused to pay up. In the attack, 12 vehicles were burnt. Similarly, on 8 August 2000, ETA murdered the president of the Asociación de Empresarios de Gipuzkoa ('ADEGI' – Business Employers' Association), José María Korta, because he had refused to accede to their demands. Besides Korta, ETA has murdered 39 businessmen since 1976 in order to reinforce their demand for the 'Revolutionary Tax'. In addition to this scheme, ETA has recently developed another, more polite letter, aimed at businesses which are known for their friendly attitude towards terrorism, asking the owner for a minor contribution (usually between €12,000 and €24,000).

There are so far no official data regarding the exact number of extortion letters sent out by ETA. Nevertheless, the detention of the terrorist, Soledad Iparraguirre, along with the papers she kept, allowed for some insights into ETA's activities. Between September and November 2003, 253 letters were sent to 95 businessmen. Assuming a constant level of activity, we may estimate that during these three decades nearly 11,000 persons have been the targets of terrorist extortion. Regarding the question of how many of them have actually paid up, 'the number of those who give in to the extortion ranges between 10 and 20 per cent'.[27] That means that if our estimations are correct, between 1,100 and 2,200 businessmen would have bought their security by financing terrorism.[28] It must also be remembered that the use of extortion letters by ETA has fluctuated heavily over time, reaching its peak between 1978 and 1986.[29]

Property raids
ETA undertook robbery and raids in order to obtain the necessary resources to commit their attacks. In its initial phase, the robbery of banks and businesses was the main procedure used to obtain liquidity. Thus, between 1965 (the year in which the group announced that it would start 'the requisition of the necessary means for the revolutionary struggle') and 1985, they perpetrated 'around 200 bank assaults and other robberies with an estimated booty of €4.2 to 4.8 million'.[30] In addition, during the 1970s ETA regularly stole explosives from quarries, the most spectacular operation being perpetrated in 1980 in the town of Soto de la Marina, where they obtained eight tons of *goma-2* explosive. Also, two years later, ETA broke into a depot of the Autonomous Basque Police, Ertzaintza, where they stole 135 Star pistols. This notwithstanding, from the mid 1980s onwards ETA decided to elaborate their own ammonal explosive from legally obtained products, thus abandoning for a time the theft/raiding strategy.[31]

---

27   J.L. Barbería, 'Una política rota' *El País*, 22 October 2004, 6.

28   A brief overview of some disclosed payments can be found in M. Buesa, *ETA S.A. El dinero que mueve el terrorismo* 87–89.

29   F. Domínguez, *ETA: Estrategia organizativa y actuaciones, 1978–1992* 141. According to an investigation by the Anticorruption Prosecution that was made public in 2004, the Basque Treasury had created a special register for 118 businessmen, mostly related to the Basque Nationalist Party, who had been victims of this extortion, and whose Fiscal Declarations were kept secret. It seems that this measure was adopted to allow them to deduct the extortion payments from their declaration without incurring a criminal offence for the financing of a terrorist group.

30   F. Domínguez, *Josu Ternera. Una vida en ETA* (Madrid: La Esfera de los Libros, 2006).

31   F. Domínguez, *ETA: Estrategia organizativa y actuaciones, 1978–1992*.

Dirty Assets

Table 13.2   Theft of explosives, weapons and other materials by ETA, 1987–2011 (€1000s in 2002 ppp)

Year	Raiding of explosives, weapons and other materials	Stolen vehicles*	Value of the explosives (€)	Value of the vehicles (€)	Total (€)
1987		19		103.9	103.9
1988		7		40.1	40.1
1989		7		41.2	41.2
1990		10		60.6	60.6
1991		17		106.8	106.8
1992		9		58.6	58.6
1993		5		34.2	34.2
1994		4		28.7	28.7
1995		4		29.8	29.8
1996		4		31.2	31.2
1997		6		51.3	51.3
1998					
1999	*Titadine (France)*: 8.350 kg. of dynamite, 11,000 m. of explosive fuse cord, 1,142 mechanical detonators and 4,612 electric detonators.		1,436.5		1,436.5
2000	*Cantera Asson (France)*: 15 kg. of dynamite, 800 m of detonator cord and 100 detonators. *Ski station Guzet-Neige (France)*: 48 kg. of dynamite.	12	27.6	112.2	139.9
2001	*Titadine (France)*: 1.600 kg. of dynamite, 20,000 detonators. *Mondragón*: A die. *San Sebastián*: Number plates of vehicles belonging to the municipal police.	16	419.8	146.6	566.4
2002	*Empresa Disprauto*: Two die castings and 250 number plates. *Abadiño*: One die and number plates. *Lasarte Enterprise*: €18,000. *Jonzac Enterprise (France)*: Hundreds of number plates.	13		116.9	116.9
2003		2		17.3	17.3

Year	Raiding of explosives, weapons and other materials	Stolen vehicles*	Value of the explosives (€)	Value of the vehicles (€)	Total (€)
2004		1		8.4	8.4
2005	*Saint-Benoit fertilizers (France)*: 4,000 kg. of sodium chlorate. *Fasver (France)*: Materials for the manufacture of ID cards. *Rouen (France)*: 1,280 kg. of aluminium powder.		205.8		205.8
2006	*Gramat (France)*: Weapons and uniforms of two gendarmes. *Replonges (France)*: Two die castings and 30,000 number plates. *Business in Vauvert (France)*: 350 pistols, ammunition and spare parts.	71		578.0	578.0
2007	*Bischoffsheim (France)*: 44 kg. of hexogen pills. *Laboratories Laberna in La Grand-Croix (France)*: 2,000 litres of nitromethane liquid.	20	201.7	161.1	362.8
2008		77		603.0	603.0
2009		51		433.6	433.6
2010	*Dammarie Les Lys (France)*: Six vehicles. *Impuls-France (France)*: Computer programs for the manufacture of ID and credit cards. Six specialist printers and 23,000 blank cards.	26		238.2	238.2
2011**		16		156.9	156.9
Total		397	2,291.5	3,158.6	5,450.1

Note: Table constructed using estimations from F. Domínguez, *ETA: Estrategia organizativa y actuaciones, 1978–1992*, the Spanish Home Office and daily press. The calculation of the value of explosives employs international prices. Regarding the vehicles, we have applied a standard mean value for a two-year old medium-sized car, accounting for the prices in the second-hand market; * Up to 2005, number of vehicles used in attacks. From 2006 on, total of vehicles stolen; ** First semester.

Nevertheless, at the end of the 1990s, and due to the more severe impact of prosecutions on the terrorist network and its subsequent lack of liquidity, ETA reactivated the strategy of robbery, illustrated by the attack against the Titadine factory in France in 1999. From then on, ETA has continued stealing explosives, weapons, number plates and identification documents.

The value of all the materials stolen by ETA exceeds €4 million, according to our estimations, all of which are represented in Table 14.3. This amount is incomplete, as it only takes into account the explosives and the related substances – which amount to €2.3 million – and to vehicles stolen (which amount to approximately €2.2 million).

Other illicit operations

Although this category of operations represents only a minor source of income for ETA, some transactions have been of notable importance. Thus, for example, the terrorist group has for many years, although only occasionally, engaged in drug trafficking.[32] Reinares[33] transcribes a very interesting conversation in which a former member of ETA confessed to him that he had participated in operations to buy weapons in which the provider required an associated purchase of cocaine. Another case in which ETA was involved with drug trafficking was the detention in 1996 of José Luis Folgueras, who was caught in possession of 150 kg of cocaine. More recently, in January 2006, the French police arrested two ETA members who had been involved in an operation in Italy to buy arms with drugs. According to one study,[34] in this operation the Genovese Camorra provided the arms and FARC in Columbia provided the drugs. There are also references to ETA participating in cocaine distribution in Spain found in the papers of the late FARC leader, Raúl Reyes.[35] ETA has also been involved in other forms of illegal trafficking, such as tobacco smuggling, although to a not very great degree.

The last relevant source of income for ETA has been the (remunerated) collaboration with other terrorist groups, especially through providing such 'services' as the training of other terrorists. Unfortunately, the information available regarding this question is very scarce[36] although it seems to have been proved convincingly that ETA has had this sort of collaboration with the Chilean MIR (Movimiento de Izquierda Revolucionaria), the Nicaraguan Sandinistas and Salvadorian guerrillas. In 1988 ETA also seems to have instructed some of Pablo Escobar's cartel members in the preparation of car bombs, charging $300,000 for its services.[37]

How important has the income generated by this activity been? It is not possible to determine, although we might conclude that it might not have been highly significant, since these activities have been only sporadic.

---

32   During some periods of its history, ETA actually hunted drug dealers as they believed them to be a cause of the weakening of Basque youth.

33   F. Reinares, *Terrorismo y antiterrorismo* 197.

34   R. Saviano, *Gomorra* (Barcelona: Debolsillo, 2008) 197–198.

35   L.A. Villamarín, *Narcoterrorismo. La guerra del nuevo siglo* (Madrid: Ediciones Nowtilus, 2005) 151–156.

36   F. Domínguez, *Josu Ternera. Una vida en ETA* 91.

37   A. Legarda, *El Verdadero Pablo. Sangre, Traición y Muerte* (Bogotá: Dipon, 2005) ch. 14.

Other Illegal Activities Related to Funding

Subventions to political parties
The political parties related to ETA have greatly benefitted from access to public funds. The Organic Law 3/1987 that regulated the financing of political parties established three ways to do so: reimbursing a part of the costs of the electoral campaign, whenever the party obtained effective representation; covering a part of the costs of parliamentary activity (either charged to the national budget or the budget of the autonomous region); and paying for their daily activity (this was done by the state). This law was soon exploited by the Basque government and Basque city councils, which started to divert additional funds to the parties. These practices were eventually even legalized,[38] much to the outrage of the Spanish Court of Audit.

All the parties related to ETA turned to this form of subvention, which has been provided by all levels of government except the Spanish central government, and which they continue to do, as can be seen in Table 14. It is important to point out that the strategy of proscribing the parties connected to ETA has been always circumvented by the creation of a new party with a very similar political configuration. Thus, Herri Batasuna was succeeded by Euskal Herritarok, later by Batasuna, the Communist Party of the Basque Country ('PCTV', Partido Comunista de las Tierras Vascas), Acción Nacionalista Vasca, Sortu, Bildu and Amaiur.[39] Depending on the respective electoral outcomes, these parties received subventions to a great or lesser degree, a point which might become even more important after the results recently obtained by Amaiur (see above). It seems clear that, although less important than in times past, during the last decades the subventions to political parties have been an important source of income for ETA. Moreover, this funding is particularly critical due to the paradox that it implies that in Spain even terrorism has been publicly subsidized.

Funds diverted to Udalbitza-Kursaal
Another political structure that has been used to finance ETA is the Assembly of Basque Municipalities (Udalbiltza). This organization was founded in 1999, joining together 1,778 mayors and town councillors of different nationalist parties. The decision to subsidize this entity convinced Euskal Herritarok (the Basque political coalition) to give it access to the Basque budget of 1999, thus allowing the Basque government (which was in a minority) to stay in power and continue governing. These subventions, which up to 2003 reached a volume of €3.27 million, with 27.6 per cent from the Basque government, 28.9 per cent as a result of the Deputies of Vizcaya and Guipúzcoa, and 42.1 per cent from 135 city

---

38   *Ley de Régimen Local*, 7/1999 and *Ley de Financiación de Partidos Políticos*, 8/2007.

39   A more detailed analysis can be found in M. Buesa, *ETA S.A. El dinero que mueve el terrorismo* 100–106.

Table 13.3 Subventions obtained by political parties related to ETA, 1992–2011 (€1000s in 2002 ppp)

Year	Subventions of regular activities					Electoral subventions			Total sum
	Basque gov't	General court	Basque parliament	Local corps	Total	Basque gov't	Basque provincial councils	Total	
1992	434.1				434.1				434.1
1993	430.9	53.5	197.4	712.9	1,394.8				1,394.8
1994	411.6	107.8	219.4	669.2	1,407.9				1,407.9
1995	346.1	112.6	292.2	506.8	1,257.7				1,257.7
1996	447.6	31.3	440.2	670.7	1,589.8	72.7		72.7	1,662.4
1997	466.3		442.9	685.6	1,594.7				1,594.7
1998	538.6		265.4	629.2	1,433.2				1,433.2
1999	614.8		55.0	790.2	1,460.0	981.7	297.7	1,279.4	2,739.4
2000	713.8		701.7	1,037.0	2,452.6				2,452.6
2001	689.8		358.2	1,209.3	2,257.3				2,257.3
2002	667.5		346.0	1,226.8	2,240.3	653.2		653.2	2,893.5
2003				617.9	617.9				617.9
2004									
2005	405.9		264.6		670.4	424.2	1.0	425.2	1,095.6
2006**	392.5		493.0		885.6				885.6
2007**	383.1		460.0	475.9	1,319.1	131.5		131.5	1,450.6
2008**	362.1		437.8	315.0	1,114.9				1,114.9
2009**	60.5		73.0	315.2	448.7				448.7
2010**				308.0	308.0				308.0
2011**				560.0	560.0	364.0		364.0	924.0
Total	7,365.2	305.2	5,046.9	10,729.7	23,447.1	2,627.2	298.7	2,925.9	26,373.0

Note: Constructed using data of the Court of Audit, Basque parliament and daily press; * Until 2004, Herri Batasuna, Euskal Herritarrok and Batasuna. From 2005 to 2009, Partido Comunista de las Tierras Vascas. From 2007 on Acción Nacionalista Vasca is added. And in 2011 also Bildu; ** Provisional estimations.

councils, were executed very haphazardly. The Basque Court of Audit[40] concluded in its report that these subventions were transferred irregularly 'without the public services having the prescriptive control' of them, thus allowing that a part of that money could flow to ETA related entities.

Table 13.4   Subventions to Udalbiltza-Kursaal, 2001–2002 (€1000s, in 2002 ppp)

Years	City councils	European Union	Total
2001	1,966.5	n.d.	1,966.5
2002	2,600.0	n.d.	2,600.0
Total	4,566.5	21,700.0	26,266.5
Annual mean	2,283.3	10,850.0	13,133.3

Note: Constructed from judicial documents (published in *El Correo*, 3 May 2003).

AEK: Publicly funded ideological indoctrination

The spread of the Basque language (Euskera), especially among the adult population, has always been a priority of the Basque nationalist government. And it has also been so for ETA, which has taken advantage of its control over the main agencies dedicated to this purpose to spread its radical and violent nationalist ideology. The medium used to fulfil this objective is 'AEK' (Coordinadora para la Alfabetización y Euskaldunización), an entity founded in 1962 as a popular initiative to promote the use of the Basque language. The documents seized from ETA clearly prove that, at least by 1992, AEK was controlled by ETA as part of the Udaletxe project.

Table 13.5   Financing of AEK, 1991–1998 (in €1000s, 2002 ppp)

Year	Basque government	Local corporations	Other entities	Raffles and others	Total
1991		219.1	383.0		602.1
1992		206.8	361.6		568.4
1993–1996					No data
1997	8,380.3	105.6	292.8	913.6	9,692.4
1998	8,228.1	103.7	287.5		8,619.3
Total	16,608.4	635.2	1,324.9	913.6	19,482.2

Note: Table constructed from judicial documents published in J. Díaz and I. Durán, *ETA. El saqueo de Euskadi* (Barcelona: Editorial Planeta, 2002).

---

40   Tribunal Vasco de Cuentas Públicas, Subvenciones a Udalbitza (Vitoria: Informe de Fiscalización, 2004) 26.

During its long history, AEK accumulated a very important patrimony in estates which, in 2000, was composed of 52 properties valued at €12 million. Also, at the time it was seized by the Supreme Court in 1998, its portfolio included around 150 schools (*euskalteguis*), mostly under the control of Batasuna.[41] In order to develop its activities, in 1996 the firm Galkaraka was set up, being in charge of hiring the teachers and subcontracting them to AEK as a form of tax avoidance (which between 1995 and 1999 amounted to at least €4.6 million). In addition, AEK managed to obtain goods from the Basque provincial administration and remit them to ETA. Although the data referring to this activity are incomplete, they seem to confirm that during the 1990s no less than €19.5 million was transferred by this mechanism to the terrorists.

The terrorist press

As soon as Spain had recovered its constitutional liberties, ETA aimed to take advantage of the new situation to obtain control over its own news media which would allow it to spread its message and justify its actions.[42] Thus, in 1976, several people close to ETA formed the limited corporation, Orain, with the aim of publishing a new, radically nationalist newspaper called *Egin*, which was launched in October 1977. A year later, the corporation expanded its capital, so that ETA, through middlemen and Herri Batasuna, acquired 40 per cent, thus giving them the power to appoint the editor-in-chief of the newspaper. Additionally, a new corporation named Ardatza was created as a vehicle to own and control the assets of *Egin* (thus saving them from possible losses of the newspaper business). The business worked properly until 1986, when the paper was split into 10 local editions, which significantly raised its costs. Hence, in 1998, the paper started to acquire heavy debts which four years later exceeded half a million euros. The most of this was covered by ETA transferring money from several other enterprises that it owned. Nevertheless, and in order to reduce its costs, Orain had stopped making regular National Insurance payments some time before. An attempt to further evade this payment was then made by creating in 1995 a new corporation (Erigane) to succeed Orain. Finally, the judicial seizure of *Egin* occurred in 1998, in reaction to which the terrorist sympathizers started a new paper, *Gara*, six months later with the same operating structure and the same personnel than *Egin*, this one being edited by the new corporation, EKHE S.A.

---

41   Ibid., 21.

42   The complex relationship between terrorism and media is studied, among others, in P. Norris, M. Kern and M. Just (eds), *Framing Terrorism. The News Media, the Government and the Public* (Abingdon: Routledge, 2003); M. Buesa, T. Baumert, A. Valiño, J. Caro and F. Roldán, 'Sangre y pixels: terrorismo, propaganda y medios de comunicación' (2011) 47 *La Ilustración Liberal* 3.

Table 13.6   Financing of *Egunkaria*, 1994–2002 (€1000s, in 2002 ppp)

Year	Subventions Basque government	Other funds	Total
1994	537.7		
1995	891.7		
1996	892.8		
1997	833.7		
1998	1,064.2		
1999	1,039.8		
2000	1,773.4		
2001	1,710.6		
2002	1,712.3		
Total	10,456.2	16,976.7	27,432.9

Note: Constructed using data of the Basque government (*ABC*, 6 March 2003) and published judicial sources (*ABC*, 17 October 2003).

Another newspaper promoted by ETA was *Euskaldunon Egunkaria*, which started publication in 1990. Unlike *Egin*, *Egunkaria* was conceived from the beginning not just as a form of communications media, but as a network aimed to obtain, transfer and launder money. For this purpose, it generated a complex and intertwined framework, that masked funds, perpetrated fiscal fraud and undertook false book-keeping. As a result, in 2000 *Egunkaria* reported losses of €24,000 which hid the real surplus of €288,000 that it had obtained. Another business belonging to the group was declared 'inactive' while actually it turned over some €4.2 million. Additionally, it falsely inflated the newspaper circulation to 5.1 million, when the actual number was below the equivalent of €3 million in revenue, in order to obtain more subventions from the Basque government. This public help was retained until 2002, when once more the business was seized by judicial order and its directors prosecuted.[43] By then, the sum obtained by the *Egunkaria* group from public sources exceeded €10.5 million, with an additional €17 million from unknown sources.

Gestoras Pro-Amnistía and relatives of imprisoned ETA members
A notably outstanding part of the terrorist network, so far, has been the societies for support of imprisoned members of ETA and their relatives. This formation not only allowed the group to maintain its internal cohesion and discipline, but also to present an image of strength to their supporters. This mission was entrusted from 1976/1977 up to its banning in 2002 to Gestoras Pro-Amnistía (subsequently substituted, in 2003, by Etxerat). The financing of Gestoras Pro-

---

43   In 2010 five members of *Egunkaria* were declared innocent of collaboration with ETA (Sentencia 27/2010 de la Sección primera de la Sala de lo Penal de la Audiencia Nacional). Nevertheless, there are still several judicial procedures ongoing.

Amnistía was based on the distribution of income in ETA's economic network, organized through the Udaletxe project in the following way: 30 per cent of the profits from this organization were destined for Gestoras, the rest flowing to Herri Batasuna (50 per cent) and KAS (20 per cent). Simultaneously, Gestoras obtained its own income through the sale of raffle tickets and the sale of drinks and snacks at stands set up at local celebrations. It is not possible to estimate the amount earned by Gestoras through such activities. When Gestoras was prohibited, it was the Basque government which took over paying the travelling costs of relatives of ETA prisoners to visit prisons throughout Spain. As can be seen in Table 13.7, the cost of this funding reached more than €1.5 million between 2003 and 2008. In addition, many city councils governed by nationalist parties (Batasuna, ANV, PCV and EA) have met different costs related to the imprisoned ETA members and their relatives from 2001 onwards.

Table 13.7   Subventions to ETA prisoners, relatives and associations of relatives, 2001–2010 (€1000s, in 2002 ppp)

Year	Basque government	City councils	Total
2001		11.4	11.4
2002		15.0	15.0
2003	191.9	20.1	212.0
2004	181.7	1.8	183.6
2005	177.0	17.7	194.7
2006	434.3	14.5	448.7
2007	213.9	37.2	251.0
2008	171.4	66.8	238.3
2009	177.3	51.2	228.5
2010		53.5	53.5
Total	1,547.4	289.2	1,836.7

Note: Constructed using data published by the Basque government and the city councils of Andoain, Azcoitia, Getxo, Ibarra, Mondragón, Zizurkil, Atxondo, Bérriz, Legázpi, Gernika, Zigoitia and Elorrio.

ETA's trading activity
As a final point, we must consider ETA's trading activities, aimed to create income for the group, give employment to their exiled sympathizers, support the salaries of the KAS-Ekin members, launder money and facilitate the logistics of the attacks committed by ETA. Although ETA had already established control over some enterprises (like Sokoa) during the 1970s, it was not until 1992 that it decided, in the context of the Udaletxe strategy to set up several mercantile corporations in

order to maintain the ETA members exiled in Latin America and to better control the logistics of the Herriko Tabernak.

Regarding the first point, many members of ETA, once they were no longer able to escape police investigation, went into 'exile' in Mexico, Cuba, Venezuela, Costa Rica, Nicaragua, Panama, Uruguay and Argentina. Thus, ETA opted to create enterprises like Ganeko, Gadusmar, Ugao and Comercial Berria, Ederra as a support mechanism offering employment to these terrorists.

Regarding the logistics and control of the Herriko Tabernak, the nucleus of organization was the Banaka S.A. corporation, which was divided into three subsidiaries: Extepare, Aixa and Hatar. The Herriko Tabernak was transformed in 1994 into cultural associations, as a means of 'whitewashing' its activities and to allow it to receive subventions from official Basque institutions. According to judicial sources, it has been estimated that these 'taverns' had an income of €15 million per year, consisting of legal activities (restaurants, caterings, terrorist merchandizing, etc.) and illegal ones (such as fraud). The detailed breakdown of these sources of income can be seen in Table 13.8 (below).

Overall Estimation

Now that we have considered all the available data on the sources of ETA's income, this section will extrapolate from this information an overall estimation of ETA's financial profile. It must be borne in mind that the sources available refer mainly to the time after the economic reorganization of the terrorist group, according to the Proyecto Udaletxe, which started in 1993. For this reason, our estimation will be constructed primarily from data referring to the period 1993–2002, the decade immediately before Batasuna was banned, and 2003–2010, the stage marked by the 'ceasefire'.

The procedure applied in order to determine ETA's financing scheme consisted of obtaining the annual average of each source and period. In those cases where the information was incomplete, we have extrapolated the average of the years for which data is available to estimate the average for the whole period. Also, when a specific source was active only during a fraction of the period, the total amount was calculated taking this fact into account. The results so obtained are presented in Table 14.9 and, in a simplified manner, in Figure 13.2 (below).

Our results evidence, first, that ETA disposed of far more income between 1993 and 2002 than subsequently. Although our estimations have to be considered incomplete due to missing data, it is striking that the total amount for the first period is quadruple that for the second one. While the terrorist network around ETA managed to generate at least €28.1 million per annum between 1993 and 2002, in more recent times this amount has only reached around €8.8. This trend

Table 13.8   Sources of ETA's income 1993–2002 and 2003–2010 (thousands of €, in 2002 ppp)

Activity	Organization	1993–2002	%	2003–2010	%
Extortion	ETA	3,787.8	13.5	2,211.5	25.2
Burglary/Raiding	ETA	245.3	0.9	305.9	3.5
Subventions to political parties	HB/PCTV/ANV	1,909.4	6.8	740.2	8.4
Subventions to the diffusion of *Euskera*	AEK	8,794.3	31.2		
Subventions to the press in *Euskera*	Egunkaria	1,045.6	3.7		
Subventions to the Basque culture	Elkargintza Elkarlenean	2,074.3	7.4		
Subventions to ETA prisoners	Etxerat	13.2	0.0	226.3	2.6
European subventions	Udalbiltza Kursaal	2,169.9	7.7		
Deviation of municipal funds	Udalbiltza Kursaal	456.8	1.6		
Social security fraud	Grupo Orain/AEK	1,456.7	5.2		
Failed credits from 'Caja Laboral Popular'	Herri Batasuna	211.4	0.8		
Funds of unknown origins	Egunkaria	2,074.3	7.4		
Benefits from mercantile activities	Herriko Tabernas	3,457.2	12.3	2,545.6	29.0
Raffles	AEK	456.8	1.6		
Affiliation fees	Batasuna			2,009.0	22.9
Donations	Herriko Tabernas			738.5	8.4
Total		28,153.0	100.0	8,777.0	100.0

Note: Constructed by the authors.

suggests that the banning of Batasuna and the judicial investigation of many of the organizations operating within ETA's orbit, significantly throttled the terrorist's economic inflow.[44]

Secondly, it should be highlighted that the model of calculation of assets in the decade before Batasuna was prohibited, was much more complex than the recent one. Thus, between 1993 and 2002 the main source of income that nourished the terrorist network was the public subventions, which amounted up to 57 per cent of the total. This means that ETA has been primarily financed by political institutions, mainly due to the fact that the strategists that head the group knew how to exploit this source effectively and that the politicians in charge have for a long time been willing to turn a blind eye to this state of affairs.

---

44   This means that other sources, mainly the ones related to the political representation in the local, regional and national Parliaments, are becoming increasingly more relevant. Other variable might be level of support for ETA and the effectiveness of counter-terrorism measures.

Also during this period, the extortion of businessmen acquired a certain importance representing around 14 per cent of the group's income together with the revenue from the firms controlled by ETA (which amounted around 12 per cent of the total). Less important sources were fraud (albeit slightly underrated) with at least 7 per cent (this includes the diversion of municipal funds and quotas not paid to the Spanish National Insurance system), an important credit given to Batasuna by the bank Caja Laboral Popular (8 per cent) and, finally, other sources like selling raffle ticket and donations, which seem to have been no more than 2 per cent of the group's total income.

The model for more recent times (2003–2010) proves to be very different. Now the main sources are represented by benefits derived from trading activities and extortion being respectively 29 and 23 per cent of ETA's total income, while the affiliation fees of sympathizers are also very important, up to 23 per cent of ETA's earnings. Public subventions drop during this period to 11 per cent, while donations and the sale of raffle tickets rise to 8.4 per cent and burglary raids only represent 3.5 per cent. It might be worth pointing out that as the income deriving from public resources has been curtailed, ETA has not only had to increase its efforts to ensure returns from fraudulent and criminal activities, but in the main has had to raise money from their sympathizers and supporters all in order to obtain only a fraction of what the group had before. It seems obvious that if all the sources of public subventions were shut off and the activities of the herriko tabernas were put under pressure, it would, by implication, mean ETA's financial collapse.[45]

A third point to be considered refers to the origin of the aforementioned public subsidies. A detailed analysis of the different origins of these sources leaves no doubt as to the singular role played in this context by the Basque government, which has complacently allowed the flow of public financial aid to the terrorist network.

As can be seen in Figure 13.2, from 1993 to 2002, three-quarters of the public funds that went to the accounts of ETA came from the Basque government. Nevertheless, we can also state that, albeit on a smaller scale, all other administrations (including the European Union), were involved in the same erroneous policy. The funds from the Basque government continued to flow even after the prohibition of Batasuna in 2003, when there could be no doubt about the connection of certain organizations with ETA. This support was either channelled through aid to the relatives of ETA prisoners (and their associations) or through endowments to the political arm of the terrorists represented in the city councils and the regional parliament.

---

45   This might encourage ETA to increase their extortion campaigns. But again, this would make them more vulnerable to judicial pressure and prosecution by the state security forces.

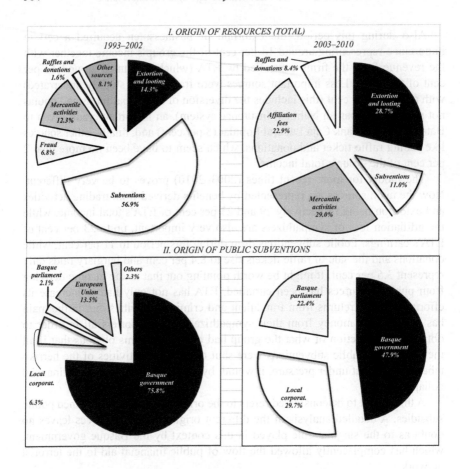

Figure 13.2   Sources of ETA's income

Conclusions

We might conclude that the sum total of all the economic inflows obtained by
ETA only represents a minimal fraction of the overall Basque economy. Between
1993 and 2002, it represented 0.07 per cent of the Gross Domestic Product of the
Basque Country; and in the period of 2003 to 2010 the amount slightly exceeded
0.01 per cent of GDP. This result is not astonishing, as it coincides closely with the
one obtained in previous studies examining other terrorist groups.[46] As we stated
at the beginning of this chapter, terrorism can be understood as a singular type of

---

46   See for this the conclusions in M. Buesa and T. Baumert, 'Untangling ETA's
finance: an in-depth analysis of the Basque terrorist's economic network and the money it
handles' (2013) 24(4) *Defence and Peace Economics* 317.

low-cost war that readily permits the mobilization of militants in order to maintain a, usually, prolonged and irregular conflict that aims to wear down its opponent until they give up. This is one reason why terrorism is so difficult to combat and to eradicate. Our study of the financial network that gives economic oxygen to ETA shows that terrorist groups have learnt to transform their sources of income into a semi-legal status, operating on the shadowy frontier between criminal, illegal and legal activities. This is the lesson that has to be learnt in fighting terrorism. One of the main instruments of effective anti-terror policies lies in a continuous economic throttling of the terrorist network, tying down the different sources of income one by one, no matter how insignificant they may seem from the overall perspective, and by all legal means available.

Chapter 14

EU Counter-Terrorist Sanctions: The Questionable Success Story of Criminal Law in Disguise

Christina Eckes[1]

Introduction

European counter-terrorist sanctions (in the form of individual sanctions) have acquired a somewhat dubious reputation. Foremost, they have been criticized for breaching fundamental rights, in particular the right to judicial review. Indeed in their current form, they breach fundamental rights because neither those sanctioned nor the judiciary possesses the necessary information to ensure effective defence rights. This is the case irrespective of whether or not individual sanctions constitute criminal law. However, the question of whether or not EU sanctions fall within the category 'criminal law' does not amount to *Begriffsjurisprudenz*.[2] The procedural protection of those listed and sanctioned depends on whether sanctions substantially amount to a criminal charge within the meaning of Article 6 of the European Convention on Human Rights ('ECHR'). Furthermore, if counter-terrorist sanctions represent criminal law, rather than temporary emergency measures, they must withstand a different type of impact assessment than emergency measures.[3] Emergency measures are not commonly subjected to elaborate efficiency assessments, considering both costs and benefits; however this becomes necessary when these measures turn into ordinary criminal sanctions of unlimited duration. In the case of counter-terrorism sanctions, the costs of adopting and enforcing them should be set against the benefits of containing terrorist activity.

The aim of this chapter is twofold. It first aims to demonstrate that autonomous EU counter-terrorist sanctions constitute criminal law in substance and that they

---

1   I would like to thank Dennis van Berkel for his insightful comments on an earlier draft. All remaining errors are of course my own.

2   'Conceptual jurisprudence' – the term is often used to criticize an overly formalistic technical approach to legal concepts that isolates them from all contexts.

3   See the Commission's usual impact assessment for structuring and developing policies http://ec.europa.eu/governance/better_regulation/impact_en.htm, accessed 19 January 2013.

are in many ways built on, and interlinked with, *national* criminal law. They have far-reaching consequences not only for those sanctioned but also for the individuals and entities that are connected to them and interact with them. Second, the chapter addresses the efficiency of sanctions. It argues that because counter-terrorist sanctions have these far-reaching consequences, and have been in place for a long period of time without any termination clause, they must be evaluated from an efficiency perspective. So far this has not been undertaken. On the contrary, even the limited effectiveness assessments that have been conducted are flawed: they take into account the wrong indicators.

Section one sets the scene by introducing the object of this research: EU counter-terrorist sanctions. Section two makes the main argument that EU counter-terrorist sanctions are criminal law in substance. It explains the nature and particularities of EU criminal law, argues that EU counter-terrorist sanctions fall within EU criminal law and constitute a criminal charge within the meaning of Article 6 of the ECHR, and examines the intricate links between EU counter-terrorist sanctions and national criminal law. Section three considers the efficiency of counter-terrorist sanctions. It highlights the lack of proper efficiency evaluation and gives pointers as to what indicators should or should not be taken into account in a cost benefit assessment. The conclusion reinforces the main argument that counter-terrorist sanctions are not emergency measures but criminal law and that consequently they should be subject to considerations of efficiency rather than only effectiveness, just as are all long-term policies.

Setting the Scene: What are Counter-Terrorist Sanctions?

European Union ('EU') counter-terrorist sanctions are essentially freezing orders adopted in directly applicable regulations, either because the UN Security Council lists the targeted person as a terrorist suspect[4] or because a 'competent national authority' in one of the Member States took a 'relevant decision' to the effect that the person is a terrorist suspect.[5] The Security Council terrorist lists are drawn up and maintained by a specialized sanctions committee created by UN Security Council ('UNSC') Resolution 1267.[6] The regime has been reformed many times, including a series of changes made to improve the procedure (introduction of the delisting

---

4 See Common Position 2002/402/CFSP (OJ 2002 L 139 p. 4) and Regulation 1286/2009 of 22 December 2009 (OJ 2009 L 346, p. 42).

5 See Common Position 2001/931/CFSP (OJ L 344, 27.12.2001, p. 93); Council Regulation (EC) No 2580/2001 (OJ L 344, 28.12.2001, p. 70).

6 S/RES/1267 (1999) of 15 Oct. 1999, given effect by the EU in CP 2002/402/ CFSP of 27 May 2002 (2002), OJ L 139/4, and Council Regulation 881/2002 of 27 May 2002 (2002), OJ L 139/9; see also EU Regulation 1286/2009 of 22 Dec. 2009 amending Regulation (EC) No. 881/2002 (2009), OJ L 346/42.

procedure;[7] the focal point;[8] regular review of the listings;[9] the ombudsperson[10]) and the respect for the substantive rights (humanitarian exemptions[11]) of those listed. In 2011, the UN list of terrorist suspects, originally containing those 'associated with Al-Qaida'[12] *and* those 'associated with the Taliban',[13] has been separated into two different regimes. This reflects the different agenda of sanctions against al-Qa'ida and sanctions against the Taliban and reduces the latter to a state-related sanctions regime,[14] similar to, for instance, sanctions against Libya. The ombudsperson is struggling to assure a minimum of fair procedures under the regime of sanctions against al-Qa'ida.[15] She has no powers under the Taliban sanctions regime or any other state-related regime. The Special Rapporteur on the promotion and protection of human rights and fundamental freedoms while countering terrorism, Ben Emmerson, has surveyed the system in 2012. In conclusion, 'the Special Rapporteur acknowledges and welcomes the significant due process improvements [...], but nevertheless concludes that the Al-Qaida sanctions regime continues to fall short of international minimum standards of due process'.[16]

The second type of sanctions consists of autonomous EU counter-terrorist sanctions based on decisions by member states' authorities. The adoption procedure exemplifies the interlocking of national and EU criminal law and will be discussed below in more detail. These sanctions target groups and individuals that the EU considers are involved in other, often regional, forms of 'terrorism'. Sanctions decisions at the EU level are often based on a national decision to instigate investigations against a person for a terrorism-related crime. For reasons of completeness, it should also be mentioned that besides these two sanctions

---

7   First introduced by: Guidelines of the Al Qaida Sanctions Committee for the conduct of its work, adopted on 7 November 2002, as amended on 10 April 2003, 21 December 2005, 29 November 2006, 12 February 2007, 9 December 2008, 22 July 2010, 26 January 2011 and 30 November 2011 ('Guidelines'), para. 7; available at: http://www.un.org/sc/committees/1267/pdf/1267_guidelines.pdf (accessed 21 March 2013).

8   UN SC Res 1730 (2006), para. 1.

9   UN SC Res 1822 (2008), paras 25–26.

10   UN SC Res 1904 (2009).

11   UN SC Res 1452 (2001).

12   UN SC Res 1989 (2011), para. 1.

13   UN SC Res 1988 (2011), para. 1.

14   UN SC Res 1988 (2011) refers explicitly to Afghanistan.

15   See the interview with Ms Kimberly Prost of 16 July 2010, available at: http://www.thenational.ae/thenational/news/world/no-fly-list-appeals-can-be-filed-online (accessed 21 March 2012). The Ombudsperson was appointed pursuant to UN SC Res 1904, extended by Res 1989 and 2083. For her work, see http://www.un.org/en/sc/ombudsperson/ (accessed 19 March 2013).

16   Report of the Special Rapporteur on the promotion and protection of human rights and fundamental freedoms while countering terrorism (A/67/396, 26 September 2012), para. 59.

regimes that target terrorist supporters, the EU has about 30 sanctions regimes in place that target the governing elites of various countries.[17] The effects on individuals are the same under the different sanctions procedures. They find all their assets are frozen and they are subject to the public accusation that they have financed illicit activities.

Since the Treaty of Lisbon has entered into force, the EU has explicit competence under Articles 75 and 215 of the Treaty on the Functioning of the European Union ('TFEU') to adopt sanctions against natural and legal persons.[18] Article 75 of the TFEU forms part of the Area of Freedom, Security and Justice ('AFSJ'). Article 215 of the TFEU deals both with trade embargoes and individual sanctions. It is in the part of the TFEU governing the Union's external actions. So far, all individual sanctions, both pre- and post-Lisbon, have been adopted in a two-tier procedure, which first requires a Common Foreign and Security Policy ('CFSP') instrument[19] containing the political decision to adopt these sanctions and then a regulation containing the actual operational measures.[20] The successor of the two-tier procedure can now be found in Article 215 of the TFEU. Post-Lisbon, the Court of Justice (hereafter also 'CJEU') has full jurisdiction to review all EU counter-terrorist sanctions, irrespective of whether they are adopted under Articles 75 and 215 of the TFEU.[21] Member States remain competent to adopt so-called secondary sanctions, which are criminal measures for the breach of EU sanctions legislation. These apply to financial institutions or third parties who do not comply with the directly applicable obligation to deny any financial assets available to those listed.

EU Counter-Terrorist Sanctions: Criminal Law in Disguise

Sanctions are imposed regardless of whether criminal proceedings can be brought. They come into play in the margins, in the grey zones where criminal prosecution

---

17   E.g. Libya: Council Decision 2011/137/CFSP of 28 February 2011, OJ 2011 L 58/53-62; Council Regulation 204/2011 of 2 March 2011, OJ 2011 L 58/1-13. Tunisia: Council Decision 2011/72/CFSP of 31 January 2011, OJ 2011 L 28/64; EU Regulation 101/2011 of 4 February 2011, OJ 2011 L 31/1-12; Council Implementing Decision 2011/79/CFSP of 4 February 2011 implementing Decision 2011/72/CFSP, OJ 2011 L 31/40-47.

18   The two separate legal bases have given rise to new problems of delimitation that go beyond the scope of the present paper, see: Case C-130/10, *European Parliament v Council of the European Union*. See on the choice of the post-Lisbon legal basis for individual sanctions: C. Eckes, 'EU Counter-Terrorist Sanctions against Individuals: Problems and Perils' (2012) 17(1) *European Foreign Affairs Review* 113.

19   Pre-Lisbon this used to be a CFSP common position; post-Lisbon the instrument is called CFSP decision.

20   See ex-Article 301 EC and Article 215(2) TFEU.

21   This includes review of both the TFEU (former Community) instrument and the CFSP decision (adopted under the TEU), see Article 275(2) TFEU.

does not bite. However, despite their preventive administrative disguise, sanctions constitute a criminal charge within the meaning of Article 6 of the ECHR (discussed below), and they are in many cases linked with criminal investigation and ultimately prosecution.

Prelude: The EU as Criminal Law Legislator

In principle, the competence to punish individuals within their jurisdiction lies with the member states. The EU is not competent to adopt a general EU criminal code. EU criminal legislation can (only) complement the existing national criminal law systems. Within this strictly limited setting, EU criminal law has come a long way in the 18 years since it was introduced under the Treaty of Maastricht. Yet, it has not achieved a great degree of harmonization.[22] The large majority of EU criminal law measures consist of measures facilitating cooperation between member states. This is partially due to its 'intergovernmental' legacy[23] and partially due to the fact that criminal law is intimately related to the state monopoly on the legitimate use of violence.[24] Despite the many changes under the Lisbon Treaty, much of EU criminal law continues to carry an 'intergovernmental' legacy of what was previously called the third pillar.[25] This meant in essence that this policy area was less integrated and subject to limited constitutional constraints. The Commission, for instance, did not have the monopoly on initiative, and the European Court of Justice did not have jurisdiction except in the limited cases set out in Article 35 of the Treaty on European Union ('TEU').

With the entering into force of the Lisbon Treaty, EU criminal law has made a leap: the EU extended its competence and more far-reaching constitutional constraints were introduced. Post-Lisbon, the EU's competences for criminal law can be divided into three categories: under Article 83(1) of the TFEU, minimum rules for a list of particularly serious areas of crime with a cross-border dimension, such as terrorism, trafficking in human beings and the sexual exploitation of women

---

22   Article 84 TFEU: exclusion of any harmonization.

23   Steve Peers identifies this as one of the four themes running through his entire account of what is now called the area of freedom, security and justice, see. Peers, *EU Justice and Home Affairs Law* (Oxford: Oxford University Press, 2010) 1. He called this the 'legal afterlife' of the former third pillar (p. 42). See also: C. Eckes, 'A European Area of Freedom, Security and Justice: A Long Way Ahead?', *Uppsala WP* 2011: http://www.jur.uu.se/LinkClick.aspx?fileticket=DBZvh%2bj7OOs%3d&tabid=5502&language=sv-SE (accessed 21 March 2013).

24   This has led to the introduction of several safeguards of state sovereignty; see Article 82(2) TFEU: 'Such rules should take into account the differences between the legal traditions and systems of the Member States.'

25   Dealing with Police and Judicial Cooperation in Criminal Matters (PJCC). See for more details on the 'intergovernmental' methods of law-making and scrutiny: V. Mitsilegas, *EU Criminal law* (Oxford: Hart Publishing, 2009) 5–57; S. Peers, *EU Justice and Home Affairs Law* 4–70.

and children, illicit drug trafficking, illicit arms trafficking, money laundering, corruption, counterfeiting of means of payment, computer crime and organized crime (so-called Euro crimes); under Article 83(2) of the TFEU, minimum rules on the definition of criminal offences and sanctions essential for ensuring the effectiveness of a harmonized EU policy;[26] and under Articles 310(6), 325, 85 and 86 of the TFEU, protection of EU public money. Most recently, the commission communicated its plans to make use of EU criminal law to ensure effective implementation of EU policies.[27] Furthermore, the EU works towards achieving common minimum standards of procedural rights in criminal proceedings more broadly.[28] Furthermore, in Article 75 of the TFEU the EU also received the explicit competence to adopt freezing measures with the aim of combating terrorism. The provision forms part of the general provisions of Title V on the AFSJ. The increased EU competence has been complemented by increased constitutional constraints. Both the European Parliament and national parliaments have been given increased powers. The European Court of Justice has comprehensive jurisdiction over EU criminal law – with the exception of pre-Lisbon instruments, for which limited jurisdiction continues under the transitional provisions until 2014.

The body of EU criminal law has been growing both in quality and in quantity. Its existence cannot be ignored even if large parts are based on cooperation rather than harmonization. The next section will position the topic of individual sanctions in this discussion. It will argue that even though individual sanctions remain in some ways an exceptional measure[29] among EU criminal law policies, they do belong in this category. This is reflected in the fact that they are dealt with in (text) books on 'EU criminal law'.[30]

---

26   This competence has been used for the first time in: Proposal for a Directive of the European Parliament and of the Council on criminal sanctions for insider dealing and market manipulation, COM(2011) 654 final 2011/0297 (COD).

27   Towards an EU Criminal Policy: Ensuring the effective implementation of EU policies through criminal law, Communication from the Commission, COM(2011) 573 final.

28   E.g. Directive 2010/64/EU of 20 October 2010 on the right to interpretation and translation in criminal proceedings, OJ 2010 L 280/1; Directive 2012/13/EU of 22 May 2012 on the right to information in criminal proceeding, OJ 2012 L 142/1 and Proposal for a Directive on the right of access to a lawyer in criminal proceedings and on the right to communicate upon arrest, COM(2011) 326 final 2011/0154 (COD).

29   C. Eckes, 'The Legal Framework of the European Union's Counter-Terrorist Policies' in C. Eckes and T. Konstadinides (eds), *Crime within the Area of Freedom, Security and Justice: A European Public Order* (Cambridge: Cambridge University Press, 2011) 127–58, Section 2.1.

30   See e.g. A. Klip, *EU Criminal Law* (Cambridge: Intersentia, 2011); E. Herlin-Karnell, *Constitutional Dimension of EU Criminal Law* (Oxford: Hart Publishing, 2012).

The Growing Realization that Sanctions are in Substance a 'Criminal Charge'

A discussion of whether counter-terrorist sanctions constitute EU criminal law cannot ignore the concept of 'criminal charge' within the meaning of Article 6 of the ECHR. Particularly in the context of EU law, where criminal law concepts are only slowly emerging, the European Court of Human Rights ('ECtHR')'s definition can be of particular guidance. The ECHR does not influence the formal classification of 'criminal' under domestic law, but it determines whether the level of procedural safeguards has to be at the level that is required for a criminal charge. The debate on whether EU counter-terrorist sanctions amount to a criminal charge within the meaning of Article 6 of the ECHR has been conducted elsewhere.[31] It will not be repeated in full. The present paper aims to outline the discussion so far and highlight more recent developments and indirect effects that are often overlooked, before considering the consequences.

Classifying counter-terrorist sanctions as a criminal charge is important because, first, stronger procedural safeguards are required in criminal proceedings, and, second, the impact assessment for open-ended criminal measures is different from the assessment of emergency measures. While Article 6(1) of the ECHR is applicable both to disputes determining civil rights and criminal charges, Articles 6(2) and (3) of the ECHR are only applicable to the latter. The presumption of innocence, for instance, applies in principle to proceedings of a criminal character only.[32] Counter-terrorist sanctions breach core fundamental rights, and their consequences for the individual listed are dire: those sanctioned are publically labelled terrorists and denied access to their financial assets. If freezing measures last indefinitely, their effects in terms of human-rights infringements cannot be distinguished from confiscations following conviction.[33] Moreover, there are other consequences that illustrate the wider destructive effect on the lives of individuals. In some countries an explicit rule excludes accepting refugees who are members or supporters of any of the groups listed under the autonomous EU sanctions regime. However, in a preliminary reference from a German court, the Court of Justice was asked to rule on the decision of a German asylum authority that membership of an organization included on the terrorist lists justified excluding the person

---

31 C. Eckes, *EU Counter-Terrorist Policies and Fundamental Rights: The Case of Individual Sanctions* (Oxford: Oxford University Press, 2009) ch. 3; see also: M. van den Broek, M. Hazelhorst and W. De Zanger, *Asset Freezing: Smart Sanction or Criminal Charge?* (Utrecht: Merkourios, 2010) 18–27.

32 See for the exceptional relevance of the presumption of innocence in civil proceedings: *Bochan v Ukraine*, App No 7577/02, 3 May 2007, para. 78; *Lutz v Germany* App No 9912/82, Ser A 123, para. 60.

33 See for a distinction between freezing and confiscation: World Bank, *Combating Money Laundering and the Financing of Terrorism* (Washington, DC, 2009), Module 3b – Compliance Requirements for Financial Institutions.

from refugee status.[34] The CJEU ruled that exclusion from refugee status must be decided on a case by case basis, but stated clearly that the inclusion is a 'factor to be considered' in evaluating whether someone has committed a 'serious non-political crime' or an 'act against the principles of the UN'.[35]

The EU institutions continue to classify counter-terrorist sanctions as preventive administrative rather than criminal measures.[36] The General Court has so far followed this line. It explicitly ruled that the listing itself is not considered a criminal charge in the recent case of *Sofiane Fahas*:[37]

> The Council's decision, which is the result of, *inter alia*, the decision of a competent national authority, does not constitute a finding that a criminal offence has in fact been committed but is adopted within the framework and for the purpose of an administrative procedure which has a precautionary function and the sole purpose of which is to enable the Council to combat the funding of terrorism in an effective manner.[38]

The court continued that 'the adoption of precautionary measures … do not constitute sanctions or prejudge in any way the innocence or guilt of the person at whom those measures are directed'.[39] This remains also the position of the Security Council, which reiterates in the preamble to Security Council Resolution 1822 of 2011 that sanctions 'are preventative in nature and are not reliant upon criminal standards set out under national law'.[40] However more recently, in the light of the long duration of counter-terrorist sanctions (many individuals have been on the list for a decade),[41] their preventive administrative nature has increasingly become contentious. Not only scholars[42] but also judicial authorities have criticized the

---

34 CJEU, C-57/09 and C-101/09, *Bundesrepublik Deutschland v B and D*, 9 November 2010.

35 Ibid., para. 90.

36 See also the preamble to the UN Security Council Resolution 1822 of 30 June 2008.

37 GC, Case T-49/07 *Sofiane Fahas v Council* [2010] ECR II-5555; see also Case T-85/09 *Kadi II* [2010] ECR II- 5177, paras 149–50.

38 See GC, Case T-49/07 *Sofiane Fahas v Council* [2010] ECR II-5555, para. 68.

39 Ibid., para. 64.

40 Reiterated on a number of occasions, see e.g.: Security Council Resolution 1822 (2008), 30 June 2008.

41 Kadi was listed for 11 years. In October 2012, following a request by the Ombudsperson, he was finally first removed from the UN lists and then from the EU lists.

42 I. Cameron, 'The European Convention on Human Rights, Due Process and United Nations Security Council Counter-Terrorism Sanctions', Report to the Council of Europe, 2006: http://www.coe.int/t/dlapil/cahdi/Texts_&_Documents/Docs%202006/I.%20Camer on%20Report%2006.pdf (accessed 19 January 2013); C. Eckes, *EU Counter-Terrorist Policies and Fundamental Rights: The Case of Individual Sanctions* ch. 3; C.C. Murphy, *EU Counter-Terrorism Law: Pre-Emption and the Rule of Law* (Oxford: Hart Publishing,

unlimited duration and have labelled sanctions 'draconian measures, unlimited as to time and quantum, constitute a serious interference with his fundamental rights, the consequences of which may be devastating'[43] or 'particularly draconian'.[44] Some went as far as designating those sanctioned 'prisoners' of the State.[45] The General Court equally voiced doubt.[46] It considered that '[i]n the scale of a human life, 10 years in fact represent a substantial period of time and the question of the classification of the measures in question as preventative or punitive, protective or confiscatory, civil or criminal seems now to be an open one'.[47] Similarly, the United Nations High Commissioner for Human Rights argued:

> [b]ecause individual listings are currently open-ended in duration, they may result in a temporary freeze of assets becoming permanent which, in turn, may amount to criminal punishment due to the severity of the sanction. This threatens to go well beyond the purpose of the United Nations to combat the terrorist threat posed by an individual case. In addition, there is no uniformity in relation to evidentiary standards and procedures. This poses serious human rights issues, as all punitive decisions should be either judicial or subject to judicial review.[48]

It is fair to conclude that the tide appears to be turning – inside and outside the judicial bodies that are asked to rule on sanctions. Increasingly the devastating effects on the lives of those listed are recognized.

2012); I. Cameron (ed.), *EU Sanctions: Law and Policy Issues Concerning Restrictive Measures* (Cambridge: Intersentia, 2013).

43   A.G. Maduro, Opinion in Joined Cases C-402/05 P and C-415/05 P Kadi I [2008] ECR I-06351, para. 47.

44   See GC, Case T-85/09 *Kadi II* [2010] ECR II- 5177.

45   *Her Majesty's Treasury v Mohammed Jabar Ahmed and others (FC); Her Majesty's Treasury v Mohammed al-Ghabra (FC); R (on the application of Hani El Sayed Sabaei Youssef) v Her Majesty's Treasury* [2010] UKSC 2, paras 60 and 192. See also: International Commission of Jurists, '*Assessing Damage, Urging Action: Report of the Eminent Jurists Panel on Terrorism, Counter-Terrorism and Human Rights*' (International Commission of Jurists, 2009), available at: http://ejp.icj.org/IMG/EJP-Report.pdf (accessed 19 January 2013).

46   See Case T-85/09 *Kadi II* [2010] ECR II-5177, which was decided earlier than *Sofiane Fahas* but by a different section of the court.

47   Ibid., para. 150.

48   Report to the General Assembly of the United Nations, 'Report on the protection of human rights and fundamental freedoms while countering terrorism' (A/HRC/12/22, 2009) point 42.

EU Sanctions and their Relationship with National Criminal Law

While the relationship between EU counter-terrorist sanctions and UN sanctions under the 1267 regime has been explored in much detail,[49] the relationship and interaction between national law and EU law has so far been largely neglected by the literature. This section examines, first, the listing procedure and the nature of the 'relevant decision' of the 'competent national authority' and, second, the effects of EU listings and sanctions under national law (post-listing), including secondary sanctions.

In the case of autonomous EU sanctions, the council lists individuals in a procedure building on, but separate from, the procedure at the national level. The council adopts autonomous sanctions following a 'relevant decision' of the 'competent national authority'.[50] This decision in turn is, 'irrespective of whether it concerns the instigation of investigations or prosecution for a terrorist act, an attempt to perpetrate, participate in or facilitate such an act[,] based on serious and credible evidence or clues, or condemnation for such deeds'.[51] The EU listing is consequently the outcome of a separate procedure with additional adverse effect for the individual.[52] The listing further pursues a different objective, namely containing terrorism rather than addressing criminal behaviour.[53] These differences in outcome and objective are admittedly limited by the General Court's ruling that 'the purpose of the national proceedings in question must none the less

---

49 C. Eckes, *EU Counter-Terrorist Policies and Fundamental Rights: The Case of Individual Sanctions*; E. Cannizzaro, 'Security Council resolutions and EC fundamental rights: Some remarks on the COJ decision in the Kadi Case' (2009) 28 *Yearbook of European Law* 593 at 599; I. De Jesus Butler, 'Securing human rights in the face of international integration' (2011) 60 *International and Comparative Law Quarterly* 125; C. Tomuschat, 'The Kadi Case: What relationship is there between the universal legal order under the auspices of the United Nations and the EU Legal Order?' (2009) 28 *Yearbook of European Law* 663; D. Halberstam and E. Stein, 'The United Nations, the European Union, and the King of Sweden: Economic sanctions and individual rights in a plural world order' (2009) 46 *Common Market Law Review* 13 at 66 et seq.; T. Tridimas, 'Economic sanctions, procedural rights and judicial scrutiny: Post-Kadi Developments' (2011) 13 *Cambridge Yearbook of European Legal Studies* 455 at 457; J. Genser and K. Barth, 'When due process concerns become dangerous: The Security Council's 1267 regime and the need for reform' (2010) 33(1) *Boston College International and Comparative Law Review* 24.

50 Article 1(4) of CP 2001/931/CFSP of 27 December 2001 on combating terrorism, OJ 2001 L 344/93.

51 Ibid.

52 See, for more detail, C. Eckes and J. Mendes, 'The right to be heard in composite administrative procedures: Lost in between protection?' (2011) 36 *European Law Review* 651.

53 See for more details: C. Eckes, *EU Counter-Terrorist Policies and Fundamental Rights: The Case of Individual Sanctions* 316 et seq.

be to combat terrorism in the broadest sense'[54] and that 'a decision of a national judicial authority' does not suffice if it rules 'only incidentally and indirectly on the possible involvement of the person concerned in such activity in relation to a dispute concerning, for example, rights and duties of a civil nature'.[55] The decisions of competent national authorities are not limited to decisions governed by criminal law,[56] but more often than not these decisions flow from criminal proceedings.[57] However, in a case where at national level police or security enquiries are closed without giving rise to any judicial consequences, the council is bound to take this status into account.[58]

Some authors even contend for the autonomous listing procedure:

> Most of the evidence that member states provide typically comes from such sources as national criminal proceedings, legal proceedings, prosecutions and sentences. The [EU] usually has no case when the basis for listing and delisting is solely intelligence information, unless that can be shown to be hard evidence.[59]

In conclusion, EU autonomous sanctions are usually added on to national criminal proceedings for terrorist (related) activities and listings are often based on national criminal proceedings giving effect to Framework Decision 2002/475/JHA on combatting terrorism. However, this dependency is not a requirement; 'clues' about terrorist connections at an early investigatory stage are in principle sufficient. Member states retain great discretion on the details of implementation, since framework decisions are 'binding upon the Member States as to the result to be achieved but shall leave to the national authorities the choice of form and methods'.[60] The definition of what constitutes a terrorist objective or a link with terrorism is consequently not necessarily identical in the different legal orders, national or European. The Dutch legislature, for instance, added specific provisions on terrorism to the existing criminal law, which allows an increase of the maximum penalty for acts with a terroristic objective by up to 50 per cent.[61] This demonstrates the circular interaction and interlocking of the EU and the national legal contexts: EU law requires member states to take action against terrorist activities, member states do so, and the EU attaches additional consequences to their action.

---

54   See GC, Case T-348/07 *Al Aqsa v Council*, not published in the ECR, para. 100.

55   See GC, Case T-348/07 *Al Aqsa v Council*, not published in the ECR, para. 101 referring to Case T-341/07 *Jose Maria Sison v Council* [2009] ECR II-03625, para. 111.

56   GC, Case T-348/07, *Al Aqsa* [2010], not published in the ECR, para. 98.

57   E.g. GC, Joined Cases T-37/07 and T-323/07 *El Morabit v Council* [2009], ECR II-00131 (summ.pub.).

58   GC, Case T-348/07, *Al Aqsa* [2010], not published in the ECR, para. 168.

59   M. Eriksson, 'In search of a due process – listing and delisting practices of the European Union' *Uppsala Working Paper* 2009, 38.

60   Article 34(2)(b) TEU (pre-Lisbon).

61   E.J. Husabø and I. Bruce, *Fighting Terrorism through Multilevel Criminal Legislation* (Leiden: Martinus Nijhhoff Publishers, 2009) 184.

Furthermore, and as acknowledged by the General Court, there are additional effects of listing, which may lead to a further circular logic of adopting a national decision 'pending the adoption' of an EU measure, which first justifies the adoption of the EU measure and then is immediately repealed when the EU measure comes into force.[62] This 'circular logic' continues where the EU law measure is then used to justify a criminal conviction or the prohibition of an organization at the national level.[63] In the Netherlands for instance, all legal persons (in other words, companies and organizations) listed by the EU pursuant to Common Position 2001/931/CFSP are prohibited *ipso jure*.[64] In Sweden and in Italy, the courts consider being on the UN list of terrorist suspects a relevant fact when, in the course of criminal proceedings, they determine whether the accused is connected with terrorism or not.[65]

Furthermore, the breach of EU sanctions legislation leads to so-called secondary sanctions under national law. Pursuant to Article 83(2) of the TFEU, minimum rules for secondary sanctions could in principle be established by the Union. However, since this has not yet happened, member states remain in charge of the adopting secondary sanctions. Secondary sanctions do not necessarily have to be criminal, but they have to be effective. Again, the specific regulations under national law differ considerably. In Austria secondary sanctions are regulated in the national sanctions law.[66] Any natural or legal person who makes funds available to a listed individual faces a fine of up to €50,000; or if more than €100,000 is made available, imprisonment of up to one year or 360 *Tagessätze*[67] may be imposed. In Germany, deliberate breaches are punishable by imprisonment for a period of between six months and five years.[68] The CJEU ruled that where the EU listing has been found flawed because the listed individuals had not been given the necessary opportunity to realize their procedural rights, the listing is illegal and cannot justify secondary sanctions under national law.[69] The case concerned the pre-trial detention of two individuals because of their alleged membership of

---

62   See GC, Case T-348/07 *Al Aqsa v Council*, not published in the ECR, para. 177.

63   See CJEU, Case C-550/09 *Generalbundesanwalt beim Bundesgerichtshof v E and F* [2010] ECR I-06213.

64   'Van rechtswege verboden', Art 2:20 Section 3 of the Civil code (Burgerlijk Wetboek).

65   See Sixth report of the Analytical Support and Sanctions Monitoring Team, UN S/2007/132, 8 March 2007, box 1, p 14.

66   See Section 12(1) Sanktionengesetz (SanktG).

67   A unit of fine calculated on the daily rate of income of the offender.

68   Section 34(4)Nr.2, (5), (6)Nr.4, (7) *Aussenwirtschafsgesetz* (AWG).

69   CJEU, Case C-550/09 *Generalbundesanwalt beim Bundesgerichtshof v E und F* [2010] ECR I-06213.

DHKP-C,[70] which had been put on the autonomous EU list of terrorist suspects.[71] The CJEU held that the EU listing 'cannot, in any circumstances, be relied upon ... as a basis for a criminal conviction in respect of facts relating to that period [in which those listed did not enjoy the necessary procedural rights], without infringing the principle of the non-retroactivity of provisions which may form the basis for a criminal conviction'.[72] The latter demonstrates the dependence of national criminal secondary sanctions on the EU listings.

Assessing the 'Success' of Counter-Terrorist Sanctions

A reliable estimation of the success (i.e., effectiveness[73]) and costs, including the economic costs, of counter-terrorist asset-freezing is very complex. Indeed, determining the true costs of counter-terrorist sanctions in terms of civil liberties and distrust or fear would require economic, sociological and psychological research, and might very well prove impossible.[74] Furthermore, EU counter-terrorist sanctions, as with many other counter-terrorist measures,[75] are part of a larger package of security-related measures.[76] This makes it difficult to isolate the impact of the individual measure. Legal analysis can only make a limited contribution to this endeavour. It can contribute to establishing the legal framework within which

---

70   See CJEU, Case C-550/09 *Generalbundesanwalt beim Bundesgerichtshof v E und F* [2010] ECR I-06213, para. 27.

71   Council Decision of 28 June 2007, implementing Article 2(3) of Regulation (EC) No 2580/2001 on specific restrictive measures directed against certain persons and entities with a view to combating terrorism and repealing Decisions 2006/379/EC and 2006/1008/EC (2007/445/EC) [2007] OJ L169/58.

72   See CJEU, Case C-550/09 *Generalbundesanwalt beim Bundesgerichtshof v E and F* [2010] ECR I-06213, para. 59 [references omitted].

73   See for an explanation of this term: E. van Um and D. Pisoiu, 'Effective counterterrorism: What have we learned so far?' *Economics of Security Working Paper* 55, September 2011.

74   See on more indirect costs of (counter)terrorism: L. Donohue, *Cost of Counterterrorism* (Cambridge: Cambridge University Press, 2008).

75   W. Wensink, M. van de Velde and L. Boer, *Estimated Costs of EU Counterterrorism Measures* (Brussels: Directorate General for Internal Policies, Policy Department C: Citizens' Rights and Constitutional Affaires Civil Liberties, Justice and Home Affairs, 2011.

76   The EU's fight against terrorist financing consists of a complex network of legal instruments. Two relevant examples are the Third Anti-Money Laundering Directive [Directive 2005/60/EC of 26 October 2005 on the prevention of the use of the financial system for the purpose of money laundering and terrorist financing, OJ 2005 L 309/15] and the Terrorist Finance Tracking Program (TFTP) Agreement [Agreement between the European Union and the United States of America on the processing and transfer of Financial Messaging Data from the European Union to the United States for the purposes of the Terrorist Finance Tracking Program, OJ 2010 L 195/5].

such an analysis should take place. It can also point out the legal costs involved in counter-terrorist measures. These are the modest objectives of this section.

First, any assessment of the success of a legal measure must be evaluated in light of its objectives. The core legal instrument of the Union's autonomous sanctions regime is Common Position 2001/931/CFSP. It states that 'the European Council has declared ... that the fight against terrorism will be a priority objective of the European Union'[77] and that 'the Council reiterated the Union's determination to attack the sources which fund terrorism, in close cooperation with the United States'.[78] It further refers to UN Security Council Resolutions 1373 (2001) and 1333 (2000), which both aim to 'suppress the financing of terrorism' and ultimately 'to combat international terrorism'.[79] The main objective of the EU autonomous sanctions is, hence, to contain terrorism by reducing the funds available for financing terrorist activity. Their success should thus be measured in terms of the reduction in terrorist activities. While no specific evaluation of the success of EU autonomous sanctions exists, some success of the broader fight against the financing of terrorism has been pointed out. A study focusing on the financing of terrorism, for instance, came to the conclusion that '[m]any independent assessments of US counter-terrorism efforts since 11 September reaffirm the importance, and at least partial effectiveness, of initiatives to target terrorist funds'.[80] Besides this main objective, other auxiliary objectives are connected with counter-terrorist sanctions. Marieke de Goede, for example, pointed out with regard to one of the groups targeted by EU autonomous sanctions (the *Hofstadgroep*) that '[t]he "assets" ... that became subject to the freezing order, such as there were any, must be estimated to be very modest. The objective of the listing order thus cannot have been the prevention of the financing of acts of terrorism but has to be understood as the societal exclusion and symbolic banishment of the affected persons, whose daily lives in the Netherlands and beyond were put on hold'.[81] Furthermore, EU counter-terrorist sanctions are adopted in order to pursue auxiliary political objectives of governments and states. The publishing of negative assessments by organizations, such as the Financial Action Task Force ('FATF'), can lead to a loss of reputation, and member states and the European Commission have a strong interest in being given good reports. These additional objectives play an important role in the adoption of sanctions. 'Success' in the context of policy justification

---

77   Common Position 2001/931/CFSP, OJ 2001 L 344/94, first recital.

78   Ibid., third recital.

79   Ibid., recital 2, 4 and 5.

80   T.J. Biersteker and S.E. Eckert, 'Conclusions: Taking stock of efforts to counter the financing of terrorism and recommendations for the way forward' in T.J. Biersteker and S.E. Eckert (eds), *Countering the Financing of Terrorism* (Abingdon: Routledge, 2007) at 289.

81   M. de Goede, *Speculative Security: The Politics of Pursuing Terrorist Money* (Minneapolis, MN: University of Minnesota Press, 2012) 157.

should be measured against the stated objective of the legal instrument rather than the auxiliary objectives of those involved in adopting them.

Second, while the legal debate focuses on the legality of sanctions and on the direct costs in terms of human-rights restrictions imposed on those who are sanctioned, some other hidden 'legal' costs are worth mentioning. Deploying a concept of 'speculative security[82] and imposing 'preventive measures' that build on, and are interlinked with, national criminal law and that are sufficiently severe to qualify as a criminal charge within the meaning of Article 6 of the ECHR lead to a *Vorfeldkriminalisierung* (criminalization at a preliminary stage). This has consequences for the legal culture, as well as for trust and confidence in the legal system, which go beyond the infringement of human rights in any particular case. For good reasons, the European Parliament pointed out that 'questions are still being asked as to what extent the UN and the EU have produced sufficient evidence of the success of these regimes in restricting the financing of acts of terrorism, bearing in mind the significant impact which these regimes have had on the credibility of the EU's and UN's commitment to fundamental rights'.[83] Furthermore, the costs of the legal challenges brought against EU sanctions are worth mentioning. This includes sanctions based on UN lists of terrorist suspects, autonomous sanctions or those directed against the regime of a particular country. Besides the pending second appeal in the well-known *Kadi* case,[84] there are many more cases that attract far less attention: five other appeals are pending before the CJEU,[85] 91 challenges are pending before the General Court[86] and both EU Courts together have already ruled in 40 cases concerning sanctions.[87] These cases have an economic cost for the EU. They are also a consequence of the widely

---

82 Ibid., at xx et seq.

83 European Parliament resolution of 16 December 2009 on restrictive measures directed against certain persons and entities associated with Usama bin Laden, the Al-Qaida network and the Taliban, in respect of Zimbabwe and in view of the situation in Somalia (2010/C 286 E/02), available at: http://eur-lex.europa.eu/LexUriServ/LexUriServ.do?uri= OJ:C:2010:286E:0005:0012:EN:PDF, at C (accessed 19 January 2013).

84 Kadi has finally been delisted but the Commission's appeal against his successful second challenge (General Court, *Kadi II*) is still pending (see AG Bot, Joined Cases C-584/10 P, C-593/10 P and C-595/10 P, *Commission, Council, United Kingdom v Kadi*, Opinion of 19 March 2013).

85 On 22 October 2012 the following appeals involving 'restrictive measures' were pending the CJEU: C-348/12 P, *Council v Manufacturing Support & Procurement Kala Naft*, Application of 7 September 2012; C-280/12 P, *Council v Fulmen and Mahmoudian*, Application of 20 July 2012; C-417/11 P, *Council v Bamba*, Application of 7 October 2011; C-584/10 P, *Commission v Kadi*, Application of 5 March 2011; C-550/10 P, *Netherlands v Al-Aqsa*, Application of 12 February 2011; C-539/10 P, *Al-Aqsa v Council*, Application of 12 February 2011.

86 List on file with author, updated on 22 October 2012.

87 Twenty-six judgments of the General Court and 14 judgments of the CJEU (list on file with author, updated on 22 October 2012).

held understanding that EU counter-terrorist sanctions, as well as certain aspects of regime sanctions (e.g. the targeting of uninvolved family members), breach fundamental rights. This has negative consequences for the EU's credibility as a Union based on the rule of law.

Third, no long-term policy should be able to avoid an impact and efficiency evaluation. Efficiency and effectiveness must be distinguished. While the first relates the success to the costs of any given policy,[88] the latter analyses whether the policy has had any success at all – irrespective of cost. The former is consequently a relevant consideration for the allocation of resources that lies behind any policy decision. In a case of emergency, when a threat to the 'life of the nation'[89] needs to be averted, it might be considered justifiable to focus on effectiveness. The threat of international terrorism however can no longer be considered an emergency. Brief duration may not be an explicit requirement of derogation under either Article 15 of the ECHR or Article 4 of the UN International Covenant on Civil and Political Rights ('ICCPR'). However, it is implied in the term 'emergency'. The UN Human Rights Committee observed with regard to Article 4 of the ICCPR that '[m]easures derogating from provisions of the Covenant must be of an exceptional and temporary nature'.[90] Similarly, the UN Human Rights Committee has frequently emphasized its concern with regard to the duration of emergency derogations.[91] Yet, the threat of terrorism is different from an 'emergency' in its ordinary meaning. It is not limited either in time or space.[92] It is an abstraction, detached from concrete attacks. Accepting an abstraction as an emergency entails a danger that the exception becomes the norm and fundamental rules are permanently suspended, until it appears to the collective memory as if they were abolished. Considerations of efficiency should become important when a policy has been in place for more than a decade, as EU

---

88   An attempt at efficiency evaluation is made by T. Sandler, D. Arce and W. Enders, 'An Evaluation of Interpol's Cooperative-based Counterterrorism Linkages' (2001) 54(1) *Journal of Law and Economics* 79.

89   In November 2001, the UK Government declared that 'a public emergency threatening the life of the nation' exists in the UK, which justified derogating from Article 5(1) of the Convention [Human Rights Act 1998 (Designated Derogation) Order 2001, SI 2001 No. 3644]. See, however, Lord Hoffmann's minority opinion, rejecting the declaration of emergency: House of Lords, *A (FC) and others; X (FC) and others v Secretary of State for the Home Department* [2004] UKHL 56 at para. 97: 'The real threat to the life of the nation ... comes not from terrorism but from laws such as these. That is the true measure of what terrorism may achieve.'

90   UN Human Rights Committee, General Comment No. 29 (24 July 2001) on Art. 4 of the International Covenant on Civil and Political Rights, para. 2.

91   See e.g. CCPR/CO/76/EGY, para. 6 (2002); CCPR/CO/71/SYR, para. 6 (2001); CCPR/C/79/Add.93, para. 11 (1998); CCPR/C/79/Add. 81, para. 19 (1997), all available at: http://www2.ohchr.org/english/bodies/hrc/index.htm (accessed 19 January 2013).

92   See also: L. Richardson, *What Terrorists Want: Understanding the Enemy, Containing the Threat* (London: Random House, 2006) ch. 7.

counter-terrorist sanctions have been.[93] The core question should become whether the benefits outweigh the costs.[94] The marginal cost of adding one 'unit' to the unlikeliness of a terrorist attack is exponential. Freezing the assets of 'obvious' suspects is a relatively low cost action. But preventing the unknown necessitates actions based on ever slimmer suspicions towards an ever-growing group of people – a growing number of whom will be innocent bystanders. Furthermore, obtaining zero risk is impossible, and every next 'unit' making a terrorist attack less likely is more costly. The total estimated EU spending on counter-terrorist measures between 2002 and 2009 increased from approximately €5.7 million in 2002 to around €93.5 million in 2009.[95] To point out the obvious, resources are limited, and money spent on countering terrorism cannot be spent again on other relevant and pressing policies that might (equally) save lives. Therefore, spending it on counter-terrorist sanctions needs to be justifiable. Indeed, while in the past most counter-terrorist measures in the EU have not been subject to a (financial) impact assessment,[96] both policymakers and academics have more recently taken a greater interest, not only in the effectiveness, but also in the efficiency of counter-terrorist measures as the attempts to contain international terrorism continue.[97]

Fourth, the causal link between particular or general counter-terrorist policies and a reduction in terrorist activity is very difficult to establish[98] when it does not concern the immediate aversion of a specific act. It is misleading to attribute any change in the frequency and intensity of terrorist activity to counter-terrorist policies because a drop in terrorist activities depends on a very large number of

---

93   UN Counter-terrorist sanctions started in 1999 with Security Council Resolution 1267; EU counter-terrorist sanctions started in 2001 with Regulation 2580/2001 of 27 December 2001.

94   B. Zycher, *A Preliminary Benefit/Cost Framework For Counterterrorism Public Expenditures* (Santa Monica, CA: RAND, 2003), summary, at x, giving a rather positive assessment of US counter-terrorist efforts: 'There is evidence that the ongoing counterterrorism effort has had important beneficial effects, but because "units" of counterterrorism are difficult to define, the more central issue of balancing marginal benefits and costs must be the subject of future research. At the same time, the rough correspondence of total benefits and costs suggests that the United States is not obviously spending too much, in that such important benefits as enhanced national pride cannot be quantified.'

95   W. Wensink, M. van de Velde and L. Boer, *Estimated costs of EU counterterrorism measures* at 10.

96   Ibid., at 17.

97   Recent examples are: W. Wensink, M. van de Velde and L. Boer, *Estimated costs of EU counterterrorism measures*; E. van Um and D. Pisoiu, 'Effective counterterrorism: What have we learned so far?'; F. Schneider, T. Brück and D. Meierrieks, 'The Economics of Terrorism and Counter-Terrorism: A Survey (Part II)' *Economics of Security Working Paper 45*, April 2011.

98   See, e.g., M. Brzoska, 'The Role of Effectiveness and Efficiency in the European Union's Counterterrorism Policy: The Case of Terrorist Financing' *Economics of Security Working Paper 51*, July 2011.

factors (context dependent). Evaluations that indicate the money that has been frozen under the different sanctions regimes or the number of people listed are of strictly limited value in assessing 'implementation effectiveness'.[99] For instance, the FATF, as well as the UN Counterterrorism Committee, have focused on the implementation effectiveness and criticized a considerable number of EU member states for not being sufficiently effective in implementing anti-terrorist financing rules.[100] Implementation effectiveness is obviously a necessary condition for a policy to be impact effective, but the attribute cannot justify adopting the policy. Relying on implementation effectiveness gives no indication of the actual impact of a policy. Indeed, it is far from certain that all this money would have benefitted terrorist activities. Counter-terrorist sanctions are part of comprehensive counter-terrorist legislation, which aims at preventing terrorist activity. If the legislation is effective as a whole, one would expect the amount of money flowing into terrorist activity to decline and consequently the amount of money frozen would decline as well. This plainly demonstrates how flawed the use of the absolute amount of frozen money is as an indicator of effectiveness. The effectiveness of police measures cannot be assessed on the basis of the number of arrests made. Only the decline in actual competition law infringements or criminal activity will reveal a 'success', though account must then be taken of independent variables.

Beyond these arguments, in the case of EU counter-terrorist sanctions additional reasons speak against the reliability of implementation effectiveness as an indicator of success. In the light of the very low evidentiary threshold for 'clues and evidence' required in order to freeze someone's financial assets under EU legislation[101] it appears particularly difficult to take frozen money as an indicator for effectiveness. Indeed, few guidelines exist, listing criteria remain vague, and the European Courts have not, so far, specified the interpretation of these criteria.[102] However, only a stronger evidentiary link between the frozen funds and terrorist financing could justify relying on implementation effectiveness as an indicator at all.

Fifth, public and private costs of regulation should both be separately considered in the estimation of the cost of any counter-terrorist policy. The latter

99   E. van Um and D. Pisoiu, 'Effective counterterrorism: What have we learned so far?'.

100   Financial Action Task Force (FATF), *Mutual Evaluation Report. Anti-Money Laundering and Combating the Financing of Terrorism. Germany*: http//www.fatf-gafi.org, 2010 (accessed 19 January 2013); see also: MONEYVAL, *Report on Fourth Assessment Visit. Anti-Money Laundering and Combating the Financing of Terrorism. Hungary*: http://www.coe.int/t/dghl/monitoring/moneyval/, 2010 (accessed 19 January 2013); Counter Terrorism Committee, *Survey of the implementation of Security Council resolution 1373 (2001) by Member States* (S/2009/620, of 3 December 2009).

101   Article 1(3) of Common Position 2001/931/CFSP.

102   C. Eckes, 'Decision-making in the Dark? – Autonomous EU Sanctions and National Classification' in I. Cameron (ed.), *Legal Aspects of EU Sanctions* (Cambridge: Intersentia, 2013).

are often disregarded and even sometimes the private bodies and individuals, such as financial institutions,[103] are unaware of their full extent.[104] In the globally interconnected world, financial institutions for instance not only have to conduct customer name checks against numerous parallel and complementary terrorist lists, they also have to monitor to whom customers transfer funds and from whom they receive funds.

Finally, effectiveness or success cannot be assessed in isolation. They must be measured against the available alternatives. While under public international law the alternatives are limited essentially either to the use of force or no action at all, domestic criminal law provides alternative mechanisms that work as an efficient deterrent in other contexts. The underlying threat of using force may explain why, from a public international law perspective, 'targeted' or even 'smart' sanctions are regularly seen as the better alternative. From an EU law perspective, they set dangerous precedents of quasi-criminal charges located in the grey zone of criminality.

Conclusion

Counter-terrorist sanctions constitute a fully harmonized EU policy and remain in this sense an exception among instruments of EU criminal law. However, this cannot justify denying the fact that their nature is that of criminal law. Several arguments support this contention: first as we have seen above, autonomous EU sanctions impose in substance sufficiently restrictive or severe consequences that they fall under the rubric of 'criminal charge' within the meaning of Article 6 of the ECHR. Second, the EU's post-Lisbon competence to adopt autonomous EU sanctions under Article 75 of the TFEU squarely falls within its criminal law competences. Third, autonomous counter-terrorist sanctions are intimately interwoven both with other instruments of EU criminal law and with national criminal law. This paper argues that autonomous EU counter-terrorist sanctions constitute criminal law, and that they should be adopted as an AFSJ policy by the Union.

Acknowledging that EU counter-terrorist sanctions have become long-term criminal, rather than short-term emergency, measures leads to the conclusion that not only the consideration of effectiveness but also of efficiency must play a role in their adoption. This is the case irrespective of the sobering conclusion that assessing the 'success' of counter-terrorist measures generally is contingent

---

103   For an impression of the complexity of combatting the financing of terrorism, see: World Bank, *Combating Money Laundering and the Financing of Terrorism*; House of Lords European Union Committee, *Money Laundering and the Financing of Terrorism* HL 132 (2008–09).

104   W. Wensink, M. van de Velde and L. Boer, *Estimated Costs of EU Counterterrorism Measures*.

on so many indeterminate factors and so many prior policy choices of what to include and exclude that estimations of effectiveness will always be political. This cannot justify the argument that the consequences of any given policy should not be taken into account in policymaking, including the marginal costs of preventing one more attack or saving one more life. Similar analyses are commonly made in areas that concern risks to human welfare, such as environmental law dealing with carcinogens or air-borne toxins.

The threat of terrorism is real and remains serious.[105] Furthermore, the links between terrorism and organized crime are increasing and the attacks claimed or attributed to separatist terrorist organizations are decreasing. In light of the continuous threat and its changing nature it is even more crucial to move away from treating counter-terrorist sanctions as emergency measures and to integrate them into existing criminal law. This includes subjecting them to ordinary efficiency evaluations.

---

105 European Parliament, *Report on the EU Counter-Terrorism Policy: Main Achievements and Future Challenges* (Committee on Civil Liberties, Justice and Home Affairs (Rapporteur: Sophia in 't Veld), A7-0286/2011); Europol, *EU Terrorism Situation and Trend Report* (The Hague: TE-SAT 2011).

Select Bibliography

The purpose of this bibliography is to give an overview of major commentaries which are directly related to the theme of the book. More detailed references may be found in individual chapters.

Abadie, A. and Gardeazabal, J., 'The economic cost of conflict: A case study of the Basque Country' (2003) 93 *American Economic Review* 113

Abrams, A., 'A new proposal for limiting private civil RICO' (1989–1990) 37 *University of California Los Angeles Law Review* 1

Akere M., *Understanding the African Union Convention on Preventing and Combating Corruption and Related Offences* (Berlin: Transparency International, 2005)

Alldridge, P., 'Money laundering and globalization' (2008) 35 *Journal of Law and Society* 437

Alldridge, P., *Money Laundering Law: Forfeiture, Confiscation, Civil Recovery, Criminal Laundering and Taxation of the Proceeds of Crime* (Oxford: Hart Publishing, 2003)

Almqvist, J., 'A human rights critique of European judicial review: Counter-terrorism sanctions' (2008) 57 *International & Comparative Law Quarterly* 303

Ashe, M. and Reid, P., 'Ireland: The Celtic Tiger bites – The attack on the proceeds of crime' (2001) 4(3) *Journal of Money Laundering Control* 253

Association of Chief Police Officers and Centrex, *Practice Advice on Financial Investigation* (Wyboston: Centrex, 2006)

Australian Crime Commission, *Organised Crime in Australia* (Canberra: 2011)

Australian Law Reform Commission, *Confiscation that Counts: A Review of the Proceeds of Crime Act 1987* (Sydney: ALRC Report 87, 1999)

Bahney, B. et al., *An Economic Analysis of the Financial Records of Al-Qa'ida in Iraq* (Santa Monica, CA: RAND, 2010)

Balsamo, A., Contraffatto, V. and Nicastro, G., *Le misure patrimoniali contro la criminalità organizzata* (Milan: Giuffré, 2010)

Bartels, L., *A Review of Confiscation Schemes in Australia.* Technical and Background Paper 36 (Canberra: Australian Institute of Criminology, 2010)

Bartels, L., 'Unexplained wealth laws in Australia', *Trends and Issues in Crime and Criminal Justice (No. 395)* (Canberra: Australian Institute of Criminology, 2010)

Basel Institute on Governance, International Centre for Asset Recovery, *Tracing Stolen Assets. A Practitioner's Handbook* (Basel: Basel Institute on Governance, 2009)

Basel Institute on Governance, *The Need for New EU Legislation Allowing the Assets Confiscated from Criminal Organisations to be Used for Civil Society and in Particular for Social Purposes* (Brussels: PE 462.437, European Parliament, 2012)

Biersteker, T.J. and Eckert, S.E. (eds), *Countering the Financing of Terrorism* (London: Routledge, 2007)

Bloodgood, E.A. and Tremblay-Boire, J., 'International NGOs and national regulation in an age of terrorism' (2011) 22 *Voluntas* 142

Bloodgood, E.A. and Tremblay-Boire, J., 'NGO responses to counter terrorism regulations after September 11th' (2010) 12(4) *International Journal of Not-for-Profit Law* 5

Blumenson, E. and Nilson, E., 'Policing for profit: The drug wars hidden economic agenda' (1998) 65 *University of Chicago Law Review* 35

Booz Allen Hamilton, *Comparative Evaluation of Unexplained Wealth Orders: Prepared for the US Department of Justice, National Institute of Justice* (Washington, DC: Department of Justice, 2011)

Borgers, M.J. and Moors, J.A., 'Targeting the proceeds of crime: Bottlenecks in international cooperation' (2007) *European Journal of Crime, Criminal Law and Criminology* 1

Bowers, C.B., 'Hawala, money lending, and terrorist financing' (2009) 37 *Denver Journal of International Law and Policy* 379

British Bankers' Association, *Guidance on the Prevention of Money Laundering and the Financing of Terrorism for the Financial Services Industry* (London: 2006)

Brück, T. (ed.), *The Economic Analysis of Terrorism* (London: Routledge, 2007)

Brzoska, M., 'The role of effectiveness and efficiency in the European Union's counterterrorism policy: The case of terrorist financing' *Economics of Security Working Paper* 51, July 2011

Buesa, M., *ETA S.A. El dinero que mueve el terrorismo y los costes que genera* (Barcelona: Planeta, 2011)

Buesa, M. and Baumert, T. (eds), *The Economic Repercussions of Terrorism* (Oxford: Oxford University Press, 2010)

Buesa, M. and Baumert, T., 'Untangling ETA's finance: An in-depth analysis of the Basque terrorists' economic network and the money it handles' (2013) 24 *Defence and Peace Economics* 1

Bullock, K., 'Enforcing financial penalties: The case of confiscation orders' (2010) 49 *Howard Journal of Criminal Justice* 328

Bullock, K., 'The confiscation investigation' (2010) 4 *Policing: An International Journal of Policy and Practice* 7

Bullock, K., Mann, D., Street, R. and Coxon, C., *Examining Attrition in Confiscating the Proceeds of Crime* (London: Home Office, 2009)

Burnett, R. and Maruna, S., 'So prison works, does it?' (2004) 43 *Howard Journal of Criminal Justice* 390

Burr, J.M. and Collins, R.O., *Alms for Jihad* (New York: Cambridge University Press, 2006)

Cabinet Office and Home Office, *Extending Our Reach: A Comprehensive Approach to Tackling Serious Organised Crime* (London: Stationery Office, 2009)

Camden Asset Recovery Inter-Agency Network (CARIN), *The History, Statement of Intent, Membership and Functioning of CARIN. Manual* (Hague: Europol, 2012)

Cameron, I. (ed.), *EU Sanctions: Law and Policy Issues Concerning Restrictive Measures* (Cambridge: Intersentia, 2013)

Campbell, L., 'Theorising asset forfeiture in Ireland' (2007) 71 *Journal of Criminal Law* 441

Cannizzaro, E., 'Security Council Resolutions and EC Fundamental Rights: Some Remarks on the COJ Decision in the Kadi Case' (2009) 28 *Yearbook of European Law* 593

Carr, I. and Goldby, M., 'Recovering the Proceeds of Corruption: UNCAC and Anti-Money Laundering Standards' (2011) *Journal of Business Law* 170

Carr, I. and Outhwaite, O., 'The OECD Anti-Bribery Convention: Ten Years On' (2009) 5 *Manchester Journal of International Economic Law* 3

Cassano, F. (ed.), *Le misure di prevenzione patrimoniali dopo il 'pacchetto sicurezza'* (Bari: Neldiritto, 1999)

Center for the Study of Democracy, *CSD Brief No 21: Investigation of Money Laundering: An Institutional Approach* (Sofia: CSD, 2010)

Center for the Study of Democracy, *CSD Brief No 33: Management and Disposal of Confiscated Criminal Assets* (Sofia: CSD, 2012)

Center for the Study of Democracy, *Examining the Links between Organised Crime and Corruption* (Sofia: CSD, 2010)

Center for the Study of Democracy, *The Hidden Economy in Bulgaria and the Global Economic Crisis* (Sofia: CSD, 2011)

Chamberlain, K., 'Recovering the proceeds of corruption' (2002) 6(2) *Journal of Money Laundering Control* 157

Charity Commission, *Compliance Toolkit: Protecting Charities from Harm* (London: 2011)

Charity Commission, *OG96: Charities and Terrorism* (London: 2007)

Cheh, M.M., 'Constitutional limits on using civil remedies to achieve criminal law objectives: Understanding and transcending the criminal-civil law distinction' (1991) 42 *Hastings Law Journal* 1325

Cole, D., 'Terror financing, guilt by association and the paradigm of prevention in the "war on terror"' in Bianchi, A., and Keller, A., (eds.), *Counterterrorism: Democracy's Challenge* (Oxford: Hart Publishing, 2008)

Cribb, N., 'Tracing and confiscating the proceeds of crime' (2003) 11 *Journal of Financial Crime* 168

Criminal Assets Bureau, *Annual Report 2010* (Dublin: Stationery Office, 2011)

Crimm, N.J., 'High Alert: The government's war on the financing of terrorism and its implications for donors, domestic charitable organizations, and global philanthropy' (2004) 45 *William & Mary Law Review* 1341

de Goede, M., 'Hawala Discourses and the war on terrorist finance' (2003) 21 *Environment Planning D: Society and Space* 513

de Goede, M., *Speculative Security: The Politics of Pursuing Terrorist Money* (Minneapolis: University of Minnesota Press, 2012)

Donohue, L.K., *The Cost of Counterterrorism: Power, Politics and Liberty* (Cambridge: Cambridge University Press, 2008)

Doyle, C., *Terrorist Material Support: An Overview of 18 USC 2339A and 2339B* (Washington, DC: Congressional Research Service CRS 7-5700, 2010)

Eckes, C., 'EU Counter-Terrorist Sanctions against Individuals: Problems and Perils' (2012) 17(1) *European Foreign Affairs Review* 113

Eckes, C., *EU Counter-Terrorist Policies and Fundamental Rights: The Case of Individual Sanctions* (Oxford: Oxford University Press, 2009)

Eckes, C., 'The Legal Framework of the European Union's Counter-Terrorist Policies' in Eckes, C. and Konstadinides, T. (eds), *Crime within the Area of Freedom, Security and Justice: A European Public Order* (Cambridge: Cambridge University Press, 2011)

Eckes, C. and Mendes, J., 'The right to be heard in composite administrative procedures: Lost in between protection?' (2011) 36 *European Law Review* 651

Edge, P.W., 'Hard law and soft power' (2010) 12 *Rutgers Journal of Law & Religion* 35

Ehrenfeld, R., *Funding Evil* (Santa Monica, CA: Bonus Books, 2003)

Enders, W. and Sandler T., *The Political Economy of Terrorism* (Cambridge, Cambridge University Press, 2006)

Eriksson, M., 'In search of a due process – listing and delisting practices of the European Union', *Uppsala Working Paper* 2009

Europol, *TE-SAT 2011: EU Terrorism Situation and Trend Report* (Hague: 2011)

Farley, T.P, 'Asset forfeiture reform: A law enforcement response' (1994) 39 *New York Law School Law Review* 149

Financial Action Task Force, *International Best Practices: Combating the Abuse of Non-profit Organisations – Special Recommendation VIII* (Paris: 2002)

Financial Action Task Force, *Terrorist Financing* (Paris: 2008)

Finklestein, J., 'The goring ox: Some historical perspectives on deodands, forfeiture, wrongful death and the western notion of sovereignty' (1973) 46 *Temple Law Quarterly* 169

Fondaroli, D., *Le ipotesi speciali di confisca nel sistema penale – Ablazione patrimoniale, criminalità economica, responsabilità delle persone giuridiche* (Bologna: Bononia University Press, 2007)

Fornari, L., *Criminalità del profitto e tecniche sanzionatorie. Confisca e sanzioni pecuniarie nel diritto penale moderno* (Padua: Cedam, 1997)

Forsaith, J., Irving, B., Nanopoulos, E. and Fazekas, M., *Study for an Impact Assessment on a Proposal for a New Legal Framework on the Confiscation and Recovery of Criminal Assets. Final Report* (Brussels: RAND Corporation, European Union, 2012)

Freeman, M., 'The sources of terrorist financing' (2011) 34 *Studies in Conflict & Terrorism* 461

Freiberg, A. and Fox, R., 'Evaluating the effectiveness of Australia's confiscation laws' (2000) 33 *Australian and New Zealand Journal of Criminology* 239

Gallant, M., 'Alberta and Ontario: Civilizing the money-centered model of crime control' (2004) 4 *Asper Review of International Business and Trade Law* 13

Gallant, M., *Money Laundering and the Proceeds of Crime: Economic Crime and Civil Remedies* (Cheltenham: Edward Elgar, 2005)

Gallant, M., 'Ontario (Attorney General) v $29,020 in Canadian currency: A comment on proceeds of crime and Provincial forfeiture laws' (2006) 52 *Criminal Law Quarterly* 64

Gantz, D.A., 'Globalising sanction against foreign bribery: The emergence of an international legal consensus' (1998)18 *North Western Journal of International Law and Business* 457

Genser, J. and Barth, K., 'When due process concerns become dangerous: The Security Council's 1267 regime and the need for reform' (2010) 33 *Boston College International and Comparative Law Review* 24

Gilmore, W.C., *Dirty Money. The Evolution of International Measures to Counter Money Laundering and the Financing of Terrorism* (4th ed., Strasbourg: Council of Europe, 2011)

Giraldo, J.K. and Trinkunas, H.A. (eds), *Terrorism Financing and State Responses* (Stanford, CA: Stanford University Press, 2007)

Golobinek, R., *Financial Investigations and Confiscation of Proceeds of Crime: Training Manual for Law Enforcement and Judiciary* (Strasbourg: Council of Europe, 2006)

Gounev, P. and Ruggiero, V. (eds), *Corruption and Organized Crime in Europe* (London: Routledge, 2012)

Gray, A., 'Forfeiture provisions and the criminal/civil divide' (2012) 15 *New Criminal Law Review* 32

Gray, A., 'The compatibility of unexplained wealth provisions and "civil" forfeiture regimes with Kable' (2012) 12 *Queensland University of Technology Law & Justice Journal* 18

Greenberg, T.S, Samuel, L.M., Grant, W. and Gray, L., *Stolen Asset Recovery. A Good Practices Guide for Non-conviction Based Asset Forfeiture* (Washington, DC: The World Bank, 2009)

Group of States against Corruption (GRECO), *Second Evaluation Report on Bulgaria*, (Strasbourg: GrecoEval II Rep (2004)13 E, Council of Europe, 2005)

Gurulé, J., *Unfunding Terrorism* (Cheltenham: Edward Elgar, 2008)

Halberstam, D. and Stein, E., 'The United Nations, the European Union, and the King of Sweden: Economic sanctions and individual rights in a plural world order' (2009) 46 *Common Market Law Review* 13

Harvey, J., 'Just how effective is money laundering legislation?' (2008) 21 *Security Journal* 189

Heidenheimer, J., Johnston, M. and Le Vine, V. (eds), *Political Corruption: A Handbook* (London: Transaction Publishers, 1989)

HM Crown Prosecution Service Inspectorate, HM Inspectorate of Court Administration and HM Inspectorate of Constabulary, *Joint Thematic Review of Asset Recovery: Restraint and Confiscation Casework* (2010) Criminal Justice Joint Inspection, report available at: http://library.npia.police.uk/docs/hmcpsi/AssetRecovery.pdf

HM Government, *A Strong Britain in an Age of Uncertainty: The National Security Strategy* (London: Cm 7953, Stationery Office, 2010)

HM Government, *Local to Global: Reducing the Risk from Organised Crime* (London: Stationery Office, 2011)

HM Inspectorate of Constabulary (HMIC), *Payback Time: Joint Review of Asset Recovery since the Proceeds of Crime Act 2002* (London: Home Office, 2004)

HM Treasury, *The Financial Challenge to Crime and Terrorism* (London: 2007)

Hobbs, D., 'Going down the glocal: The local context of organised crime' (1998) 37 *Howard Journal of Criminal Justice* 407

Hodgson, D., *Profits of Crime and their Recovery* (London: Heinemann, 1984)

Home Office, *National Best Practice Guide to Confiscation Order Enforcement* (London: Home Office, 2010)

Home Office, *New Powers Against Organised and Financial Crime* (London: Stationery Office, 2006)

Home Office, *One Step Ahead: A 21st Century Strategy to Defeat Organised Crime* (London: Stationery Office, 2004)

Home Office and HM Treasury, *Review of Safeguards to Protect the Charitable Sector (England and Wales) from Terrorist Abuse* (London: 2007)

House of Lords European Union Committee, *Money Laundering and the Financing of Terrorism* HL 132 (2008–09) and HL 11 (2010–11)

Independent Reviewer of the Terrorism Legislation (D. Anderson), *First and Second Reports on the Operation of the Terrorist Asset Freezing etc Act 2010* (London: 2011, 2012) and HM Treasury, *Responses* (London: Cm 8287 and 8553, 2012 and 2013)

International Commission of Jurists, *Assessing Damage, Urging Action: Report of the Eminent Jurists Panel on Terrorism, Counter-Terrorism and Human Rights* (International Commission of Jurists, 2009), available at: http://ejp.icj.org/IMG/EJP-Report.pdf

Ivanova, I., Todorova, V. and Kolarov, T., 'Гражданската конфискация vs. организираната престъпност' ['Civil forfeiture vs. organised crime'], *Obektiv*, Bulgarian Helsinki Committee, 26 April 2012: http://www.bghelsinki.org/bg/

publikacii/obektiv/obektiv/2012-04/grazhdanskata-konfiskaciya-vs-organizi ranata-prestpnost/

Jaggar, T. and Sutherland Williams, M., 'Civil recovery: Then and now' (2010) *Criminal Bar Quarterly* 5

Keene, S., *Hawala and Related Informal Value Transfer Systems* (Shrivenham: Defence Academy Journal, 2007)

Kennedy, A., 'An evaluation of the recovery of criminal proceeds in the United Kingdom' (2007) 10 *Journal of Money Laundering Control* 33

Kilchling, M., 'Tracing, seizing and confiscating proceeds from corruption (and other illegal conduct) within or outside the criminal justice system' (2001) 9 *European Journal of Crime, Criminal Law and Criminal Justice* 264

King, C., 'Using civil processes in pursuit of criminal law objectives: A case study of non-conviction-based asset forfeiture' (2012) 16 *International Journal of Evidence and Proof* 337

Klein, S., 'Civil in rem forfeiture and double jeopardy' (1996–1997) 82 *Iowa Law Review* 183

Lawrence, I., 'Draconian and manifestly unjust: How the confiscation regime has developed' (2008) 76 *Amicus Curiae* 22

Lea, J., 'Hitting criminals where it hurts: Organised crime and the erosion of due process' (2004) 35 *Cambrian Law Review* 81

Lee, R., *Terrorist Financing: The US and International Response* (Washington, DC: Congressional Research Service RL31658, 2002)

Legal Department of the IMF, *Suppressing the Financing of Terrorism: A Handbook for Legislative Drafting* (Washington, DC, 2003)

Levi, M., 'Combating the financing of terrorism' (2010) 50 *British Journal of Criminology* 650

Levi, M., 'New frontiers of criminal liability: Money laundering and proceeds of crime' (2000) 3(3) *Journal of Money Laundering Control* 223

Levi, M., 'Pecunia non olet? The control of money-laundering revisited' in Bovenkerk, F. and Levi, M. (ed.), *The Organised Crime Community* (New York: Springer, 2007)

Levi M., 'Taking the profit out of crime' (1997) 5 *European Journal of Crime, Criminal Law and Criminal Justice* 228

Levi, M. and Maguire, M., 'Reducing and preventing organised crime: An evidence-based critique' (2004) 41 *Crime, Law and Social Change* 397

Levi, M. and Osofsky, L., *Investigating, Seizing and Confiscating the Proceeds of Crime* (London: Home Office, Police Research Group Crime, Detection and Prevention Series Paper 61, 1995)

Levitt, M., *Hamas, Politics, and Charity* (New Haven: Yale University Press, 2006)

Levy, L., *A License to Steal: The Forfeiture of Property* (Chapel Hill: University of North Carolina Press, 1996)

Lloyd's, *Under Attack? Global Business and the Threat of Political Violence* (London, 2007). Available at: http://www.lloyds.com/~/media/lloyds/reports/ 360/360%20terrorism%20reports/globalbusinessunderattack.pdf

Lusty, D., 'Civil forfeiture of proceeds of crime in Australia' (2002) 5 *Journal of Money Laundering Control* 345

Lusty, D., 'Taxing the untouchables who profit from organised crime' (2003) 10 *Journal of Financial Crime* 209

Lynch, G., 'RICO: The crime of being a criminal, Parts I & II' (1987) 87 *Columbia Law Review* 661

Matrix Insight, *Assessing the Effectiveness of EU Member States' Practices in the Identification, Tracing, Freezing and Confiscation of Criminal Assets* (London: Matrix Insight, 2009)

Maugeri, A. (ed.), *La riforma delle misure di prevenzione patrimoniali* (Milan: Giuffré, 2008)

Maxeiner, J., 'Bane of American forfeiture law: Banished at last?' (1977) 62 *Cornell Law Review* 768

Mazzarese, S. and Aiello, A., *Le misure patrimoniali antimafia* (Milan: Giuffré, 2010)

McKeachie, J. and Simser, J., 'Civil asset forfeiture in Canada' in Young, S. (ed.), *Civil Forfeiture of Criminal Property: Legal Measures for Targeting the Proceeds of Crime* (Cheltenham: Edward Elgar, 2009)

Meade, J., 'Organised crime, moral panic and law reform: The Irish adoption of civil forfeiture' (2000) 10(1) *Irish Criminal Law Journal* 11

Meade, J., 'The disguise of civility: Civil forfeiture of the proceeds of crime and the presumption of innocence in Irish law' (2000) 1 *Hibernian Law Journal* 1

Mitsilegas, V., 'The constitutional implications of mutual recognition in criminal matters in the EU' (2006) 43 *Common Market Law Review* 1277

Murphy, C.C., *EU Counter-Terrorism Law: Pre-Emption and the Rule of Law* (Oxford: Hart Publishing, 2012)

Murphy, S., 'Tracing the proceeds of crime: Legal and constitutional implications' (1999) 9 *Irish Criminal Law Journal* 160

Naylor, R.T., *Satanic Purses* (Montreal: McGill-Queen's University Press, 2006)

Naylor, R.T., 'Wash-out: A critique of follow-the-money methods in crime control policy' (1999) 32 *Crime, Law and Social Change* 1

Naylor, T., 'Criminal profits, terror dollars, and nonsense' (2007) 23 *Crime & Justice International* 27

Nelen, H., 'Hit them where it hurts most? The proceeds-of-crime approach in the Netherlands' (2004) 41 *Crime, Law and Social Change* 517

Nicol, N., 'Confiscation and the profits of crime' (1988) 52 *Journal of Criminal Law* 75

Nikolov, N., 'General characteristics of civil forfeiture' (2011) 14 *Journal of Money Laundering Control* 16

Nikolov, N., *Гражданската конфискация по Закона за отнемане в полза на държавата на незаконно придобито имущество. Тематичен коментар на новите моменти* [*Civil forfeiture according to the Law on forfeiture of illegally acquired assets. Thematic comments on the new aspects*] (Sofia: Fenea, 2012)

OECD, *Behind the Corporate Veil: Using Corporate Entities for Illicit Purposes* (Paris: OECD, 2001)

Parliament Joint Standing Committee on the Corruption and Crime Commission, *Proceeds of Crime and Unexplained Wealth: A Role for the Corruption and Crime Commission?* (Perth: Parliament of Western Australia, 2012)

Parliamentary Joint Committee on the Australian Crime Commission, *Inquiry into the Legislative Arrangements to Outlaw Serious and Organised Crime Groups* (Canberra: Commonwealth of Australia, 2009)

Parliamentary Joint Committee on Law Enforcement, *Inquiry into Commonwealth Unexplained Wealth Legislation and Arrangements* (Canberra: Commonwealth of Australia, 2012)

Passas, N., *Informal Value Transfer Systems, Terrorism and Money Laundering* (Washington, DC: Report to the National Institute of Justice, 2003)

Performance and Innovation Unit (PIU), *Recovering the Proceeds of Crime* (London: Cabinet Office, 2000)

Petrunov, G., *Money Laundering in Bulgaria: The Policy Response* (Sofia: RiskMonitor Foundation, 2010)

Pieth, M. (ed.), *Financing Terrorism* (Heidelberg: Springer, 2010)

Piety, T.R., 'Scorched Earth: How the expansion of civil forfeiture doctrine has laid waste to due process' (1991) 45 *University of Miami Law Review* 911

Pollock, S.J., 'Proportionality in civil forfeiture: Towards a remedial solution' (1994) 62 *George Washington Law Review* 456

Rees, E., Fisher, R. and Bogan, P., *Blackstone's Guide to the Proceeds of Crime Act* (4th ed., Oxford: Oxford University Press, 2011)

Rider, B., 'Cost effectiveness – a two edged sword!' Editorial (2009) 12 *Journal of Money Laundering Control*

Ryder, N., 'The Financial Services Authority and money laundering: A game of cat and mouse' (2008) 67 *Cambridge Law Journal* 635

Sandler, T., Arce, D. and Enders, W., 'An evaluation of Interpol's cooperative-based counterterrorism linkages' (2001) 54 *Journal of Law and Economics* 79

Schecter, M., 'Note: Fear and loathing and the forfeiture laws' (1990) 74 *Cornell Law Review* 1151

Schneider, F., Brück, T. and Meierrieks, D., 'The Economics of Terrorism and Counter-Terrorism: A Survey (Part II)', *Economics of Security Working Paper 45* (Berlin: 2011)

Sharman, J., 'Power and discourse in policy diffusion: Anti-money laundering in developing states' (2008) 52 *International Studies Quarterly* 635

Sheptycki, J.W.E., 'Global law enforcement as a protection racket: Some sceptical notes on transnational organized crime as an object of global governance' in Edwards, A. and Gill, P. (eds), *Transnational Organised Crime: Perspectives on global security* (London: Routledge, 2003)

Sheptycki, J.W.E., *Review of the Influence of Strategic Intelligence on Organized Crime Policy and Practice* (London: Home Office, 2004)

Sherman, T., *Report on the Independent Review of the Operation of the Proceeds of Crime Act 2002 (Cth)* (Canberra: Commonwealth of Australia, 2006)

Sidel, M., 'Counter-Terrorism and the enabling legal and political environment for civil society' (2008) 10(3) *International Journal of Not-for-Profit Law* 7

Sidel, M., 'The Third Sector, human security, and anti-terrorism' (2006) 17 *Voluntas* 199

Simser, J., 'Money laundering and asset cloaking techniques' (2008) 11 *Journal of Money Laundering Control* 15

Smith, I., Owen, T. and Bodnar, A., *Asset Recovery, Criminal Confiscation, and Civil Recovery* (2nd ed., Oxford: Oxford University Press, 2007)

Smith, R.G., Walters, J., Smith, E., et al., *Australian Anti-money Laundering and Counter-terrorism Financing Reporting and Regulatory Review* (Canberra: Australian Institute of Criminology, 2013)

Special Rapporteur on the promotion and protection of human rights and fundamental freedoms while countering terrorism, *Promotion and Protection of Human Rights and Fundamental Freedoms while Countering Terrorism* (New York: United Nations A/67/396, 2012)

Spencer, J. and Broad, R., 'Lifting the veil on SOCA and the UKHTC: Policymaking responses to organised crime' in van Duyne, P., Antonopoulos, A., Harvey, J., et al. (eds), *Cross-Border Crime Inroads on Integrity in Europe* (Tilburg: Wolf Legal, 2010)

Sproat, P., 'The new policing of assets and the new assets of policing: A tentative financial cost-benefit analysis of the UK's anti-money laundering and asset recovery regime' (2007) 10 *Journal of Money Laundering Control* 277

Stephenson, K.M, Grey, L., Power, R., et al., *Barriers to Asset Recovery. An Analysis of the Key Barriers and Recommendations for Action* (Washington, DC: World Bank, 2011)

Stoychev, S., Petrunov, G., Velev, A. and Veselinova, M., *Civil Confiscation in Bulgaria (2005–2010)* (Sofia: RiskMonitor Foundation, 2011)

Sutton, R.H., 'Controlling corruption through collective means: Advocating the Inter-American Convention against corruption' (1997) 20 *Fordham International Law Journal* 1427

Tartaglia, R. (ed.), *Codice delle confische e dei sequestri* (Rome: Neldiritto, 2012)

Thompson, E.A., 'Misplaced blame: Islam, terrorism and the origins of Hawala' (2007) 11 *Yearbook of UN Law* 279

Tridimas, T., 'Economic sanctions, procedural rights and judicial scrutiny: Post-Kadi developments' (2011) 13 *Cambridge Yearbook of European Legal Studies* 455

Vaccini, M., *Alternative Remittance Systems and Terrorist Finance* (Washington, DC: Paper No. 180, World Bank, 2009)

van den Broek, M., Hazelhorst, M. and De Zanger, W., *Asset Freezing: Smart Sanction or Criminal Charge?* (Utrecht: Merkourios, 2010)

van der Does de Willebois, E., Halter, E.H., Harrison, R.A., et al., *The Puppet Master* (Washington, DC: World Bank, 2011)

van Duyne, P. and Vander Beken, T., 'The incantation of the EU organised crime policy making' (2009) 51 *Crime, Law and Social Change* 261

van Duyne, P., Harvey, J., Maljevic, A., et al. (eds), *Crime, Money and Criminal Mobility in Europe* (Tilburg: Wolf Legal, 2009)

van Duyne, P., Harvey, J., Maljevic, A., et al. (eds), *European Crime-markets at Cross-roads: Extended and Extending Criminal Europe* (Tilburg: Wolf Legal, 2008)

van Duyne, P.C., Groenhuijsen, M.S. and Schudelaro, A.A.P., 'Balancing financial threats and legal interests in money-laundering policy' (2005) 43 *Crime, Law and Social Change* 117

van Duyne, P., von Lampe, K. and Newell, J. (eds), *Criminal Finances and Organising Crime in Europe* (Nijmegen: Wolf Legal Publishers, 2003)

Vergine, F., *Confisca e sequestro per equivalente* (Milan: Ipsoa, 2009)

von Lampe, K., 'Making the second step before the first: Assessing organized crime: The case of Germany' (2004) 42 *Crime, Law and Social Change* 227

Walker, C., 'Conscripting the public in terrorism policing' (2010) *Criminal Law Review* 441

Walker, C., *Terrorism and the Law* (Oxford: Oxford University Press, 2011)

Wensink, W., van de Velde, M. and Boer, L., *Estimated Costs of EU Counterterrorism Measures* (Brussels: Directorate General for Internal Policies, Policy Department C: Citizens' Rights and Constitutional Affairs Civil Liberties, Justice and Home Affairs, 2011)

Williams, M.R., Holcomb, J.E., Kovandic, T.V. and Bullock, S., *Policing for Profit: The Abuse of Civil Asset Forfeiture* (Arlington: Institute for Justice, 2010)

Woodiwiss, M. and Hobbs, D., 'Organized evil and the Atlantic Alliance: Moral panics and the rhetoric of organized crime policing in America and Britain' (2009) 49 *British Journal of Criminology* 106

World Bank, *Combating Money Laundering and the Financing of Terrorism* (Washington, DC: 2009)

Worrall, J., 'Addicted to the drug war: The role of civil asset forfeiture as a budgetary necessity in contemporary law enforcement' (2001) 29 *Journal of Criminal Justice Studies* 171

Young, S. (ed.), *Civil Forfeiture of Criminal Property. Legal Measures for Targeting the Proceeds of Crime* (Cheltenham: Edward Elgar, 2009)

Index

Page numbers in **bold** refer to tables, page numbers in *italics* refer to figures.